Empirical Foundations of Household Taxation

A National Bureau
of Economic Research
Project Report

Empirical Foundations of Household Taxation

Edited by Martin Feldstein and
James M. Poterba

The University of Chicago Press

Chicago and London

MARTIN FELDSTEIN is president of the National Bureau of Economic Research and the George F. Baker Professor of Economics at Harvard University. JAMES M. POTERBA is director of the Public Economics Research Program at the National Bureau of Economic Research and professor of economics at the Massachusetts Institute of Technology.

The University of Chicago Press, Chicago 60637
The University of Chicago Press, Ltd., London
© 1996 by the National Bureau of Economic Research
All rights reserved. Published 1996
Printed in the United States of America
05 04 03 02 01 00 99 98 97 96   1 2 3 4 5
ISBN: 0-226-24097-5 (cloth)

Library of Congress Cataloging-in-Publication Data

Empirical foundations of household taxation / edited by Martin Feldstein
    and James M. Poterba.
        p.   cm.—(National Bureau of Economic Research project report)
        Includes bibliographical references and index.
        1. Taxation—United States—Statistics.   2. Households—Economic
    aspects—United States—Statistics.   3. Tax incentives—United
    States—Statistics.   4. Income tax—United States—Statistics.   5. La-
    bor supply—Effect of taxation on—United States—Statistics.   6. Tax-
    ation—Law and legislation—United States.   I. Feldstein, Martin S.
    II. Poterba, James M.   III. Series.
    HJ2381.E49   1996
    336.2′00973—dc20   95-53960
                                                                                CIP

Relation of the Directors to the
Work and Publications of the
National Bureau of Economic Research

1. The object of the National Bureau of Economic Research is to ascertain and to present to the public important economic facts and their interpretation in a scientific and impartial manner. The board of Directors is charged with the responsibility of ensuring that the work of the National Bureau is carried on in strict conformity with this object.

2. The President of the National Bureau shall submit to the Board of Directors, or to its Executive Committee, for their formal adoption all specific proposals for research to be instituted.

3. No research report shall be published by the National Bureau until the President has sent each member of the Board a notice that a manuscript is recommended for publication and that in the President's opinion it is suitable for publication in accordance with the principles of the National Bureau. Such notification will include an abstract or summary of the manuscript's content and a response form for use by those Directors who desire a copy of the manuscript for review. Each manuscript shall contain a summary drawing attention to the nature and treatment of the problem studied, the character of the data and their utilization in the report, and the main conclusions reached.

4. For each manuscript so submitted, a special committee of the Directors (including Directors Emeriti) shall be appointed by majority agreement of the President and Vice Presidents (or by the Executive Committee in case of inability to decide on the part of the President and Vice Presidents), consisting of three Directors selected as nearly as may be one from each general division of the Board. The names of the special manuscript committee shall be stated to each Director when notice of the proposed publication is submitted to him. It shall be the duty of each member of the special manuscript committee to read the manuscript. If each member of the manuscript committee signifies his approval within thirty days of the transmittal of the manuscript, the report may be published. If at the end of that period any member of the manuscript committee withholds his approval, the President shall then notify each member of the Board, requesting approval or disapproval of publication, and thirty days additional shall be granted for this purpose. The manuscript shall then not be published unless at least a majority of the entire Board who shall have voted on the proposal within the time fixed for the receipt of votes shall have approved.

5. No manuscript may be published, though approved by each member of the special manuscript committee, until forty-five days have elapsed from the transmittal of the report in manuscript form. The interval is allowed for the receipt of any memorandum of dissent or reservation, together with a brief statement of his reasons, that any member may wish to express; and such memorandum of dissent or reservation shall be published with the manuscript if he so desires. Publication does not, however, imply that each member of the Board has read the manuscript, or that either members of the Board in general or the special committee have passed on its validity in every detail.

6. Publications of the National Bureau issued for informational purposes concerning the work of the Bureau and its staff, or issued to inform the public of activities of Bureau staff, and volumes issued as a result of various conferences involving the National Bureau shall contain a specific disclaimer noting that such publication has not passed through the normal review procedures required in this resolution. The Executive Committee of the Board is charged with review of all such publications from time to time to ensure that they do not take on the character of formal research reports of the National Bureau, requiring formal Board approval.

7. Unless otherwise determined by the Board or exempted by the terms of paragraph 6, a copy of this resolution shall be printed in each National Bureau publication.

(Resolution adopted October 25, 1926, as revised through September 30, 1974)

Contents

Acknowledgments

This volume is part of a multiyear research program on Behavioral Responses to Taxation that is being conducted under the auspices of the National Bureau of Economic Research (NBER). This project draws together researchers with a wide range of interests in tax policy issues. The development and maintenance of the NBER TAXSIM program, a detailed computer algorithm for computing household tax liabilities under actual and various alternative tax regimes, is one of the centerpieces of this research project. Many of the research studies in this volume involve calculations with the TAXSIM program. We are grateful to the Lynde and Harry Bradley Foundation, the Starr Foundation, the John M. Olin Foundation, and the Dean Witter Foundation for financial support of this research.

We are grateful to many members of the NBER staff for their assistance with the planning and execution of this research, and of the research meetings and the January 1995 conference at which the findings in this volume were presented. The NBER Conference Department, under the direction of Kirsten Davis, provided its usual, outstanding level of logistical support for the meeting at which these papers were presented. We are particularly grateful to Lauren Lariviere, who served as conference coordinator, for assistance with this project. Deborah Kiernan and Mark Fitz-Patrick of the NBER Publications Department have carefully guided the manuscript through various stages of the editorial process, and we are grateful for their assistance at every stage.

Introduction

Martin Feldstein and James M. Poterba

Tax policy debates depend critically on estimates of how alternative tax rules would affect household and firm behavior. Studies suggesting that reductions in marginal tax rates would increase household labor supply and saving were key components of the case for tax reform that resulted in the 1981 Economic Recovery Tax Act. Research indicating that capital gain realizations were very sensitive to capital gains tax rates played a similar role in the 1978 capital gains tax reform. In the early 1990s, federal tax policy debates focused on a related question, the effect of raising marginal tax rates on household behavior and reported taxable income.

Despite decades of interest in the effect of tax policy on household behavior, there remains substantial controversy on key empirical links between tax rates, household behavior, and revenue collections. The papers in this volume are the product of an ongoing NBER study of the effects of tax policies on household behavior. They present new statistical findings on how taxes affect household behavior or new analytical results on the effects of different types of tax policy. All of this research relies on household-level data, either drawn from public-use tax return files provided by the U.S. Treasury or from large household-level surveys, to explore various aspects of the relationship between taxes and household behavior. Most of the studies employ the TAXSIM model, an NBER-supported computer program that facilitates study of how changing tax rates or tax rules would affect the tax liabilities of taxpayers in different circumstances.

The eight studies can be broadly classified into three groups. The first set

Martin Feldstein is president of the National Bureau of Economic Research and the George F. Baker Professor of Economics at Harvard University. James M. Poterba is director of the Public Economics Research Program at the National Bureau of Economic Research and professor of economics at the Massachusetts Institute of Technology.

considers the effect of tax policy on labor market activity. Nada Eissa's paper on "Labor Supply and the Economic Recovery Tax Act of 1981" utilizes the tax rate reductions associated with this major tax reform to explore how after-tax wages affect the labor supply of married women. Her results suggest that raising after-tax wages encourages labor force participation and increases the number of hours worked by women who participate, although the estimated effects are relatively small. There is some evidence (Eissa 1995) that labor supply responses by women who experienced large tax rate reductions in 1986 were larger than those associated with the 1981 tax reform, perhaps because the 1986 tax rate reductions were part of a revenue-neutral tax reform.

Martin Feldstein and Dan Feenberg's paper, "The Taxation of Two-Earner Families," investigates how changing the current tax rules associated with joint filers would affect the labor supply of married women and the efficiency cost of the tax code. Drawing on previous estimates of the labor supply behavior of married women, this paper uses the TAXSIM program along with data from the Current Population Survey to estimate how several potential tax reforms would affect the hours of work and labor force participation of married women. The paper shows that policies that reduce the marginal tax rate on such earners, even if they are enacted in a revenue-neutral way, might substantially reduce the efficiency cost of the current tax system.

The third paper, by Gilbert Metcalf, investigates "Labor Supply and Welfare Effects of a Switch from Income to Consumption Taxation." This paper uses data from the Consumer Expenditure Survey to explore the welfare gains associated with a shift from income to consumption taxation. The usual argument for such a switch is that an income tax creates an efficiency loss by taxing capital income; a consumption tax such as a value added tax (VAT) avoids this. Metcalf points out that in practice most VATs exclude a number of goods from taxation, which induces an efficiency cost. Exemptions and exclusions distort consumer choices between the taxed and untaxed goods. The paper illustrates the potential magnitude of these effects and suggests that the welfare gain from reduced intertemporal distortions is likely to exceed the welfare loss from distortions among consumer goods.

A second set of papers is concerned with the effect of special tax provisions on household behavior. William Gentry and Alison Hagy's paper, "The Distributional Effects of the Tax Treatment of Child Care Expenses," studies the tax reductions received by households in different income and family status categories as a result of current tax expenditures for child care expenses. The authors focus on the child care tax credit and the dependent care allowance. Gentry and Hagy use data from tax return filings as well as from the National Child Care Survey to estimate the distribution of child care expenses, as well as the extent of utilization of these tax-based subsidies by parents with children. The study concludes that contrary to some previous claims, once one focuses on taxpayers with children, the benefits from these programs decline as household income rises.

Jonathan Gruber and James Poterba develop a new framework for measuring the net tax subsidy to purchasing health insurance in their paper, "Tax Subsidies to Employer-Provided Health Insurance." They argue that the current income and payroll tax systems embody substantial subsidies to employer-provided insurance but that these are frequently overstated. Not all of the costs of employer-provided insurance are paid on a pretax basis, and not all medical costs that might be incurred if a household were not insured can be deducted from taxable income. The authors combine data from the TAXSIM program with survey data from the National Medical Expenditure Survey to estimate the distribution of employer-provided insurance spending across households. They use these data to analyze the effects of various tax reforms, such as capping the amount of employer provided insurance that can be excluded from taxable income, on the demand for such insurance.

A third set of studies focuses on the effect of recent tax reforms on reported taxable income and tax revenues. Joel Slemrod's paper, "High-Income Families and the Tax Changes of the 1980s: The Anatomy of Behavioral Response," explores the effect of marginal tax rate reductions in 1981 and 1986 on the distribution of taxable income across taxpayers in different income groups. His starting point is Feenberg and Poterba's (1993) observation that after the Tax Reform Act of 1986 (TRA86), the share of taxable income reported by very high income taxpayers, those in the top 0.5 percent of the income distribution, rose substantially. Slemrod shows that some of this increase is due not to the same households reporting higher income after TRA86 than before, but to a shift in the set of households with very high incomes. He then tries to relate the share of taxable income reported by high-income taxpayers to a variety of factors, such as interest rates and stock market appreciation, that might affect this distribution. The results of this analysis suggest that the rise in taxable income among the highest income group after TRA86 cannot simply be attributed to the continuation of underlying economic trends of the 1970s and 1980s.

A second paper on a related topic, Andrew Samwick's "Tax Shelters and Passive Losses after the Tax Reform Act of 1986," attempts to determine which part of the 1986 tax reform was responsible for the sharp decline in tax shelter activity in the late 1980s. TRA86 included a number of provisions designed to curb tax shelters, including a reduction in marginal tax rates on interest and dividend income, an increase in capital gains tax rates, and limitations on taxpayers' ability to use passive losses to offset income from nonpassive activities.

The last paper in the volume, James Alm, Brian Erard, and Jonathan Feinstein's paper on "The Relationship between State and Federal Tax Audits," is difficult to group with any of the other studies. It is an analysis of the potential efficiency gains from greater coordination in tax administration between state tax agencies and the Internal Revenue Service. The authors use a unique data set from Oregon to show that in many cases state and federal tax administrators audit the same taxpayer without sharing information from their audits, even though such sharing would substantially increase total revenue collections at very little incremental administrative cost.

The NBER's research project on the effects of taxation on household behavior is an ongoing effort. Researchers affiliated with the project are continuing to explore the effects of tax reforms on various dimensions of household behavior and the efficiency costs of current tax provisions and their alternatives. Findings from these studies will be reported in the future.

References

Eissa, Nada. 1995. Taxation and labor supply of married women: The Tax Reform Act of 1986 as a natural experiment. NBER Working Paper no. 5023. Cambridge, Mass.: National Bureau of Economic Research.

Feenberg, Daniel R., and James M. Poterba. 1993. Income inequality and the incomes of high-income taxpayers: Evidence from tax returns. In *Tax policy and the economy,* vol. 7, ed. James Poterba, 145–73. Cambridge: MIT Press.

1   Labor Supply and the Economic Recovery Tax Act of 1981

Nada Eissa

1.1 Introduction

U.S. personal income tax rates changed dramatically during the 1980s, especially at the top of the income distribution. In 1980, the top marginal tax rate (at the federal level) was 70 percent. The Economic Recovery Tax Act of 1981 (ERTA) reduced that rate to 50 percent, and the Tax Reform Act of 1986 (TRA86) reduced it further to 28 percent. A dominant motivation for the initial law was to alleviate the disincentives for individuals to supply labor and to save that were generated by the high marginal tax rates. For labor supply, ERTA pursued this goal by introducing a deduction for the secondary earner in the household and, more generally, by reducing marginal tax rates by 23 percent within each tax bracket.

By providing large and potentially exogenous variation in marginal tax rates, these tax laws provide fertile ground for analyzing the responsiveness of individual behavior to taxes. Evidence suggests that individual behavior did respond to the incentives in these tax laws. Lindsey (1987) and Navratil (1994) use tax return data and find that the marginal tax rate reductions in ERTA had a significant effect on taxable income. Feldstein (1993) and Auten and Carroll (1994) find similar results for TRA86. Burtless (1991) and Bosworth and Burtless (1992) study the labor supply responses to the tax reforms of the 1980s. These studies analyze the trend in labor supply for different demographic groups using Current Population Survey (CPS) data for 1968–88 and 1968–90, respectively. They find significant responses in hours of work (relative to trend)

Nada Eissa is assistant professor of economics at the University of California, Berkeley, and a faculty research fellow of the National Bureau of Economic Research.

The author is grateful to Dan Feenberg for assistance with the TAXSIM calculations, to conference participants for useful suggestions, and to David Cutler, Douglas Elmendorf, and Martin Feldstein for helpful comments.

by married women at the top and bottom of the income distribution. Eissa (1995) also finds a strong response by upper-income women to TRA86.

This paper examines whether married women responded to the incentives to increase labor supply in ERTA, using individual-level data rather than aggregated data (as in the case of Bosworth and Burtless 1992). I focus on married women for two reasons. First, ERTA implicitly targeted this group in the introduction of the secondary earner deduction. Second, this group is believed to be more responsive to changes in the tax rate than any other group (men and female heads of households). While the empirical literature is in less agreement on the overall responsiveness of married women than of other groups, it is generally accepted that it is the participation decision rather than the hours-of-work decision for working women that is responsive. I therefore analyze these two margins separately.

I use the time variation in marginal tax rates to estimate both difference-in-difference regression models (where I compare the change in labor supply for upper-income women with the change in labor supply for lower-income women) and standard labor supply models (where labor supply is a function of the after-tax wage). This approach is appealing in that it allows me to address a standard criticism of the empirical analysis of taxation and labor supply. Because cross-sectional variation in marginal tax rates derives primarily from differences in income and family structure, the existing literature faces an identification problem. Separating the tax effect from a nonlinear income (or family structure) effect is difficult in the cross section. ERTA, however, generated potentially exogenous time variation in marginal rates that can be used to evaluate the responsiveness of labor supply to taxes.

Using data from the 1981 and 1985 CPS, I find weak evidence that labor force participation of upper-income married women is responsive to taxes. The point estimates suggest that following ERTA, upper-income married women increased their labor force participation by up to 2.6 percentage points (from a predicted base of 47 percent). That estimate suggests an elasticity of 0.79. For working women, the most likely values show a response of between 20 and 49 hours per year, but these are estimated with such imprecision that it is not possible to rule out no response at all. Finally, standard labor supply estimates predict participation and hours-of-work responses for upper-income women that are at the lower end of the observed responses.

This paper is organized as follows: Section 1.2 presents a quick review of the tax and labor supply literature. To motivate the regressions estimated in the paper, I first review the basic model of labor supply and outline some basic assumptions maintained for the analysis of labor supply within the household. To place the current paper in context, I present a brief review of the empirical labor supply literature. Section 1.3 reviews the provisions in ERTA relevant for the treatment of earned income. Section 1.4 presents the identification strategy, with particular attention to the difference-in-difference approach. Section 1.5

discusses the data and presents basic labor supply results. The difference-in-difference specification and regression results are presented in section 1.6, and the standard labor supply estimates are presented in section 1.7. Finally, section 1.8 concludes.

1.2   Tax and Labor Supply Literature

1.2.1   Model of Labor Supply

To motivate the labor supply equations that I estimate, I sketch below the simple model of taxes and labor supply. I use the basic static, two-good labor supply model. In this model, the worker has a utility function defined over consumption and leisure and chooses her hours of work at a fixed wage. The optimization problem is typically characterized as follows:

$$(1) \qquad \max u(c,l) \text{ such that } [wh - G(wh,y)] + y = c,$$

where $u(c, l)$ is the utility function, c is consumption of a composite commodity (the numeraire), l is leisure, wh is the woman's labor income (the product of the wage and hours of work), y is unearned income, and $G(wh, y)$ is the tax liability. The partial derivative of utility with respect to leisure, u_l, is positive, and the second partial, u_{ll}, is negative.

The function $G(\cdot)$ can incorporate nonlinearities and nonconvexities of the budget set due to several features of the tax system, such as the social security payroll tax, the earned income tax credit, and transfer programs. The marginal tax rate, θ, is the derivative of the function $G(\cdot)$ with respect to labor income. At interior solutions, the equality of the marginal rate of substitution between consumption and leisure (MRS) and the net wage determines labor supply: $u_l/u_c = w(1 - \theta)$.

With a nonlinear budget set, the choice of hours and consumption determines the segment of the budget constraint on which the individual locates. For local movements, behavior is equivalent to that arising from utility maximization subject to a linear budget constraint with the net wage, $w(1 - \theta)$, and "virtual" income given by the intercept of that budget segment with the consumption axis. Theory predicts that the income effect is negative because greater income leads one to purchase more leisure (assuming that leisure is a normal good). Theory provides little guidance on the effect of the net wage, however, because the substitution effect from a tax cut leads to an increase in labor supply while the income effect leads to greater consumption of leisure.

This paper analyzes separately two measures of labor supply: participation and hours of work conditional on working. Because no attempt is made to explicitly address the nonlinearity of the budget set, one can characterize the participation decision as a function of the MRS at zero hours and the after-tax market wage.[1] If the individual has unearned income, an uncompensated change in the tax rate has an ambiguous effect on the participation margin.

Unearned income for a married woman includes her spouse's earned income and is therefore affected by the spouse's labor supply decisions. I assume that the interaction between the husband's and wife's labor supply is governed by the chauvinist model. In that model, the wife conditions her labor supply on her spouse's labor supply decision, making her the secondary earner in the household. The husband's earned income affects the wife's labor supply only through an income effect. This model is useful for two reasons: the household's capital income and the husband's total labor income generate an exogenous measure of unearned income, and the first-hour marginal tax rate faced by the wife is her spouse's last-hour marginal rate. The chauvinist model is clearly not valid for some households. One could use more general models that allow, for example, an interaction between one partner's wage and the other partner's labor supply. Evidence suggests, however, that such models do not produce very different estimates of the wage elasticity of labor supply (Hausman and Ruud 1984).

1.2.2 Empirical Labor Supply Literature

The empirical literature on taxation and labor supply is extensive and employs several approaches to estimating labor supply equations. The early literature posited a linear budget constraint (i.e., a proportional tax) and estimated a structural labor supply equation of the form

$$(2) \qquad h_i = \delta_0 X_i + \delta_1 w_i^n + \delta_2 y_i + \varepsilon_i \, ,$$

where h_i is annual (or weekly) hours of work, X_i is a set of individual characteristics, w_i^n is the after-tax hourly wage, and y_i is unearned income.

Researchers used ordinary least squares (OLS) and two-stage least squares (2SLS) to estimate the hours-of-work equations (Boskin 1973; Hall 1973). Estimates from this early work generally found large wage and income elasticities for married women. Killingsworth and Heckman's (1986) review of the literature cites a range of estimated wage elasticities of -0.3 to 14, with a tendency toward 1. More specific to taxation, Hausman (1985) cites a range of estimates of -0.3 to 2.3. Mroz (1987) showed that this elasticity is closer to zero for *working* married women, but his estimates also suggest that the participation decision may be quite sensitive to the wage. This result is also found in recent work using the nonlinear budget set approach identified with Hausman (1981).

Hausman (1981) assumes a functional form for taxpayers' preferences and then estimates preference parameters by solving an optimizing model in which the nonlinear and nonconvex budget constraints facing taxpayers are carefully

---

1. Nonconvexities in the budget constraint invalidate this decision process because the entire budget constraint and not just the marginal tax rate on the participation margin determine whether the individual enters the labor force (Hausman 1980).

modeled. Using maximum likelihood methods and cross-sectional data from the 1975 Panel Study of Income Dynamics (PSID), Hausman estimates a net wage elasticity of approximately 1 for married women. Using a similar methodology and 1984 PSID data, Triest (1990) estimates a total labor supply elasticity of 1.1 for married women. However, he estimates an elasticity of only 0.2 for *working* married women. Triest's results provide further support for the view that the participation decision is more responsive to changes in the net wage than are hours conditional to working.

While the careful modeling of the nonlinearity of the budget set is appealing, this approach faces two critical problems. First, the results are quite sensitive to the specification of preferences chosen (Blundell and Meghir 1986), and even under similar preference specifications, results do not seem to be replicable across different data sets and time periods (MaCurdy, Green, and Paarsch 1990). Second, constraints that make the models tractable appear to be binding and heavily influence the results (Heckman 1982; MaCurdy et al. 1990). MaCurdy et al. show that the nonlinear budget set approach imposes the Slutsky condition, which amounts to restricting the income effect to be negative. Even when the nonlinear budget constraint approach is not used, structural labor supply models are extremely sensitive to the specification chosen (Mroz 1987).

An alternative approach to identifying labor supply responsiveness is to examine the response of taxpayers to changes in tax laws (Eissa 1995; Blundell, Duncan, and Meghir 1995). Eissa analyzes the responsiveness of upper-income married women to the large tax reductions in TRA86. That paper uses a difference-in-difference approach and compares the labor supply response of married women at the 99th percentile of the CPS income distribution to women at the 75th and 90th percentiles of the same distribution. Blundell et al. use the several tax reforms in England during the 1980s to estimate a structural model of labor supply that allows them to distinguish between income and substitution effects. The advantage of this approach is that it relies on minimal and transparent assumptions for identification.

This paper follows in the line of the natural experiment approach. Before I discuss the methodology, I review the relevant features of ERTA.

1.3   Economic Recovery Tax Act of 1981

Before 1981, the U.S. federal tax schedule consisted of 16 brackets, ranging from 11 to 70 percent. The highest rate applied to individuals with taxable income over $215,400. Table 1.1 presents the statutory federal income tax schedule for 1980. At higher income tax brackets, earned income was taxed at a lower rate than unearned income. The lower tax rate on earned income was due to the "maximum tax," passed as part of the Tax Reform Act of 1969. The maximum tax provided tax relief to taxpayers with substantial earned income so that the marginal rate on earned income did not exceed 50 percent. In fact,

Table 1.1   **Statutory Federal Individual Income Tax Schedule for Married, Joint Tax Filers, 1980 and 1984**

Taxable Income (nominal dollars)	Tax Year	
	1980	1984
0–3,400	0	0
3,400–5,500	14	11
3,400–7,600	16	12
7,600–11,900	18	14
11,900–16,000	21	16
16,000–20,200	24	18
20,200–24,600	28	22
24,600–29,900	32	25
29,900–35,200	37	28
35,200–45,800	43	33
45,800–60,000	49	38
60,000–85,600	54 (50)	42
85,600–109,400	59 (50)	45
109,400–162,400	64 (50)	49
162,400–215,400	68 (50)	50
215,400 and over	70 (50)	50
CPI adjustment factor (1980 $)	1.00	1.26

Sources: Tax schedule, Pechman (1987); CPI, *Economic Report of the President 1994* (Washington, D.C.: Government Printing Office, 1994).

complications in the law meant that the maximum tax on *earned* income could have exceeded 50 percent.[2]

In addition to the federal income tax, taxpayers faced the social security payroll tax (equal to 6.13 percent on the employee)[3] and state taxes. Although the statutory state tax rate could have been as high as 16 percent (in Minnesota), the deductibility of state taxes from federal taxable income reduces the effective marginal tax rate. Nonetheless, for many secondary earners in high-income households, the marginal tax rate for the first hour of work could have far exceeded the federal rate of 50 percent.[4]

2. Not all taxpayers with taxable income in the relevant brackets were eligible for the maximum tax: married taxpayers had to file joint tax returns and have taxable earned income more than the amount that faced the 50 percent rate ($60,000 in 1980) to be eligible. In addition, eligible taxpayers who were in the relevant brackets because they had substantial unearned income did not see marginal tax rates on earned income fall to 50 percent (see Lindsey 1981 for a discussion of the workings of the maximum tax). Lindsey estimates that most taxpayers eligible for the maximum tax faced marginal rates of more than 50 percent in 1977.

3. The social security tax is a payroll tax and therefore applies even to secondary earners in the highest tax brackets if their own earnings are below the social security maximum taxable earnings ($25,900 in 1980).

4. For a taxpayer with $55,000 of taxable earned (and $25,000 unearned) income, the marginal tax rate on earned income would be 69 percent ((55 percent federal tax + 12.26 percent FICA tax + 6 percent state tax)/1.0613).

ERTA reduced marginal tax rates by 23 percent within each bracket over a period of three years: by 10 percent in 1982, another 10 percent in 1983 (such that they were 19 percent below their pre-ERTA levels), and by 5 percent in 1984.[5] ERTA abolished the maximum tax on earned income and set the top marginal tax rate at 50 percent as of 1982. ERTA also provided two-earner married couples with a deduction equal to 10 percent of the income of the lower-earning spouse (up to $30,000).[6] The aim of this provision was to reduce the disincentive effects of high marginal rates on secondary earners. In effect, the deduction provided larger tax reductions for secondary earners at higher levels of the income distribution: it reduced the marginal rate by 5 percentage points for a secondary earner in the 50 percent bracket, but only 1 percentage point for a secondary earner in the 11 percent bracket. The federal statutory income tax schedule for 1984 is also presented in table 1.1.

Because the tax code was not indexed for inflation during this period, taxpayers were likely to find themselves in higher brackets with no real increase in income. In practice, bracket creep is important in this analysis for two reasons. First, inflation was high during the period in which ERTA took effect: between 1980 and 1984, prices increased by 26 percent. Second, jumping into higher brackets was easy because income tax brackets were narrow. Table 1.1 includes the CPI adjustment factor for 1984 to allow comparison of marginal tax rates between years. Consider the taxpayer with taxable income of $20,000 in 1980. Her marginal tax rate was 24 percent in 1980. If her income increased by the CPI each year and ERTA was not passed, she would have faced a marginal rate of 32 percent in 1984. ERTA reduced the marginal rate in the 32 percent bracket to 25 percent. Rather than fall by 23 percent, this taxpayer's federal marginal rate *increased* by 4 percent, from 24 to 25 percent.[7] In effect, bracket creep eroded most of the tax gains for lower-income and middle-income taxpayers (Lindsey 1987), thus leaving upper-income taxpayers as the main beneficiaries of the 1981 tax law. How much very high income individuals gained from ERTA depends heavily on whether the maximum tax capped marginal rates at 50 percent in 1980, however.

Unlike TRA86, ERTA represented an uncompensated tax change. ERTA contained few provisions that affected the tax base except for the expanded eligibility for IRAs and the secondary earner deduction. Thus, net-of-tax incomes rose because the tax on the family fell. Lindsey (1987) estimates that ERTA reduced tax liability by 26.8 percent in 1984. This feature of the tax law generates an income effect and affects the interpretation of the results, an issue I return to later.

---

5. In 1981 a credit of 1.25 percent was given against regular taxes.
6. The secondary earner deduction was only 5 percent in 1982.
7. If eligible for the secondary earner deduction, her marginal tax rate in 1984 would have been 22.5 percent.

1.4   Identification Strategy

I compare the change in labor supply of women "most" affected by ERTA (the treatment group) with women "less" affected by the law (the control group) before and after the tax reform. The treatment here is the change in the marginal tax rate, or more generally the change in the budget set. Marginal tax rates are not available in the survey data, however. I use income as a proxy for the marginal tax rate because ERTA provided greater tax reductions for women in higher-income households than for women in lower-income households.

The choice of groups from different points on the income distribution generates a potential endogeneity problem. If the allocation is made based on family income, those who respond to the tax changes (high earners after 1981) are the treatment group. This selection process biases upward the estimated response and labor supply elasticity of the treatment group. To remove this bias, the choice of the treatment and control groups before and after the tax law is based on "other household income"—the sum of husband's labor income and any nonlabor income received by the family. I choose women with real other household income of at least $50,000 as the treatment group and women with other household income between $30,000 and $50,000 as the control group.[8] The effect of the tax law is then the difference between the change in labor supply of these two groups.

This difference-in-difference approach requires that assignment into the treatment and the control groups be random. Since these groups are at different points along the income distribution, there are likely to be systematic differences in their characteristics. In addition, the composition of working women may change over the period if there is a participation response and new entrants are different from those already in the labor force. With nonrandom assignment, differences in labor market outcomes may reflect the noncomparability of the two groups rather than the effect of the tax law. To guard against this possibility, I estimate regressions in which I control for the relevant demographic characteristics.[9] With this adjustment, we need a weaker assumption: conditional on observable characteristics, allocation into the treatment and the control groups is random.

Identification is based on the assumption that there is no contemporaneous shock to relative labor market outcomes of women with large tax cuts and women with small tax cuts. This assumption is somewhat fragile in this period. Evidence suggests that wage inequality grew significantly between 1979 and 1987 (Katz and Murphy 1992). In addition, women with higher-income husbands tend to be more educated on average than women whose husbands have

---

8. The choice of the treatment group is guided by data limitations, which I describe in the next section.

9. Controlling demographic characteristics in a regression framework will solve the problem if new participants differ only in observable characteristics from those in the labor force.

less income. A rise in the relative wages of more-educated individuals would generate a response similar to that of a relative reduction in tax rates (Rosen 1976). Only part of the estimated response would be due to tax reductions in that case. I test for shocks to *relative* labor market outcomes by allowing the impact of education on labor market outcomes to vary over the period of the reforms. If upper-income women increase their participation or work more hours because there is greater demand for them, this test will generate a more precise estimate of the tax effect. This test will also produce better estimates of the tax effect if there are any unobservable shocks to labor supply over the period that are correlated with education. An example of such a shock would be that higher-income women prefer to work more hours at any wage following the tax law.

A more basic identification condition is that the difference in the *change* in the after-tax wage for the two groups is not zero. Wages for nonparticipants do not exist, however. To avoid imputing market wages to nonparticipants, I assume instead that the difference in the after-tax share (1-marginal tax rate) between the two groups is not zero. In other words, I implicitly assume that relative wages remain unchanged. This assumption may not be valid given the endogeneity of the wage to tax reforms and the changes in returns to education during this period. I test this assumption later using the sample of working women.

Under the identifying assumptions, I can calculate the uncompensated elasticity of labor supply for the upper-income group as

$$(3) \qquad \eta = \frac{\Delta l_{\mathrm{H}}^{s} - \Delta l_{\mathrm{L}}^{s}}{\Delta(1 - \theta)_{\mathrm{H}} - \Delta(1 - \theta)_{\mathrm{L}}},$$

where H indexes the treatment group (high income), L indexes the control group (lower income), η is the elasticity of labor supply, l^{s} refers to the labor supply measure, $1 - \theta$ is the after-tax share (1-marginal tax rate), and Δx is the percentage change in x.

Because ERTA reduced the tax liability of taxpayers, the tax law has an income effect and we estimate an uncompensated elasticity. This uncompensated elasticity is relevant for estimating tax revenue. Estimates of the elasticity are presented in the next section. I do not attempt to isolate the compensated effect, which is what matters for deadweight loss calculations. Eissa (1995) estimates compensated labor supply elasticities using TRA86, which was a revenue-neutral and a distributionally neutral tax change.

1.5   Data and Basic Difference-in-Difference Results

1.5.1   Sample

The data I use come from the 1981 and 1985 March CPS. The CPS provides annual labor market and income information for the year preceding the survey, so the data are for tax years 1980 and 1984. I use 1984 as the postreform period because ERTA was phased in over three years, with most of the reductions taking place by 1983.

The advantage of the CPS is that it is the largest data set with income and hours information available for the relevant years. The disadvantage is that income fields are top-coded and the top code changes between 1980 and 1984, from $50,000 to $100,000. The low top code in 1980 affects the marginal tax rate calculation for that year and therefore biases estimates of the effect of ERTA on marginal tax rates. The direction of the bias is not clear, however. On one hand, the top code leads one to underestimate the marginal tax rate in 1980 and thus the reduction in the tax rate over the period. On the other hand, top-coding of income leads one to overestimate the marginal tax rate if these tax-payers are eligible for the maximum tax.[10] Approximately 29 percent of the 1980 sample with real other income of at least $50,000 has wage and salary income that is top-coded. To avoid misclassifying individuals because of top-coded income, I define the treatment group to have at least $50,000 in other income, the sum of both husband's earned income and family unearned income.[11]

The CPS has information on households, families, and individuals. However, the relevant unit of analysis for this study is the tax-filing unit. The tax-filing unit is based on CPS families. Therefore, subfamilies (both related and unrelated) are allocated to separate tax-filing units from the primary family. Any member of the tax-filing unit who is under age 19 (or under age 24 and a full-time student) is considered a dependent child for tax purposes. Tax-filing unit income does not include children's earned income or unearned income.

The sample is made up of married women between ages 19 and 64, residing with their employed spouses at the time of the interview. I exclude women who report being self-employed because interpreting hours of work for this group is difficult. I also exclude women who report being out of the labor force because of an illness or disability, or who report working more than 4,160 hours per year (52 weeks at 80 hours per week). Finally, I exclude women with zero or negative other household income since these women are primary earners. The resulting sample size is 54,381 observations.

Table 1.2 presents the characteristics of the sample. Column (1) presents the

10. Recall that to be eligible for the maximum tax, a married taxpayer filing a joint return had to have taxable earned income in excess of $60,000 in 1980. An individual with $75,000 of taxable earned income will be classified as having $50,000 in my data. This individual's calculated marginal tax rate is higher than his true marginal rate.

11. Individuals may also be misclassified if they misreport their income to the CPS. Here, the difference-in-difference estimates of the labor supply response are inconsistent. Scholz (1990) finds that tax units with wage and salary income more than $50,000 reported, on average, less income to the CPS than to the Internal Revenue Service (IRS) in 1984. Tax units with wage and salary income between $25,000 and $50,000 reported very similar incomes in the two data sets. The estimate of the tax effect is biased downward if individuals underreport income to the CPS. Without a match between IRS and CPS data, however, correcting for this bias is difficult.

Table 1.2   **Summary Statistics of Data Sample**

	All		Employed	
Variable	Before ERTA81 (1)	After ERTA81 (2)	Before ERTA81 (3)	After ERTA81 (4)
Age	38.45	38.61	37.32	37.56
	(11.77)	(11.38)	(11.28)	(10.78)
Education	12.28	12.56	12.58	12.87
	(2.61)	(2.63)	(2.48)	(2.50)
Nonwhite	.083	.090	.090	.098
	(.275)	(.029)	(.029)	(.030)
Preschool children	.419	.416	.344	.357
	(.72)	(.712)	(.636)	(.650)
Family size	3.323	3.233	3.210	3.142
	(1.31)	(1.24)	(1.24)	(1.16)
Other household income	20,819	21,574	19,656	20,430
	(12,393)	(15,341)	(11,313)	(13,737)
Interest and dividend income	741.4	1,219.2	630.0	1,018.8
	(3,176)	(5,153)	(2,825)	(4,287)
Labor force participation	.656	.687	1	1
	(.475)	(.464)	(0)	(0)
Hours	948.6	1,039.5	1,447.1	1,512.5
	(912.2)	(931.0)	(740.3)	(738.7)
Observations	29,269	25,112	19,186	17,259

Notes: All income figures are in 1980 dollars. Numbers in parentheses are standard deviations. Means are unweighted.

characteristics of all married women before ERTA. The average married woman in the pretax change period is 38.45 years old, has a high school degree, and has approximately 1.3 children. Her family has approximately $21,000 of other household income (defined as tax-filing unit income less the wife's wage income) and $740 of interest and dividend income. The probability that she is employed is two-thirds. Column (2) shows that after ERTA, she has similar characteristics.[12]

Because I analyze the hours response for working married women, I present their characteristics as well. Column (3) of table 1.2 shows that working women are not very different from nonworking women: they are younger, are more educated, have a smaller family size, and are less likely to be white but only slightly so. Also, employed women have less other household income than women out of the labor force.

Columns (1) and (2) show that the participation rate of all married women increased following the tax change: after ERTA, the labor force participation of married women increased by 3.1 percentage points, from 65.6 to 68.7 per-

12. The tax reductions, and especially the secondary earner deduction, should reduce the marriage penalty and therefore affect marriage incentives. Therefore, either there was no marriage response, or newly married women are similar to those already married.

cent. The increase in labor force participation suggests that the populations of working women before and after the tax reforms may not be directly comparable. New participants may enter the labor force at different points on the hours-of-work distribution. For the analysis, however, I assume that the distribution of hours of work for new entrants is similar to that of the pre-ERTA participants. While verifying this assumption with repeated cross-sectional data is impossible, we can check that the demographic characteristics of the two groups look similar. Columns (3) and (4) show that the two populations are quite similar, except for the number of preschool children they have. Whereas all married women have fewer preschool children after 1981, working married women have more preschool children. Therefore, new entrants into the labor force are more likely to be women with young children.[13]

1.5.2 Marginal Tax Rate

I define the marginal tax rate variable as the sum of the federal, state, and social security payroll taxes on the individual's marginal revenue product:

$$tmtr = [fmtr + (1 - pitem \cdot fmtr) \cdot smtr + 2 \cdot ssmtr]/(1 + ssmtr),$$

where tmtr is the total marginal tax rate, fmtr is the federal tax rate, pitem is the probability that the individual itemizes deductions for the federal income tax, smtr is the state tax rate, and ssmtr is the employer's (also employee's) share of the social security payroll tax.

The federal and state income tax rates are calculated using the NBER TAX-SIM model. Several income sources are used in the calculation: wage and salary, interest, dividend, pension, self-employment, farm, and public assistance income. The CPS does not provide information on tax-filing status; therefore I assume that all couples file jointly.[14] TAXSIM computes the marginal tax rate from the tax liability incurred from an additional $100 of wage and salary income. The deductibility of state taxes from the federal tax for taxpayers who itemize their deductions reduces the contribution of the state marginal tax rate. Since the CPS does not have information on itemization and deductions, I impute the probability that the individual itemizes from the *Statistics of Income* as the share of tax returns that itemize deductions within each income class.[15]

I assume full incidence of the FICA payroll tax on the worker.[16] In 1980, the

---

13. Women with preschool children tend to work fewer hours than women with no young children once they enter the labor force. Thus new participants should be entering at a lower point in the hours distribution, shifting it to the left and reducing the estimated hours response.

14. In 1980, 96.8 percent of married couples filed a joint tax return; in 1984, 98.2 percent did (*Statistics of Income*).

15. The income classes (in thousands of dollars) are 0–5, 5–10, 10–20, 20–30, 30–50, 50–75, 75–100, 100–200, and 200–500.

16. The social security payroll tax is a tax only to the extent that the present value of taxes exceeds that of benefits. Feldstein and Samwick (1992) argue that married women face the full social security tax.

rate was 12.26 percent (6.13 percent on the employer). In 1984, the rate was 14.00 percent. These rates are zero for any woman whose earnings exceed the social security maximum taxable earnings.

Between 1980 and 1984, the average federal marginal rate for women in the sample fell by only 1 percentage point, from 40.2 to 39.2 percent. The average reduction in the sample is much smaller than the statutory reduction contained in ERTA because of bracket creep and increases in the social security payroll tax.

In the estimation, I rely on variation in marginal tax changes across the income distribution. Table 1.3 presents data on marginal tax rates before and after ERTA, disaggregated by the tax unit's other household income. Two observations are noteworthy. First, the largest tax reduction went to individuals at the top of the income distribution: 5.2 percentage points for women in families with at least $50,000 in other household income. Second, bracket creep and the social security tax completely offset the reductions in ERTA for women in the $10,000–$20,000 and $20,000–$30,000 income groups. At the very bottom of the other-income distribution, taxpayers received a 0.6 percentage point reduction. Table 1.4 transforms these figures to percentage changes in the after-tax share (1-marginal tax rate). It shows that women at the top received a 12.33 percent increase in the after-tax share, whereas those at the very bottom received a 1.12 percent increase.

1.5.3   Basic Labor Supply Results

In this section, I present basic results on labor force participation and hours of work for married women at different points along the income distribution.

Table 1.3   **Marginal Tax Rate**

Group[a]	Before ERTA81	After ERTA81	Change
$y \geq 50$	.599	.547	−.052
	(.001)	(.001)	(.001)
$30 \leq y < 50$	.520	.496	−.024
	(.001)	(.001)	(.001)
$20 \leq y < 30$	.437	.437	.00
	(.001)	(.001)	(.001)
$10 \leq y < 20$	.364	.364	.00
	(.001)	(.001)	(.001)
$y < 10$	.274	.268	−.006
	(.002)	(.001)	(.002)

Notes: Federal and state tax rates are calculated by TAXSIM. I assume all couples file jointly and assign each unit the average itemized deductions for the income class. I assume that the full incidence of the payroll tax falls on the worker. See text for details. Numbers in parentheses are standard errors.

[a]Other household income in thousands of dollars.

Table 1.4   **After-Tax Share**

Group[a]	Change (%)
$y \geq 50$	12.33
$30 \leq y < 50$	5.44
$20 \leq y < 30$	.22
$10 \leq y < 20$	.17
$y < 10$	1.12

Note: I assume that the growth rate of the real market wage is constant across groups. The reported figure is the difference in the group average of the log of the after-tax share between 1980 and 1984.

[a]Other household income in thousands of dollars.

Table 1.5   **Labor Supply of Married Women Before and After ERTA81**

Group[a]	Before ERTA81	After ERTA81	Change
	A. *Labor Force Participation*		
$y \geq 50$	.419 (.014)	.499 (.015)	.080 (.020)
	[1,221]	[1,143]	{19.0}
$30 \leq y < 50$	.563 (.008)	.618 (.008)	.055 (.011)
	[3,947]	[3,644)	{9.7}
$20 \leq y < 30$	.649 (.005)	.695 (.006)	.046 (.008)
	[8,307]	[6,512]	{6.9}
$10 \leq y < 20$	.704 (.004)	.723 (.005)	.019 (.007)
	[11,313]	[9,072]	{2.7}
$y < 10$	.690 (.007)	.707 (.007)	.017 (.010)
	[4,481]	[4,739]	{2.5}
	B. *Annual Hours Conditional on Working*		
$y \geq 50$	1,265.9 (35.6)	1,395.9 (34.7)	129.0 (49.7)
	[512]	[570]	{10.3}
$30 \leq y < 50$	1,369.7 (16.3)	1,428.6 (16.5)	58.9 (23.2)
	[2,223]	[2,253]	{4.3}
$20 \leq y < 30$	1,432.6 (10.1)	1,527.5 (10.8)	94.9 (14.8)
	[5,396]	[4,525]	{6.6}
$10 \leq y < 20$	1,488.7 (8.0)	1,535.9 (8.9)	47.2 (12.0)
	[7,692]	[6,558]	{3.2}
$y < 10$	1,450.7 (13.6)	1,522.6 (12.7)	71.9 (18.6)
	[3,093]	[3,352]	{5.0}

Notes: Each cell contains the mean for that group, along with standard error in parentheses, and number of observations in brackets or percentage increase in braces. Means are unweighted.

[a]Other household income in thousands of dollars.

Table 1.5 contains those results. The sample is disaggregated in the same way as in tables 1.3 and 1.4 to allow for comparison. Panel A presents participation results, and panel B presents hours of work for working women. Each cell presents the average participation rate (or hours of work) for that group, standard errors, and size of the sample.

The primary observation from panel A is that labor supply of married women was changing dramatically during the period for nontax reasons. Labor force participation increased even for those groups that saw no change in the marginal tax rate.

The second observation is that women whose marginal rates fell showed larger increases in labor force participation than those whose marginal rates were unchanged: those with spouses earning more than $50,000 increased their labor force participation by 8 percentage points, from 41.9 to 49.9 percent.[17] Those with spouses earning between $30,000 and $50,000 increased their participation rate by 5.5 percentage points.

Clearly the 8 percentage point increase in participation at the top of the income distribution reflects factors other than the effect of ERTA. Using women below that income bracket, one can generate several different estimates of the response to ERTA. Each estimate entails different assumptions about the comparability of the groups. I use the $30,000–$50,000 group because it is closest to the treatment group. While having a control group whose marginal tax rate is unaffected by the tax law (such as the $20,000–$30,000 group) is preferable, the raw means suggest that the results would be similar.

A comparison of the treatment and control groups suggests that participation of upper-income married women increased by 2.5 percentage points, or 6 percent. Over the same period, the relative after-tax share increased by approximately 6.9 percent. The implied elasticity of participation is 0.86.[18]

Panel B of table 1.5 presents average annual hours of work for *working* women. It shows that, while the highest income group increased their hours of work significantly over the period (129.4 hours), so did working women married to the poorest men (72 hours). This pattern is similar to that found by Bosworth and Burtless (1992) using data stratified into quintiles by family income. Overall, the pattern of annual work hours is far less continuous than that of participation. Recall, however, that it is a different group of women working after 1981 and that new participants may work fewer hours than existing participants.

A comparison of the treatment and control groups suggests that annual hours of work by upper-income married women increased by 70.1 hours. This figure represents a 5.5 percent increase in annual hours of work. Dividing by the corresponding relative increase in the after-tax share for working women (7.2 percent) produces an elasticity of 0.77. The question to ask is whether this is a response to tax reduction or to a combination of wage growth and tax reductions. If wages grew faster for the treatment group than the control group, estimates of the effect of ERTA are biased upward. Table 1.6 shows that the *relative* gross hourly wage increased by 2.2 percent between 1980 and 1984 for

17. All dollar amounts are in 1980 dollars.
18. An alternative measure of the effect of the tax law is the share of *non*participants drawn into the labor force. Because the two groups have different participation rates before the tax law, this measure need not generate similar conclusions. In this sample, the elasticity of nonparticipation is 0.62.

Table 1.6   Change in Gross Hourly Wage

Group[a]	Change (%)
$y \le 50$	7.25
$30 \le y < 50$	5.02
$20 \le y < 30$	4.93
$10 \le y < 20$	2.29
$y < 10$	−.57

Note: Reported figures are for workers with hourly wages between $1 and $100 (1980 dollars). The change is the difference in the average log gross wage between 1980 and 1984.
[a]Other household income in thousands of dollars.

the relevant groups.[19] The relative increase in the after-tax wage for upper-income women becomes 9.4 percent. Using the difference in the after-tax wage suggests an annual hours-of-work elasticity of 0.58 (5.5/94).[20]

Even after adjusting the estimates for wage growth, the responses suggested by the raw means are much larger than expected. Using very different methodologies, Mroz (1987) and Triest (1990) estimate uncompensated hours-of-work elasticities that are close to zero for working married women. In the next section, I address the concern that differences in observable characteristics or changes in these characteristics over time may bias both the hours-of-work and the participation responses.

1.6   Difference-in-Difference Regressions

Because women in the treatment group differ from women in the control group in characteristics that are relevant for labor supply, the observed relative differences in participation and hours of work may reflect the noncomparability of the groups rather than a response to ERTA. I control for such a possibility in this section. After presenting the specification used, I discuss the regression results.

1.6.1   Specification

Assuming that disutility of labor is normally distributed in the population generates the probit model for participation, specified as follows:

$$(4) \qquad P(\text{lfp}_{it}) = \Phi(\alpha_1 Z_{it} + \alpha_2 T_t + \alpha_3 \text{High}_k + \alpha_4 (T*\text{High})_{kt}).$$

The hours-of-work equation is specified as follows:

19. This number cannot be added to the results in table 1.4 because it is based on the sample of working women. Table 1.4 presents the figures for the entire sample.

20. If lower taxes lead women to choose better-paying but less-attractive jobs, and the higher wage represents a compensating differential, then hours of work should not adjust to the higher wage. Here the response is both the higher hours and the greater pay per hour. The hours-of-work increase is 30 percent higher (2.2/7.2), and the elasticity remains 0.77.

(5) $h_{it} = \beta_1 X_{it} + \beta_2 T_t + \beta_3 \text{High}_k + \beta_4 (T^*\text{High})_{kt} + \mu_{it}$,

where i indexes individuals, t indexes time, k indexes the group, Z_{it} and X_{it} are individual characteristics, T_t is a dummy equal to 1 for 1984 and equal to 0 for 1980, High_k equals 1 if real other household income is at least $50,000 (1980 dollars) and equals 0 if real other household income is between $30,000 and $50,000, and μ_{it} is an error.

The set of covariates Z and X are assumed to adequately control for allocation into the treatment group. The variables included are age, age squared, education, education squared, the number of preschool children, family size, a dummy for self-employed spouse, a race dummy (equal to 1 if the woman is nonwhite), 50 state dummies, and a dummy for residence in a central city. Any unobservable differences in labor supply preferences between the various groups will be picked up by the income class dummy High_k. The coefficient on this variable is expected to be negative because higher-income women will purchase more leisure than their counterparts further down the income distribution. To control for common macroeconomic factors affecting the labor supply of married women, I include a year dummy. Because participation and hours are increasing over time, α_2 and β_2 should be positive. The behavioral response to ERTA will be reflected in the coefficients on the interaction $T^*\text{High}$. A test that ERTA increased the labor supply of upper-income women is a test that α_4 and β_4 are greater than zero.

Thus far, the tax unit's other income determines the group assignment. Because the income distribution shifts over time with productivity growth, the number of families with real other household income of at least $50,000 should be greater in 1984 than in 1980. Classifying individuals using income may generate groups that differ in characteristics over the period. Note that if the included covariates capture all differences, estimates of the labor supply response will not be biased. Nonetheless, I generate different estimates by sorting individuals based on their percentile position in the income distribution. I classify women at or above the 95th percentile of the other income distribution as the treatment group and women between the 80th and 95th percentiles of the income distribution as the control group.

1.6.2   Difference-in-Difference Regression Results

Labor Force Participation

Table 1.2 showed that ERTA reduced taxes most for women with real other household income of at least $50,000. The raw data show that this group increased its participation by 6 percent and hours of work (by those employed) by 5.5 percent following the passage of the tax law.

This section presents results for regressions that control for various observable characteristics. Two sets of estimates are presented in table 1.7. In the first set of regressions, women are classified by their tax unit's real other household

Table 1.7   **Difference-in-Difference Probit Results: Labor Force Participation**

	Level Classification			Percentile Classification	
Variable	Coefficient (1)	Marginal Effect (2)	Coefficient (3)	Coefficient (4)	Coefficient (5)
Age	.038 (.012)	−.0116	.038 (.012)	.036 (.011)	.036 (.012)
Age^2	−.001 (.000)		−.001 (.000)	−.001 (.000)	−.001 (.000)
Education	−.010 (.046)	.0284	−.010 (.046)	.001 (.044)	.001 (.044)
Education^2	.003 (.002)		.003 (.002)	.003 (.002)	.003 (.002)
Children under age 6	−.440 (.029)	−.1732	−.440 (.029)	−.443 (.028)	−.443 (.028)
Nonwhite	.183 (.069)	.0709	.184 (.069)	.206 (.065)	.206 (.065)
Education*T			.012 (.012)		.010 (.011)
T	.098 (.030)	.0386	−.058 (.161)	.073 (.029)	−.059 (.153)
High	−.410 (.044)	−.1621	−.404 (.044)	−.392 (.041)	−.388 (.041)
T*High	.080 (.062)		.071 (.062)	.039 (.058)	.030 (.059)
Log-likelihood	−6,242		−6,242	−6,805	−6,804
Observations		9,995		10,871	
Predicted responses	.030 (.023)		.026 (.023)	.014 (.021)	.011 (.022)
Implied elasticity	0.91		0.79	0.42	0.33

Notes: Regressions include family size, 50 state dummies, a central city dummy, and a dummy for self-employed spouse. Data are from March CPS 1981 and 1985. High$_1$ equals 1 if real other household income exceeds $50,000 in cols. (1)–(3) (the control group is women with other income between $30,000 and $50,000) and at or above the 95th percentile in cols. (4) and (5) (the control group is women with other income between the 80th and 95th percentiles). Numbers in parentheses are standard errors.

income. These results are comparable to those generated from tables 1.3, 1.4, and 1.5. The treatment group is women with real other household income of at least $50,000. The control group is women with real other household income between $30,000 and $50,000. In the second set of regressions, women are classified by their tax unit's position in the other-income distribution. Columns (1)–(3) present the former set of results, and columns (4) and (5) present the latter set of results.

Column (1) presents the probit coefficients for equation (4). Because the probit is a nonlinear model, these coefficients are not equivalent to the marginal effects of the variables on participation. Column (2) presents the marginal probabilities.[21] All estimated coefficients in the regression have the expected signs. Older women are less likely to be in the labor force: the marginal probability is −1.16 percentage points. One year of education increases the probability of entering the labor force by 2.84 percentage points. The number

21. To generate the marginal effects, I multiply the normal density function (evaluated at the individual characteristics) by the coefficient on the after-tax share. The estimates presented are sample averages.

of preschool children reduces the likelihood that the mother enters the labor force, as does having a high-income spouse.

The probit coefficient for the interaction variable is 0.080 (with a standard error of 0.062). I generate the treatment effect using the sample of upper-income married women observed after the tax change. For each woman in that sample, I predict participation assuming that β_4 is zero; I then predict participation at the estimated value of β_4. The difference in the sample average of the participation probabilities is the treatment effect. The predicted increase in participation is 3.0 percentage points (from a base of 47 percent), with a standard error of 2.3 percentage points.[22] A simple calculation shows that the implied elasticity of labor force participation with respect to the after-tax share is 0.91 (6.3/6.9).[23]

These calculations assume that the distribution of potential market wages of the treatment and the control group grew at the same rate between 1980 and 1984. I test that labor demand explains part of the response by adding a variable that interacts education with the time dummy (T). The results are in column (3).

The education interaction is small and statistically insignificant and does not alter the overall results. The predicted response at the top of the income distribution falls to 2.6 percentage points (with a standard error of 2.3), and the implied participation elasticity falls to 0.79. Changes in the returns to education, therefore, explain only 13 percent of the estimated response. This finding should not be surprising. The difference in average education between two groups is very small, less than one year. It seems that distinguishing between a common time effect and a differential education response in this sample is not possible. Note that the inclusion of the education interaction makes the time dummy negative and insignificant. In fact, when evaluated at the average education level in the sample (13.58), the sum of the time and the education coefficients (0.105) is very similar to the time coefficient in the basic regression (0.098).

Using income percentiles to define the various groups generates insignificant participation responses that are of the same order of magnitude. Women at or above the 95th percentile of other-income distribution constitute the high-

---

22. The asymptotic variance of the estimated treatment effect is given by

$$V(G(\theta)) = \left[\frac{\partial G(\hat{\theta})}{\partial \hat{\theta}}\right] V(\hat{\theta}) \left[\frac{\partial G(\hat{\theta})}{\partial \hat{\theta}}\right]',$$

where $G(\hat{\theta})$ is the treatment effect given by

$$G(\hat{\theta}) = \frac{1}{N}\sum_{i=1}^{N}[\Phi(X_i\hat{\theta}\,|\,D = 1) - \Phi(X_i\hat{\theta}\,|\,D = 0)]$$

and $\hat{\theta}$ = estimated parameters, Φ = normal cumulative distribution function, D = treatment interaction dummy, X_i = regressors for individual i, and ϕ = normal density function.

23. Note that this estimate does not necessarily imply that a 1 percent rise in the marginal tax rate will reduce participation by 0.91 percent.

income group. Women who fall between the 80th and 95th percentiles of the distribution constitute the control group. The results are presented in columns (4) and (5). The predicted response falls to a statistically insignificant 1.4 percentage points. Accounting for changes in the returns to education reduces those figures further to 1.1 percentage points. These results imply a participation elasticity of 0.33 with respect to the after-tax share.

Controlling for demographic characteristics does not alter the basic difference-indifference estimates of ERTA's effect on married women's labor force participation. The range of participation responses is 1.1 to 2.6 percentage points.

Specification checks. There remains significant variation in income, both within groups and over time. Part of the time variation in income is artificial, however. The change in the top code (from $50,000 in the 1981 March CPS to $100,000 in the 1985 March CPS) increases the treatment group's other income relative to that of the control group. This spurious increase in income generates a reduction in participation by upper-income women (by the income effect) and, as a result, increases the estimated effect of ERTA. To remove this bias, I top-code the husband's wage and salary income at $50,000 (adjusted for inflation) in the 1985 March CPS and generate an adjusted other income, which I then include as a regressor in the participation equation. The inclusion of the adjusted measure of other income does not affect the results. The estimated treatment effect increases to 3.2 percentage points in the level classification and 1.6 percentage points in the percentile classification.

That upper-income women are observationally different from lower-income women leaves open the possibility that the estimated responses are due to a contemporaneous shock correlated with observable characteristics. If the estimated response varies by race, we would be suspicious of the interpretation that ERTA caused the observed shift in labor supply. To check this possibility, I interacted age, race, family size, and children younger than six variables with the time dummy. The predicted response to ERTA remained unaffected. The results are also not sensitive to the use of education and cohort dummies.

An additional concern is that the nonlinearity of the probit model drives the estimated response. The difference-indifference approach relies heavily on the linearity of the model. To gauge the bias from the nonlinearity of the model, I estimate linear probability models of the participation decision. The estimated responses mimic closely the predicted responses using the probit model: 3.2 percentage points using the level classification and 1.4 percentage points using the percentile classification.

Annual Hours of Work

Table 1.8 presents the hours-of-work regression results for *working* married women. Because the evidence suggests a participation response, we should be careful in interpreting the hours results without any correction for the selection

Table 1.8   **Differences-in-Differences OLS Results: Annual Hours Conditional on Employment**

	Level Classification		Percentile Classification	
Variable	(1)	(2)	(3)	(4)
Age	35.30 (9.23)	35.89 (9.23)	33.17 (8.75)	32.98 (8.75)
Age^2	−.449 (.109)	−.446 (.109)	−.422 (.104)	−.420 (.104)
Education	−147.33 (42.66)	−146.35 (42.42)	−123.49 (39.81)	−122.16 (39.48)
Education^2	6.29 (1.51)	5.91 (1.51)	5.51 (1.41)	5.13 (1.41)
Children under age 6	−125.23 (24.02)	−126.59 (24.01)	−133.80 (22.49)	−135.06 (21.48)
Nonwhite	221.61 (45.20)	222.51 (45.15)	220.92 (42.09)	221.88 (42.06)
Education*T		18.49 (9.07)		18.17 (8.53)
T	24.15 (22.39)	−228.89 (124.42)	24.74 (21.41)	−223.42 (117.85)
High	−124.66 (38.37)	−118.66 (38.56)	−111.04 (35.21)	−105.01 (35.36)
T*High	61.76 (52.15)	49.91 (52.65)	32.89 (48.72)	21.02 (49.12)
R^2	.090	.091	.089	.089
Observations		5,558		6,146
Elasticity	0.56	0.45	0.34	0.22

Notes: Regressions include family size, 50 state dummies, a central city dummy, and a dummy for self-employed spouse. Data are from March CPS 1981 and 1985. High$_1$ equals 1 if real other household income exceeds $50,000 in cols. (1) and (2) (the control group is women with other income between $30,000 and $50,000) and at or above the 95th percentile in cols. (3) and (4) (the control group is women with other income between the 80th and 95th percentiles). Numbers in parentheses are standard errors.

effect. If one could identify a shock to participation but not to hours of work, one could identify a selection model. ERTA, however, does not include any provisions that affect participation separately from hours of work. With that caveat in mind, I present the regression results.

Column (1) of table 1.8 presents results of equation (5) using OLS. The evidence for an hours-of-work response is weak. The table shows that, relative to women in the next income group, upper-income married women worked 61.76 more hours per year (with a standard error of 52.15). Purging the effect of changes in returns to education reduces the response to 48.8 hours. Using the percentile definitions, the estimate falls to 20 hours per year (with a standard error of 49.12). Simple calculations suggest that the uncompensated elasticity of hours of work is between 0.22 and 0.45. Therefore, controlling for observable characteristics reduces the hours-of-work response at the top of the income distribution.

1.7 Standard Labor Supply Estimates

I have argued that the difference-in-difference approach is preferable to the more standard approach of estimating labor supply equations because it does not rely explicitly on any measure of the net wage. That is an advantage because the net wage is measured with error. Heckman (1993) notes that "CPS-type wage measures have a very low signal-to-noise ratio." Of course, the marginal tax rate will also be measured with error since survey data generally does not include deductions or exemptions. Therefore, the net wage coefficient in a standard labor supply equation will be biased downward. If the measurement error averages to zero in the defined income classes, however, then the difference-in-difference results are unbiased. In this section, I compare the previous results with standard labor supply estimates.

1.7.1   Labor Force Participation

Table 1.9 presents the results for the labor force participation equation:

$$(6) \qquad P(\text{lfp}_{it} = 1) = \Phi(\beta_1 Q_{it} + \beta_2 \ln(1 - \theta)_{it} + \beta_3 y_{it}).$$

The covariate set Q includes the same covariates as in the difference-in-difference regressions, θ is the marginal tax rate on the participation margin,

Table 1.9   **Standard Labor Supply Model Probit Results: Labor Force Participation**

Variable	Coefficient (1)	Marginal Effect[a] (2)	Coefficient (3)	Coefficient (4)
Age	.053 (.004)	−.0076	.052 (.004)	.052 (.004)
Age^2	−.001 (.000)		−.001 (.000)	−.001 (.000)
Education	.046 (.010)	.0327	.037 (.010)	.037 (.010)
Education^2	.002 (.000)		.003 (.000)	.003 (.000)
Children under age 6	−.374 (.011)	−.1318	−.376 (.011)	−.376 (.011)
Nonwhite	.161 (.024)	.0547	.164 (.024)	.164 (.024)
After-tax income (thousand $)	−.001 (.001)	−.0047	.001 (.002)	.001 (.002)
log (After-tax share)	.622 (.078)		.330 (.095)	.293 (.099)
High*log(After-tax share)				.375 (.315)
Time dummy	Yes		Yes	Yes
Income dummies	No		Yes	Yes
Log-likelihood	−30,684		−30,607	−30,606
Observations		54,373		
Marginal effect of tax variable	.219 (.027)		.116 (.033)	.213 (.112)
Elasticity	0.32		0.17	0.32[b]

Notes: Other covariates include family size, a dummy for self-employed spouse, 50 state dummies, and a central city dummy. Data are from March CPS 1981 and 1985. In cols. (3) and (4), I include 10 income class dummies (see text for definition). Numbers in parentheses are standard errors.

[a]Marginal effect is given by $[\phi(x\beta)]*\beta$, where ϕ is the standard normal density evaluated using the estimated parameters and β is the estimated coefficient.

[b]The elasticity in col. (4) refers to high-income women (other income of at least $50,000).

and y_{it} is the tax unit's after-tax income, excluding the wife's income. I estimate several specifications of this model.

The probit coefficients of equation (6) are in column (1) of table 1.9, and the marginal probabilities are in column (2). The marginal effects are similar to those estimated in the difference-in-difference regression. The estimate suggest that an additional year of education increases the likelihood that a married woman enters the labor force by 3.27 percentage points, as compared to 2.86 percentage points in the difference-in-difference regression. Older, white women with preschool children are less likely to be in the labor force, again in similar magnitudes to what the previous estimates suggest.

The coefficient on the log of the after-tax share is 0.622, with a standard error of 0.078. The marginal effect, presented at the bottom of the table, is 0.219 (with a standard error of 0.027).[24] To calculate the elasticity of participation, I divide the marginal probability by the average participation rate in the sample (0.671). A 1 percent increase in the after-tax share leads to a 0.32 percent increase in labor force participation.[25]

Both cross-sectional and time variations in marginal tax rates identify the tax effect. The cross-sectional variation in taxes derives largely from differences in income and family size, creating a potential identification problem. If the relationship between these variables and hours of work is nonlinear, then the after-tax share variable may reflect these nonlinearities rather than the tax effect. To account for this possibility, I reestimated the participation equation with 10 dummies for other-household income.[26] Column (3) of table 1.9 shows that the tax coefficient declines by almost 50 percent, from 0.622 to 0.330 (with a standard error of 0.095). Including income class dummies reduces the marginal effect to 11.6 percentage points and the elasticity to 0.17.

One explanation for these results might be that income dummies removed time (and cross-sectional) variation in marginal tax rate. Tables 1.3 and 1.4 show that the tax changes were correlated with income. If this were the entire story, however, we should have observed an increase in the standard error and no change in the tax coefficient. The more plausible explanation is that the relationship between other household income and labor force participation

---

24. The result is not very different if calculated at the characteristics of the average woman.

25. It is convenient to use the after-tax share because wages are not observed for those who are not working. Nonetheless, wages can be imputed for nonworkers. I do so by using Heckman's (1979) technique for correcting for sample selection bias. I predict the hourly wage by estimating a wage equation (using the sample of working women) in which I include the following demographic variables: age and education (in levels and higher-order terms), an age-education interaction, dummies for time, state, race, and central city residence, and a sample selection term. Using the estimated coefficients from the wage equation, I predict an hourly wage for each woman in the sample. The results for the regression that includes the net wage variable suggest that taxes have a much stronger effect on participation: the elasticity on the participation margin is 0.59. The problem with this procedure is that identification is derived from functional form assumptions.

26. The dummies are defined for the following group: $y \geq \$50,000$, and at \$5,000 intervals for incomes below \$50,000. The excluded dummy is $\$40,000 \leq y < \$45,000$.

is nonlinear and that the coefficient on the after-tax share reflects this non-linearity.

The difference-in-difference results suggest a participation elasticity much larger than the 0.17 estimated here. Might it be the case that upper-income women are more responsive than the "average" woman? The results in column (4) show that upper-income women do, in fact, have higher participation elasticities than the average woman, although the difference is not statistically significant. The coefficient on the after-tax share (for high-income women) is 0.668, and the implied elasticity is 0.32.

Measurement error in the after-tax share resulting from the fact that deductions and exemptions are imputed may still bias this estimate downward. If this measurement error averages to zero in the defined income classes, then the difference-in-difference estimates are preferable to the standard model estimates.

1.7.2   Annual Hours of Work

Table 1.10 presents results for the hours-of-work equation:

$$(7) \qquad (h_{it} \,|\, X_{it}, w_{it}^n, y_{it}, h_{it} > 0) = \alpha_1 X_{it} + \alpha_2 \ln(w_{it}^n) + \alpha_3 y_{it} + \varepsilon_{it},$$

where X_{it} includes the same covariates as the participation regression. The income variable used in these regressions is "virtual" income. The wage variable is constructed in the usual method: by dividing wage and salary income by annual hours of work. The after-tax wage is the product of the hourly wage and the after-tax share.

Table 1.10 presents the basic regression results.[27] Column (1) presents the OLS results. Again all estimated coefficients in the regression have the expected signs. Women work fewer hours as they get older. Nonwhite women and women with preschool children also work fewer hours, as do women with more virtual income.

I estimate the regressions using the observed net wage without correcting for self-selection. This regression produces an after-tax wage coefficient of 53.89 hours. To translate this into an elasticity, I divide the coefficient by the average annual hours worked in the sample (1,478). The uncompensated elasticity of hours of work with respect to the after-tax wage is 0.03.

To address the endogeneity of the marginal tax rate and virtual income to hours worked, I use the net wage and the unit's after-tax income at the zero hours margin as instrumental variables.[28] The 2SLS estimates are presented in

---

27. The sample size for these regressions is smaller than that reported in table 1.2 because the log of the wage is undefined for women who have a zero wage (volunteers).

28. The first-hour marginal tax rate is a valid instrument if it is correlated with the actual marginal rate and uncorrelated with the error in the hours equation. In my sample, it is easy to defend the first assumption: the correlation between the marginal rate and its instrument is 0.44. It is not so easy to defend the second assumption, however. The error in the labor supply equation may be correlated with the first-hour rate if we imagine an assortative mating process. Suppose that higher-

Table 1.10   **Standard Labor Supply Model OLS and 2SLS Results: Annual Hours Conditional on Employment**

Variable	OLS (1)	2SLS (2)	2SLS (3)	2SLS (4)
Age	54.34 (2.80)	52.27 (2.81)	52.11 (2.83)	52.02 (2.83)
Age^2	−.688 (0.04)	−.662 (0.04)	−.660 (0.04)	−.659 (0.04)
Children under age 6	−134.54 (7.24)	−136.79 (7.25)	−137.56 (7.25)	−137.56 (7.25)
Nonwhite	135.34 (13.86)	133.19 (13.88)	134.58 (13.89)	134.00 (13.89)
Virtual income (thousand $)	−6.03 (0.45)	−6.00 (0.46)	−6.09 (1.69)	−5.75 (1.69)
log (Net wage)	53.89 (4.69)	102.88 (4.72)	102.39 (4.73)	106.09 (4.90)
High*log(Net wage)				−54.18 (18.15)
Time dummy	Yes	Yes	Yes	Yes
Income dummies	No	No	Yes	Yes
Adjusted R^2	.085	.082	.084	.083
Observations			35,851	
Elasticity	0.03	0.07	0.07	0.04[a]

Notes: Regressions also include family size, a dummy for self-employed spouse, 50 state dummies, and a central city dummy. Data are from March CPS 1981 and 1985. Numbers in parentheses are standard errors. The sample here includes only women with hourly wages between $1 and $100 (1980 dollars). The instrument in the 2SLS regression is the first-hour, after-tax wage. In cols. (3) and (4), I include 10 income class dummies (see text for definition).

[a]The elasticity in col. (4) refers to high-income women (other income of at least $50,000).

column (2). The coefficient on the log of the net wage increases to 102.88 (statistically significant at the 99 percent confidence interval). Nonetheless, the elasticity of hours of work, 0.07, remains very small. In column (3), I reestimate the hours-of-work equation by adding 10 income class dummies (defined as in the participation equation). Here, time variation in after-tax wages rather than cross-sectional variation identifies the hours equation. The inclusion of income dummies does not affect the results: the after-tax wage coefficient remains 102.39 (with a standard error of 4.73). The hours-of-work equations do not seem to exhibit the nonlinear relationship with income found in the participation equations.

The uncompensated elasticity estimates in columns (2) and (3) predict hours-of-work responses to ERTA that are much smaller than those estimated in table 1.8. Moreover, allowing a separate coefficient for upper-income women does not reduce this divergence (col. [4]). The coefficient on the interaction variable (High*log(Net wage)) is negative and statistically significant:

---

income men have stronger tastes for work and they tend to marry women that are like them. Because it implies a positive correlation between tastes for work and first-hour tax rates, assortative mating would bias the coefficient on the net wage variable upward.

the elasticity of labor supply for high-income women is only 0.04, smaller than for the "average" woman in the sample.

Elasticities derived from basic hours-of-work equations are generally lower than those generated using difference-in-difference methods. One explanation for this divergence is measurement error in the net wage. Evidence suggests that there is significant measurement error in the wage and that it is negatively correlated with hours of work (Mroz 1987). Such error would bias the coefficients in the standard model toward zero. If this measurement error averages to zero in the income classes defined, then the difference-in-difference regression results are unbiased (Wald 1940; Angrist 1991). In addition, the standard labor supply models estimated were the most basic models. No attempt was made to address biases due to wage endogeneity or sample selection in the hours-of-work equations. Nonetheless, the results generated are consistent with those of Mroz (1987), who carefully controlled for sample selection and wage endogeneity.

1.8 Conclusion

The Economic Recovery Tax Act of 1981 reduced marginal tax rates by 23 percent within each tax bracket. In addition, ERTA introduced a tax deduction of 10 percent of the secondary earner's income up to $30,000. Together, these changes produced a significant reduction in marginal tax rates for upper-income individuals and a smaller reduction for lower-income individuals. I use the variation in marginal tax rates to estimate both difference-in-difference regression models (where I compare the change in labor supply for upper-income women with change in labor supply for lower-income women) and standard labor supply models (where labor supply is a function of the after-tax wage).

Using data from the 1981 and 1985 Current Population Survey, I find weak evidence that labor force participation of upper-income married women is responsive to taxes. The point estimates suggest that following ERTA, upper-income married women increased their labor force participation by up to 2.6 percentage points (from a predicted base of 47 percent). That estimate suggests an elasticity of 0.79. For working women, the most likely values show a response between 20 and 49 hours per year, but these are estimated with such imprecision that it is not possible to rule out no response at all. Finally, standard labor supply estimates predict participation and hours-of-work responses for upper-income women that are at the lower end of the observed responses. A likely explanation for the divergence between the difference-in-difference results and the standard model results is measurement error in the marginal tax rate and in the gross wage. This measurement error biases the standard estimates downward. The difference-in-difference results, however, would be unbiased if the measurement error averages to zero for the income groups defined.

References

Angrist, Joshua. 1991. Grouped-data estimation and testing in simple labor supply models. *Journal of Econometrics* 47:243–66.

Auten, Gerald, and Robert Carroll. 1994. Taxpayer behavior and the 1986 Tax Reform Act. Washington, D.C.: Department of the Treasury, Office of Tax Analysis. Mimeograph.

Blundell, Richard, Alan Duncan, and Costas Meghir. 1995. Estimating labour supply responses using tax reforms. London: Institute for Fiscal Studies. Mimeograph.

Blundell, Richard, and Costas Meghir. 1986. Selection criteria for a microeconometric model of labour supply. *Journal of Applied Econometrics* 1:55–80.

Boskin, Michael. 1973. The economics of labor supply. In *Income maintenance and labour supply,* ed. Glen Cain and Harold Watts. Chicago: Markam.

Bosworth, Barry, and Gary Burtless. 1992. Effects of tax reform on labor supply, investment, and saving. *Journal of Economic Perspectives* 6(1): 3–26.

Burtless, Gary. 1991. The supply side legacy of the Reagan years: Effects on labor supply. In *The economic legacy of the Reagan years: Euphoria or chaos?* ed. A. Sahu and Ronald Tracy. New York: Praeger.

Eissa, Nada. 1995. Taxation and labor supply of married women: The Tax Reform Act of 1986 as a natural experiment. NBER Working Paper no. 5023. Cambridge, Mass.: National Bureau of Economic Research.

Feenberg, Daniel, and James Poterba. 1993. Income inequality and the incomes of very high income taxpayers. In *Tax policy and the economy,* vol. 7, ed. James Poterba, 145–77. Cambridge: MIT Press.

Feldstein, Martin. 1993. The effect of marginal tax rates on taxable income: A panel study of the 1986 Tax Reform Act. NBER Working Paper no. 4496. Cambridge, Mass.: National Bureau of Economic Research.

Feldstein, Martin, and Andrew Samwick. 1992. Social security rules and marginal tax rates. *National Tax Journal* 45(1): 1–22.

Hall, Robert. 1973. Wages, income and hours of work in the U.S. labor force. In *Income maintenance and labor supply,* ed. Glen Cain and Harold Watts. Chicago: Markam.

Hausman, Jerry. 1980. The effects of wages, taxes, and fixed costs on women's labor force participation. *Journal of Public Economics* 14:161–94.

———. 1981. Labor supply. In *How taxes affect economic behavior,* ed. Henry Aaron and Joseph Pechman. Washington, D.C.: Brookings Institution.

———. 1985. Taxes and labor supply. In *Handbook of public economics,* vol. 1, ed. Alan Auerbach and Martin Feldstein. Amsterdam: Elsevier.

Hausman, Jerry, and James Poterba. 1987. Household behavior and the Tax Reform Act of 1986. *Journal of Economic Perspectives* 1(1): 101–20.

Hausman, Jerry, and Paul Ruud. 1984. Family labor supply with taxes. *American Economic Review* 74(2): 242–49.

Heckman, James. 1979. Sample selection as a specification error. *Econometrica* 47(6):153–61.

———. 1982. Comment. In *Behavioral simulation methods in tax policy analysis,* ed. Martin Feldstein. Chicago: University of Chicago Press.

———. 1993. What has been learned about labor supply in the past twenty years? *American Economic Review* 83(2): 116–21.

Katz, Lawrence, and Kevin Murphy. 1992. Changes in relative wages, 1963–1987: Supply and demand factors. *Quarterly Journal of Economics* 107(1): 35–78.

Killingsworth, Mark. 1983. *Labor supply.* Cambridge: Cambridge University Press.

Killingsworth, Mark, and James Heckman. 1986. Female labor supply: A survey. In

Handbook of labor economics, vol. 1, ed. Orley Ashenfelter and Richard Layard. Amsterdam: Elsevier.

Lindsey, Lawrence. 1981. Is the maximum tax on earned income effective? *National Tax Journal* 34(2): 249–55.

———. 1987. Individual taxpayer response to tax cuts, 1982–1984: With implications for the revenue maximizing tax rate. *Journal of Public Economics* 33:173–206.

MaCurdy, Thomas, David Green, and Harry Paarsch. 1990. Assessing empirical approaches for analyzing taxes and labor supply. *Journal of Human Resources* 25(3): 415–90.

Mroz, Thomas. 1987. Sensitivity of an empirical model of married women's hours of work to economic and statistical assumptions. *Econometrica* 55(4): 765–99.

Murphy, Kevin, and Finis Welch. 1992. The structure of wages. *Quarterly Journal of Economics* 107(1): 285–326.

Navratil, John. 1994. Evidence of individual taxpayer behavior from panel tax return data. Cambridge: Harvard University. Mimeograph.

Pechman, Joseph. 1987. *Federal tax policy.* Washington, D.C.: Brookings Institution.

Rosen, Harvey. 1976. Taxes in a model of joint wage-hours determination. *Econometrica* 44(3): 485–508.

Scholz, John Karl. 1990. The participation rate of the earned income tax credit. Discussion Paper no. 928-90. Madison: University of Wisconsin, Institute for Research on Poverty.

Triest, Ronald. 1990. The effect of income taxation on labor supply in the United States. *Journal of Human Resources* 25(3): 491–516.

Wald, Abraham. 1940. The fitting of straight lines if both variables are subject to error. *Annals of Mathematical Statistics* 11:284–300.

Comment   James J. Heckman

This paper adopts an atheoretical stance toward measuring the effect of taxes on labor supply. It offers a dramatic contrast to the paper by Hausman that I discussed at the 1981 NBER conference held in Florida on measuring the effect of taxes on behavior (see Heckman 1982).

The earlier Hausman paper offered a tightly structured model of taxes and labor supply that exploits all the information in the data and in the theory and adds a lot of econometric structure to produce tax estimates that are not credible. I pointed out that Hausman lacked information about the true budget constraint facing potential workers and his assumptions produced statistically inconsistent estimators even granting the arbitrary distributional and functional form assumptions. My concerns were validated in a paper by MaCurdy, Green, and Paarsch (1990) who found (1) that they could not even reproduce Hausman's estimates using Hausman's methods and Hausman's sample, (2) that ro-

James J. Heckman is professor of economics at the University of Chicago and a research associate of the National Bureau of Economic Research.

The author thanks Jim Poterba for advice on ERTA and for general comments and Ann Ferris for editorial assistance. This work was supported by NSF-93-21-048 and a grant from the Russell Sage Foundation.

bust estimates show essentially zero wage and income effects for male labor supply, and (3) that simpler and more plausible methods of estimation produce estimates of labor supply that agree with the estimates from the complex methods properly applied.

The absurd labor supply estimates produced by the "structural" econometric approach led a whole generation of empirically oriented scholars to reject formal econometric methods and to adopt a series of substitutes for rigorous econometrics. The move toward social experiments, natural experiments, difference-in-difference methods, and Wald estimators represents a yearning for simplicity, familiarity, and robustness in frameworks for conducting empirical work in economics.

In contrast to a more economically explicit style of doing empirical work, the economics in this new empirical methodology is kept implicit, and the discussion of crucial identifying assumptions is also kept implicit. Many people like to keep their econometrics at an intuitive level and to agree, collectively, on what constitutes a "natural experiment" or an "instrument." Given the power of networks in our profession, this agreement to suppress explicit discussion of identifying assumptions and to suppress use of explicit economic measuring frameworks is likely to have a long life.

The new conventions should be recognized as just that: agreements among groups of like-minded persons to keep things simple and intuitively plausible. There is another way to settle these issues, however, and that is to uniformly apply the standards of credibility. Thus while Hausman's framework and empirical evidence is properly dismissed as arbitrary and unconvincing, it should also be noted that the widely used difference-in-difference method is also strongly functional form dependent. It requires additive separability between observed and unobserved variables. It requires that the unobservables have a special time-series structure. It assumes that common trends operate on both treatments and controls, and it rarely identifies parameters of economic interest. Blundell, Duncan, and Meghir (1995), cited by Eissa, demonstrate how very strong functional form assumptions are required to justify the application of difference-in-difference methods to estimate economically interpretable parameters. I amplify this point below. The available experimental evidence speaks strongly against the difference-in-difference method. LaLonde's widely acclaimed study (1986), which contributed to the distrust of econometric methods and the call for experiments, documented that the method gave very poor estimates. Heckman and Smith (1995) report similar evidence. The only thing going for the method and the closely related fixed-effects strategy is computational convenience.

The economic parameter being estimated is never defined in terms of conventional income and substitution effects measured in other studies. Thus it is difficult to compare Eissa's estimates with those from other studies, even other difference-in-difference studies, since the method is so strongly dependent on particular sample paths for conditioning variables. The 1981 tax reform had the effect of raising the after-tax wages of women from families with high income compared to those from families with low income. It also had the effect of raising the after-tax income of their husbands. It reduced the marginal tax rate on capital income from a top rate of 70 percent to 50 percent and changed other rates below the top as well. The net effect of the reforms on labor supply is ambiguous because the after-tax wage of women was higher, encouraging an increase in their labor supply, but the after-tax income of their husbands was higher, encouraging a reduction in female labor supply. The labor supply response estimated by Eissa is neither a compensated nor an uncompensated effect of taxes on female labor supply as conventionally defined because different tax changes apply to wage and capital gains income. Therefore, the author cannot reasonably compare her estimates to those from the previous literature that identified those effects.

The estimation strategy adopted in this paper relies critically on the classification of women into "high" and "low" cells based on pretax household income, excluding the wife's earnings but including other joint capital income, and assumes that taxes do not affect membership in this classification—the conditions required for application of the Wald estimator. Even if male labor supply has a zero wage elasticity, as the author assumes and as MaCurdy et al. effectively demonstrate, capital income is well known to have a high tax elasticity. If some women change categories as a result of the reduced tax on asset income, the effect is to violate the fixed grouping assumption of the Wald estimator. Presumably the net shift is that some "low" women become "high" women as their families adjust capital incomes.

Bias in the Estimator

To be more precise about the nature of the bias resulting from this violation, consider the following table for log hours of work:

	Low Income	High Income
New tax	C	A
Old tax	D	B

Let P_T be the proportion of women who move from D to A in response to the effect of the tax change on capital gains and other income. Assume no shifting across other cells. Let E be log labor supply. $E^0(l, T)$ is the log of hours worked under the old tax regime by low-income people who will transfer to the high-income group. $E^0(l, \tilde{T})$ is the log hours worked in the old tax regime by low-income people who will stay in the low regime. $E^n(l, \tilde{T})$ is the labor supply in the new regime for those initially low-income people who do not switch status. Let $E^0(h)$ be the log hours worked by high-income people in the old tax regime. Let $E^n(h)$ be the log hours worked in the new regime.

Eissa defines her parameter of interest to be

$$[(A - B) - (C - D)]/[\Delta\ln(1 - t)(h) - \Delta\ln(1 - t)(l)]$$

where A, B, C, and D stand for mean of log hours worked in each cell. Define

$$\Delta\ln(1-t)(h) - \Delta\ln(1-t)(l) = \Delta t$$

to be the change (in logs) of the after-tax share of wages between high income women and low income women.

$$A = E^n(h), \qquad B = E^0(h)$$

$$C = P_T E^n(1, T) + (1 - P_T)E^n(1, \tilde{T})$$

$$D = P_T E^0(1, T) + (1 - P_T)E^0(1, \tilde{T}).$$

For simplicity I use geometric means. What Eissa actually estimates is

$$[(A^* - B) - (C^* - D)]/\Delta t,$$

where, letting N_h be the number of people in the high-income regime and N_l the number in the low-income regime, both measured in the base state,

$$A^* = wE^n(h) + (1 - w)E^n(1, T),$$

$$C^* = E^n(1, \tilde{T}),$$

and

$$w = \frac{N_h}{N_h + P_T N_l}.$$

Then the bias for her parameter is

$$\{[(A^* - B) - (C^* - D)] - [(A - B) - (C - D)]\}/\Delta t$$

$$= [(A^* - A) - (C^* - C)]/\Delta t$$

$$= [(1 - w)(E^n(1, T) - E^n(h)) - P_T(E^n(1, \tilde{T}) - E^n(1, T))]/\Delta t.$$

It is plausible that income effects on labor supply yield the ordering $E^n(1, T) - E^n(h) > 0$, but it is also plausible that $E^n(1, \tilde{T}) - E^n(1, T) > 0$. Thus the direction of the bias for Eissa's parameter depends on the disparity in the new tax situation between the mean log labor supply of the transferees relative to those who stay in the high and low cells. The women shifting into cell A raise the labor supply there but by leaving cell C they raise the average there as well. The larger the transferees are as a proportion of women in the postreform high cell, and the larger the gap is between transferee labor supply and the labor supply of the initially high-income women, the more likely it is that her estimate is upward biased. The smaller the transferees are as a proportion of the pretax low-income households, and the farther apart the new tax regime labor supply of transferees and nontransferees is, the more likely it is that her estimate is downward biased for her parameter.

Dependence on Functional Form and Assumptions about Time Paths of Regressors

The extreme dependence of the difference-in-difference estimator on the functional form of the labor supply equation and implicit assumptions about movement of the exogenous variables over time between the high and low groups can also be exhibited within this framework. To discuss this issue, I ignore the crossover problem just discussed.

Write $\Delta E(h)$ as the change in log labor supply between the old and new tax regime for persons in the high group. $\Delta E(l)$ is the change in log labor supply for the low group. As before, $\Delta\ln (1 - t)(h)$ is the change in log marginal tax rates for the high group, and $\Delta\ln (1 - t)(l)$ is the change in the log marginal tax rate for the low group. Let $\Delta\ln X(h)$ be the change in other characteristics for the high group, and let $\Delta\ln X(l)$ be the change in the other characteristics for the low group. Let $\Delta U(h)$ be the change in the unobservables for the high group, and $\Delta U(l)$ be the change in the unobservables for the low group.

In finite changes,

$$\Delta E(h) = \alpha_1(h)\Delta\ln (1 - t)(h) + \alpha_2(h)\Delta\ln X(h) + \Delta U(h)$$

$$\Delta E(l) = \alpha_1(l)\Delta\ln (1 - t)(l) + \alpha_2(l)\Delta\ln X(l) + \Delta U(l) .$$

Eissa's estimator of wage response is the difference of the average of the changes within each group:

$$\frac{\overline{\Delta E(h)} - \overline{\Delta E(l)}}{\Delta\ln (1 - t)(h) - \Delta\ln (1 - t)(l)} = \frac{\overline{\Delta E(h)} - \overline{\Delta E(l)}}{\Delta t},$$

where the overbar denotes average. She implicitly assumes that $\alpha_1(h) - \alpha_1(l)$ (no wealth effect on the response of a change in taxes on labor supply), $\alpha_2(h) = \alpha_2(l)$ (other variables have the same marginal effect on log labor supply at different wage levels), and $\Delta\overline{\ln X}(h) = \Delta\overline{\ln X}(l)$ (the other characteristics, such as child bearing, age, wages, etc. change in the same way in logs between the groups) and

$$\plim_{N\to\infty} [\overline{\Delta U}(h) - \overline{\Delta U}(l)] = 0,$$

so that sample differences in the changes in unobservables between high and low converge to zero. Thus she implicitly makes strong functional form assumptions as well as assumptions about the time profiles in logs of the explanatory variables $X(h)$ and $X(l)$ in the two groups. She ignores the effects of taxes on the entry and exit of persons into the workforce and the effects of these compositional changes on estimated labor supply parameters—a major theme of the literature on selection bias surveyed in Killingsworth's survey of labor supply.

By adopting an atheoretical approach, the author throws away a potentially important source of information for identifying wage and tax effects on labor supply: the demand-induced change in real wages that highly educated women experienced in her sample period. The only advantages in not using the wage information are that she can assume that her women suffer from tax illusion and she can avoid standard measurement error and simultaneous equation problems in the use of wages in labor supply equations. However, all the evidence in the literature argues that the after-tax wage is relevant to labor supply decisions. Wage and tax effects in logs should have the same effects on labor supply. Averaging as she does should greatly attenuate mean zero measurement error and simultaneous equations problems. Thus it is not clear that she gains anything by not using the wage data.

Instead of using wage growth to help identify tax effects on labor supply, she adopts an ad hoc method for eliminating the effects of demand growth on wages and hence on labor supply. She throws wages into the $X(h)$ and $X(l)$ variables and therefore is forced to take steps to undo the consequences of the false assumption that high-income women have had the same wage growth as low-income women. Positive assortative mating on education coupled with the greater trend in wage growth for more educated women argues strongly against such an assumption. Part of her estimated tax effect is due to differential wage growth, but it would be better to constrain the tax coefficients and the wage coefficients to allow the variation in the wage growth to inform the estimation of tax effects.

The pendulum has swung too far away from using economics as a means of interpreting economic data. Wage variation should be used as a source of identifying information and not as a problem to be eliminated, especially when a substantial component of the growth is demonstrably exogenous to individual decisions, as was the wage growth of 1980s. Trends and demand shocks would provide "natural instruments" for wages.

Finally, the comparison of Eissa's estimate with those obtained from her interpretation of conventional econometric models of labor supply is not convincing. Econometrics has advanced beyond the simple probit model, and discrete-choice models that allow for more general forms of nonlinearity are now widely available.[1] Even the probit model could be made more flexible by incorporating nonlinearities in the arguments of the model. It is not an essential feature of probit analysis to constrain the estimates to be linear functions within the probit argument or to make tax or wage effects uniform across income levels. The contrast between the constrained probit estimates and her estimates is thus somewhat contrived.

Many methods are available for handling the problem of measurement error in wages. The labor supply equation estimated in this paper is much more like the "first generation" studies (as labeled by Killingsworth) than like the second-generation studies which consider simultaneity, selectivity, and measurement error. Her specification does not distinguish between self-selection effects of wages and the effects of wages on labor supply. Models and methods

1. See Todd (1995), who demonstrates that in many cases the models of nonparametric discrete choice make little difference in a wide array of applications. Her results suggest that probit models are not restrictive.

for estimating labor supply functions under more robust conclusions are available. It would be of interest to estimate these models before the strategy of estimating interpretable economic models is rejected out of hand.

Summary

Difference-in-difference methods are functional form dependent and produce interpretable economic parameters only under very special conditions. Difference-in-difference estimates are not even comparable across studies of the same type because policy-invariant structural parameters are not estimated and different studies condition on different variables and different levels of the variables. In this application, the estimates produce a tax effect on labor supply that has no clear economic interpretation and that cannot be compared with estimates from the structural labor supply literature. Moreover, the classification scheme of "high" and "low" family incomes is likely to be affected by taxes, violating a key assumption of the Wald estimation method used in this paper.

The reaction to the implausible labor supply models of the early 1980s has gone too far. It is time to bring economics back to the study of labor supply and taxes. Credible methods exist to estimate economically interpretable labor supply parameters that can be compared across studies and that can be used to address problems of economic interest.

References

Blundell, Richard, Alan Duncan, and Costas Meghir. 1995. Estimating labour supply responses using tax reforms. London: Institute for Fiscal Studies. Mimeograph.

Heckman, James. 1982. Comment. In *Behavioral simulation methods in tax policy analysis,* ed. Martin Feldstein. Chicago: University of Chicago Press.

Heckman, James, and Jeffrey Smith. 1995. Ashenfelter's dip and the determinants of program participation. Chicago: University of Chicago, March. Manuscript.

LaLonde, Robert. 1986. Evaluating the econometric evaluations of training programs with experimental data. *American Economic Review* 76(4): 604–20.

MaCurdy, Thomas, David Green, and Harry Paarsch. 1990. Assessing empirical approaches for analyzing taxes and labor supply. *Journal of Human Resources* 25(3): 415–90.

Todd, Petra. 1995. Estimation of binary choice models under choice-based sampling by semiparametric least squares. Chicago: University of Chicago. Manuscript.

2 The Taxation of Two-Earner Families

Martin Feldstein and Daniel R. Feenberg

More than two-thirds of married women under age 65 are now working outside the home. The tax treatment of married women is therefore a subject of substantial importance not only to the women themselves but also to anyone concerned about the operation of our labor markets and the efficiency of our tax system.

The U.S. system of taxing the earnings of married women is very different from the methods used in most other major industrial nations. Among the OECD countries, the most common procedure is to tax each married taxpayer separately, thereby giving married women the same tax schedule that they would face if they were single.[1] In contrast, the personal income tax in the United States taxes married couples on their combined income, thus not distinguishing between an increase in family income due to higher earnings of the husband and an increase in family income due to the wife's earnings. As a practical matter, the wife's marginal personal income tax rate on her first dollar of earnings is frequently the marginal *income tax* rate on her husband's last dollar of earnings.

More important, however, the overall marginal tax rate of the married working woman is substantially higher than her husband's marginal tax rate because of the rules governing social security taxes and retirement benefits. Married

Martin Feldstein is president of the National Bureau of Economic Research and the George F. Baker Professor of Economics at Harvard University. Daniel R. Feenberg is a research associate of the National Bureau of Economic Research.

The authors are grateful to Jeffrey Liebman, Harvey Rosen, and other members of the NBER Public Economics Program and the Harvard-MIT Public Finance Seminar for comments on an earlier draft.

1. See Munnell (1980) for a summary of the tax treatment of married couples in other countries. These rules have been revised in several countries in recent years. Britain and Canada have recently adopted new rules in which married women are taxed separately.

women and married men are both subject to the same 15.3 percent payroll tax on earnings (including the portion paid by employers). Because the level of future retirement and survivor benefits depends on the level of earnings during working years, the effective social security tax rate is the difference between the statutory 15.3 percent and the present actuarial value of the future benefits that the employee can expect per additional dollar of his or her earnings. The rules governing retirement and survivor benefits mean that the expected present value of these benefits is generally substantially higher per marginal dollar of a husband's earnings than for a marginal dollar of a wife's earnings. Feldstein and Samwick (1992) show that, for a typical middle-income married couple in their forties, the net social security OASI payroll tax rate in 1990 (excluding the disability and hospital insurance portions) was the full statutory rate of 11.2 percent for the wife but only about 3.8 percent for the husband.[2]

The current U.S. system of taxing married women has been criticized for three weaknesses. First, the high marginal tax rates on married women inappropriately distort their decisions about whether to work and, if they work, about how much to work. The basic theory of optimal taxation implies that the total deadweight loss of the tax system is reduced if marginal tax rates are lower on those individuals whose labor supply is more sensitive to marginal tax rates. Since there is substantial evidence that the labor supply elasticities of married women are substantially greater than the labor supply elasticities of their husbands,[3] the theory of optimal taxation implies that married women should be taxed at a lower marginal tax rate than their husbands.[4] In contrast to this optimality condition, the social security tax and benefit rules make the marginal tax rates on married women's earnings substantially higher than on

2. The difference reflects the fact that husbands generally have higher average lifetime earnings than their wives and that retiree wives are entitled to the greater of their own benefit and 50 percent of their husband's benefit. Since wives generally outlive their husbands, it is also important that a surviving wife is entitled to the higher of the benefits based on her own lifetime earnings and her husband's full benefit. Feldstein and Samwick (1992) present calculations of the net present value of retirement benefits for a variety of different combinations of income, demographic status, and discount rates.

3. See, e.g., the survey by Triest (1990) and the more recent study by Eissa (1995).

4. This conclusion is emphasized by Boskin and Sheshinski (1983). The relevant labor supply elasticities are the compensated elasticities of labor supply with respect to the net-of-tax share, i.e., to one minus the marginal tax rate. The proposition that applying a lower marginal tax rate to married women than to their husbands reduces the overall deadweight loss of the tax system depends on the cross-elasticities of labor supply as well as on the own elasticities; to the extent that there is evidence on this cross-elasticity (see, e.g., Triest 1990; Hausman and Ruud 1984) it appears to be sufficiently small so that it does not change the basic result.

A more general analysis of the deadweight loss of the income tax recognizes that it depends on distortions to the pattern of consumption (in favor of deductible items like mortgage interest and excludable items like fringe benefits) and to the nature of labor supply (effort, location, risk taking, etc., in addition to participation and hours). Feldstein (1995c) shows that this more comprehensive measure of deadweight loss can be evaluated in terms of the elasticity of taxable income with respect to the net-of-tax share. We plan to use the broader measure to evaluate alternative tax treatments of two-earner families in a future study.

their husbands' earnings.[5] The calculations developed in this paper show that the overall deadweight loss of the tax system could probably be reduced by lowering the marginal tax rate of married women even though there is a deadweight loss associated with the taxes needed to replace the lost revenue.

A second common criticism of the current system is that it imposes a "marriage penalty" on some married couples by taxing them more than the same two individuals would pay on the same income if they were single.[6] The marriage penalty is seen as unfair because it violates the basic principle of taxing equals equally by imposing different tax burdens on two otherwise identical couples. Although it could be argued that the two couples are not identical because one couple has chosen to live together without marrying while the other couple has called upon the state to provide the legal benefits of marriage, it seems contrary to general public policy to impose a fiscal charge on individuals for choosing to marry rather than living together without marrying. Moreover, as living together without marriage becomes more common, the effect of the marriage tax on the decision to marry is also likely to become more substantial.[7]

Finally, the current system is considered unfair because it imposes the same tax burden on a married couple with one earner as it does on a two-earner couple with the same income.[8] The two-earner couple will in general have more total hours of work and less of the untaxed home services of the second earner.

The present paper examines the efficiency and revenue effects of several alternative tax treatments of two-earner families. These options also have the effect of reducing the marriage penalty and of reducing the tax on two-earner couples relative to the tax on single-earner couples with the same total income. In addition to these new options, the present paper is distinguished from previous contributions to the analysis of two-earner families by four technical improvements:

1. The analysis uses new, and we believe more reliable, estimates of the compensated elasticities of the labor supply of married women based on the experience with the 1986 tax rate reductions.[9]

5. Previous discussions have ignored the important effect of net social security taxes; see, e.g., Rosen (1987).

6. See the discussions in Feenberg and Rosen (1983, 1994), Munnell (1980), and Rosen (1987).

7. Although there appears to be no direct research on this point, it is noteworthy that in 1992 there were 3.3 million unmarried couples (defined as two unrelated adults of the opposite sex sharing the same household) and that 1.1 million of these couples had at least one child under the age of 15. This compares to approximately 56 million married couples. Among 25–44-year-olds, there were 2.0 million unmarried couples and 26 million married couples, a ratio of 7.6 percent.

8. In fact, because of the social security tax and benefit rules, a couple with two earners is likely to pay more net tax than a couple with one earner and the same total income. The two-earner couple will pay more in tax (net of the present value of future social security benefits) unless the husband and wife have the same earnings in every year.

9. These elasticities have been estimated by Eissa (1995). We believe that her difference-in-difference estimates are more reliable than previous estimates based on cross-sectional variation

2. The marginal tax rates explicitly incorporate the social security payroll taxes net of the present actuarial value of future retirement benefits.

3. The analysis of alternative options is based on the NBER TAXSIM model which has been modified for this study to incorporate separate estimates of the earnings of husbands and wives.

4. Explicit estimates of the effects of the alternative options on the dead-weight loss of the tax system are presented. These reflect separately the changes in labor force participation and in average hours among those who are working. The analysis is based on the Harberger-Browning local approxima-tion and therefore does not require any assumption about the form of the util-ity function.

Section 2.1 of the paper presents a simple heuristic calculation that indicates that reducing the marginal income tax rate on a representative married women to what it would be if she were single would substantially reduce the dead-weight loss of the tax system as a whole. Section 2.2 extends this simple analy-sis to reflect changes in labor force participation as well as in average hours among those who are employed. This disaggregated analysis confirms the gen-eral estimates of the simpler model of the previous section.

Section 2.3 then describes the augmented TAXSIM model that is used to evaluate a variety of alternative options for the entire population of married taxpayers. The options are specified and the simulation results are presented in section 2.4. There is a brief concluding section.

2.1   Effect of Reducing the Marginal Tax Rate on Married Women: A Simplified Calculation

In 1994, a married woman in a couple with taxable income between $38,000 and $91,850 had a marginal federal personal income tax rate of 28 percent. In addition, she and her employer paid a social security payroll tax (including the Medicare portion) of 15.3 percent for which she can generally expect to re-ceive little or no incremental benefit (Feldstein and Samwick 1992). She was also likely to face a state marginal income tax rate of 5 percent or higher. Her combined marginal tax rate was therefore approximately 48 percent of her taxable income.[10]

---

in after-tax wage rates. Since previous estimates of labor supply behavior have been shown to be sensitive to the choice of functional form, it is significant that the difference-in-difference ap-proach avoids the need to specify an explicit functional form. A further advantage of this approach is that it is not necessary to impute a wage rate to the women who are out of the labor force.

Eissa's overall estimated supply elasticity, including the effects of both participation and hours, is not substantially different from the central tendency of the general body of previous work. See, e.g., the recent survey by Triest (1990). The confirmation of these earlier cross-sectional results by the more reliable difference-in-difference estimates is nevertheless very reassuring.

10. Because the employer's half of the 15.3 percent payroll tax is not included in the individual's taxable income, the combined tax of 48 percent is equivalent to $48/(1.0765) = 45$ percent of the full pretax wage. The deadweight loss depends therefore on this marginal tax rate although applied

Most married women would have faced a marginal federal personal income tax rate of only 15 percent if they were taxed as single individuals on their own income.[11] If they were taxed in this way, their total marginal tax rate would be reduced from 48 percent to 35 percent.

This section presents a simplified but very detailed estimate of the effect of reducing the tax rate on married women from 48 percent to 35 percent. The analysis suggests that this rate reduction would reduce the deadweight loss by substantially more than the decline in revenue. More specifically, the parameter values based on the estimated behavior of labor supply imply that, for such women, the deadweight burden of the tax would decline by $2.74 for each dollar of revenue loss. Since there are other ways of raising revenue with a substantially smaller relative deadweight loss, reducing the marginal tax rate on married women could be part of a broader tax reform that reduces the overall deadweight loss of the tax system.

Reducing the marginal income tax rate on married women would also address (but not completely remedy) the other two criticisms of the existing tax rules. It would reduce the marriage penalty and would tax a two-earner couple less than a single-earner couple with the same income.

Our analysis focuses on the effect of taxes on labor force participation and average hours. A more comprehensive analysis would recognize that changing tax rates affects taxable income through a number of other channels, including the intensity of work effort, the form of compensation, the use of tax-deductible expenditures, and various aspects of nonlabor income and expenses.[12] By focusing just on the traditional labor supply measures of participation and hours we understate the deadweight loss of the current situation and the potential gain from reform. We return to this subject in the concluding section.

The current analysis uses the labor supply elasticities recently estimated in Eissa's (1995) study of the response of married women to the 1986 tax rate reductions. In contrast to previous cross-sectional studies, Eissa used the natural experiment of the 1986 rate reductions to study how married women responded to differences in the marginal rate reductions associated with differences in their husbands' pre-1986 income levels. This difference-in-difference approach, based on successive Current Population Surveys, found a compensated elasticity of the participation rate with respect to the net of tax wage (i.e.,

---

to a tax base that is larger by a factor of 1.0765. Since the net effect is to reduce the deadweight loss by less than one-tenth, we postpone taking this into account until we get to the detailed TAXSIM calculations in section 2.4. This makes the illustrative calculations in the first two sections easier to follow.

11. Under the tax schedule for single individuals, the taxpayer would pay a 15 percent marginal tax on taxable income up to $22,750. Since the median money income of year-round full-time female workers was only $22,167 in 1992, a substantial majority of working wives in 1994 would have earnings below $22,750.

12. See Feldstein (1995a, 1995c, 1996) for a more complete discussion of the importance of this broader definition of taxpayers' responses to higher marginal tax rates.

to $(1 - t)w$, where t is the marginal tax rate and w is the pretax wage) of 0.42 and a compensated elasticity of the hours worked among those who are employed of 0.45.[13] Although the next section will study the separate responses of participation and hours, the simpler model in the current section uses a single overall elasticity of total hours with respect to the net of tax share.

The effect of the tax rate reduction on revenue depends on the corresponding *un*compensated elasticity of total hours with respect to the net-of-tax share. The usual Slutsky decomposition implies

$$(1) \qquad dL/(1 - t) = \{dL/d(1 - t)\}_{COMP} + (dL/dy)[dy/d(1 - t)],$$

where L is hours worked, t is the marginal tax rate, and dy is the rise in income that results from the tax rate reduction with no behavioral response. Multiplying both sides by $(1 - t)/L$ gives the corresponding elasticity expressions:

$$(2) \quad [(1 - t)/L][dL/d\,(1 - t)] = [(1 - t)/L]\,\{dL/d(1 - t)\}_{COMP} \\ + [(1 - t)/L]\,(dL/dy)[dy/d(1 - t)].$$

Writing η for the uncompensated supply elasticity on the left-hand side of equation (2) and ε for the compensated supply elasticity (the first term on the right-hand side) and noting that $dy/d\,(1 - t) = -dy/dt = wL$, where w is the pretax wage, allows us to rewrite equation (2) as

$$(3) \qquad\qquad\qquad \eta = \varepsilon + (1 - t)wdL/dy.$$

Eissa's estimates of compensated elasticities of participation and hours of 0.45 and 0.42 imply a total compensated labor supply elasticity of about $\varepsilon = 0.9$. Previous estimates imply that the income effect, that is, the net-of-tax expenditure on leisure per dollar of additional exogenous income, $-(1 - t)w(dL/dy)$, is approximately 0.10, implying that $\eta = \varepsilon - 0.10 = 0.80$.

With this information in mind, recall the traditional Harberger-Browning formula[14] for the deadweight loss of the income tax with a marginal tax rate of t is

$$(4) \qquad\qquad\qquad DWL = 0.5\varepsilon t^2 wL/(1 - t).$$

Thus, with a marginal tax rate of 0.48, the deadweight loss is

---

13. These estimates use the difference-in-difference framework combined with regression equations to control for demographic differences to reduce the bias and the variance of the parameter estimates. The raw difference-in-difference estimates are 0.35 for participation and 0.38 for hours, so the effect of the regression adjustment is a small increase in the estimated elasticities. Elasticities are calculated at the mean participation rate (0.464) and mean hours of those who worked (1,283 hours per year) among the women with high-income husbands.

14. Browning (1987) showed that the original Harberger (1964) formula for the deadweight loss (DWL = $0.5t^2\varepsilon wL$) has to be modified when the elasticity and the labor supply are not measured at the undistorted no-tax point. Since the elasticity estimate that we use and the initial labor supply are both measured at the with-tax distorted point, the traditional Harberger formula must be modified by dividing by $1 - t$. See Browning (1987, 13) and the derivation of eq. (7) below.

$$\text{DWL} = 0.5\ (0.48)^2 \varepsilon wL\ (1 - 0.48)^{-1}.$$

The corresponding formula for the reduction in the deadweight loss if the marginal tax rate is reduced from 48 to 35 percent is

(5) $\Delta\text{DWL} = -0.5[(0.48)^2 - (0.35)^2]\varepsilon wL/(1 - 0.48)$

$$= -0.093wL.$$

If the woman pays the same tax rate on all of her income,[15] a change in the marginal tax rate alters her tax liability at the rate of

(6) $d(twL)/dt = [1 - (t/(1 - t))\ \eta]wL.$

A tax reduction of $dt = 0.13$ from $t = 0.48$ implies a revenue loss of $0.034wL$.

Thus, every dollar of revenue loss reduces the deadweight loss by $0.093/0.034 = \$2.74$. Stated differently, this calculation implies that the total cost (including both the resource transfer and the deadweight loss) of taxing married women at 48 rather than 35 percent is \$3.74 for each extra dollar of revenue collected because the higher rate is used. Reducing the marginal tax rate from 48 percent to 35 percent would reduce the total deadweight loss of the tax system as a whole if the decline in revenue can be offset from some other source with a deadweight loss of less than \$2.74 per dollar of revenue.

The estimated loss of revenue caused by the reduction of the tax rate is based on the assumption that the woman's entire income was initially taxed at 48 percent. Recall that a 48 percent marginal tax rate for married women is based on a 28 percent federal marginal income tax rate and that the 28 percent rate begins at \$38,000 of taxable income for a married couple. With one child and the standard deduction, this is equivalent to a gross income of \$51,700. As a result, in many cases only a fraction of the wife's initial earnings will be subject to the full 48 percent rate. This would not affect the reduction in the deadweight loss since the deadweight loss depends only on the marginal tax rate. But when only a fraction of the women's income is originally taxed at the higher rate, the net revenue loss is reduced and may even be reversed to produce a revenue gain.

Consider for example a couple with one child in which the husband initially earns \$40,000 and the wife initially earns \$25,000. Their gross income is \$65,000, and their taxable income is \$51,300. She initially pays a 48 percent tax on \$13,300 of her earnings (the excess over \$38,000) and a 35 percent tax on the remaining \$11,700. Reducing her tax rate to 35 percent on all of her income only reduces her tax liability by \$1,729 on her original earnings. With a marginal tax rate reduction from 48 percent to 35 percent and an uncompensated elasticity of 0.8, she increases her pretax earnings from \$25,000 to

15. If the 48 percent initial marginal tax rate is paid on only part of her income, the revenue loss from reducing her tax rate to 35 percent would be less while the improvement in the deadweight loss would be unchanged. We return to this in the text below.

$30,000 and pays a tax of $1,750 on the incremental earnings. Her net tax payment therefore actually rises by $21. The reduction in the deadweight loss remains unchanged at $0.093wL = \$2,325$. Thus in this realistic case the deadweight loss reduction is substantial even though there is no revenue loss at all.

Before exploring these issues further with the help of the TAXSIM model's simulations, we consider in detail a more analytically complete model that distinguishes the separate effects of the tax rate on women's participation decisions and on the average hours worked by those who do participate.

2.2 Effects of Participation and Hours Responses to Marginal Tax Rate Reductions

Calculating the deadweight loss and the revenue effects of tax-induced changes in the married women's labor force participation rate is quite different from calculating the deadweight loss and revenue effects of tax-induced changes in average working hours among the employed women. It is useful therefore to consider each component of total labor supply separately and then to combine the separate results. We also show how the change in the deadweight loss and in revenue are related to the household's welfare gain.

2.2.1 Effect of the Hours Distortion on Deadweight Loss, Revenue, and Household Welfare

We begin with the effects of the marginal tax rate on the hours worked by those wives who are employed. To illustrate the calculation we again assume that a representative married woman initially pays a marginal tax rate of 48 percent on her entire earnings and that this is reduced to 35 percent by the change in tax rules. As already noted, if the 48 percent rate applies to only part of her earnings, this assumption causes us to overstate the revenue loss but not the improvement in the deadweight loss. Following Eissa (1995) we take the elasticity of hours with respect to the net of tax share to be $\varepsilon_H = 0.45$. Since the change in the deadweight loss and in the revenue are both proportional to the initial wage income, we need not specify numerical values for either the wage (w) or the initial hours (H_1).

Figure 2.1 illustrates the reduction in the deadweight loss as the marginal tax rate is reduced from $t_1 = 0.48$ to $t_2 = 0.35$ and hours increase on the compensated supply curve from H_1 to H_2. The deadweight loss reduction is equivalent to the shaded trapezoid bounded by the labor supply curve (SS) and the wage line (w) between the initial hours H_1 and the final hours H_2:

$$\Delta\text{DWL} = -[t_2 w(H_2 - H_1) + 0.5(t_1 - t_2)w(H_2 - H_1)]$$

$$(7) \qquad = -[t_2 w + 0.5(t_1 - t_2)w][dH/d(1-t)w](t_1 - t_2)w$$

$$= -[t_2 + 0.5(t_1 - t_2)](t_1 - t_2)(1 - t_1)^{-1}\varepsilon_H wH_1,$$

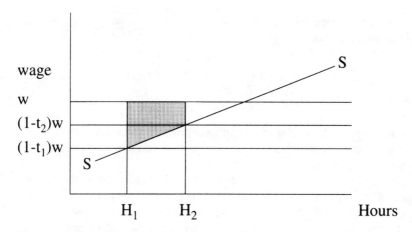

Fig. 2.1 Deadweight loss—participants

where $\varepsilon_H = [(1 - t_1)w/H_1][dH/d(1 - t)w]$. Substituting $t_1 = 0.48$, $t_2 = 0.35$, and $\varepsilon_H = 0.45$ implies $\Delta DWL = -0.047wH_1$.

The revenue effect of reducing the marginal tax rate from t_1 to t_2 is

(8) $$\Delta \text{Rev} = (t_2 - t_1)\, wH_1 + t_2 w\Delta H,$$

where ΔH is the increase in hours implied by the uncompensated labor supply function. That is, the revenue effect is the combination of the revenue loss from the reduced tax rate applied to the initial labor income offset in part by the additional revenue that results from the increased number of hours worked. Following the usual Slutsky decomposition,

(9) $$\Delta H = \{dH/d(1 - t)\}_{\text{COMP}} d(1 - t) + (dH/dy)dy,$$

where dy is the decrease in taxes with no behavioral response: $dy = (t_1 - t_2)wH_1$. Thus

(10) $$\Delta H = \varepsilon_H H_1[d(1 - t)/(1 - t)] + w^{-1}(dwH/dy)(t_1 - t_2)wH_1.$$

Since those who are not initially participating do not have any income effect, the entire effect of a change in exogenous income is concentrated on those who are already working. Previous estimates of this income effect suggest $dwH/dy = -0.15$.[16] Substituting this into equation (10) and using $\varepsilon_H = 0.45$ and $d(1 - t)/(1 - t) = 0.25$ implies

$$\Delta H = [0.45(0.25) - 0.15(0.13)]H_1 = 0.093H_1.$$

16. This is analogous to the simplifying assumption in the previous section that $(1 - t)dwL/dy = 0.10$.

Finally, substituting this expression for the change in hours into equation (8) yields the change in revenue:

$$\Delta\text{Rev} = (t_2 - t_1)wH_1 + t_2w\Delta H$$
$$= [-0.13 + 0.35\,(0.093)]wH_1$$
$$= -0.0975wH_1.$$

Thus, among those who are already working, the reduction in the marginal tax rate from 48 percent to 35 percent reduces revenue by $0.0975wH_1$ and reduces the deadweight loss by $0.047wH_1$.

When there is already a tax in place, the reduction in the deadweight loss that follows from a decline in the tax rate is not the same as the direct gain in the welfare of the individual household. If the decline in the deadweight loss is accompanied by a loss of revenue to the Treasury, that revenue is still a gain to the household although not to society as a whole. The reduction of the deadweight loss therefore understates the gain to the household. Conversely, if the decline in the deadweight loss is accompanied by a rise in revenue, the decline of the deadweight loss overstates the gain to the household.[17] Figure 2.1 shows that the net welfare gain to the woman has two components. First, on her initial earnings she would pay less tax; her net income would rise by $(t_1 - t_2)wH_1$. To this extent, her gain is the Treasury's loss. But the increased hours that she works are compensated at a net of tax wage $(1 - t_1)w$ that exceeds her required supply price along the SS compensated supply curve. Her surplus on these incremental hours is the triangle $0.5(t_1 - t_2)w(H_2 - H_1)$.

Thus, the working woman's total gain is

$$(11) \quad \Delta W = (t_1 - t_2)wH_1 + 0.5(t_1 - t_2)w(H_2 - H_1)$$
$$= (t_1 - t_2)wH_1 + 0.5(t_1 - t_2)\varepsilon_H[(t_1 - t_2)/(1 - t_1)]wH_1.$$

Substituting numerical values for $t_1 = 0.48$, $t_2 = 0.35$, and $\varepsilon_H = 0.45$ yields $\Delta W = 0.137wH_1$. The additional hours that the woman works increases her welfare by an amount equal to a little more than 5 percent of her pretax labor income.

Note that the triangle that represents the woman's surplus gain from working more hours is equal to the decline in the deadweight loss reduced by the gain in revenue that the government receives $t_2w(H_2 - H_1)$ as a result of the increased work along the compensated supply curve. The government's net revenue gain (excluding the revenue impact of the income effect on work) is this increased revenue $(t_2w(H_2 - H_1))$ minus the revenue lost on the initial earnings $((t_1 - t_2)wH_1)$. Thus the woman's gain is equal to the decline in the deadweight

---

17. More precisely, these statements are true if the revenue changes associated with changes in labor supply are measured along the compensated labor supply curve. This is explained further in the text that follows.

loss minus the net revenue gain of the government (excluding the revenue impact of the income effect on work).

We now turn to the corresponding calculations for the effect of the tax on participation and then combine the effects for the two groups.

2.2.2   Effect of the Participation Distortion on Deadweight Loss, Revenue, and Household Welfare

A reduction in the tax rate faced by married women increases the number of women who choose to work. More formally, it increases the number of women for whom the net-of-tax wage exceeds the reservation wage. Eissa (1995) estimates that the elasticity of participation with respect to the net-of-tax share is 0.42, implying that reducing the tax rate from 48 percent to 35 percent would increase the participation rate from 0.46 (in her sample) to about 0.51.[18]

There is of course no change in the deadweight loss among women who remain out of the labor force after the reduction in the tax rate. All of the deadweight loss reduction among those who are initially nonparticipants is among those women who go from being nonparticipants to being participants.

Modeling the reduction in the deadweight loss is complicated by two factors. First, we do not know how many hours would be worked by those women who would enter the labor force if their tax rate were reduced. In the current analysis we therefore assume that those who enter the labor force in response to the lower marginal tax rate would then choose to work the same number of hours that previous participants work, H_2.

The second complication is that we do not know the reservation wage of those who shift into the labor force when the tax rate declines. All we know is that the net reservation wage is higher than $(1 - t_1)w$ since they did not work at that wage and that it is not higher than $(1 - t_2)w$ since they do work at that wage. Fortunately, although the precise magnitude of the deadweight loss depends on the level of the reservation wage, the analysis in this section and the simulations in section 2.4 show that for many possible tax changes the uncertainty about the reservation wage produces only a relatively small uncertainty about the magnitude of the deadweight loss. We calculate the deadweight loss at the extreme values of the reservation wage (i.e., at $(1 - t_1)w$ and $(1 - t_2)w$).

These issues are illustrated in figure 2.2. The pretax wage is shown as w. The individual initially faces a net wage of $(1 - t_1)w$ at which she chooses to work zero hours. Her reservation wage is shown as $(1 - t^*)w$, where t^* is unknown to us as analysts. Increases in the net wage above $(1 - t^*)w$ induce her to move to higher desired hours along the labor supply curve S that starts

---

18. This reflects the fact that there is no income effect since those women who are not working initially do not have a change in tax revenue unless they change their behavior.

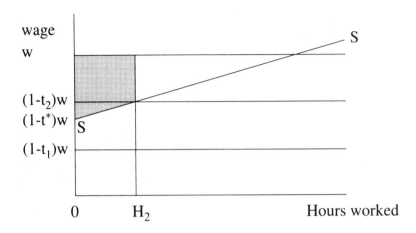

Fig. 2.2   Deadweight loss—nonparticipants

at the point with zero hours and net wage $(1 - t^*)w$ and passes through the point with coordinates $(1 - t_2)w$ and H_2. We do not observe intermediate points on that labor supply curve because her labor supply jumps to H_2 hours when the available wage jumps to $(1 - t_2)w$.

The reduction of the deadweight loss consists of the shaded trapezoid bounded by the gross wage level and the labor supply line between labor supply of zero and H_2. For all of those who are induced to participate, the deadweight loss falls by at least the rectangle t_2wH_2, the revenue that the government collects when people are no longer discouraged from participating in the labor force. In addition, the deadweight loss falls by the amount indicated by the triangle with area $0.5(t^* - t_2)wH_2$. Since the reservation wage is unknown, we will write this as $0.5\lambda(t_1 - t_2)wH_2$ where $0 < \lambda < 1$.

Combining the two parts shows that the total change in the deadweight loss is given by

(12)
$$\Delta DWL = -[t_2wH_2 + 0.5\lambda(t_1 - t_2)wH_2]$$
$$= -[t_2 + 0.5\lambda(t_1 - t_2)]wH_2.$$

Since $t_2 = 0.35$ and $0.5(t_1 - t_2) = 0.065$, the uncertainty about the magnitude of the reservation wage cannot influence the deadweight loss estimate by more than 19 percent (i.e., $0.065/0.35 = 0.19$) for those women who are initially nonparticipants. For those who become employed, the reduced deadweight loss lies between $0.35wH_2$ and $0.415wH_2$. More general tax reforms can create greater uncertainty about the reservation wage and the deadweight loss if the resulting value of t_2 is substantially less than t_1, for example, a separate filing system that reduces the personal income tax for the married women to zero.

To aggregate this with the deadweight loss calculated for those who were initially employed and changed their hours (i.e., the $0.047wH_1$ reported above)

the postchange hours H_2 in equation (12) must be restated in terms of the initial hours, H_1. Since equation (10) implies that the increase in hours among participants was equal to $0.093H_1$, it follows that $H_2 = 1.093H_1$ and therefore that the reduced deadweight loss among those who were not initially in the labor force but who are induced by the tax reduction to join the labor force lies between $0.35(1.093)wH_1 = 0.38wH_1$ per new participant and $0.45wH_1$ per new participant. The actual aggregation is discussed below after we comment on the revenue effect of the reduced tax rate for this group.

The revenue effect of the lower tax rate for those who are initially not in the labor force is unambiguously positive. Since none of these women were employed before the tax rate reduction, there is no decrease in initial tax revenue. The revenue effect for each woman who shifts from not working to working H_2 hours is

(13) $$\Delta Rev = t_2 w H_2.$$

Restating H_2 as $1.093H_1$ implies that $\Delta Rev = 0.38H_1$ for each new participant.

The welfare gain to the individual household depends on the woman's reservation wage. If the reservation wage is almost exactly equal to the net wage after the tax reduction ($t^* = t_2$), virtually the entire reduction in the deadweight loss accrues to the government in the form of increased revenue. This is a special case of the statement made earlier that, for those women who were initially working, the gain to the woman is the reduction in the deadweight loss minus the government's net revenue gain (excluding the revenue impact of the income effect on work effort.) In this case, the reduced deadweight loss is just the government revenue gain so there is no gain (i.e., no reduced deadweight loss) for the woman. Of course, if the reservation wage is lower, there will be a net gain to the woman equal to the area of the triangle $0.5(t^* - t_2)wH_2$ in figure 2.2, and the deadweight loss reduction exceeds the government's revenue gain by that amount.[19]

2.2.3   Combined Effect on Deadweight Loss and Revenue for All Married Women

The total of the effect on those who are initially employed and the effect on those who enter the labor force depends on the initial distribution between those who are in the labor force and those who are not and the increase in the fraction in the labor force that results from the tax rate reduction. To illustrate this calculation we use the figures based on Eissa's sample: 46 percent of women are initially in the labor force so that, with a participation elasticity of 0.42 with respect to the net-of-tax rate, the tax rate reduction from 48 percent to 35 percent raises the participation rate to 51 percent.

We can now put the pieces together and calculate the reduced deadweight

---

19. In the case of women who were previously nonparticipants, there is no income effect of the tax rate reduction.

loss per 100 married women. Since the deadweight loss per employed woman is reduced by $0.047wH_1$ and there are 46 employed women per 100 married women, the reduced deadweight loss from this source is $0.047(46)wH_1 = 2.16wH_1$ per 100 women. Similarly, since the deadweight loss is reduced by between $0.38wH_1$ and $0.45wH_1$ for each woman who enters the labor force and 5 women per 100 married women are induced to enter the labor force by the reduced tax rate, the reduced deadweight loss among initial nonparticipants is equal to between $1.90wH_1$ and $2.25wH_1$ per 100 women. Combining these two shows that the overall deadweight loss reduction per 100 married women is between $4.06wH_1$ per 100 married women and $4.41wH_1$ per 100 married women. In this case, the uncertainty introduced by not knowing the reservation wage is less than 10 percent of the total reduced deadweight loss.

The revenue effect of the reduced tax rate can be calculated in the same way. Since lowering the tax rate from 48 to 35 percent reduces tax revenue among employed women by $0.0975wH_1$ and there are 46 employed women per 100 married women, the revenue loss among those who are initially employed is $4.48wH_1$ per 100 married women. Among those who are not initially employed, the rate reduction induces a revenue gain of $0.38wH_1$ per newly employed person. Since the lower tax rate induces 5 women per 100 married women to join the labor force, the increased revenue is $1.90wH_1$. The combined revenue effect is therefore a net loss of $2.58wH_1$ per 100 married women.

Comparing the change in the deadweight loss and the change in the revenue shows that reducing the marginal tax rate from 48 to 35 percent would reduce the deadweight loss by at least $4.06wH_1$ per 100 married women while reducing revenue by $2.58wH_1$ per 100 married women. In rough terms, there is $1.57 of deadweight loss avoided for every dollar of lost revenue. Equivalently, there is a real net resource loss of $1.57 for every dollar of revenue raised by taxing married women at 48 instead of 35 percent. Since the revenue loss could presumably be offset with a much smaller deadweight loss by other tax changes, a reform that reduces the marginal federal income tax rate on married women from 28 to 15 percent (and therefore reduces the overall marginal tax rate from 48 to 35 percent) could increase the overall efficiency of the income tax.

It is worth emphasizing that, among women who are initially out of the labor force, the participation effect not only reduces the deadweight loss but actually increases revenue at the same time. Since some previous estimates of the response of married women to taxes suggest that the participation response is even more important than the 0.42 elasticity that we have assumed,[20] our calculations here may underestimate the relative advantage of lowering the marginal tax rate on married women. This is reinforced to the extent that the initial

---

20. Triest (1990) suggests that the response of total hours to increases in the net-of-tax share is about the same as Eissa's estimates but that almost all of that response comes through increased participation. The TAXSIM simulations presented below include an explicit analysis of the sensitivity of the results to the estimated elasticity.

average tax rate on those married women who are working is less than their marginal rate so that the rate reduction involves a smaller loss of revenue.

2.3   Adapting the TAXSIM Model to Analyze the Effects of Tax Reforms on Married Women

Although the detailed examination of a group of representative middle-class married women in section 2.2 indicates that there may be substantial efficiency gains from changing the tax rules that apply to two-earner families, it is important to go beyond these simplified examples and consider how changes in tax rules would affect the entire population of married women. Microsimulation analysis with the NBER TAXSIM model permits taking into account a variety of complexities, including the initial pattern of labor force participation and the relations between wives' earnings and other family income.

To carry out this analysis, the usual TAXSIM model had to be augmented in several ways. These changes are described in the current section. The TAXSIM model combines a stratified random sample of more than 100,000 tax returns provided by the Internal Revenue Service with a computer program that incorporates the current income tax rules and the ability to modify those rules and calculate the effects of alternative tax rules on taxable income, deadweight loss, and the like. The model can reflect the behavioral responses of taxpayers to changes in tax rates and tax rules. As noted above, the behavioral responses that we study in the current paper focus on changes in married women's labor supply through changes in participation and in average hours worked.[21]

The TAXSIM model used in the current paper incorporates the Treasury's public-use sample of individual tax returns for 1991, the most recent sample that is currently available. Since this study is concerned exclusively with alternative tax rules for married women, the usual TAXSIM sample is reduced to married couples. These tax returns are augmented with data from the March 1992 Current Population Survey (CPS) in order to have information on the separate earnings of husbands and wives and to go beyond the very limited information on taxpayer age provided in the Treasury's public-use sample (whether the taxpayer claims one or more age exemptions for being over age 65). When this information has been added to the tax return file we can use earlier estimates by Feldstein and Samwick (1992) of the present value of social security retirement and survivor benefits to calculate the net marginal social security payroll tax for each individual.

---

21. Although the basic TAXSIM model and data are very similar to those used by the Office of Tax Analysis at the Treasury Department and by the staff of the Congressional Joint Tax Committee, the nature of our simulations is very different. The official revenue estimators impose on themselves the restriction that the behavioral responses that they estimate must not change nominal GDP. See Feldstein (1994, 1996) for a discussion of the current procedures of the revenue estimators and of the reasons for looking beyond the narrow range of behavior that they do take into account.

Data from the CPS is added to the tax return information by matching each couple in the tax file to a couple in the CPS. To do this, the CPS couples are cross-classified into 109 types by four criteria: total wages of the husband and wife together, interest and dividend income, number of children, and whether the taxpayer and/or the spouse is over age 65. Each TAXSIM record is then matched to a CPS record randomly selected from among the CPS records whose wage category, interest and dividend income category, number of dependents, and age 65-plus status match the TAXSIM record exactly. The earnings of the husband and of the wife are then imputed to the TAXSIM record in a way that preserves the taxpayer's combined wage and salary income (line 1 of form 1040) while making the ratio of the wife's wage and salary to the combined wage and salary conform to the ratio in the CPS data. The CPS record was also used to impute the age of the primary earner.

The resulting data for 1991 were "aged" to 1994 to reflect the expected increase in the number of tax returns and the rise in incomes. In addition, the 1994 baseline incomes were adjusted to reflect taxpayers' assumed responses to the four major aspects of the 1993 tax legislation:[22] (1) the increase in the top marginal tax rate from 31 to 36 percent on taxable incomes between $140,000 and $250,000 and to 39.6 percent on taxable incomes over $250,000,[23] (2) the elimination of the $135,000 ceiling on the tax base for the Medicare (health insurance) payroll tax, (3) the changes in the alternative minimum tax, and (4) the changes in the earned income tax credit.

The TAXSIM analysis of alternative tax rules for married women follows the simplified assumption of focusing exclusively on the participation and hours decisions of the married women. We ignore other changes in their behavior that alter taxable income as well as all changes in the behavior of men and single women. We assume also that the pretax wage rate is constant. The two key behavioral elasticities, based on Eissa (1995), are the compensated elasticities of hours with respect to the net-of-tax wage among women who work under existing tax rules ($\varepsilon_H = 0.45$) and the elasticity of the participation rate with respect to the net-of-tax share ($\varepsilon_P = 0.42$). As discussed above, we take the effect of exogenous income on the demand for leisure hours consumed to be $0.15 of foregone wage income per incremental dollar of exogenous income.

Because the TAXSIM model does not currently incorporate 1994 state income tax rates, they are ignored in the current analysis. This reduces the initial and final overall tax rate levels and therefore decreases the reduction in the deadweight loss that results from reducing the tax rate.

In contrast to the simplified analyses of sections 2.1 and 2.2, we now incorporate a more realistic treatment of the social security tax to reflect the present

22. This adjustment follows the procedures described in Feldstein (1995c).
23. These are the changes for married couples filing joint tax returns. Other changes were made for single individuals and other filing categories.

actuarial value of future benefits. We also recognize that the taxpayer's income is defined net of the employer's share of the social security payroll tax. Each $100 of taxable wage income up to a maximum taxable wage level of $60,600 for 1994 is subject to an extra tax of $7.65. This indicates that the full gross wage is $107.65 per $100 of taxable wage income, implying that $100 of taxable wage income corresponds to a marginal product of labor of $107.65.

We now make this more precise by describing the explicit calculation used to evaluate the deadweight loss and revenue effects of the existing tax rules and of potential alternative tax rules. We follow the framework of section 2.2 by dividing the sample of married couples into those with a working spouse (i.e., a wife with wage and salary income in 1994) and those in which the wife was not in the labor force.

2.3.1   Subsample of Working Wives

The initial marginal tax rate of the working wife is

$$(14) \qquad t_1 = t_1^{PIT} + t_1^{HI} + t_1^{SSN}$$

where t_1^{PIT} is the marginal tax rate under the personal income tax, t_1^{HI} is the employer-employee combined payroll tax for health insurance (Medicare), and t_1^{SSN} is the net employer-employee payroll tax for social security. The subscript 1 indicates that this is the initial tax rate; a subscript 2 is used to denote the postreform tax rate. Each of these components needs some further comment.

The marginal tax rate under the personal income tax is defined as a fraction of the full gross wage (the marginal product of labor). If the woman earns less than the $60,600 (the social security maximum covered earnings in 1994), the employer pays a payroll tax of 7.65 percent, implying that each dollar of taxable income corresponds to $1.0765 of marginal product. A 28 percent statutory tax rate on taxable income therefore corresponds to a tax rate of $0.28/1.0765 = 0.26$ on the marginal product of labor. For such an individual, we therefore write $t_1^{PIT} = 0.26$. If the woman's income exceeds $60,600, she is no longer subject to the social security payroll tax on marginal earnings but is still subject to the 2.9 percent Medicare payroll tax. For such women, the employer pays a marginal payroll tax of 1.45 percent, implying that a 28 percent tax on taxable income is equivalent to $t_1^{PIT} = 0.28/1.0145 = 0.276$ on the marginal product of labor.

The health insurance payroll tax is $t_1^{HI} = 0.029/1.0765 = 0.0269$ if the woman's income is less than $60,600 and is $t_1^{HI} = 0.029/1.0145 = 0.0286$ if the woman's income exceeds $60,600.

The social security payroll tax that influences the taxpayer's behavior should reflect the present actuarial value of the future benefits that are accrued by earning an additional dollar of wage and salary income.[24] For married women,

---

24. The simplified calculations of sections 2.1 and 2.2 ignored this aspect of the social security tax.

assessing the value of this incremental benefit is complicated by the fact that a woman may claim benefits at retirement based on her own earnings history or may claim benefits as her husband's dependent spouse. Since a dependent spouse's benefits are equal to 50 percent of the benefits of the primary retiree, a wife will choose to receive benefits as a retired worker (rather than as a dependent spouse) if her own lifetime earnings record implies a benefit level greater than 50 percent of her husband's benefit level.[25] A second complication in calculating the present actuarial value of benefits is that a surviving spouse can receive benefits equal to 100 percent of her husband's benefit or can receive the benefit to which she is entitled as a retired worker. Most married women will find it advantageous to claim such survivor benefits and therefore will get no extra benefit during the years that she is a widow for the taxes that she paid while she was working.

Feldstein and Samwick (1992) estimated the present actuarial value of benefits for employees classified by age, sex, income, and prospective benefit status (e.g., male retiree with dependent spouse or female retiree without dependents). Although it is not possible for us to reflect all of the complexities of the social security benefit rules on the basis of the information that we have in the augmented TAXSIM file, we do use the Feldstein-Samwick calculations to estimate the present actual value of retirement benefits for each woman in our sample.[26] For this purpose, we classify a woman as a potential retired worker who will claim benefits on the basis of her own earnings only if her current wage and salary places her at a point in the earnings distribution at which her individual benefit would exceed the benefit to which she would be entitled as a dependent spouse.

The marginal social security tax rate t_1^{SSN} is the difference between the gross social security tax rate (0.124 if her wage and salary income is less than the \$60,600 social security maximum and zero if her wage and salary income is higher) and the present actuarial value of benefits (pavb) derived by Feldstein and Samwick divided by the marginal product of labor per dollar of taxable income. Thus a woman with wage and salary income below \$60,600 has $t_1^{SSN} =$ $(0.124 - \text{pavb})/1.0765$. If her income exceeds the maximum taxable earnings under social security, $t_1^{SSN} = 0$.

Equation (7) in section 2.2.1 shows that the change in the deadweight loss due to a change in the marginal tax rate on married women workers is given by

$$(15) \qquad \Delta DWL = -[t_1 + 0.5(t_1 - t_2)](t_1 - t_2)(1 - t_1)^{-1}\varepsilon_H E_1,$$

where t_1 is the marginal tax rate described in equation (14), t_2 is the corresponding marginal tax rate after the change in tax rules, ε_H is the compensated

25. The analysis is complicated further by her ability to retire earlier than her husband, claiming benefits at that time on her own record, and then shift to dependent spouse status when her husband retires.

26. The Feldstein-Samwick estimates do not include the value of disability benefits. Such benefits are about 10 percent of the total social security OASDI benefits.

elasticity of hours with respect to the net-of-tax share, and E_1 is the woman's initial wage and salary income (corresponding to wH_1 of eq. [7]). TAXSIM evaluates equation (15) for each individual in the subsample of married women who work.

Calculating the revenue effect for each woman of a change in the tax rule can be conceptually divided into two parts: (1) the "static" tax change and (2) the effect on revenue of the induced change in earnings. The static tax change calculation begins with the total tax paid under existing tax rules, T_1, defined to exclude the payroll taxes on the husband's earnings. Thus the T_1 tax measure consists of the couple's initial personal income tax liability, plus the woman's initial health insurance tax $(0.029\ E_1)$ and the woman's initial social security payroll tax $(0.124E_1$ if $E_1 < \$60,600$ and zero if $E_1 > \$60,600)$. The tax rules and tax rates are then revised, and the TAXSIM program is used to recalculate the corresponding tax liability under the new rules and rates but with no changes in the initial incomes. We denote this tax burden under the new rules with the old income as T_2. The static change in the individual's tax is therefore $T_2 - T_1$.

Although behavior is appropriately modeled in terms of the social security tax net of the present actuarial value of benefits, the Treasury's *current* revenue receipts depend only on the gross social security tax. Since government budget accounting generally ignores the present value of future taxes and outlays, we calculate both a net revenue and a gross revenue change that ignores the present actuarial value of future benefits. More specifically, we take the value of benefits into account in modeling individual behavior but then calculate the revenue implications based only on the gross tax. Section 2.4 presents alternative revenue estimates based on net and gross social security revenue.

Calculating the revenue effect of the individual change in earnings is based on equation (10) of section 2.2. Since we assume that the wage rate per hour (w) is fixed, we can multiply all of the terms in equation (10) by w and therefore rewrite equation (10) in terms of earnings $(E = wH)$ as

$$(16) \qquad \Delta E = \varepsilon_H E_1 (t_1 - t_2)/(1 - t_1) + (dE/dy)(T_1 - T_2).$$

Equation (16) states the change in earnings as the sum of the compensated percentage change in hours multiplied by the initial level of earnings plus the income effect on earnings of the reduction in taxes with no behavioral response. As we noted earlier, previous research indicates the income effect is commonly estimated at about $dE/dy = -0.15$. The total revenue effect is therefore calculated by TAXSIM with the new tax rules and tax rates applied to the new level of earnings, $E_1 + \Delta E$.

2.3.2   Subsample of Wives Initially out of the Labor Force

If the proportion of women under age 65 who are initially employed is p_1, the participation elasticity implies

(17) $$\Delta p = p_1 \, \varepsilon_P \, (t_1 - t_2)/(1 - t_1).$$

For any woman who is initially out of the labor force, the probability of entering the labor force is $\Delta p/(1 - p_1)$.

In calculating the deadweight loss and the revenue, our baseline assumption is that women who shift from being out of the labor force to being employed have the same pretax earnings when they are employed as the average earnings of the previously employed women under the new tax rules (i.e., the mean of $E_1 + \Delta E$).[27] We also present simulation results that assume that new entrants have only one-half of the average earnings of previously employed women under the new tax rules.

From the analysis of section 2.2.2, the reduced deadweight loss for new participants lies between a lower bound that is just equal to the tax that they pay under the new tax rules and an upper bound that is an unweighted average of that tax and the tax that they would pay on the same earnings under the old tax rules.[28] TAXSIM therefore derives the lower bound on the change in the deadweight loss for those who shift into employment by calculating, under the new tax rules, the change in the couple's personal income tax associated with the wife's new employment plus her payroll tax payments. The upper bound on the change in the deadweight loss is calculated by averaging the lower bound figure with the taxes that would occur under the old tax rates and rules with the new participation and hours.

Our TAXSIM procedure multiplies the potential reduced deadweight loss for each woman who is initially out of the labor force by the probability that she will enter the labor force. TAXSIM can therefore simply add these probability-weighted deadweight loss reductions over all of the observations in the sample of nonworking wives.

The revenue changes and deadweight loss reductions for the two subsamples taken together give the total changes in revenue and deadweight loss for all married women.

2.4   Tax Reform Options

In this paper, we analyze four different types of alternatives to the current method of taxing two-earner couples. Section 2.4.1 discusses proposals to reinstate the secondary earner deduction that was repealed in the 1986 tax reform legislation. Section 2.4.2 considers other innovations within the framework of joint filing that have the effect of reducing the marginal tax rate on married

---

27. This is analogous to the assumption of section 2.2.2 that those women who enter the labor force work the same H_2 hours as previous employees. This subject could obviously benefit from more extensive analysis based on panel data. It may also be possible to refine the analysis of the probability of shifting from out of the labor force to employment to reflect information about the individual's spouse, children, age, etc., that are in the TAXSIM file but not currently taken into account.

28. See eq. (12) of section 2.2.2 and note that $\lambda = 1$ implies $\Delta \text{DWL} = -0.5 \, (t_1 + t_2) \, wL$.

women. Section 2.4.3 then discusses separate filing as an alternative to the current joint filing rule. Finally, section 2.4.4 analyzes the effect of eliminating the extra marginal tax rate imposed by social security on married women.

For each option, we calculate the effects on earnings, on tax revenue, and on the deadweight loss of the tax system. Finally, we examine the impact on the marriage penalty as well as on the marriage bonus. For the secondary earner deduction, we also discuss the sensitivity of the analysis to alternative values of the labor supply elasticities and present disaggregated results by income class.

Before looking at any of the alternative tax rules, we present estimates of the current tax situation of married taxpayers that can serve as a background for putting the effects of the individual options in perspective. Table 2.1 shows 1994 average and aggregate tax revenues for married taxpayers (with tax liabilities greater than zero) in each taxable income class starting with $10,000 of adjusted gross income (AGI).[29] The table presents the personal income tax (PIT), the employee-employer payments of the social security payroll tax (OASDHI^G), and the total federal tax (the sum of the personal income tax and the employer-employee payroll tax).

In the aggregate, these 51 million married taxpayers paid total personal income taxes of $384 billion, approximately 70 percent of the estimated personal income taxes paid by all taxpayers. Similarly, these couples and their employers paid OASDHI payroll tax of $292 billion, about 63 percent of the estimated 1994 total OASDHI receipts for all taxpayers.

Table 2.2 presents comparable baseline figures for the marriage penalty, showing, by AGI class, the number of couples that are now paying a marriage penalty (i.e., that pay more personal income tax than they would if they were unmarried) and the average penalty among such couples. Similarly, the table shows the number of couples that are now enjoying a marriage bonus (i.e., paying less personal income tax than they would if they were not married) and the average bonus for such couples. In the aggregate, there are now 20 million couples (40 percent) paying marriage penalties that total $37 billion while there are also 27 million couples (54 percent) receiving marriage bonuses that total $41 billion. Thus for married taxpayers as a whole, the effect of marriage is to reduce taxes. Among taxpayers with AGIs over $50,000, however, the opposite is true.

2.4.1 Secondary Earner Deduction

A 10 percent "secondary earner deduction" was a feature of the income tax law from 1981 until it was repealed in the Tax Reform Act of 1986. It allowed the couple to deduct from taxable income 10 percent of the wage and salary income of the spouse with the lower earnings, up to a maximum deduction of

---

29. A married couple with AGI below $10,000 owes no tax because the combination of two personal exemptions and the standard deduction for a joint return together exceed $10,000.

Table 2.1   Distribution of Aggregate and Average Tax Revenues: Joint Tax Returns, 1994

AGI Class (thousands $)	Number of Returns (thousands)	Averages per Return			Aggregates		
		PIT	OASDHI[G]	PIT+ OASDHI[G]	PIT	OASDHI[G]	PIT+ OASDHI[G]
10–	9,258	166	1,759	1,926	1.5	16.2	17.8
25–	16,968	3,092	4,610	7,702	52.4	78.2	130.6
50–	16,408	8,398	8,495	16,893	137.7	139.3	277.1
100–	3,389	23,640	12,609	36,249	80.1	42.7	122.8
200+	795	144,491	15,225	159,717	114.8	12.1	126.9
Total	50,731	7,575	5,754	13,329	384.2	291.9	676.2

Source: Estimates are based on TAXSIM model calculations using the 1991 Treasury public-use sample aged to 1994 levels.
Note: Averages per return are in dollars. Aggregates are in billions of dollars. All figures for 1994.

Table 2.2   Couples with Marriage Penalties and Marriage Bonuses

AGI Class (thousand $)	Number of Returns (thousands)	Couples with Marriage Penalty		Couples with Marriage Bonus	
		Number (1)	Average Amount (2)	Number (3)	Average Amount (4)
10–	9,258	1,527	1,729	7,102	730
25–	16,968	7,774	1,413	9,156	1,332
50–	16,408	8,328	1,542	7,991	2,122
100–	3,389	2,164	3,062	1,224	4,079
200+	795	399	9,648	368	4,080
Mean			1,833		1,533
Total	50,731	20,270	37.1[a]	26,975	41.3[a]
		(40.0 percent)		(53.2 percent)	

Source: Estimates are based on TAXSIM model calculations using the 1991 Treasury public-use sample aged to 1994 levels.
Note: Averages per return are in dollars. All figures for 1994.
[a]In billions of dollars.

$3,000. For married women with wage and salary income below $30,000, the deduction of 10 percent of earnings is equivalent to a 10 percent reduction in the tax rate on those earnings.[30]

In addition to analyzing the original pre-1986 plan, we recognize that nominal per capita income has nearly doubled since the $30,000 limit was set in

---

30. Since the secondary earner deduction reduces taxable income but not AGI, it does not affect any of the tax deductions that themselves depend on the level of AGI. The secondary earner deduction is discussed in detail with an explicit example in Feldstein (1995b) as an illustration of the importance of taking taxpayer labor supply behavior into account in evaluating tax proposals.

1981. We therefore consider the effect of raising the maximum deduction to $5,000 (i.e., a deduction of 10 percent of the first $50,000 of wage and salary income).

Row 1 of table 2.3 presents the results of our analysis of the original secondary earner deduction with the $3,000 limit. The reduced marginal tax rate would cause the pretax earnings of married women with earnings below $30,000 to increase while those with incomes over $30,000 would decline (by $450 each) because of the income effect. The aggregate effect of this would be a $5.7 billion net increase in pretax earnings, shown in column (1).

This increase in earnings is reflected in the difference between the static revenue change shown in column (2) and the revenue change with behavior shown in columns (3), (4), and (5). With no change in behavior, the static revenue loss is $7.2 billion. The $5.7 billion net increase in earnings cuts the loss of personal income tax revenue from $7.2 to $6.1 billion, shown in column (3).[31] In addition, the increased earnings that result from greater labor force participation and greater working hours also increase the payroll taxes that these women and their employers pay. This revenue gain is shown in column (4) as the positive change in OASDHI[G]; the superscript G identifies this as the change in full payroll tax revenue without any offset for the present actuarial value of future retirement benefits. The total increase in OASDHI payroll tax revenue that results from the higher earnings is $0.9 billion (col. [4]), bringing the net revenue loss of the secondary earner deduction down to $5.2 billion (col. [5].)[32] In this case, the static revenue loss overstates the estimated net loss by $2.0 billion, or 38 percent.

Columns (6) and (7) report the aggregate change in the deadweight loss of the tax system, giving both a lower bound estimate and an upper bound estimate.[33] Since the reductions in marginal tax rates are relatively small, the range of possible reservation wages for new participants is also small. Our inability to know the reservation wage precisely therefore does not affect any conclu-

---

31. It is wrong to interpret the ratio of the additional income tax to the additional earnings (0.193) as an average marginal tax rate of 19.3 percent since the $5.7 billion earnings increase is the net effect of earnings increases of women with lower earnings and earnings decreases of women with higher earnings (and typically higher marginal tax rates).

32. The difference between the gross OASDHI revenue and the corresponding revenue net of the present value of future benefits is very small because most married women, and particularly those with the lower earnings who increase their earnings in response to the deduction, will claim retirement benefits as dependent spouses. We estimate that the present value of the benefits offsets only about 10 percent of the extra gross payroll tax revenue. If the present value of future social security retirement benefits is taken into account, the net OASDHI revenue is reduced to $0.8 billion and the overall net revenue loss rises to $5.3 billion.

33. The lower and upper bounds on the deadweight loss reduction reflect the uncertainty of the reservation wage of those who shift from nonparticipants to participants (as explained in sec. 2.2 of this paper). The lower bound estimate corresponds to $\lambda = 0$ in eq. (11), and the upper bound estimate corresponds to $\lambda = 1$. The lower bound assumes that the woman is just indifferent between working and not working after the tax change, while the upper bound estimate assumes that she was just indifferent between working and not working before the tax change. In the lower bound case, all of the reduced deadweight loss accrues in the form of increased tax revenue.

Table 2.3 Revenue and Deadweight Loss Effects of Alternative Tax Rules

Description	Change in Earnings (1)	Static Revenue Change (2)	Revenue Change with Behavior			Change in Deadweight Loss		Change in Deadweight Loss per Dollar of Revenue Loss		Marriage Penalty		Marriage Bonus	
			PIT (3)	OASDHI[a] (4)	PIT+OASDHI[a] (5)	Lower Bound (6)	Upper Bound (7)	Lower Bound (8a)	Upper Bound (8b)	Percentage (9)	Average (10)	Percentage (11)	Average (12)
1. Secondary earner deduction: 10 percent of first $30,000	5.7	−7.2	−6.1	0.9	−5.2	−3.1	−3.2	0.60	0.62	36	1,627.0	56	1,465.0
2. Secondary earner deduction: 10 percent of first $50,000	7.4	−7.9	−6.3	1.1	−5.2	−3.8	−3.9	0.72	0.73	36	1,593.0	56	1,468.0
3. Flat rate on secondary earner wages: Optional 15 percent rate on first $50,000	27.9	−27.1	−23.0	4.2	−18.8	−11.5	−12.9	0.61	0.69	31	1,242.0	62	1,623.0
4. Flat rate on secondary earner wages: Optional 20 percent rate on first $50,000	14.7	−14.9	−12.0	2.2	−9.8	−7.0	−7.6	0.71	0.77	35	1,409.0	58	1,499.0

5. Special secondary earner tax schedule: 60 percent of single-filer tax rate	65.6	−65.2	−59.0	9.5	−49.5	−18.4	−27.3	0.37	0.55	39	1,464.0	53	1,149.0
6. Special secondary earner tax schedule: 80 percent of single-filer tax rate	55.6	−54.5	−48.2	8.1	−40.1	−15.4	−24.2	0.38	0.60	20	1,444.0	72	989.0
7. Mandatory separate filing: Rescaled 1994 joint-return tax rates	45.5	−12.5	−6.9	6.9	0.0	−13.2	−19.3	n.a.	n.a.	22	1,062.0	60	1,869.0
8. Mandatory separate filing: Rescaled 1994 single-filer rates	43.7	−11.8	−6.4	6.5	0.1	−12.5	−18.3	n.a.	n.a.	33	1,074.0	44	1,325.0
9. Eliminate social security burden: No secondary earner OASDHI tax	37.9	0.0	8.5	−51.4	−42.9	−17.1	−19.7	0.39	0.46	39	1,833.0	53	1,533.0

Source: Estimates are based on TAXSIM model calculations using the 1991 Treasury public-use sample aged to 1994 levels.

Note: Amounts are in billions of dollars. All figures for 1994.

sions about the desirability of reviving the secondary earner deduction. We also report (col. [8]) the ratio of the reduction in the deadweight loss to the net revenue loss ($5.2 billion), a ratio of 0.60 with the lower bound estimate and 0.62 with the upper bound estimate, implying that each dollar of revenue loss reduces the deadweight loss of the tax system by between 60 and 62 cents.

Columns (9) through (12) show the effect of the secondary earner deduction on the marriage penalty and bonus. The secondary earner deduction reduces the marriage penalty for all taxpayers who currently face a marriage penalty since all married couples receive some tax reduction, including those with incomes over $30,000. Column (9) shows that the percentage of couples with a marriage penalty falls from the initial 40 percent shown in table 2.2 to 36 percent. The average dollar amount per couple with a marriage penalty also falls, from $1,833 to $1,627. Finally, the couples with a marriage bonus rises from the initial 54 percent with an average bonus of $1,533 to 56 percent with an average bonus of $1,465.

The second simulation (shown in row 2) examines the effect of a more generous secondary earner deduction: a deduction of 10 percent of earnings up to a $5,000 limit. The surprising feature of this analysis is that the plan with the higher ceiling dominates the original secondary earner deduction: it has the same revenue loss but a greater reduction in the deadweight loss. This occurs because the pre-1986 secondary earner deduction plan shown in row 1 has no favorable effect on the incentives of women with initial earnings above $30,000 while nevertheless reducing the tax that they pay. Raising the ceiling to $50,000 provides favorable incentives to enough women with initial earnings between these two limits to make the additional earnings of these higher-earning women pay for the entire increased static revenue loss.

More specifically, the higher deduction limit raises the static revenue loss by approximately $700 million, from $7.2 to $7.9 billion (col. [2]). But the induced rise in earnings of $7.4 instead of $5.7 billion (col. [1]) brings enough extra tax revenue to offset the $700 million static revenue loss. Although the personal income tax revenue still declines by about $200 million (col. [3]), this is offset by the greater payroll tax revenue (col. [4]).

With an overall revenue loss of $5.2 billion and a deadweight loss reduction of $3.8 billion, the deadweight loss reduction is about 72 cents per dollar of revenue loss (col. [8]). Raising the maximum secondary earner deduction also reduces the average marriage penalty.

Table 2.4 disaggregates these results by five AGI class brackets. Although earnings rise at all income levels, more than half of the increase is among taxpayers with AGIs between $50,000 and $100,000. An additional one-third of the additional earnings is by couples with AGIs below $50,000. The distribution of the static tax reductions is also concentrated on taxpayers with AGIs between $50,000 and $100,000. They receive more than half of the total static tax reduction. Less than $500 million of the $7.9 billion static revenue loss accrues to taxpayers with incomes over $200,000.

Table 2.4   Distributional Effects of the Secondary Earner Deduction: 10 Percent of First $50,000

AGI Class (thousand $)	Number of Returns (thousand)	Change in Earnings (1)	Static Revenue Change (2)	Revenue Change with Behavior			Change in Deadweight Loss		Change in Deadweight Loss per Dollar of Revenue Loss		Couples with Marriage Penalty		Couples with Marriage Bonus	
				PIT (3)	OASDHI^G (4)	PIT+OASDHI^G (5)	Lower Bound (6)	Upper Bound (7)	Lower Bound (8a)	Upper Bound (8b)	Number (9)	Average Amount (10)	Number (11)	Average Amount (12)
10–	9,258	0.6	−0.1	0.0	0.1	0.1	0.3	0.3	−3.36	−3.43	1,519	2.5	7,108	5.2
25–	16,968	1.5	−1.4	−1.2	0.2	−0.9	0.7	0.8	0.82	0.84	6,807	9.6	10,069	12.3
50–	16,408	4.1	−4.3	−3.5	0.6	−2.8	2.0	2.1	0.74	0.75	7,829	8.9	8,576	17.3
100–	3,389	0.8	−1.5	−1.3	0.1	−1.2	0.5	0.4	0.39	0.40	2,076	5.2	1,312	5.0
200+	795	0.2	−0.4	−0.4	0	−0.36	0.2	0.2	0.48	0.50	398	3.4	369	1.8
Total	50,731	7.4	−7.9	−6.3	0.9	−5.2	−3.8	−3.9	0.73	0.74	18,706	mean 1,593[a] 29.8	28,571	mean 1,467[a] 41.9

Source: Estimates are based on TAXSIM model calculations using the 1991 Treasury public-use sample aged to 1994 levels.

Note: Amounts are in billions of dollars. All figures for 1994.

[a]In dollars.

It is interesting to compare the distribution of the static revenue loss and the distribution of the revenue loss with the behavioral change. In the lowest income class, the induced increase in earnings is enough to cause total taxes to rise. The middle-bracket taxpayers still receive 50 percent of the overall tax reduction.

Comparing column (9) with column (1) of table 2.2 shows that the largest relative reduction in couples paying a marriage penalty occurs among those in the $25,000–$50,000 AGI class. The decline in the number of marriage penalty couples in this group from 7.8 to 6.8 million is about two-thirds of the overall decline in those paying a marriage penalty.

Table 2.5 shows the sensitivity of the revenue and deadweight loss estimates of the second-earner deduction to alternative assumptions about labor supply elasticities. Row 1 repeats the baseline estimates shown in row 2 of table 2.3. Row 2 shows the effect of reducing the behavioral elasticities (both compensated and uncompensated) by 50 percent. The change in earnings is of course reduced by 50 percent, from $7.4 to $3.7 billion. Since the static revenue estimate does not depend on behavior, it remains unchanged. The revenue loss with behavior is now larger. Cutting the behavioral elasticities in half reduces the difference between the static revenue changes and the behavioral revenue

Table 2.5   Sensitivity Analysis of Secondary Earner Deduction

| Description | Change in Earnings (1) | Static Revenue Change (2) | Revenue Change with Behavior | | | Change in Deadweight Loss: Upper Bound (6) | Change in Deadweight Loss per Dollar of Revenue Loss (7) |
			PIT (3)	OASDHI^G (4)	PIT+ OASDHI^G (5)		
1. Baseline	7.4	−7.9	−6.3	1.1	−5.2	−3.8	0.72
2. Reduce elasticities by 50 percent	3.7	−7.9	−7.1	0.6	−6.6	−2.8	0.42
3. Raise elasticities by 50 percent	11.0	−7.9	−5.5	1.7	−3.8	−4.8	1.26
4. No behavior among AGI <$50,000	5.2	−7.9	−6.7	0.8	−5.9	−2.7	0.46
5. Reduce hours of new entrants by 50 percent	5.9	−7.9	−6.7	0.9	−5.8	−2.9	0.50

Source: Estimates are based on TAXSIM model calculations using the 1991 Treasury public-use sample aged to 1994 levels.
Note: Amounts are in billions of dollars. All figures for 1994.

changes with the baseline elasticities by 50 percent. But even with the elasticities reduced by 50 percent, the total revenue loss of $6.6 billion is one-sixth smaller than the static revenue loss. The reduction in the deadweight loss declines from $3.8 billion with the baseline elasticities to $2.8 billion with the reduced elasticities. The reduction in deadweight loss per dollar of revenue loss is thus still 42 cents.

The effect of an increase in the behavioral elasticities is symmetrically higher. Earnings rise by $11 billion, and the revenue loss is limited to only $3.8 billion. The change in the deadweight loss is $4.8 billion, implying a reduction in deadweight loss of $1.26 per dollar of revenue loss.

Because the estimates of the behavioral elasticities that we use are based on Eissa's analysis of the experience of relatively high income taxpayers, we consider another and more radical sensitivity analysis: assuming no behavioral response among taxpayers with incomes below $50,000. The results are shown in row 4. Even with no behavioral response among taxpayers with AGI below $50,000, the secondary earner deduction causes earnings to rise by $5.2 billion, or 70 percent of the total for all taxpayers. The revenue loss with the baseline elasticities for those with AGIs over $50,000 and zero elasticities for those with AGIs below $50,000 is $6.7 billion, or $0.4 billion more than when everyone is assumed to behave in the same way. The total revenue loss with behavior is $5.9 billion, or $0.7 billion more than when all are assumed to act in the same way. Thus, even if we ignore the behavior of all taxpayers with AGIs less than $50,000, behavior reduces the estimated revenue loss by 25 percent. The reduction in the deadweight loss is restricted to those with AGIs above $50,000 since all others are assumed not to respond to the initial taxes. The resulting deadweight loss decline is $2.7 billion, implying a deadweight loss reduction of 46 cents per dollar of revenue loss.

The final analysis examines the sensitivity of the calculations to the assumption that individuals who are induced to enter the labor force by the secondary earner credit work the same number of hours as the existing employees. Row 5 shows the effect of reducing the average hours of these new entrants by 50 percent. The additional earnings induced by the more favorable tax rules are reduced by one-fifth, and the revenue loss with behavioral responses increases from $5.2 to $5.9 billion. The improvement in the deadweight loss declines from $3.8 to $2.7 billion. Thus, even with this reduction in hours for new participants, the second-earner credit reduces the deadweight loss by 46 cents per dollar of revenue loss.

2.4.2   Special Secondary Earner Flat Rate Tax Schedules

The secondary earner deduction is an example of the differentially lower tax rate on secondary earners that optimal tax theory suggests. It achieves a significant reduction in the deadweight loss with a relatively modest cost in foregone revenue. We now present an alternative way of giving a lower tax rate to secondary earners by allowing the secondary earner to choose between her usual tax (up to the first $50,000 of her wage income) and an optional flat rate tax on that income.

The first such option that we consider is an optional flat rate tax of 15 percent on the first $50,000 of the secondary earner's wage income. Unlike the 10 percent deduction for secondary earners, this option is valuable only to a secondary earner who pays a marginal personal income tax rate in excess of 15 percent on at least part of her income. This is true only if the couple has taxable income of at least $38,000; with two children, this corresponds to AGI of at least $54,150. For those who do qualify, the marginal tax rate is reduced from 28 percent (or higher) to 15 percent unless the woman's earnings exceed $50,000. Such a marginal tax rate reduction brings a substantial reduction in deadweight loss.[34]

The results are summarized in row 3 of table 2.3. The deadweight loss is reduced by at least $11.5 billion (col. [6]) and perhaps by as much as $12.9 billion (col. [7]). The greater relative gap between the lower and upper bounds reflects the larger reduction in the marginal tax rate, making it more difficult to be precise about the reservation wage for those who are not working now but who enter the labor force in response to the tax rate reduction. The substantial decline in the marginal tax rate also induces a $27.9 billion rise in earnings, enough to reduce the revenue loss from the static $27.1 billion (col. [2]) to a net loss of only $18.8 billion (col. [5]). The optional 15 percent flat rate tax thus reduces the deadweight loss by between 61 and 69 cents per dollar of revenue loss.

The flat rate tax is more effective at reducing the marriage penalty, cutting the number of marriage penalty couples to 31 percent from the 36 percent with the secondary earner deduction and the 40 percent under current law. This of course reflects not only the targeting of this tax reduction but also the much larger cost of this tax change.

The cost of an optional flat rate tax on part of the secondary earner's wage income can be reduced while maintaining the same simple structure of the plan by increasing the tax rate on the alternative flat rate tax. With an optional flat rate of 20 percent (instead of the 15 percent), a woman will choose the optional tax only if her average effective tax rate on the first $50,000 of her income exceeds 20 percent.[35] The results of this plan are shown in row 4 of table 2.3. The static revenue loss is cut nearly in half to $14.9 billion and, with the $14.7

---

34. The woman might choose the optional tax even if it implied a higher tax burden at her initial level of earnings because it gives her the opportunity to increase her earnings at a lower marginal tax rate. Our analysis therefore understates both the efficiency gain and the revenue loss by assuming that taxpayers only take the optional rate when it lowers their tax liability on their original level of earnings.

35. Once again, she might prefer the optimal tax because it allows her to earn a higher net wage even if she had to accept a smaller net-of-tax income on her initial earnings. The higher optional marginal tax rate would however still reduce the number of women who take the optional plan.

billion projected rise in earnings, the net decline in total revenue is only $9.8 billion. The static revenue loss overstates this projected revenue loss by more than 50 percent.

The efficiency gain is smaller than with the 15 percent flat tax but still implies a reduced deadweight loss between $7.0 and $7.6 billion. Comparing this to the $9.8 billion net revenue loss indicates a reduction in the overall deadweight loss of between 71 and 77 cents per dollar of lost revenue.

2.4.3 Separate Filing by Husbands and Wives

The most obvious alternative to the current tax treatment of two-earner families is a rule that requires each individual to file a separate tax return. Designing a system of separate filing involves decisions about the division between the husband and wife of nonlabor income and of itemized deductions. One option is to base the division of income on the ownership of underlying assets and the division of deductions on the individual who incurs the deductible expense. The income from jointly owned property would be divided in half as would joint deductible expenses (e.g., mortgage interest on a jointly owned house). Although advocates of this method recognize that couples could use interspousal transfers to reduce tax liabilities, they argue that such transfers of assets are real transfers, not likely to be entered into lightly in an age in which the ratio of divorces to marriages has reached 50 percent and more than a third of women in their forties who have been married have also been divorced. The alternative is to use arbitrary rules for dividing property income and deductions, either automatically assigning them to minimize tax burdens or merely dividing everything equally between the two spouses.

We do not have the underlying data on intrafamily asset ownership and expense patterns with which to allocate them between the spouses. Moreover, even if we had current information on income and expenses, it would not be appropriate to use that information to measure how those assets and expenses would be divided under a system that required separate filing based on the individual ownership of assets and individual deductions. We therefore adopt the rule that divides all nonlabor income, adjustments to gross income, deductible expenses, personal exemptions, and tax credits equally between the husband and wife.

A shift from the current joint filing requirement to mandatory separate filing also requires a decision about the tax rates to be used at each level of income. We present four alternative analyses. The first permits the primary earner to continue to use the current schedule for joint filers while the secondary earner uses a special new schedule equal to 60 percent of the current single filer's rate at each level of taxable income. For many women, filing a separate tax return with half of the deductions and exemptions for the family means paying no tax at all. The marginal tax rate drops from 15 percent, 28 percent, or higher to zero. Although the lower marginal tax rate can induce a substantial reduction in deadweight loss, it also involves a very large revenue loss. Since much of that loss is associated with the decrease from the 15 percent tax bracket, it is a relatively inefficient way of reducing deadweight loss. These characteristics are reflected in the estimates presented in row 5 of table 2.3.

Column (2) shows that the static revenue loss would be $65.2 billion. Although the reduced marginal tax rates induce an earnings rise of $65.6 billion, the personal income tax loss is only reduced very slightly (to $59.0 billion, as shown in col. [3]) because much of the additional earnings are earned by women who, after the reform, would not be subject to any tax at all because they would file separately with half of the deductions and exemptions of the family. Even with additional payroll tax revenue of $9.5 billion, the net revenue loss is $49.5 billion.

The reduction in the deadweight loss is at least $18.4 billion and could be as large as $27.3 billion. The much greater uncertainty about the magnitude of the reduced deadweight loss reflects the sharp drop in the marginal tax rate, often from 28 percent or higher to zero. The lower and upper bounds imply that this option would reduce the deadweight loss by between 37 and 55 cents per dollar of revenue, substantially less than the other proposals that did not involve the possibility of a zero tax rate.

Option 6 is similar to option 5 but only reduces the tax rates on the single-earner schedule to 80 percent of their current values. Although this seems like a substantial reduction in the tax advantage to the secondary earner, that is not true for those who do not have taxable income. Similarly, the primary earner continues to get the advantage of paying tax on a much reduced taxable income at the joint-filer tax rates. The result is a continued large revenue loss and a relatively unfavorable ratio of efficiency gain per dollar of revenue loss.

Row 6 of table 2.3 shows that the $55.6 billion increase in earnings only induces a net increase in revenue of $6.3 billion, a clear indication that most of the increased earnings are to women in the zero marginal tax rate bracket. Even when the additional payroll tax revenue is recognized, the net revenue loss is still $40.1 billion. The change in deadweight loss is therefore only between 38 and 60 cents per dollar of revenue loss.

The final two rules are designed to be revenue neutral when the behavioral response of the married women is taken into account. The first of these requires mandatory separate filing by husbands and wives using the tax brackets of the joint return but with all tax rates multiplied by 1.11. The results are shown in row 7 of table 2.3. The women's earnings rise by $45.5 billion, cutting the loss in personal income tax revenue from the $12.5 billion static estimate to $6.9 billion. This is completely offset by the additional $6.9 billion of payroll tax revenue. Despite the revenue neutrality, the deadweight loss is reduced by between $13.2 and $19.3 billion. Since many women would still find themselves paying no tax, the revenue neutrality is achieved by increasing the tax rates on their husbands who face the rescaled single-earner schedule instead of the more favorable joint-filer schedule. The remaining small static revenue loss in the income tax is just offset by the additional OASDHI tax collected as a result of the higher earnings of the married women. This analysis does of course reflect the strong (but traditional) assumption that the labor supply of husbands is completely inelastic.[36]

The final revenue-neutral income splitting option that we present (row 8 of table 2.3) uses the tax rate brackets of the single-taxpayer schedule but reduces all rates to 92.9 percent of existing statutory rates. The results are quite similar to those of row 7 based on the joint-taxpayer schedule.

2.4.4   Eliminating the Secondary Earner Social Security Tax Burden

The current method of calculating social security benefits has the effect of giving married women very little additional benefit in return for the extra payroll taxes that they pay when they work more. As we noted earlier in the paper, this has the effect of making the married woman's marginal tax rate substantially higher than her husband's. In this section we consider the effect of eliminating the actuarially unfair burden of social security on married women by excluding married women from the OASDHI tax base.[37]

The final row of table 2.3 shows that the resulting reduction in marginal tax rates would cause earnings to rise by $37.9 billion and would reduce the deadweight loss of the tax system by at least $17.1 billion. Eliminating the social security tax on married women does however reduce payroll tax revenue by $51.4 billion. The offsetting revenue gain of $8.5 billion of additional personal income tax revenue leaves a net revenue loss of $42.9 billion, implying that the deadweight burden reduction is between 39 and 46 cents per dollar of revenue loss, similar to the efficiency of the separate filing options and less cost-effective than the secondary earner deduction.

2.5   Concluding Comments

Three general conclusions emerge from analyzing the simulations of the various options presented in this paper. First, the existing high marginal tax rates on married women cause substantial deadweight losses that can be reduced by alternative tax rules that lower their marginal tax rates. Second, the behavioral responses to the lower marginal tax rates induce additional tax payments that offset large fractions of the "static" revenue losses. Third, there are substantial differences in cost-effectiveness among these options, that is, in the

---

36. We recognize that the assumption that husbands do not respond to their higher marginal tax rates is unrealistic. A realistic analysis would recognize that husbands as well as wives respond to changes in marginal tax rates by altering the character of their work and the pattern of their consumption. We will provide a more realistic analysis in a future paper that takes such broader behavior into account.

37. This could be achieved in practice by a rebatable credit equal to the full social security tax liability. Married women would continue to receive benefits on the basis of their husbands' income as most of them now do. We do not consider the effect of the tax paid by the married woman in other years when she was not married.

revenue cost per dollar of reduced deadweight loss. Several of the options are sufficiently cost-effective that they could probably be combined with other ways of raising revenue to produce a net reduction in the deadweight loss of the tax system as a whole.

We are aware however that the current framework is very restrictive in three important ways. First, it ignores the response of the primary earner in the couple to any change in tax rates or spousal income. Second, it defines the labor supply response very narrowly in terms of participation and hours, excluding such important dimensions of labor supply as choice of occupation and of particular job, effort, location, travel requirements, risk bearing, assumption of responsibility, and so forth. More generally, taxes affect not only the labor supply of men and women but also change taxable income through changes in excluded income (fringe benefits, etc.) and in taxpayer deductions. These changes in taxable income are the key variable for influencing tax revenue. Moreover, the deadweight loss of the tax system depends not just on the change in the amount of labor that individuals choose to supply but also on the induced changes in the amounts of excludible income and deductible expenses (Feldstein 1995c). We plan to extend the current work to merge the evidence on the effects of taxes on the hours and participation of married women with the more general evidence on the sensitivity of taxable income to marginal tax rates.

References

Boskin, Michael J., and Eytan Sheshinski. 1983. Optimal tax treatment of the family: Married couples. *Journal of Public Economics* 20: 281–97.

Browning, Edgar K. 1987. On the marginal welfare cost of taxation. *American Economic Review* 77(1): 11–23.

Eissa, Nada. 1995. Taxation and labor supply of married women: The Tax Reform Act of 1986 as a natural experiment. NBER Working Paper no. 5023. Cambridge, Mass.: National Bureau of Economic Research.

Feenberg, Daniel R., and Harvey S. Rosen. 1983. Alternative tax treatments of the family: Simulation methodology and results. In *Behavioral methods in tax policy analysis*, ed. Martin Feldstein. Chicago: University of Chicago Press.

———. 1994. Recent developments in the marriage tax. *National Tax Journal* 48(1): 91–101.

Feldstein, Martin. 1994. The case for dynamic analysis. *Wall Street Journal*, December 14.

———. 1995a. The effect of marginal tax rates on taxable income: A panel study of the 1986 Tax Reform Act. *Journal of Political Economy* 103, no. 3 (June): 551–72.

———. 1995b. Revenue estimates should reflect the effect of taxes on work and saving. Testimony to the U.S. Congress, Joint Hearing of the Senate Budget Committee and the House Budget Committee, January 10. 103d Cong., 2d sess.

———. 1995c. Tax avoidance and the deadweight loss of the income tax. NBER Working Paper no. 5055. Cambridge, Mass.: National Bureau of Economic Research.

———. 1996. Revenue estimation and tax policy. *National Tax Journal,* forthcoming.
Feldstein, Martin, and Andrew Samwick. 1992. Social security rules and marginal tax rates. *National Tax Journal* 45(1): 1–21.
Harberger, Arnold. 1964. Taxation, resource allocation, and welfare. In *The role of direct and indirect taxes in the Federal Revenue System,* ed. John Due. Princeton, N.J.: Princeton University Press.
Hausman, Jerry, and Paul Ruud. 1984. Family labor supply with taxes. *American Economic Review* 74(2): 242–48.
Munnell, Alicia. 1980. The couple versus the individual under the personal income tax. In *The economics of taxation,* ed. Henry Aaron and Michael Boskin. Washington, D.C.: Brookings Institution.
Rosen, Harvey. 1976. A methodology for evaluating tax reform proposals. *Journal of Public Economics* 6(1–2): 105–21.
———. 1987. The marriage tax is down but not out. *National Tax Journal* 40(4): 567–76.
Triest, Ronald. 1990. The effect of income taxation on labor supply in the United States. *Journal of Human Resources* 25(3): 491–516.

Comment   Harvey S. Rosen

The taxation of the family is an important topic that raises a variety of fascinating technical, political, and social issues. The Feldstein-Feenberg paper advances our understanding of several of the key economic questions relating to the tax treatment of the family. Specifically, they examine how alternative policies would affect labor supply, tax revenues, and excess burden. The basic tack is to take elasticity estimates of female labor supply from the literature and use them to infer behavioral changes associated with the various tax regimes. With the behavioral changes in hand, Feldstein and Feenberg can compute tax revenue changes and changes in consumer surplus.

Feldstein and Feenberg use the conventional consumer surplus framework in a careful and creative way. I would like to discuss four technical issues that might be relevant in thinking about their procedure.

Welfare economics with discrete choices.   As Feldstein and Feenberg stress, changes in the taxation of married women affect not only the supply of hours conditional on working but also the labor force participation decision. The conventional consumer surplus framework does not allow for the analysis of discrete choices. It turns out, however, that the conventional framework can easily be generalized to accommodate the fact that the probability that an individual works may depend on the tax system (see Small and Rosen 1981). One needs to compute the expected change in labor supply under a given tax re-

Harvey S. Rosen is the John L. Weinberg Professor of Economics and Business Policy at Princeton University and a research associate of the National Bureau of Economic Research.

gime, which requires estimates of the probability that the individual works under that regime and the number of hours conditional on working.

Instead of following this approach, Feldstein and Feenberg in effect try to bracket the "true" answer by assuming different values of the reservation wage. Further, they assume that if the current nonparticipants worked under a particular tax regime, they would all work the same number of hours. Feldstein and Feenberg go to a considerable amount of effort to motivate their procedure and argue that it is robust with respect to reasonable changes in assumptions. It would be interesting to see how their results would change if they based their analysis on expected values. To do so, they would need equations for the probability of working and the number of hours worked conditional on being in the labor force.

Elasticities.   The key behavioral parameters are based on Eissa's (1995) study of married women's labor supply responses to the Tax Reform Act of 1986. It is important to note that Eissa's analysis focused on the behavior of high-income women. While Feldstein and Feenberg provide us with some sensitivity analysis, it would be useful to see the work done with elasticities calculated for women lower in the income scale.

Before-tax wages.   Married women have been an important part of the labor force for a number of years now, and one would expect that substantial changes in their labor supply could induce changes in before-tax wage rates. It would be useful to incorporate such changes into the analysis.

Perception of net social security tax rates.   An innovative and important part of the analysis is the inclusion of net social security tax rates. Feldstein and Feenberg take into account not only social security taxes but the present actuarial value of the benefits associated with these taxes. These net benefit rates play an important part in the analysis, and it would be nice if there were some research indicating whether they are perceived correctly by workers.

I would like to turn now to some political and social questions raised by the paper. The normative framework behind the paper is optimal tax theory. Any change in the tax system that reduces excess burden, ceteris paribus, is "good." Hence, the paper is subject to the usual criticisms of this framework. For example, from a political point of view, a prescription based on the goal of a "level playing field" might make more sense than one which differentiates among spouses. Once politicians are given scope to make distinctions, they may make distinctions that lead to worse situations than the status quo. In the current context, certain proposals now circulating to make the tax system more "profamily" might end up making the system even more inefficient than it is now.

Like the optimal tax literature, the paper also ignores nonutilitarian considerations that might be important. Ultimately, one has to deal with the question of what the correct unit of taxation is, the family or the individual. One's views about the role of the family in society will have a heavy weight in determining one's views about the appropriate tax treatment of the family. Having said all of this, computations of excess burden are an important component of any analysis of the taxation of the family, and this paper provides the best estimates to date.

References

Eissa, Nada. 1995. Taxation and labor supply of married women: The Tax Reform Act of 1986 as a natural experiment. NBER Working Paper no. 5023. Cambridge, Mass.: National Bureau of Economic Research.

Small, Kenneth A., and Harvey S. Rosen. 1981. Applied welfare economics with discrete choice models. *Econometrica* 49(1): 105–30.

3   Labor Supply and Welfare Effects of a Shift from Income to Consumption Taxation

Gilbert E. Metcalf

3.1 Introduction

In the past few years there has been increasing interest in shifting from an income-based tax system in the United States to a consumption-based system. These tax reforms take a number of forms. Many advocate an increase in the availability of tax-sheltered savings (e.g., expanded IRAs), while others advocate value added taxation. Still others argue for either a broad-based consumption tax or a consumed income tax.[1] All argue that substantial welfare gains result from the reduction in taxation of capital income. On the other hand, some have argued that a shift from income to consumption taxation will lead to a lower real wage, which in turn will decrease labor supply.

The purpose of this paper is to investigate the labor supply and welfare effects of a shift from income to consumption taxation. The first point of the paper is that labor supply effects of a shift to consumption taxation are likely to be small. As part of that discussion, I identify the significant parameters that analysts must know in order to identify the labor supply effects. It turns out that our knowledge of the relevant parameters is sketchy at best and a better understanding of labor supply responses is unlikely to occur without more empirical work.

Gilbert E. Metcalf is assistant professor of economics at Tufts University and a faculty research fellow of the National Bureau of Economic Research.

The author appreciates the thoughtful comments and suggestions of Gary Burtless, Martin Feldstein, James Poterba, and conference participants.

1. Rep. Dick Armey has proposed the "Freedom and Fairness Restoration Act," a Hall-Rabushka–style flat consumption tax. Senators Nunn and Domenici's proposed "USA Tax System" is a consumed income tax. The Republican Congress's "Contract with America" would extend IRA treatment to all families and allow withdrawals for first-time home purchases, higher education expenses, medical expenses, or long-term care insurance premiums. The Contract would also provide a 50 percent long-term capital gains deduction (see U.S. Congress 1995 for a description of the tax proposals contained in the Contract with America).

Second, I note that the welfare effects of a change from income to consumption taxation depend importantly on the breadth of consumption taxation. Previous investigations of a shift from income to consumption taxation have assumed that all income was taxed under the former tax system and all consumption is potentially taxed under the latter system. In the real world, not all income is taxed. Specifically, not all saving is taxed. Moreover, not all consumption is necessarily taxed under consumption taxation. As Metcalf (1995) notes in a survey of value added taxation, a wide range of consumption goods are zero rated in European value added taxes (VATs). The Nunn-Domenici consumed income tax plan explicitly exempts housing consumption from the tax base (see Christian and Schutzer 1995 for details of this plan). Hence the shift from income to consumption taxation may not reduce the intertemporal consumption distortion at the same time that it may dramatically increase the intracommodity distortion. The welfare effects of the change depend to a large degree on which goods are untaxed; conceivably, the tax-preferred consumption goods are untaxed based on optimal tax considerations. A more cynical perspective suggests that there may be little correlation between optimal tax rates and actual tax rates in a narrow-based consumption tax.

I present a number of simulation results to illustrate these points. The simulations build on a particular structure of preferences, and no attempt is made to claim generality in the results. Rather the point is to make plausible statements about behavioral responses and welfare effects and to identify the various elasticities that researchers need to measure in order to make definitive statements about the effects of a shift from income to consumption taxation. If anything, this paper identifies what we do not know more than it adds to what we do know. But before we can answer questions we need to know what questions to ask.

Section 3.2 provides some theoretical considerations relevant to a shift from income to consumption taxation, followed by section 3.3., which develops a specific example using a nested constant elasticity of substitution (CES) utility function. Sections 3.4 and 3.5 consider the welfare effects of a change from incomplete income to incomplete consumption taxation. The last section concludes with thoughts about directions for research.

3.2   Labor Supply, Welfare, and a Revenue-Neutral Tax Reform

I begin by considering a general two-period model in which an individual maximizes utility of consumption and leisure over two periods. I assume that all labor supply occurs in the first period. The individual maximization problem is

$$\max U(C_1, C_2, 1 - L) \quad \text{subject to}$$

(1)
$$wL = C_1 + pC_2,$$

$$w = 1 - \tau_w, \quad p = \frac{1}{1 + (1 - \tau_s)r}.$$

I have normalized the gross wage rate and the price of current consumption to 1. There is a total of one unit of time endowment that can be allocated to labor (L) or leisure $(1 - L)$. The price of future consumption is determined by the after-tax rate of return $(1 - \tau_s)r$. In this simple framework, we can implement a consumption tax either by taxing consumption directly or by taxing wage income.[2] The fact that a consumption tax decreases the real wage creates the possibility that a VAT could have labor supply effects. To reiterate, the key difference between a consumption tax and an income tax is the tax treatment of savings. The former does not tax savings while the latter does.

There are a number of tax reforms incorporating a consumption tax that could be implemented. One reform would be to shift from the current hybrid income-consumption tax system to a consumed income tax. That could be done by eliminating the tax on interest income (setting τ_s to 0) and increasing the tax on wage income (τ_w) to maintain revenue neutrality. Alternatively, a number of different VATs could be implemented with their key distinguishing feature being the extent of zero-rated commodities.

How will a general tax reform (dR) affect labor supply? Slemrod (1987) considers this issue in a model in which cross-price effects are ignored.[3] Following Slemrod, we can decompose the individual labor supply response (dL) as follows:

$$(2) \qquad \frac{dL}{dR} = \frac{\partial L^c}{\partial w}\frac{dw}{dR} + \frac{\partial L^c}{\partial p}\frac{dp}{dR} + \frac{\partial L}{\partial Y}\frac{dY}{dR},$$

where the superscript c indicates a compensated response and Y is income. We can add up over individuals to measure the aggregate labor supply response:

$$(3) \qquad \sum \frac{dL}{dR} = \sum \frac{\partial L^c}{\partial w}\frac{dw}{dR} + \sum \frac{\partial L^c}{\partial p}\frac{dp}{dR} + \sum \frac{\partial L}{\partial Y}\frac{dY}{dR}.$$

If the tax reform is revenue neutral, then $\sum dY/dR$ will equal zero, and the last term in equation (3) is proportional to Cov $(\partial L/\partial Y, dY/dR)$. The presence of this covariance term in equation (3) means that aggregate revenue neutrality does not imply the lack of an income effect on labor supply from a tax reform. For example, if the tax reform shifted the tax burden from groups with large income elasticities to those with small income elasticities, the aggregate income effect would be to increase aggregate labor supply. The ability to shift burdens across taxpayer groups allows for this possibility. If, however, the addi-

---

2. I am ignoring transitional issues by levying the tax at the beginning of the individual's life.
3. His analysis looks at tax reforms that are unlikely to have significant price effects across commodities.

tional restriction of distributional neutrality is imposed, then the scope for aggregate income effects on labor supply is reduced. Distributional neutrality means that revenue collected from narrower income groups (e.g., quintiles) must be unaffected by the reform. Now, only shifts in tax burden within the narrower group can be used to generate an aggregate income effect. It is unlikely that there will be sufficient systematic variation in income elasticities within groups to generate an aggregate income effect. In this case, changes in aggregate labor supply will be driven by compensated responses:

$$\text{(4)} \qquad \sum \frac{dL}{dR} = \sum \frac{\partial L^c}{\partial w} \frac{dw}{dR} + \sum \frac{\partial L^c}{\partial p} \frac{dp}{dR}.$$

Equation (4) tells us that the response of labor supply to changes in the tax system will be driven by (1) the compensated elasticity of labor supply with respect to the net wage *and* (2) the compensated cross-price elasticity of labor supply with respect to the price of future consumption.

Our choice of first-period consumption as the numeraire is arbitrary. If we had chosen labor as the numeraire, then labor supply responses would be driven by changes in the prices of first- and second-period consumption. Therefore, the direction of labor supply effects will be driven by the relative complementary of current and future consumption with labor supply. That aggregate labor supply response depends on cross-price elasticities is troubling. Our knowledge of these elasticities is sketchy at best. One effort to measure cross-price effects suggests that they may be important. Using 12 years of panel data from the Panel Study of Income Dynamics (PSID), Fullerton and Skinner (1985) estimate a demand system for consumption and leisure in which they include cross-price effects (lead and lags in wages and interest rates) in both equations. They find that cross-price effects are generally statistically significant. Focusing on their leisure equation, a fall in future consumption prices (rise in the real rate of return one or two periods ahead) increases labor supply—leisure and future consumption appear to be substitutes.

The importance of cross-price elasticities can be seen by considering a shift from our current tax system to a consumed income tax system. The tax rate on interest income (τ_s) is set to zero, and τ_w is increased to maintain budget neutrality. This corresponds to the wage rate and the price of future consumption falling. If labor supply (leisure) is a complement (substitute) to future consumption (as suggested by Fullerton and Skinner 1985), then this tax reform could increase labor supply.[4]

An example with Stone-Geary utility illustrates how these two components

4. This was pointed out early on by Atkinson and Stiglitz (1976), who note in the optimal tax context that "whether there should be an interest income tax or subsidy depends on the complementarity or substitutability (in the Edgeworth sense) between the first-period consumption and labor" (69).

of the labor supply response can work at cross-purposes. Assume that utility is given by

(5) $U = \beta_1 \ln(C_1 - \gamma_1) + \beta_2 \ln(C_2 - \gamma_2) + \beta_3 \ln((1 - L) - \gamma_3).$

The γs are the required consumption parameters of current and future consumption and leisure, while the βs are share parameters and are assumed to add to 1. As is well known, a limitation of the Stone-Geary utility system is that all goods must be substitutes. In that case the first term in equation (4) will be negative (wage reduction reduces labor supply) while the second term will be positive (the decrease in the price of future consumption will lead to a substitution away from leisure: labor supply increases).[5] For a revenue-neutral tax response, these two effects will exactly offset, leading to a zero labor supply response. This simply follows from the weak separability between leisure and consumption in the linear expenditure system. If we are going to get any labor supply response at all, we must choose preferences in which we have not built in weak separability.

As noted in the discussion of equation (1), a consumption tax is equivalent to a wage tax (ignoring transitional issues). An income tax, on the other hand, amounts to a commodity tax with a higher tax rate on future consumption. Nearly 20 years ago, Atkinson and Stiglitz (1976) characterized conditions under which uniform treatment of present and future consumption is optimal. If (1) preferences are weakly separable between leisure and consumption and (2) nonlinear income taxes are possible, then there should be no differentiated tax rates on present and future consumption. This result has been extended to allow for linear income taxes if preferences also exhibit linear Engle curves.[6]

This separability result initially led public finance economists to conclude that income taxation was inefficient and undesirable. Weak separability was enshrined in the discipline because it followed directly from the most commonly employed utility functions (Cobb-Douglas, CES, and Stone-Geary). Of course, this is a limitation, and economists began to seek more flexible functional forms that do not impose an optimal tax result from the outset. Deaton and Muellbauer (1980) provide one example with the almost ideal demand system (AIDS). More to the point, the data do not support weak separability (see, e.g., Browning and Meghir 1991). Hence whether a switch from an income tax to a consumption tax would improve welfare is an empirical matter. The presumption in favor of consumption taxation must also be tempered by

5. It is easy to show that the compensated effect of the tax reform for the Stone-Geary system is given by

$$\frac{dL^c}{dR} \left(\frac{\beta_1 + \beta_2}{w} \frac{dw}{dR} - \frac{\beta_2}{p} \frac{dp}{dR} \right) (l^c - \gamma_3),$$

where l is leisure.

6. Among other sources for this result, see Deaton (1976).

the likelihood that a considerable fraction of consumption is unlikely to be taxed under any of the schemes under discussion.

3.3 Simulations and Labor Supply

I model consumer behavior with a time separable nested CES function. Utility for an individual is given by

$$(6) \qquad U = [\alpha^{1/\rho} v_1^{(\rho-1)/\rho} + (1 - \alpha)^{1/\rho} v_2^{(\rho-1)/\rho}]^{\rho/(\rho-1)},$$

where aggregate consumption in each period (v_i) is modeled as

$$(7) \qquad v_i = [\beta_i^{1/\sigma_i} C_i^{(\sigma_i-1)/\sigma_i} + (1 - \beta_i)^{1/\sigma_i} l_i^{(\sigma_i-1)/\sigma_i}]^{\sigma_i/(\sigma_i-1)},$$

subject to the lifetime budget constraint

$$(8) \qquad w_1 T_1 + w_2 T_2 = w_1 l_1 + w_2 l_2 + p_1 C_1 + p_2 C_2.$$

Consumers optimize by choosing consumption in each of two periods (C_i) along with leisure (l_i). They face consumption prices p_i and wage rates w_i. Their time endowment in each period equals T_i.

This formulation is quite general; nesting consumption and leisure within each time period allows the possibility of leisure affecting the marginal rate of substitution between current and future consumption. That is, weak separability is not built into this model. The parameter ρ measures the intertemporal elasticity of substitution between aggregate consumption bundles, while σ_i measures the elasticity of substitution between leisure and consumption in each time period.

We can compute the marginal rate of substitution between current and future consumption directly. It is given by

$$(9) \qquad \text{MRS}_{12} = \left(\frac{\alpha}{1 - \alpha}\right)^{\rho^{-1}} \left(\frac{\beta_1^{\sigma_1^{-1}}}{\beta_2^{\sigma_2^{-1}}}\right) \left(\frac{v_1^{\sigma_1^{-1} - \rho^{-1}}}{v_2^{\sigma_2^{-1} - \rho^{-1}}}\right) \frac{C_1^{-\sigma_1}}{C_2^{-\sigma_2}}.$$

Since v_i is a function of l_i, weak separability between consumption and leisure is avoided so long as the intertemporal elasticity of substitution is not equal to either of the intracommodity elasticities of substitution.

The budget in equation (8) says that the value of the lifetime time endowment can be allocated to leisure and consumption in each period. The wage rate in each period is net of the tax on labor income. Taking the first-period price of consumption as the numeraire, w_2 equals the second-period net-of-tax wage discounted to the first period by the after-tax rate of return. Similarly, the price of C_2 is the period-two price discounted by the after-tax return. At this stage, I will treat consumption as a composite good with price 1. Thus C is the expenditure on consumption in each period. If we define Y as lifetime full income (net of tax) and q_i as the (shadow) price of aggregate consumption, we can rewrite the lifetime budget constraint in equation (8) as

(10) $$Y = q_1 v_1 + q_2 v_2.$$

Solving the first-stage maximization problem (treating aggregate consumption as the argument) yields demand functions

(11) $$v_1 = \frac{\alpha Y}{q_1^\rho [\alpha q_1^{1-\rho} + (1 - \alpha) q_2^{1-\rho}]},$$

$$v_2 = \frac{(1 - \alpha) Y}{q_2^\rho [\alpha q_1^{1-\rho} + (1 - \alpha) q_2^{1-\rho}]}.$$

Ignoring time subscripts, the within-period optimization problem uses the budget constraint

(12) $$pC + wl = qv.$$

The demand functions for C and l are given by

(13) $$C = \frac{\beta(qv)}{p^\sigma [\beta p^{1-\sigma} + (1 - \beta) w^{1-\sigma}]},$$

$$l = \frac{(1 - \beta)(qv)}{w^\sigma [\beta p^{1-\sigma} + (1 - \beta) w^{1-\sigma}]}.$$

To run simulations, we need values for the parameters of the utility functions. I will choose parameter values in part based on estimates in the literature and in part based on calibration using data from 1989 Consumer Expenditure Survey (CEX).

Auerbach and Kotlikoff (1987) review the literature on the intertemporal elasticity of substitution and note that parameter estimates range from 0.07 to over 1.00. I follow Auerbach and Kotlikoff and choose $\rho = 0.25$.

The parameters σ_i and β_i will affect the household's labor supply elasticity and labor-leisure allocation. The leisure-consumption elasticity (σ) can perhaps be best chosen by determining the resultant labor supply elasticities. The elasticity σ measures the percentage change in the leisure consumption ratio in any year following a 1 percent change in the wage-price ratio, holding other prices constant. If consumption were unchanged, σ would measure the labor supply elasticity directly. However, since consumption will adjust as the wage changes, we need to measure the labor supply responsiveness explicitly to relate the elasticity of labor supply to the elasticity of substitution between consumption and leisure. I follow Auerbach and Kotlikoff (1987) and choose a value of σ equal to 0.8. Finally, the parameter α measures time preferences for the individual, and I choose a central value for this parameter equal to 0.50.

Equations (13) can be combined to provide an expression for β:

(14) $$\beta = \frac{p^\sigma C}{p^\sigma C + w^\sigma l}.$$

Average expenditures on consumption when young provide a value for C_1, while p equals 1 in period one.[7] To complete our computation of β, we need estimates of wage rates and leisure.

To compute leisure, I turn to the CEX. The CEX asks household members how many hours they worked in the past week. I take this from the family file for the reference member of the household and the spouse (if present). I check for the presence of regular work and adjust the reported labor supply figure accordingly.[8] To simplify the analysis, I assume that second-period labor supply equals zero. Based on CEX data for 1989, a small percentage of elderly households report hours (29 percent), and their average—conditional on working—is roughly 30 hours per week. Within this group, many will only work for a small part of the year.

I assume a time endowment of 5,000 hours per year and subtract the estimated labor supply from the endowment to compute leisure. Table 3.1 provides some distributional information on labor supply across different categories of workers. Roughly 70 percent of the household heads age 30 or over in the CEX family file report hours worked. Conditional on reporting hours, the mean hours are 2,055 per year, with the median occurring at 2,000 hours per year.[9] Nearly 93 percent of the households with household head between ages 30 and 60 report hours, with mean hours just under 2,000 per year.

To compute the gross (of tax) wage rate, I use data from the CEX household member file. Those household members currently working are asked how large their most recent paycheck was. I divide this amount by the number of hours worked in the previous week after adjusting the paycheck by the frequency of payment. I then regress the log of the wage on age, age squared, and dummy variables for sex and race, as well as indicators for whether the household member is divorced or single. There are 6,072 usable observations with which I can run the regression. Results are reported in table 3.2. Wage increases with age until about age 46, after which it begins to fall. At age 30 wages are increasing a bit less than 4 percent per year. Women have wages roughly 30 percent lower than men after controlling for age, race, and marital status. Nonwhites earn roughly 6 percent less, as do divorced and single men. The results are statistically significant and plausible.

The regression results from table 3.2 are applied to the reference person and spouse (if present) in the family files. Column (1) of table 3.3 reports summary statistics on the generated wage used in the wage regression in table 3.2. Col-

7. I consider time periods of 30 years so that effective adult life equals 80 years. Think of an individual living for 20 years as a child followed by two 30-year periods of different work amounts. Death occurs at age 80 (60 in economic years). For purposes of compounding savings, I take the midpoint of the first time period.

8. The CEX asks household members how many weeks they worked the previous year. It also asks if they worked part or full time for part or all of the previous year.

9. The CEX reports weekly hours. I multiply by 50 to obtain annual values.

Table 3.1   **Labor Supply Statistics across Age Groups**

	All	Young[a]
Average labor supply	1,439	1,996
	(1,080)	(776)
Average labor supply conditional on $L > 0$	2,055	2,152
	(633)	(492)
Percentage with $L > 0$	70.0	92.7
25th Percentile[b]	2,000	2,000
50th Percentile[b]	2,000	2,000
75th Percentile[b]	2,375	2,400
N	1,422	918

Source: Data from 1989 CEX family file.
Note: Numbers in parentheses are standard deviations.
[a]Age 30–60.
[b]Percentiles are conditional on $L > 0$.

Table 3.2   **Wage Regressions: Dependent Variable = Log (wage)**

Variable	Coefficient
Age	.097
	(.004)
Age squared	−.001
	(.000)
Female	−.299
	(.017)
Nonwhite	−.059
	(.024)
Divorced	−.060
	(.028)
Single	−.061
	(.025)
Intercept	.603
	(.087)
R^2	.18
N	6,072

Source: Data from 1989 CEX household member file.
Note: Wage is computed as last gross paycheck divided by the number of hours in the pay period. Numbers in parentheses are standard errors. All estimated coefficients are significant at the 95 percent level.

umn (2) presents summary statistics for the reference member in the family file. The mean wage is roughly $1.50 per hour lower in the family file, reflecting the fact that wages are being imputed to workers and nonworkers alike. Also, the age distribution of individuals differs across the family and member files. The mean age in the family file equals 36.9 years, while it equals 49 years

Table 3.3   Imputed Wage from CEX

	Member (1)	Family (2)
Mean	10.38	8.88
Standard deviation	9.77	2.86
25th Percentile	5.25	6.91
50th Percentile	8.29	8.95
75th Percentile	13.00	11.50
N	6,072	1,957

Source: Wage imputed from information in 1989 CEX household member file. See text for details of construction. Col. (2) gives imputed wage from regression in table 3.2 applied to household heads in CEX family file.

in the member file. There is virtually no skew in the distribution. If it were important to model variation in wages across the entire population then this would be troubling. However, I will be using mean wages within various age groups for purposes of calibrating β so that the lack of skew is less problematic. Isolating the individuals in the family file who are "young" (age 30–60), the mean wage (age) is $10.10 (40.2).

The final step to constructing a value for w is to compute the marginal tax rate on wage income for households in the CEX. I use the NBER TAXSIM tax calculator for this purpose. I feed income and household data from the family file to TAXSIM and compute a federal tax liability.[10] I then recompute the tax liability after adding $100 of wage income to the return. The difference in tax liabilities divided by 100 is the marginal tax rate on wage income. The median tax rate is 15 percent with an interquartile range running from 10.4 to 28 percent. The correlation between gross wage and tax rate is .46.

We now have the pieces to estimate values of β. For this two-period model, I select households in the CEX sample in which the reference person is between ages 30 and 60. I take averages of per capita consumption, leisure, and net wage rates across this group. Table 3.4 gives average values, and the resulting value of β_1 equals .43. To account for the absence of labor supply in the second period, I set β_2 below β_1 at .33. Parameterizing the model as I have leads to negligible labor supply elasticities. The uncompensated wage elasticity for the young equals -0.07 while the compensated elasticity equals 0.44.

3.4 Simulation Results and Sensitivity Analysis

I now consider the experiment of switching from a tax on capital income and increasing the tax on consumption to maintain revenue neutrality over the

---

10. For completeness, I should compute a marginal tax rate using federal and state income tax codes. However, it is difficult to impossible to determine the state in which CEX households live.

Table 3.4   **Commodity-Leisure Weight Parameter**

Variable	Average Value
p_1	1
$\bar{W}_1$	8.55
C_1	12,785
l_1	3,004
σ_1	.80
β_1	.43
N	918

Source: Averages are taken from 1989 CEX family file for households with reference person in age range 30–60 (period one).
Note: $\bar{W}$ is the wage net of tax. N is the number of observations in the group.

Table 3.5   **Shift to Consumption Taxation**

	Tax Base			
Variable	Capital Income (1)	Consumption (2)	Capital Income (3)	Consumption (4)
C_1	15,090	14,164	14,815	13,065
C_2	18,273	20,808	14,503	18,862
L_1	1,986	1,954	2,040	1,971
S	6,056	5,279	6,914	5,257
τ_k	.25		.50	
τ_c		.097		.205
EV_1		.19		.78
EV_2		5.64		11.75

Notes: Results of simulations with $\rho = .25$, $\sigma_1 = .80$, $\sigma_2 = .80$, $\alpha = .50$, $\beta_1 = .43$, and $\beta_2 = .33$. The consumption tax rate is adjusted to collect the same lifetime tax revenue as under the capital income tax. EV_1 measures the equivalent variation of the change from the income tax expressed as a percentage of lifetime resources, while EV_2 measures equivalent variation as a percentage of lifetime discounted tax revenue.

individual's lifetime.[11] I begin with a tax rate of 25 percent on capital income. Table 3.5 presents results.

Column (1) gives information about consumption, labor supply, and savings under the capital income tax. The individual consumes roughly 70 percent of first-period income, saving the remaining 30 percent. The large amount of sav-

---

11. The issue of revenue neutrality is an important one. Typically policymakers consider revenue neutrality in a limited sense, for example over a five-year period. Neutrality here means that the present discounted value of tax revenue, discounted at the before-tax return, is unchanged. As Summers (1981) has noted, equivalent tax rates on wage and consumption taxation will not necessarily achieve revenue neutrality in the steady state given the different composition of savings over the lifetime arising from the two different tax systems.

ing means that a nontrivial consumption tax will be needed to recoup the revenues lost when capital income is untaxed.

Column (2) presents a shift to a comprehensive consumption tax. The effect of this tax reform is to increase the price of current consumption while decreasing the price of future consumption. This is borne out by a moderate decrease in current consumption (-6 percent) and a large increase in future consumption (14 percent).

A consumption tax rate of 9.7 percent suffices to balance the government's budget. There is a modest welfare gain from this reform. Expressed as a fraction of potential lifetime income, the welfare gain equals 0.19 percent of income. Alternatively, the gain is equal to roughly 5 percent of lifetime tax collections. Perhaps surprisingly, savings falls under this tax reform by over 10 percent. One of the arguments in favor of a shift to consumption taxation is the favorable effects on capital accumulation. For example, Summers (1981) finds a highly sensitive response of savings to changes in the tax treatment of capital income, which in turn leads to substantial welfare gains from shifting to consumption taxation. However, there is no theoretical basis for expecting savings to rise with a switch from income to consumption taxation (see Feldstein 1978 for an extended discussion of this point).

Column (3) increases the initial capital income tax rate from 25 to 50 percent. Comparing columns (3) and (1), the most significant difference is the 21 percent drop in second-period consumption. Shifting to a consumption tax from a capital income tax leads to a larger percentage increase in future consumption (relative to the 25 percent capital income tax) and a larger percentage drop in current consumption. Doubling the tax rate on capital income leads to roughly a quadrupling of the excess burden (expressed as a percentage of a lifetime earnings), as one would expect from the quadratic deadweight loss rule.[12]

Concerns about the labor supply effects of a shift from capital income to consumption taxation are misplaced if the results from this analysis are correct. Labor supply falls somewhat—on the order of 1–3 percent. The labor supply effects seem small relative to the welfare gains from shifting tax bases.

Table 3.6 presents some sensitivity analyses for the results. The first set indicates that changes in the intertemporal elasticity parameter (ρ) can have significant welfare effects. Halving the parameter cuts the welfare gains in half, while doubling the parameter doubles the welfare gain. Labor supply is also affected. If ρ equals 0.125, labor supply falls over 4 percent.

The results are also somewhat sensitive to changes in α, the intertemporal weight parameter. Welfare gains from a shift to consumption taxation fall as α rises, reflecting the lower weight placed on future consumption (and any distortions arising from the capital income tax). Altering σ_1 has modest effects

---

12. The equivalent variation as a fraction of tax revenue only doubles because the tax revenue itself roughly doubles when the capital income tax rate is doubled.

Table 3.6   **Sensitivity Analysis**

ρ	α	σ_1	σ_2	$\%\Delta L$	EV_1
.25	.50	.80	.80	−3.4	.78
.125	.50	.80	.80	−4.4	.35
.50	.50	.80	.80	−1.8	1.45
.25	.35	.80	.80	−4.6	.84
.25	.65	.80	.80	−1.7	.35
.25	.50	.95	.80	−4.0	.87
.25	.50	.65	.80	−2.4	.72

Note: Results of simulations corresponding to shifting from a 50 percent capital income tax to a consumption tax; $\beta_1 = .43$, $\beta_2 = .33$, and the interest rate equals 5 percent.

on labor supply and welfare effects. The welfare gains from the tax shift rise with σ_1, though the gains are not dramatic.[13]

3.5   Narrowing the Tax Base

One of the main attractions of a consumption tax is the elimination of the intertemporal distortion. Table 3.5 suggests that significant welfare gains result from the elimination of this distortion. However it comes at the cost of possibly creating intracommodity distortions if various items are excluded from the tax base. Typically, European VATs exclude housing, food consumed at home, and medical care from the tax base. Moreover, in this country much of personal saving is not subject to taxation. According to the most recent *Flow of Funds* report, net acquisition of financial assets in the derivation of personal saving equaled $526 billion in 1993. Of that, roughly 65 percent was flows into life insurance and pension reserves.[14] On a levels basis, between one-third and one-half of all financial assets are held as nontaxable assets. Therefore, a change from income to consumption taxation creates the possibility of generating a small intertemporal welfare gain while creating a large intracommodity welfare loss. I now turn to simulations in which I explore this possibility.

I modify the utility function in equation (7) above to allow for nontaxed consumption goods. The v functions now include taxed (C_i) and nontaxed (D_i) consumption goods and leisure with share parameters β_{ci}, β_{di}, and $1 - \beta_{ci} - \beta_{di}$, respectively. The values of β are calibrated in a similar fashion as in equation (14) for a VAT that zero rates food consumed at home, shelter, and medical

---

13. Changing σ_2 has negligible effects on welfare or labor supply.

14. This likely understates tax-exempt savings. While there was a net decumulation of tax-exempt securities in 1993 ($16 billion), $187 billion was invested in mutual funds, some of which was invested in tax-exempt securities. Overall, mutual funds increased their holdings of tax-exempt securities by $45 billion in 1993; it is likely that the bulk of that addition came from the household sector.

Table 3.7   Consumption Expenditures for Selected Categories in 1989

Category	Consumer Unit Spending ($)	Percentage
Food at home	2,390	9
Shelter	4,660	17
Health care	1,407	5
All three categories	8,457	30

Source: 1989 CEX.

Table 3.8   Zero Rating with a VAT

Variable	Capital Income (1)	Comprehensive VAT (2)	Partial VAT (3)
C_1	10,335	9,115	8,496
C_2	10,107	13,146	12,239
D_1	4,478	3,950	4,582
D_2	4,398	5,716	6,622
L_1	2,040	1,971	1,972
S	6,915	5,257	5,255
τ_k	.50		
τ_c		.205	.315
EV_1		.78	.52
EV_2		11.75	7.81

Notes: Results of simulations with $\rho = .25$, $\sigma_1 = .80$, $\sigma_2 = .80$, $\alpha = .50$, $\beta_{c1} = .30$, $\beta_{d1} = .13$, $\beta_{c2} = .23$, and $\beta_{d2} = .10$. The consumption tax rate is adjusted to collect same lifetime tax revenue as under capital income tax. See table 3.5 for definitions of EV_1 and EV_2.

costs. In 1989 these three consumption categories accounted for 30 percent of total consumption expenditures (see table 3.7).

Table 3.8 reports results of the simulation. Column (1) assumes a capital income tax of 50 percent. Prior to the VAT, the commodity that will be subject to the partial VAT accounts for roughly 70 percent of total consumption. The share parameters were chosen to generate a 30 percent nontaxable consumption fraction, with total consumption, labor supply, and savings to correspond to column (1) of table 3.5.

Column (2) of table 3.8 assumes that all consumption is taxed. Hence the results are equivalent to those in column (4) of table 3.5. A tax rate of 20 percent suffices to replace the capital income tax. A partial VAT is modeled in column (3).

If a partial VAT is employed, the welfare gains from shifting from capital income to consumption taxation are reduced by over 30 percent. The equivalent variation (as a fraction of lifetime income) falls from 0.78 to 0.52. The

Table 3.9   **Extent of Zero Rating and Welfare**

Percentage of Untaxed Commodity[a]	τ_c[b]	EV_1	EV_2
0	20.5	.78	11.75
30	31.5	.52	7.81
50	48.4	.15	2.28
60	66.3	−.20	−2.03

Note: See table 3.5 for definitions of EV_1 and EV_2.

[a]Fraction of consumption under the capital income tax that will be untaxed with a shift to a partial consumption tax.

[b]Tax rate necessary on the taxed commodity to balance the budget.

tax rate on consumption must now rise to 31.5 percent to maintain revenue neutrality. There is a larger fall in consumption of the tax good and a small increase in the consumption of the untaxed good, particularly in the second period.

Despite the fact that 30 percent of consumption is untaxed (introducing a substantial intracommodity distortion), the welfare gains from shifting from capital income to partial consumption taxation are still positive and substantial. To examine the relative importance of the intracommodity and intertemporal distortion, I redid the analysis allowing for increasingly greater fractions of consumption to be untaxed. Table 3.9 presents the results.

If 50 percent of consumption is untaxed, a tax rate of 48 percent on the remaining goods is required to balance the government's budget. The welfare gains from not taxing capital income fall sharply with EV_2 dropping from 11.75 percent (no exclusions) to 2.28 percent. Once excluded consumption exceeds 60 percent of total consumption, the capital income tax becomes preferable from a welfare perspective to a consumption tax. At the untaxed fraction of 60 percent, a VAT rate of 66.3 percent is required to balance the budget and there is a welfare loss of 3 percent from the reform.

These results suggest that the benefits from removing the intertemporal distortion swamp any distortions that arise from taxing only a fraction of consumption (unless the fraction of untaxed consumption exceeds one-half). While some sensitivity analysis should be carried out to consider the robustness of this conclusion, the fact that welfare losses only occur with very narrow consumption tax bases suggest that this is not an important distortion (relative to the intertemporal distortion).

Some rough calculations suggest that this is likely to be a robust result. The effect of eliminating the capital income tax is to decrease the price of future consumption. Let p_1 be the price of future consumption under the capital income tax and p_2 the price once the tax is eliminated. Similarly, C_2^1 is the amount of future consumption under the capital income tax and C_2^2 the amount once the tax is eliminated. An approximation for the deadweight loss reduced by eliminating the tax is given by[15]

(15) $$\Delta DWL_s = \frac{1}{2}(p_1 - p_2)(C_2^1 - C_2^2).$$

The price of future consumption equals $[1 + (1 - \tau)r]^{-30}$. Given an interest rate of 5 percent, $p_1 = 0.48$ and $p_2 = 0.23$. The price is effectively cut in half by eliminating the capital income tax. What is the effect on future consumption? The change in saving in the simulations is on the order of 25 percent. That is, $S_2 = 0.75S_1$. Since $S_i = p_iC_2^i$, $0.23C_2^2 = (0.75)(0.48)C_2^1 = 1.56C_2^1$. Therefore, the change in consumption is $C_2^1 - C_2^2 = 0.56C_2^1$. Consumption in the first period in this model is on the order of 70 percent of income (Y). Hence, the change in consumption is approximately $- 0.56(0.70Y) = -0.39Y$. Thus, $\Delta DWL_s = \frac{1}{2}(0.48 - 0.23)(0.39Y) = -0.049Y$.

Now consider the consumption tax. The former capital income tax collected is $[(0.23)^{-1} - (0.48)^{-1}]S_1$ in future consumption units. Savings is roughly 20 percent of wage income in the model, yielding tax revenue of roughly $0.45Y$. In present value terms, that equals $(0.23)(0.45Y) = 0.10Y$. If current consumption is roughly 70 percent of income, then the consumption tax rate required to replace the capital income tax is $0.10Y/0.70Y = 14$ percent. With a partial VAT covering 70 percent of consumption, the required tax rate would be $0.10Y/[(0.70)(0.70Y)] = 20$ percent. The deadweight loss associated with the increase in the partial consumption tax would equal

(16) $$\Delta DWL_c = -\frac{1}{2} \varepsilon t^2 C_1,$$

where ε is the compensated elasticity of demand for consumption. The change in the deadweight loss thus equals $\frac{1}{2}(0.20)^2(0.49Y)\varepsilon = 0.0098\varepsilon Y$. Assuming a demand elasticity of 1, the reduction in deadweight loss from eliminating the capital income tax is roughly five times the increased deadweight loss from the partial consumption tax. Put slightly differently, the difference in deadweight loss between a comprehensive consumption tax and the partial consumption tax equals

$$\frac{1}{2}\varepsilon Y[(0.20)^2 (0.49) - (0.14)^2 (0.70)] = 0.0029\varepsilon Y.$$

Deadweight loss increases by about 40 percent with the partial consumption tax; however, the magnitudes are quite small relative to the deadweight loss from the capital income tax.

---

15. Feldstein (1978) provides an extensive analysis of welfare costs using Harberger deadweight loss triangles. As he points out, the formula requires the analysis of the tax system as a whole, and separate analysis of each tax component is inappropriate. For my purposes, I am only demonstrating the relative importance of the individual components of a reform rather than rigorously measuring excess burden with this formula.

3.6 Conclusion

Let me begin by noting that this analysis has taken the production side of the economy as given. Factor prices and commodity prices are assumed to be unaffected by the tax reform. This is clearly unrealistic. A partial consumption tax is likely to lead to an increase in the price for the untaxed commodity relative to the price of the tax commodity. This will serve to make the partial consumption tax look more like a comprehensive consumption tax and reduce the losses arising from the presence of untaxed commodities.

I began this paper by making two points on the subject of consumption versus income taxation. First, labor supply effects—when they are considered at all—are generally thought to be negative with a consumption tax. The shift from income to consumption taxation involves a narrowing of the tax base and the effective tax on wage income must rise. However, as I have shown, labor supply effects are likely to be quite small, and moreover, labor supply can increase or decrease in response to a shift to consumption taxation.

The second point that I have made in this paper is that the welfare gains from a shift to consumption taxation may be overstated if there is only partial taxation of consumption. However, the reduction in gains from partial consumption taxation are not very large, and over plausible ranges of parameter estimates, the gains from removing the intertemporal distortion exceed the losses from the intracommodity distortion.

Overall, there are two reassuring messages that come out of this paper for supporters of consumption taxation. First, a shift from income to consumption taxation is not likely to have large adverse labor supply effects. Second, the welfare losses from partial consumption taxation are relatively unimportant compared to the gains from removing the intertemporal distortion. While there are many good reasons to avoid zero rating and exemption of goods in a consumption tax, welfare reasons are not paramount. Administrative and distributional concerns are likely to loom much larger than welfare concerns.

References

Atkinson, A., and J. Stiglitz. 1976. The design of tax structure: Direct versus indirect taxation. *Journal of Public Economics* 6:55–75.

Auerbach, A., and L. Kotlikoff. 1987. *Dynamic fiscal policy.* New York: Cambridge University Press.

Auerbach, A., L. Kotlikoff, and J. Skinner. 1983. The efficiency gains from dynamic tax reform. *International Economic Review* 24:81–100.

Browning, M., and C. Meghir. 1991. The effects of male and female labor supply on commodity demands. *Econometrica* 59:925–51.

Christian, E., and G. Schutzer. 1995. Unlimited savings allowance (USA) tax system. *Tax Notes* 66(10 March): 1485–1575.

Deaton, A. 1976. Optimally uniform commodity taxes. *Economics Letters* 2:357–61.
Deaton, A., and J. Muellbauer. 1980. An almost ideal demand system. *American Economic Review* 70:312–36.
Feldstein, M. 1978. The welfare cost of capital income taxation. *Journal of Political Economy* 86:S29–S51.
Fullerton, D., and D. Rogers. 1993. *Who bears the lifetime tax burden?* Washington, D.C.: Brookings Institution.
Fullerton, D., and J. Skinner. 1985. Cross price effects and capital taxation. In *National Tax Association–Tax Institute of America Proceedings of 1984,* 292–99. Columbus, Ohio: National Tax Association.
Metcalf, G. 1995. Value added taxation: A tax whose time has come? *Journal of Economic Perspectives* 9:121–40.
Slemrod, J. 1987. Can a revenue-neutral, distributionally-neutral tax reform increase labor supply? Ann Arbor: University of Michigan, Department of Economics. Mimeograph.
Summers, L. 1981. Capital taxation and accumulation in a life cycle growth model. *American Economic Review* 71:533–44.
U.S. Congress. Joint Committee on Taxation. 1995. *Description of tax proposals contained in the "Contract with America"* (JCS-1-95). Washington, D.C., 9 January.

Comment   Gary Burtless

Many economists—and a smaller number of politicians—favor replacing the present income tax system with a partial or comprehensive tax on household consumption. The claimed advantages of a consumption tax include a reduction in the distortion of consumers' allocation decision between consuming today and consuming in the future. Because it taxes the return on savings, an income tax favors current over deferred consumption. A consumption tax would reduce or eliminate this distortion.

Gilbert Metcalf examines the potential effect of a consumption tax on labor supply, saving, and consumer well-being within a stylized model of consumer behavior. The effects of the tax are measured relative to those of a capital income tax that raises the same amount of revenue over each consumer's life span. In comparison with an income tax, the consumption tax induces consumers to work less and save less. It also improves consumer welfare because agents are permitted to allocate consumption across different periods of their lives without tax penalty.

Metcalf's conclusions rest on several clearly stated assumptions. Individuals are assumed to live for two periods and to consume completely their net lifetime incomes by the time they expire. That is, they do not share their incomes with relatives, nor do they leave bequests. Their consumption and labor supply over the two periods of their lives are determined by a time-separable constant

Gary Burtless is a senior fellow in economic studies at the Brookings Institution.

elasticity of substitution (CES) utility function. Metcalf assumes the values of the critical variables in this utility function or infers their values based on observed consumption and labor supply patterns in the Bureau of Labor Statistics Consumer Expenditure Survey (CEX). To simplify the analysis, the author also assumes that individuals do not work during the second period of their lives. This is not entirely consistent with evidence in the CEX, which suggests that nearly a third of older family heads are employed and that employed older people work approximately two-thirds as much as younger workers. I doubt that Metcalf's simplification leads to a major distortion in his qualitative results, given the other assumptions in his model.

The other assumptions of the model are clearly open to question, however. The substantial amount of work effort among a minority of older CEX respondents reflects a substantial diversity in individual circumstances (such as wealth and labor market opportunities) and individual preferences (i.e., utility functions). Metcalf's analysis ignores the diversity in circumstances and preferences to focus on the response of a representative agent, who is assigned a wage and preference function that is thought to reflect the population average.

I suspect that the main limitation in this study for practical policy making is its focus on a single representative agent. Population responses may differ from those of a single representative agent because some groups in the population are almost certainly more responsive to taxation than others. If the most responsive groups are also ones that have a high wage or an exceptional propensity to save, the economy-wide effects of a tax change will not be accurately reflected by the responses of a single representative member of the population who has average characteristics and preferences. However, Metcalf's focus permits us to see clearly how aspects of the tax system and the individual preference function can affect individual welfare and behavioral response.

The sensitivity analysis shown in tables 3.5, 3.6, 3.8, and 3.9 is straightforward and illuminating. Compared with a capital income tax that raises the same discounted revenue over each taxpayer's life span, a consumption tax reduces labor supply. The intuition behind this result is plain. In Metcalf's model a consumption tax is equivalent to a tax on wages, so workers are modestly discouraged from working. Because the assumed labor supply elasticity is very low, however, the reduction in labor supply is small, so Metcalf finds only a small decline in lifetime earnings.

The consumption tax also yields a reduction in first-period consumption *and* saving, in large measure because it increases tax burdens in the first period. The wage earner has less net income in the first period to divide between consumption and saving. However, the worker has more net income in the second period, and hence she consumes more in that period than she would under a capital income tax. When consumers are permitted to allocate freely their consumption between the two periods without special tax penalty, they choose to defer consumption to the second period. The improvement in consumers' welfare from this reallocation of consumption between periods more than offsets the loss of welfare from reduced lifetime earnings, yielding an improvement in consumer well-being. Metcalf's sensitivity analyses suggest that this improvement will likely remain even if the consumption tax is not uniform across commodities. However, this conclusion is probably sensitive to changes in preference parameters about which economists know little.

As noted in the paper, these results do not come out of a general equilibrium model that includes the production side of the economy. Workers reduce their labor supply and saving under a consumption tax, so it would be surprising if the economy could produce as much output as under an income tax. Nor does the paper consider the formidable problem of shifting from an income tax to a consumption tax system. In Metcalf's stylized model it might seem feasible to impose a consumption tax starting with a particular cohort, rather than imposing it on all generations at the same time. This simple solution to the transition problem is not available to policymakers, because most taxpayers' life spans last longer than two periods. A transition rule that is fair to retired 70-year-olds and to 20-year-olds just entering the labor force may not be fair to 50-year-olds who have accumulated assets under an income tax system for 30 years and face the prospect of working for 15 additional years and drawing retirement benefits for 20 years under a consumption tax system. Any transition rule will create winners and losers. Practical efforts to minimize the number of losers or the size of their losses may involve imposing burdens on taxpayers who cannot vote, namely, future workers who are left with a larger public debt.

The paper is convincing in showing the long-run advantages of a consumption tax under sensible assumptions. Even a consumption tax involves distortions, of course. The tax is imposed on goods and services that are purchased in the market, but it exempts goods and services produced in the home as well as leisure consumption. Decisions about home production and labor supply behavior will therefore be distorted by a consumption tax just as they are by an income tax. In addition, as Metcalf points out, almost no existing consumption tax is uniformly imposed on all goods and services. Some market goods and services are more lightly taxed than others; some goods and services are exempt from taxes altogether. Thus, consumption taxes that are politically feasible may cause distortions in budget allocation across different classes of commodities, even though they lessen the distortion in allocations across time periods.

As actually implemented in current tax law, the income tax introduces a comparable distortion. Different classes of income are subject to differing tax rates. Imputed rent on owner-occupied homes and unrealized gains on capital income are exempt from the income tax. Employer contributions to medical insurance are also untaxed. Several forms of capital income, in addition to unrealized capital gains, are lightly taxed in comparison with an identical stream of money wages. For example, assets held in qualified pension plans, 401(k) plans, and individual retirement accounts (IRAs) generate returns that are untaxed until withdrawals from the plan begin sometime during retirement.

Like a consumption tax which imposes differing rates on different classes of commodities, an income tax that imposes differing rates on different classes of income can distort agents' behavior. Actual income tax systems favor certain kinds of income-generating activities over others, just as most implemented consumption tax systems favor certain kinds of consumption over others. In the case of the U.S. income tax, two of the most costly tax preferences are aimed at boosting particular forms of household saving. The preferences to encourage home ownership and qualified pension plans are expensive to the Treasury, but they may induce taxpayers to save more in their homes and in company pension plans than taxpayers would save under an income tax system in which all forms of income were subject to a uniform tax rate.

In fact, of course, the present U.S. income tax contains elements of a consumption tax as well as an income tax. The tax preference for pensions exempts contributions to pension plans and income earned in the plans from taxes until money is withdrawn in retirement. For workers who are contributing less to pension plans than allowed by their employer and by current law, the present income tax system causes no distortion in the intertemporal allocation of resources. Workers are free at the margin to increase their consumption in old age without any special tax penalty. The specific income-tax-induced distortion treated in this paper is not relevant in this case. The number of workers who can make additional tax-preferred contributions to pension plans is very large since many workers do not make the largest allowed contribution to 401(k) or IRA plans. Even those workers who cannot make additional tax-preferred contributions to pension plans are less constrained than it may appear. Workers with a strong preference for deferring compensation into the future have the option of seeking an employer who offers a pay package with less current money compensation and more deferred compensation. While it is more costly for workers to find employers offering the optimal mix of current and deferred compensation than it is for them to allocate their consumption under a consumption tax, the present income tax system certainly offers workers rich opportunities for deferring taxes on compensation until the compensation is used for consumption. In view of this feature of the U.S. income tax, the welfare gains of moving to a comprehensive consumption tax are likely to be noticeably smaller than suggested in this paper.

4 The Distributional Effects of the Tax Treatment of Child Care Expenses

William M. Gentry and Alison P. Hagy

The child care tax credit (CCTC) is the largest federal government program in the United States aimed at helping families with child care expenses.[1] In 1991, over 5.9 million households took the CCTC, costing the government $2.8 billion in tax revenues (Internal Revenue Service 1993). This paper measures the distributional effects of the CCTC and dependent care assistance plans (DCAPs), an alternative tax-relief program administered as an employee benefit that allows families to pay for child care with pretax income.

The tax credit's critics claim that it is regressive because it benefits middle- and upper-income families without offering relief to less-advantaged families.[2] Yet, previous research by Dunbar and Nordhauser (1991) and Altshuler and Schwartz (1996) using tax return data shows that the tax credit is progressive. As with any government program targeted at child care, this tax relief will redistribute resources from households without children to households with children. However, as discussed by Altshuler and Schwartz, much of this redistribution cancels out over the life cycle: families with young children may receive tax relief now but will not receive relief when their children are older. Since this type of redistribution is transitory, we focus on measuring the redistribution of benefits within the population of families with children. This redistribution comes from the various tax rules pertaining to tax relief for child

William M. Gentry is assistant professor of finance and economics at the Graduate School of Business, Columbia University, and a faculty research fellow of the National Bureau of Economic Research. Alison P. Hagy is assistant professor of economics at Pomona College.

The authors thank Rosanne Altshuler, David Bradford, Phil Cook, Charlie Clotfelter, Doug Holtz-Eakin, Jean Kimmel, Brigitte Madrian, Margie McElroy, Gib Metcalf, Jim Poterba, and participants at the NBER Summer Institute and Tax Policy Analysis Conference for helpful comments. The authors remain responsible for any errors.

1. For a review of the numerous government programs aimed at child care, see Robins (1990).
2. See Garfinkel, Meyer, and Wong (1990) for simulations of how various expansions of the CCTC would affect poverty and welfare recipiency.

care, how child care expenditures vary with income, and differences in family choices regarding child care.

Our primary data source is the National Child Care Survey (NCCS), although when possible we compare our results with those obtained using a sample of tax returns. The NCCS surveys families with at least one child under age 13 and thus isolates a cohort of families with children of eligible ages for tax relief. In addition, the NCCS includes information that is not available from the previously analyzed tax return data. For example, it has information on access and participation in DCAPs and details on family structure, labor force participation, and child care expenses. This information allows us to investigate what family characteristics affect whether a family receives tax relief and, if so, how much tax relief it receives. We can also construct an alternative ability-to-pay measure, "potential labor income," based on wage and individual characteristic data. The advantage of this alternative measure of ability to pay is that it is related to a family's labor market opportunities rather than its preferences for leisure.

Our results suggest that a broad cross section of Americans benefit from tax relief for child care. However, tax relief does not reach the bottom 10 percent of the income distribution primarily because the CCTC is nonrefundable. Despite this regressivity at low income levels, we find that above the bottom quintile of the income distribution, tax relief is progressive: the effective subsidy rate (i.e., tax relief benefits divided by income) steadily declines with income. We attribute this progressivity to a combination of progressive features of the tax rules (e.g., the CCTC rate declines with income) and the income inelasticity of child care expenses. Finally, we find tax relief to be more progressive when we use potential income as a measure of ability to pay.

Among families that receive tax relief for child care expenses, the tax benefits average 1.24 percent of family income. While our results on the progressivity of tax relief indicate that this percentage varies systematically across income groups, tax relief is too small to influence the income distribution dramatically. However, tax relief also varies substantially across families with the same income. This variation within income groups suggests that tax relief for child care changes household tax liabilities (and after-tax incomes), depending on the ages and number of children in the family, marital status of the parents, parent's education, and choice of child care arrangements.

Our results using potential income suggest that household labor supply decisions are an integral part of how tax relief for child care is distributed. By reducing the after-tax price of child care, tax relief for child care can affect the labor market and child care decisions of households. In response to the lower price of child care, families may choose paid care over nonpaid care, a different mode of market-provided care (e.g., child care center vs. family day care home), or a higher-priced option within a particular mode of child care. Reducing the cost of child care may also affect the labor force participation or hours decisions of parents, especially mothers, because it raises the net of child care wage. To the extent that tax relief induces significant changes in household labor supply and child care decisions, these behavioral responses will have implications for the distributional effects of any changes in the tax treatment of child care.

The remainder of the paper is organized as follows. Section 4.1 briefly describes the different features of tax relief. Section 4.2 discusses various rationales for tax relief for child care. Section 4.3 presents evidence on the progressivity of tax relief, providing a comparison of results from the NCCS and tax return data. Section 4.4 explores the determinants of the distribution of tax relief, including the various rules pertaining to tax relief for child care, how child care expenditures vary with income, and differences in family choices regarding child care. Section 4.5 discusses the results of using potential income to measure ability to pay. Section 4.6 discusses the implications of recent estimates of the demand for child care for how tax relief for child care can affect family behavior. The last section summarizes our results.

4.1 Tax Relief for Child Care

The U.S. income tax code has had special provisions for child care expenses since 1954.[3] Initially, work-related child care expenses incurred by low-income families were deductible from the tax base. In 1971, Congress expanded deductibility to cover a broader range of income groups, allowing families with an adjusted gross income (AGI) up to $27,600 to receive benefits. The Tax Reform Act of 1976 replaced the deductibility of expenses with a flat 20 percent credit for work-related child care expenses. The Economic Recovery Tax Act of 1981 (ERTA) modified the credit by introducing the current declining rate credit. ERTA also introduced DCAPs, which are employer-provided benefits that effectively give some taxpayers the choice between claiming the CCTC and deducting child care expenses from their taxable income. Subsequent tax reforms have made minor changes to the tax relief provisions, but they are substantially the same as enacted in 1981. Below, we describe current features of the tax treatment of child care expenses.

In terms of eligibility, the two tax relief programs, the CCTC and DCAPs, are similar and have several features in common: (1) Only the expenses for children under age 13 qualify. (2) Both parents, or the single parent, must work or be enrolled in school. (3) Child care expenses must be work related. (4) Eligible expenses are limited to the earned income of the parent with the least income.

The programs differ in the amount of eligible expenses, the value of the reduction in taxes, and in their administration. For the CCTC, qualified expenses are limited to $2,400 for families with one child under age 13 and

---

3. Wolfman (1984) discusses the legislative history of child care provisions in the tax code and the legal debate surrounding the tax treatment of child care.

$4,800 for families with more than one child under age 13. The amount of the credit depends on family income and child care expenses. For families with AGI below $10,000, the credit is 30 percent of qualified expenses. The rate of the credit falls by 1 percentage point for every $2,000 of AGI until AGI equals $28,000. For families with AGI above $28,000, the credit rate is 20 percent. The credit is nonrefundable so the total credit is limited to the family's tax liability.

In contrast to the CCTC, DCAPs are flexible spending accounts by which employees can reduce their pretax income and use the reduction to pay for child care expenses. Employees cannot unilaterally create DCAPs; instead, employers must offer the plans as part of a fringe benefit package. Total family contributions to DCAPs are limited to $5,000. Contributions are subject to neither income nor payroll taxes. The employee chooses a contribution level at the beginning of the year and contributions are subject to a "use it or lose it" rule: the employee loses any contributions that are not withdrawn for child care expenses during the year. Since DCAP contributions lower taxable income, the DCAP's value roughly equals the family's marginal tax rate times the DCAP contribution.

A dollar of child care expenses cannot be subsidized through both the CCTC and the DCAP. However, using a DCAP does not completely preclude using the CCTC: each dollar contributed to a DCAP lowers the maximum expense qualifying for the CCTC by a dollar. Whether a family benefits more from a DCAP or the CCTC depends on its credit rate and its marginal tax rate. Because higher income families have lower credit rates and higher marginal rates, they may find it advantageous to use the DCAP rather than the CCTC. Consequently, the distribution of tax relief for child care is likely to be even more skewed toward middle- and upper-income families than the distribution of the benefits of the CCTC alone.

4.2 Rationales for the Tax Treatment of Child Care

In discussing the appropriate tax treatment of different items under an income tax, economists often start from the Haig-Simons definition of income: income is the monetary value of increases in potential consumption net of the costs incurred to earn that income. Under this definition, one could argue that work-related child care expenses should be tax deductible. Yet, the Haig-Simons criterion is not so easily applied in this case. For example, from the standpoint of a family with children in which both parents work, child care may be considered a necessary business expense. However, from the standpoint of a family deciding whether to have children, the future costs of childrearing, including work-related child care, are arguably more a personal consumption decision than a necessary business expense. Despite the ambiguity under the Haig-Simons criterion, it is interesting to note that this argument for tax relief supports deductibility rather than a tax credit.

A broad range of other arguments can be made for and against tax provisions for child care. We divide these normative rationales into two groups: equity and efficiency (or incentive) arguments.

4.2.1 Equity and the Tax Treatment of Child Care

One goal of income taxation is to levy taxes in relation to a household's ability to pay. Yet, annual income is not necessarily a good measure of ability to pay. For example, a two-parent family with both parents in the labor force could have the same inherent ability to pay as a two-parent family with only one parent in the labor force, but its measured income would be different because of its labor supply choices. By giving the two-earner family tax relief for their child care expenses, the tax system makes a crude adjustment for this discrepancy between measured and actual ability to pay. A major flaw in this argument is that targeting child care is an imprecise way of distinguishing between one-earner and two-earner families because many two-earner families do not have child care expenses. A more precise adjustment would be a partial deduction of the earnings of the secondary earner as was the case in the United States in the early 1980s (see Feldstein and Feenberg, chap. 2 in this volume).

Another possible justification for tax relief for child care is that differences in child care expenses drive a wedge between otherwise similar families. For example, the income tax code already recognizes that ability to pay can depend on family size by allowing personal exemptions. However, a uniform personal exemption does not distinguish between families with different costs of raising children, for example, if younger children are more expensive to raise than older school-aged children. Yet, this is more of an argument for making the personal exemption related to age than for special treatment for child care expenses.[4] Another example would be that some families have access to low-cost, high-quality child care (e.g., care provided by a relative) while otherwise similar families do not have access to such care (see Krashinsky 1981). In this case, tax relief for child care adjusts tax payments to reflect differences in ability to pay driven by variation in the costs of care. Both of these arguments (distinguishing between two-earner and one-earner families and families with different child care expenses) are horizontal equity arguments for tax relief for child care.

In contrast to horizontal equity arguments, the notion of vertical equity is implicit in claims by critics of the CCTC that most of the benefits of tax relief accrue to middle- and upper-income families.[5] These critics are often most

---

4. One obvious difference between making the personal exemption related to age and tax relief for child care is that targeting child care increases the chance that part of the additional after-tax income is spent on children. This concern is analogous to the sentiment that some people are more willing to have welfare for children than for parents. Of course, since money is fungible it is unclear whether this targeting changes overall expenditure patterns.

5. See, e.g., the statement of Douglas J. Besharov before the Senate Finance Committee (U.S. Congress 1988).

concerned with the quality of child care in low-income households. Thus, they compare the distribution of benefits generated by direct expenditure programs targeted at low-income families (e.g., Head Start) with the much less targeted tax relief programs. Vertical equity considerations have obviously affected the design of tax relief programs, including the declining credit rate and the limits on qualified expenditures.

4.2.2   Efficiency and Tax Relief for Child Care

In addition to horizontal and vertical equity rationales, tax relief for child care may be justified on efficiency (or incentive) grounds. One of the often-cited goals of subsidizing child care (whether through the tax system or direct expenditure programs) is to improve the quality of care received, particularly by children in low-income families. Society may care about the quality of care received by children in low-income families for equity reasons or because quality care generates social benefits, just as we believe education generates benefits beyond the individual. If these external benefits are large, which may be especially likely for children from disadvantaged families, then subsidizing child care may increase efficiency. Tax relief for child care reduces the marginal cost of care for many working families,[6] which may encourage families to spend more per hour of care or to purchase more hours of care (if the child does not already have paid care for all of the parents' working hours). Higher-cost care is commonly presumed to be of higher quality. Also, if market-provided care is of higher quality than the alternative form of care (e.g., self-care), then increasing the number of hours of paid care (for a given number of hours of parents' labor supply) increases the quality of care received.

Another often-cited goal of subsidizing child care is to influence the labor force participation and hours-of-work decisions of parents. A common assumption is that parents' labor supply decisions depend on the net-of-tax wage after accounting for child care expenses (the effective wage rate). Tax relief that is tied to labor force participation, under certain assumptions, increases the effective wage rate of the recipient (often the mother).[7] Thus, tax relief is likely to influence the mother's labor force participation decision as well as her decision regarding how many hours to work. Changes in labor supply could affect efficiency in two ways.[8] First, as is sometimes argued in the policy de-

---

6. For families that do not have tax liabilities or exceed the qualified expense limits, tax relief does not affect the marginal cost of child care.

7. In particular, it is necessary to assume that for every hour worked, an hour of child care is needed.

8. For a more detailed efficiency argument, see Krashinsky (1981), which presents a model with household production of child care and adult consumption. In the presence of a wage tax, the deductibility of child care expenses is the largest subsidy that can be justified on efficiency grounds. The optimal child care subsidy rate relative to the marginal wage tax rate depends on the relative elasticities between goods for time in the production of child care and adult consumption. He argues that reasonable assumptions about the substitutability of time and goods for producing child care and adult consumption leads to deductibility being close to optimal.

bate, if the tax treatment of child care induces low-income parents to work, then these parents may learn work skills that lead them to self-sufficiency. Second, for higher-income families, the tax treatment of child care could mitigate some of the inefficiencies created by the current tax treatment of two-income families (see Feldstein and Feenberg, chap. 2 in this volume, for details on possible efficiency gains of alternative tax rules for families).

4.3 Distribution of Tax Relief for Child Care

As discussed above, rationales for tax relief for child care include both vertical and horizontal equity arguments. The limited previous literature has focused solely on vertical equity. In this section, we address the vertical equity of tax relief for child care by evaluating the progressivity of tax relief using new data and a somewhat different methodology. In the next section, to address some of the horizontal equity concerns, we examine the distribution of tax relief for child care across family characteristics, such as marital status and the number of children.

4.3.1 Measuring Progressivity

Tax relief for child care has been criticized as regressive because it is predominantly used by middle- and upper-income families (Robins 1990). Critics point to nonrefundability of the credit as a particularly regressive feature. Yet, other features of the CCTC, such as the credit rate declining with income, are progressive. Contrary to the claims of regressivity, using 1979–86 tax return data Dunbar and Nordhauser (1991) find that the tax system with the CCTC is more progressive than without the CCTC.

Several methodological points may help explain this controversy over the progressivity of the CCTC. First, instead of focusing on families with children, Dunbar and Nordhauser study all households. Therefore, part of the CCTC's progressivity may simply be from the transfer of income from older families to families with children. This redistribution may increase the measured annual progressivity of the tax credit because older families are likely to have higher annual incomes than families with young children, for life-cycle reasons. However, in the long run (assuming the tax credit stays in place), all families with children have an opportunity to qualify for the tax credit when their children are young. The effects of these transfers may be large since 6.5 percent of 1989 tax returns claim the CCTC (Internal Revenue Service 1991–92) compared with 29.9 percent of our sample of families with children.

Altshuler and Schwartz (1996) also examine the progressivity of the CCTC using tax return data. Unlike Dunbar and Nordhauser, they use average income over a number of years as a way of removing some transitory income shocks. Even with this alternative measure of ability to pay, they find results similar to Dunbar and Nordhauser's. Yet, this approach still fails to capture life-cycle differences in income. Altshuler and Schwartz mitigate these life-cycle issues by restricting their sample to tax returns with dependent children. The NCCS gives us better information on family characteristics for determining whether a family is eligible for tax relief.

Second, Dunbar and Nordhauser use average measures of progressivity rather than estimating progressivity at different points in the income distribution. The CCTC could, on average, be progressive while still being regressive for low income groups. To measure progressivity at different points in the income distribution, we focus on how the average effective subsidy rate varies with income.[9] The effective subsidy rate is the ratio of dollars of tax relief to household income. The average effective subsidy rate is the mean value of this ratio for the families in each income group. If the subsidy rate increases with income, then tax relief is regressive because higher income families are receiving proportionately more benefits. This measure of tax relief progressivity is the analog to average rate progression commonly used in tax analysis.

Finally, the progressivity of tax relief depends on the relationship between child care expenditures and income. If lower-income families spend a larger fraction of their incomes on child care than higher-income families, then, ceteris paribus, a subsidy to child care will be progressive. Unfortunately, the all-else-equal assumption fails to hold: labor force participation, household income, and child care expenses are endogenously determined (see Connelly 1992; Blau and Robins 1988). Therefore, income is a flawed ability-to-pay criterion for measuring progressivity.[10]

As an alternative ability-to-pay criterion, we construct a measure of household potential labor income. By eliminating differences in labor supply decisions from the ability-to-pay measure, our potential income measure assigns the same ability to pay to one-earner and two-earner families that have the same labor market opportunities. For the one-earner family, the ratio of actual income to potential income is low relative to the two-earner family. However, the two-earner family is more likely to benefit from tax relief. By treating these two families as equal, using potential income as a measure of ability to pay may reduce the perception that tax relief benefits are concentrated among relatively well off families.

4.3.2 Distribution of Benefits: NCCS Data

The NCCS includes 4,397 families with at least one child under age 13 (see Hofferth et al. 1991 for details on the NCCS). Along with demographic and labor market data, the NCCS has data on the families' child care arrangements. The survey, conducted from October 1989 to April 1990, asked whether the family planned to use the CCTC for 1989, whether either parent had access to

9. Altshuler and Schwartz examine progressivity at different points in the income distribution and find that the CCTC is progressive on average but regressive at low income levels.

10. Atkinson and Stiglitz (1980, chap. 9) discuss the logic of wanting to measure interpersonal differences in ability rather than outcomes for distributional issues.

a DCAP, and if the family used the DCAP, the family's contribution level. We exclude families with missing information on (1) whether they plan to use the credit for 1989, (2) whether they paid for child care, (3) marital status, (4) employment status, (5) household income, or (6) whether they use a DCAP (given that they have access to a DCAP). This leaves a sample of 3,526 families.

The NCCS data have a number of advantages over tax return data. First, the NCCS isolates a cohort of families with children of eligible ages for tax relief. Second, in addition to information on the CCTC, the NCCS has information on access and participation in DCAPs. Third, the NCCS includes details on family structure, labor force participation, and child care expenses. This detailed demographic, labor market, and expenditure data set allows us to separate eligible households from ineligible households. It also enables us to uncover whether certain types of families benefit more from tax relief than others, and it allows us to examine how the income elasticity of child care expenditures influences the distribution of benefits. A disadvantage of the NCCS for studying tax relief is the need to impute tax liabilities and the value of tax relief.

Table 4.1 presents the take-up rates for each type of tax relief by income level. Since some families use both programs, the table also reports the take-up rate for families using either form of tax relief. For the overall sample, 29.9 percent of families claim the CCTC but only 1.6 percent of families use DCAPs. Overall, 30.6 percent of families claim some form of tax relief. This percentage increases with income: 25.6 percent of families with incomes below $25,000 (about the bottom third of the income distribution) claim tax relief, compared with 30.0 percent of families with incomes between $25,000 and $40,000 (roughly the middle third of the income distribution), and 36.5 percent of families with incomes about $40,000. Tax relief from DCAPs goes to an affluent minority: only 1.6 percent of families use DCAPs but almost two-thirds (63.8 percent) of these families have incomes above $50,000. Since DCAPs are such a small fraction of total tax relief, the pattern of the take-up rates for the CCTC mirror the take-up rates for all tax relief.

The main reason DCAPs are such a small fraction of tax relief is that few families have access to them. In our NCCS sample, only 7.7 percent of the households (272/3,526) report having access to a DCAP.[11] Data from employer-based surveys suggest that more than 7.7 percent of families had access to DCAPs in the late 1980s; Hayes, Palmer, and Zaslow (1990, 203)

---

11. One problem with self-reported data is that some people may be unaware of whether their employers offer DCAPs. We classify these families as not having access. In part, knowledge of access to DCAPs may be correlated with overall awareness of tax relief programs. In the NCCS data, families with access to DCAPs have a higher propensity to use the CCTC than families without access. While 29.9 percent of all families take the CCTC, 60.3 percent (35/58) of families that use DCAPs also plan to use the CCTC for 1989. For families with access to DCAPs that do not contribute to the DCAP, 41.6 percent (89/214) use the CCTC.

Table 4.1   Tax Relief by Income Level for 1989

Income (thousand $)	Cumulative Percentage of Income Distribution (1)	Percentage Taking CCTC (2)	Percentage Using DCAP (3)	Percentage with Some Tax Relief (4)	Mean Tax Relief for Families with Tax Relief ($) (5)	Mean ESR for Families with Tax Relief (6)	Mean ESR for All Families (7)
Under 5	3.4	21.0	0.0	21.0	0.00	0.0	0.00
5–7.5	5.9	15.7	0.0	15.7	0.00	0.0	0.00
7.5–10	9.9	26.4	0.0	26.4	12.00	0.14	0.02
10–12.5	13.3	30.6	0.0	30.6	147.44	1.31	0.30
12.5–15	17.0	24.8	0.0	24.8	309.26	2.25	0.38
15–17.5	20.0	29.0	0.0	29.0	545.86	3.36	0.69
17.5–20	23.5	25.6	0.0	25.6	465.99	2.49	0.46
20–25	35.1	26.8	0.5	26.8	425.53	1.89	0.40
25–30	47.4	27.7	1.2	28.4	404.03	1.47	0.33
30–35	57.7	28.4	0.8	29.0	410.53	1.26	0.28
35–40	67.6	32.8	1.4	33.0	461.41	1.23	0.33
40–45	74.8	26.1	2.0	27.3	484.64	1.14	0.23
45–50	81.2	36.7	0.4	36.7	486.85	1.02	0.30
50–75	93.4	37.8	4.9	40.1	558.19	0.89	0.31
75–100	97.3	44.5	8.0	46.7	617.43	0.71	0.30
100–125	98.3	27.8	5.6	30.6	730.93	0.65	0.16
125–150	99.0	30.4	8.7	30.4	633.14	0.46	0.14
Over 150	100.0	27.8	2.8	27.8	640.44	0.37	0.09
Total		29.9	1.6	30.6	446.02	1.24	0.30

Notes: The sample includes 3,526 families. The take-up rates in cols. (2)–(4) are from responses to questions on whether the family takes the CCTC or uses a DCAP. Cols. (5) and (6) condition on whether a family claims to receive either form of tax relief and reports paying for some regular child care. ESR stands for the effective subsidy rate expressed as a percentage of income. Col. (7) is the ESR averaging over all families and assigning an ESR of zero to families that claim to use tax relief but do not report child care expenses.

report that approximately 14 percent of large and small employers offered DCAPs. More recent data indicate that access to DCAPs is growing rapidly; according to a survey by Foster Higgins, benefits consultants, 45 percent of large employers offer DCAPs (reported in Rowland 1994). Access to DCAPs is skewed toward higher-income households. Relative to families in the bottom third of the income distribution, families in the top third of the income distribution are almost four times more likely to report having access to a DCAP.[12] Furthermore, since DCAPs are less valuable than the CCTC for lower-income households, the DCAP take-up rate among families with access to DCAPs rises sharply with income: 4.8 percent (2/42) of households in the bottom third of the income distribution (and no families with income below $20,000), 16.3 percent (13/80) of the middle third, and 28.7 percent (43/150) of the top third use DCAPs.

The overall pattern of take-up rates of tax relief reflects several differences between high- and low-income families. First, at very low incomes, the take-up rate is low for working families because they have zero tax liability. Second, low-income families are less likely to work and be eligible for tax relief. However, conditional on all parents in the family working during the previous year, the differences in take-up rates persist (not shown in the table). Third, low-income working families are less likely to use paid child care and be eligible for tax relief. Conditioning on working and paying for child care, the take-up rates are similar across income groups: 50.5 percent of families in the bottom third of the income distribution claim tax relief, compared with 54.2 percent of families in the top third. Thus, differences in family choices regarding child care and labor force participation at least partially explain the distribution in benefits across families of different income levels.

While the take-up rates increase with income, progressivity depends on the relationship of dollars of tax relief to income. Since the NCCS only asks whether a family takes the CCTC and not the value of the credit, we must impute the value of tax relief. First, we calculate the family's tax liability before the CCTC. Since the CCTC is nonrefundable, this tax liability is an upper bound for the value of the tax credit. We start by assuming that a family's AGI is the midpoint of their reported income range. Next, we impute taxable income by assuming that the standard deduction is taken and basing the value of exemptions on the number of people in the household.[13] The tax liability depends on taxable income and the rate schedule.

---

12. For the bottom third of the income distribution, 3.4 percent (42/1,237) of households report having access to DCAPs, compared with 7.0 percent (80/1,147) of the families in the middle third, and 13.1 percent (150/1,142) of the families in the top third of the income distribution.

13. The assumption that all families take the standard deduction is unlikely to affect the results because the CCTC subsidy rate is based on AGI, which is calculated before taking either itemized or standard deductions. In some cases, we may understate the effect of the credit being nonrefundable since families with exceedingly high itemized deductions may not have taxable income to offset against the credit. Also, we may overstate the marginal tax rates of some families who itemize, which would overstate the value of their using a DCAP.

The value of the CCTC is the maximum of either the family's tax liability before the CCTC or the product of the family's credit rate and their qualifying annual expenses. The family's credit rate depends on AGI. We assume that all reported child care expenses are work related and qualify for the credit.[14] For families using DCAPs, the value of the DCAP is the family's marginal tax rate times their DCAP contribution. The total value of tax relief is the sum of the values of the CCTC and the DCAP after accounting for the provision that each dollar spent can receive only one form of relief.

Column (5) of table 4.1 reports the average dollar value of tax relief by income level for families claiming tax relief and reporting positive child care expenses during the last year.[15] The average value of all tax relief is $446 per recipient, while the average value of just the CCTC is $429 (not shown in the table). The dollar value of tax relief is zero or quite small for families with incomes under $10,000, reflecting nonrefundability of the CCTC.[16] The value of tax relief rises quickly over the first few income groups and then flattens out over a broad range of incomes. The decline in the value of the credit between $17,500 and $30,000 may be partly explained by the credit rate declining with income. In addition, part of the increase in the value of tax relief at the top of the income distribution most likely reflects the increasing propensity to use DCAPs, which are more valuable than the CCTC. We return to explanations for the observed distribution of benefits in the next section.

Column (6) presents the mean effective subsidy rate (ESR) conditional on claiming tax relief. Overall, tax relief for child care is 1.24 percent of the income of those taking the credit. For the bottom quintile of the income distribution, the subsidy rate increases with income suggesting that tax relief is indeed regressive. The ESR reaches a maximum of 3.4 percent of income for the $15,000–$17,500 income group. Above this income level, the mean ESR steadily falls with income, suggesting that over most of the income distribution tax relief is progressive.

While the ESR declines with income for families with tax relief (col. [6]), the propensity to receive tax relief increases with income (col. [4]). The prod-

---

14. The NCCS allowed respondents to report child care expenditures over different intervals (e.g., weekly, monthly, or annually). Therefore, we calculate annual expenditures by multiplying weekly expenditures by 44 and monthly expenditures by 12. The choice of 44 weeks per year is somewhat arbitrary but reflects the fact that most families do not purchase work-related child care every week because of holidays and vacations. The choice of 12 months per year is also somewhat arbitrary. Nevertheless, it reflects our belief that expenditures reported on a monthly basis more accurately reflect days missed than expenditures reported on a weekly basis. As noted below, these assumptions lead to imputed tax credits that are similar to those found in tax return data.

15. The numerator of the take-up rates includes all families claiming to use tax relief. However, some of these families reported having no paid child care during the previous year. We exclude these families from the calculations in cols. (5), (6), and (7) because we cannot impute the value of tax relief.

16. A puzzle in the data is why so many families with low incomes report receiving tax relief when their incomes suggest that the CCTC has no value to them. One possible explanation is that the respondents confused the CCTC with the refundable earned income tax credit.

uct of these two columns (col. [7]) is the unconditional ESR and may be interpreted as the mean ESR for all families.[17] As with column (6), the unconditional ESR increases through the bottom quintile of the income distribution and falls through the rest of the income distribution. Unlike the numbers in column (6), the unconditional ESR is roughly constant between incomes of $25,000 and $100,000, which suggests that tax relief is proportional to income through much of the income distribution. Therefore, even without conditioning on receiving tax relief, the tax programs are at least proportional over most of the income distribution of families with children.

4.3.3 Distribution of Benefits: Tax Return Data

In using the NCCS data to measure the distribution of tax relief, we must impute the value of tax relief using self-reported information on income and expenditures. This imputation may differ from the actual tax situation of the household because either income or child care expenses reported on tax returns differ from the survey responses. Since the quality of our data may affect our conclusions, we construct similar statistics to those presented in table 4.1 from tax return data for 1989. The tax return data are from the public-use sample prepared by the Statistics of Income (SOI) Division of the Internal Revenue Service (IRS). In order to be as comparable to the NCCS data as possible, we use a sample of 39,459 tax returns of families with dependent children living at home. As discussed above, tax return data has the advantage of precisely measuring the value of the CCTC but has several disadvantages, such as not being able to isolate a cohort of families with children of eligible age for tax relief or measure tax relief from DCAPs. Therefore, our analysis of tax return data focuses entirely on the CCTC.

Before comparing the distribution of the CCTC in the two data sets, it is instructive to compare the NCCS responses with the aggregate number of families taking the credit reported by the IRS. Using the entire NCCS sample and sample weights that correct for potential nonresponses, the NCCS data imply that 6.01 million families took the credit in 1988 and 7.09 million families planned to take the credit in 1989.[18] In contrast, the SOI tax return samples indicate that 8.82 million families took the credit in 1988 but only 5.92 million

---

17. The numbers in col. (7) are not exactly equal to the product of cols. (4) and (6) since col. (6) is conditional on the family reporting paid child care expenses. In col. (7), we treat families that claim to receive tax relief but report no paid child care expenses as having an ESR of zero. This assumption may lead to col. (7) understating the mean ESR for all families.

18. We can offer two explanations for the 18 percent increase in claimants between 1988 and 1989 in the NCCS. First, families whose only child was under age 1 at the time of the survey could not have qualified for the CCTC in 1988. This accounts for 430,000 claimants in 1989 but is offset by claimants eligible in 1988 but not surveyed by the NCCS (e.g., families with a youngest child who was 13 years old in 1988). This offset is probably small because families with youngest children aged 13 rarely take the credit. Second, we expect that some respondents who did not know about the CCTC at the time of the survey said that they did not take it in the past but would take it in the future; that is, the NCCS raised these families' awareness of the CCTC.

families did in 1989. The dramatic 33 percent decline in CCTC filers in the tax return data is most likely a response to changes in the tax rules that took effect in 1989 (e.g., claimants were required to report the social security number of the child care provider).[19] In contrast, tax credit benefits grew steadily at an average 19 percent nominal growth rate between 1980 and 1988, and the number of claimants grew by about 10 percent per year according to data from the IRS *Statistics of Income*. Also there is no evidence of any significant change in actual child care arrangements at this time. The proportion of children cared for either by a parent or by a relative stayed about the same between 1985 and 1990 (Hofferth et al. 1991, 101). Thus, the decline in CCTC filers likely reflects reduced tax evasion. That the NCCS coincides with these legislated changes complicates comparisons of the two data sets. Nevertheless, averaging across the two years, the two data sets produce similar numbers of total claimants.

Table 4.2 reports statistics on the distribution of the CCTC from the tax return data.[20] For the sake of comparison, table 4.2 reports the same income ranges as in table 4.1; however, here we use each family's reported AGI as their household income rather than the midpoint of their income range as was necessary in table 4.1. In addition, since the tax return data do not precisely identify children's ages, the take-up rates in table 4.2 use all tax returns with dependent children living at home as the denominator.

Despite the differences in the definition of the take-up rate, the take-up rates in the two samples have a similar pattern. It generally increases with income but declines slightly for households with incomes over $100,000. In addition, the average value of the CCTC is quite similar in the two data sets, though the value of the credit is slightly lower in the tax return data than in the NCCS data ($404 vs. $429 per recipient). As with the NCCS data, the tax return data indicate that the dollar value of tax relief is zero or quite small for low-income families and that the benefits rise quickly before flattening out over a broad range of incomes. As a percentage of income, the CCTC rises through incomes of $15,000 and falls fairly steadily for the rest of the income distribution. While the mean ESR peaks at a lower income in the tax return data, this income level represents a larger fraction of the population than it does in the NCCS data. Thus, the general conclusion that tax relief is regressive at low income levels and progressive for most of the income distribution holds using tax return data, as well as with the NCCS data.

Despite these similarities, there are some notable differences between the two data sets. Unlike the NCCS data, the tax return data do not show a positive

19. The NCCS may not reflect this decline because at the time of the survey the respondents had not yet filed their 1989 tax returns, which would require the information reporting. Also, in responding to the NCCS, families that fraudulently claimed the CCTC might not say that they claimed it on their tax returns.

20. Since the sample oversamples high-income tax returns, we use sampling weights to create statistics that are representative of the overall population.

Table 4.2   CCTC by Income Level for 1989, Tax Return Data

Income (thousand $)	Cumulative Percentage of Income Distribution (returns with dependents) (1)	Percentage Taking CCTC (returns with dependents) (2)	Mean CCTC for Families Taking CCTC ($) (3)	Mean ESR for Families Taking CCTC (4)	Percentage for Which Refundability Binds (5)	Percentage for Which Expense Limit Binds (6)	Percentage for Which Earnings Limit Binds (7)
Under 5	5.8	0.00	0.00	0.0	–	–	–
5–7.5	9.9	0.00	0.00	0.0	–	–	–
7.5–10	14.4	2.80	129.49	1.37	66.5	13.9	3.16
10–12.5	19.6	10.09	289.33	2.54	61.2	25.4	3.38
12.5–15	24.7	12.25	412.11	3.02	35.2	27.4	1.41
15–17.5	29.4	16.15	401.97	2.48	15.3	16.6	2.23
17.5–20	33.8	18.56	465.80	2.50	12.4	20.1	4.95
20–25	42.4	20.27	436.04	1.96	3.8	23.2	3.25
25–30	50.1	18.67	388.64	1.41	0.53	22.1	1.56
30–35	57.8	20.64	356.12	1.10	0.41	15.2	2.15
35–40	65.0	18.58	416.64	1.12	0.0	25.3	1.26
40–45	71.6	19.31	374.07	0.88	0.36	17.2	2.59
45–50	76.9	18.58	379.25	0.80	0.0	21.1	1.18
50–75	91.6	21.60	421.90	0.71	0.0	23.5	1.16
75–100	95.9	19.90	445.19	0.53	0.0	27.5	2.13
100–125	97.4	12.56	491.50	0.44	0.0	36.1	2.54
125–150	98.2	12.88	475.98	0.35	0.0	34.7	2.04
Over 150	100.0	9.74	484.19	0.23	0.0	38.6	5.27
Total		15.72	404.06	1.32	5.9	22.2	2.13

Notes: The sample includes 39,459 tax returns from the public-use sample prepared by the SOI Division of the IRS with dependent children living at home. Income ranges refer to AGI. The take-up rates in col. (2) use all tax returns as the denominator. Cols. (3) and (4) condition on whether a family receives a CCTC.

take-up rate at low income levels. This suggests that either the low-income families who claim to receive tax relief in the NCCS answered the tax relief question incorrectly or their AGI exceeds what they reported in the NCCS. At high income levels, the imputations using the NCCS overstate the value of tax relief relative to the tax return data.[21] Also, in the various income ranges, the mean dollars received can vary substantially between the two data sets. These differences are most noticeable at the tails of the income distribution, where some of the sample sizes are quite small.[22]

4.4   Determinants of the Distribution of Tax Relief

Several factors combine to generate the pattern of benefits from tax relief described above. These factors include the various rules pertaining to tax relief for child care, how child care expenditures vary with income, and differences in family choices regarding child care. In this section, we explore each of these determinants of the distribution of benefits from tax relief for child care.

4.4.1   Program Features

In addition to the declining credit rate, these features of tax relief affect the distribution of benefits: (1) nonrefundability, (2) limits on the maximum qualified expense, and (3) the earnings test that limits qualified expenses to the earnings of the parent with the lowest earnings. We examine the first and second of these features with both the NCCS and tax return data; for the earnings test, we use only the tax return data because the earnings data in the NCCS is subject to relatively large measurement error.

Nonrefundability restricts the CCTC's benefits to low-income families with positive tax liabilities. As a consequence, it is difficult to measure how nonrefundability affects the take-up rate. Changing the tax rules may induce several types of behavioral responses, such as more parents working, more children being cared for by paid child care providers, and more families filing tax returns. These behavioral responses may be especially important for families that do not have a positive tax liability. We do not impute any behavioral changes. Instead, we calculate the fraction of families that have a positive tax liability before the CCTC but do not owe taxes after the credit. For these families,

---

21. A small portion of this difference is from including DCAPs in our measure of tax relief in table 4.2. Since the number of families using both a DCAP and the CCTC is small, the NCCS imputations for just the CCTC are typically similar to the imputations for all tax relief. However, for the $125,000–$150,000 income range, the NCCS data suggest a mean value of all tax relief of $633 for families taking tax relief but a mean value of the CCTC of $256 for families taking the CCTC. This difference highlights the importance of examining both programs simultaneously.

22. To test whether these differences are statistically significant, we compare the sample of CCTC observations in the two samples with a Mann-Whitney rank sum test for each income range. The null hypothesis of this nonparametric test is that the two samples are drawn from the same distribution. We reject this null hypothesis at the 95 percent confidence level in 8 of the 18 income ranges: $7,500–$10,000, $15,000–$17,500, and all of the ranges between $30,000–$100,000. In these higher-income groups, our imputations from the NCCS overstate the value of the credit, which would tend to bias the results toward finding the credit to be regressive.

nonrefundability binds at the margin. Using the NCCS data, we estimate that half of the families with incomes below $17,500 with positive tax liabilities before the CCTC paid no taxes after the CCTC. Thus, nonrefundability promotes regressivity at low incomes. The tax return data, in column (5) of table 4.2, suggest that nonrefundability binds less frequently: 29.5 percent of families with incomes below $17,500 who take the CCTC have a credit that is at least as large as their tax liability before the credit.[23]

Qualified expense limits place an upper limit on the amount of tax relief a family can receive.[24] Since higher-income families typically spend more on child care, one would expect these limits to have a greater impact on higher-income families. Using the NCCS data, we estimate that the expense limits bind for 29.1 percent of all families. The fraction of families for whom the limits bind increases substantially with income: for families in the bottom third of the income distribution, we estimate that the limits bind for 20.2 percent of families, compared to 35.9 percent of families in the top third of the income distribution. By limiting the benefits of the relatively well-off, these expense limits increase the progressivity of tax relief. As reported in column (6) of table 4.2, the tax return data confirm this result. Overall, the limit binds for 22.2 percent of all families, but it binds for 36.7 percent of families with AGI above $100,000.

The earnings test could affect the distribution of benefits if secondary earners in certain income ranges tend to have lower earnings than secondary earners in other income ranges. Column (7) of table 4.2 does not suggest a systematic link between the earnings test binding and the level of income. Overall, the earnings test binds for 2.1 percent of families who take the CCTC. This limit binds most frequently for the bottom third of the income distribution and for the highest income groups.

4.4.2 Income Elasticity

The distribution of tax relief benefits for child care also depends on the income elasticity of expenditures. Subsidizing a good at a constant rate can be either progressive or regressive depending on whether the good is income inelastic or elastic. As a simple measure of the income elasticity of child care purchases, we calculate how the median expenditure share varies with income. The median expenditure share for families with child care expenses falls from 9.1 percent in the lowest third of the income distribution to 2.8 percent for the top third. While child care expenditures rise with income, this falling expendi-

---

23. However, the $17,500 income cutoff represents 30 percent of the population in the tax return data, compared to only 20 percent of the NCCS sample.

24. For families with only one child under age 13, the DCAP limit of $5,000 is considerably greater than the CCTC limit of $2,400. Of the 38 families that report their annual DCAP contributions, 21 have only one eligible child. Of these one-child families, two report contributions of $2,400 and eight report contributions greater than $2,400. Thus, for these families, the ability to use the DCAP for more expenses than the CCTC is an important difference between the two programs.

ture share suggests that child care expenses are income inelastic. Thus, it is not surprising that in the portion of the income distribution that faces a constant subsidy rate, we find that tax relief for child care is progressive.

4.4.3   Family Characteristics

While the tax code specifies the maximum value of tax relief, the actual tax benefit a family receives depends on certain family characteristics, such as the number of children, and on the family's labor supply and child care choices. Many of these decisions are endogenous to government policies toward child care. We do not attempt to examine specific behavioral responses with respect to tax policy. Instead, in an effort to address horizontal equity concerns, our goal is simply to uncover whether certain types of families benefit more from tax relief than others. Therefore, in this section, we examine the distribution of tax relief for child care across family characteristics.

A parent's marital status is likely to have a strong influence on the household's labor supply and child care decisions. As a consequence, the benefits of tax relief for child care are likely to vary according to marital status. Table 4.3 presents the NCCS information from table 4.1 for single- and two-parent (married) families. Several differences emerge: First, the income distributions of the two types of households are dramatically different. Over half of single-parent families have incomes below $17,500, while over half of married households have incomes over $35,000. Second, 38.4 percent of single parents report receiving tax relief, a substantially higher percentage than the 28.3 percent of married households that report receiving tax relief. This greater propensity to claim tax relief probably means that more single-parent households meet the work requirements than married couples. Third, the mean value of tax relief for married families receiving relief exceeds that of single-parent families receiving relief ($467 vs. $392). However, conditional on income, single-parent families typically receive more tax relief than two-parent families. This difference is most prominent at low incomes, where differences in the value of exemptions for single heads of households and married families mean that single-parent families have higher tax liabilities for any given level of AGI. Also, married couples may rely less on market-provided child care than single parents because couples can share child care responsibilities. Finally, the mean ESR for single parents is 1.7 percent of income, much larger than the mean ESR for married couples of 1.1 percent of income. The differences in take-up rates and ESRs suggest that tax relief for child care redistributes income from married households to single-parent households within the cohort of families with children.[25]

As a way of characterizing the relationships between family characteristics and tax relief for child care, we regress whether a family claims tax relief and

---

25. In terms of progressivity or regressivity within each sample, the two samples display the same peaked-shape pattern of ESRs as in the combined sample.

Table 4.3 Tax Relief by Income Level for 1989, by Marital Status

	Single				Married			
Income (thousand $)	Cumulative Percentage of Income Distribution (1)	Percentage with Some Tax Relief (2)	Mean Tax Relief for Families with Tax Relief ($) (3)	Mean ESR for Families with Tax Relief (4)	Cumulative Percentage of Income Distribution (5)	Percentage with Some Tax Relief (6)	Mean Tax Relief for Families with Tax Relief ($) (7)	Mean ESR for Families with Tax Relief (8)
Under 5	11.7	21.7	0.00	0.0	1.0	18.5	0.0	0.0
5–7.5	20.1	13.6	0.00	0.0	1.8	21.7	0.0	0.0
7.5–10	31.4	28.1	15.79	0.18	3.7	23.5	0.0	0.0
10–12.5	39.3	38.7	241.08	2.14	5.8	22.0	2.73	0.02
12.5–15	46.3	34.6	423.08	3.08	8.5	17.6	65.47	0.48
15–17.5	51.3	57.5	601.23	3.70	11.0	11.9	296.73	1.83
17.5–20	57.1	44.4	478.45	2.55	13.9	15.0	437.50	2.33
20–25	71.6	46.5	471.84	2.10	24.6	19.1	374.70	1.67
25–30	79.8	47.7	465.38	1.69	38.1	25.0	378.24	1.38
30–35	86.3	41.2	436.88	1.34	49.6	27.0	404.14	1.24
35–40	91.4	50.0	484.11	1.29	60.8	30.8	456.99	1.22
40–45	94.3	52.2	440.63	1.04	69.2	24.8	493.03	1.16
45–50	95.9	53.9	425.87	0.90	77.0	35.7	493.05	1.04
50–75	98.2	61.1	609.52	0.98	92.1	39.2	554.47	0.89
75–100	99.3	62.5	606.40	0.69	96.8	45.7	618.25	0.71
100–125	99.5	0.0	—	—	98.0	32.4	730.93	0.65
125–150	99.6	100.0	0.0	0.0	98.8	27.3	738.67	0.54
Over 150	100.0	33.3	480.00	0.27	100.0	27.3	660.50	0.38
Total		38.4	391.94	1.70		28.3	467.19	1.07

Notes: The sample includes 3,526 families of which 787 are single-parent families and 2,739 are two-parent families. The columns correspond to the columns in table 4.1.

the value of this tax relief (conditional on receiving tax relief) on various family characteristics. We include information on the age of the youngest child in the family, the number of children in each of four age groups (0–2 years old, 3–5 years old, 6–12 years old, and 13–18 years old), the mother's age and number of years of schooling (for families with missing information on the mother, we use the father's age and years of schooling), marital status, whether a relative is available who could assist with child care, the primary child care arrangement of the youngest child in the family, and the logarithm of the midpoint of the family's reported income range.[26]

Column (1) of table 4.4 presents results from a probit regression of whether a family claims to receive tax relief. The results indicate that a family whose youngest child is older is less likely to receive tax relief. Thus, at a point in time, tax relief is associated with families with younger children. Families with more children tend to be less likely to receive tax relief (though this relationship is not statistically significant for children ages 3–5). Conditional on income, more-educated mothers are more likely to receive tax relief, although this finding may reflect differences in labor force participation based on education levels.[27] Consistent with the results in table 4.3, single-parent families are more likely to receive tax relief than two-parent families. Relative to families who report parental care as the primary arrangement of the youngest child (the omitted category), families who use child care centers or family day care homes are the most likely to receive tax relief.[28]

Column (2) of table 4.4 reports the results from regressing the value of tax relief on family characteristics for families that claim tax relief. The dependent variable is the logarithm of the imputed value of tax relief for the family. The results indicate that families with more younger children receive more tax relief. For example, adding a four-year-old to a family that already receives tax relief will increase their tax relief by 26.2 percent. Again consistent with the results in table 4.3, two-parent families claiming tax relief receive lower benefits than single-parent families claiming tax relief. In addition, families using either child care centers or family day care homes as the primary arrangement for their youngest child receive the largest benefits.[29] The model excludes a

26. Since the income variable is reported as a range, we include separate variables for each income group that are equal to the logarithm of the midpoint of the range for people reporting income in that range and zero for families reporting income outside of the range.

27. The interpretation of this coefficient is complicated by the fact that the family's income depends on each parent's labor force participation decision and education level.

28. Since the primary arrangement variable applies only to each family's youngest child but tax relief may result from expenditures on older children, we tried two types of sensitivity analysis. First, we excluded the primary arrangement variables. Second, we used a sample of families with only one child, which required excluding the variables on the number of children in different age categories. For both of these alternative specifications, the remaining coefficients have a similar pattern to the reported results.

29. As with the probit, we estimated two alternative specifications: (1) excluding the primary arrangement variables and (2) using families with only one child but excluding the age category variables. Again, these alternative specifications yield similar results to those reported in table 4.2.

Table 4.4   **Regression Analysis of Take-up Rates and Value of Tax Relief**

Independent Variable	Take-up Rate Probits (1)	Value of Tax Relief, If Relief > 0 (2)
Youngest child's age	−0.076* (0.015)	−0.021 (0.021)
No. children age 0–2	−0.302* (0.078)	0.179 (0.101)
No. children age 3–5	−0.058 (0.053)	0.262* (0.066)
No. children age 6–12	−0.097* (0.035)	0.012 (0.048)
No. children age 13–18	−0.133* (0.042)	−0.294* (0.066)
Parent's age	0.0001 (0.005)	0.005 (0.007)
Parent's education	0.044* (0.013)	0.032 (0.017)
Married (yes = 1)	−0.405* (0.071)	−0.225* (0.084)
Relative present (yes = 1)	−0.060 (0.055)	0.021 (0.068)
Main arrangement		
Center	1.238* (0.072)	0.811* (0.096)
Relative	0.389* (0.076)	0.463* (0.123)
Sitter	0.540* (0.146)	0.433* (0.182)
Family day	1.222* (0.085)	0.867* (0.106)
Self-care	0.305 (0.226)	−0.560 (0.436)
Other	0.158 (0.099)	0.254 (0.167)
Income 1	−0.003 (0.038)	
Income 2	−0.035 (0.035)	
Income 3	0.008 (0.031)	0.235* (0.043)
Income 4	0.030 (0.031)	0.375* (0.038)
Income 5	0.016 (0.030)	0.454* (0.039)
Income 6	0.042 (0.030)	0.503* (0.038)
Income 7	0.017 (0.029)	0.464* (0.037)
Income 8	0.030 (0.026)	0.468* (0.033)
Income 9	0.043 (0.025)	0.455* (0.033)
Income 10	0.032 (0.025)	0.438* (0.034)
Income 11	0.049* (0.025)	0.464* (0.033)
Income 12	0.036 (0.025)	0.444* (0.034)
Income 13	0.056* (0.025)	0.451* (0.033)
Income 14	0.054* (0.023)	0.444* (0.033)
Income 15	0.064* (0.024)	0.447* (0.033)
Income 16	0.039 (0.030)	0.457* (0.040)
Income 17	0.019 (0.032)	0.454* (0.041)
Income 18		0.426* (0.037)
Intercept	1.027 (0.368)	
Adjusted R^2		0.98

Notes: The sample size is 3,438 for the take-up probit and 764 for the value of tax relief regression. Parental care is the omitted category for primary arrangement. Numbers in parentheses are standard errors.

*Statistically significant at the 95 percent confidence level.

constant but has a full set of income variables because no families in the first two income groups receive tax relief. Conditional on other family characteristics, the income coefficients for the different income variables are typically around 0.44 and do not vary much by income. These coefficients suggest that the elasticity of tax benefits with respect to income is around 0.44, which is substantially less than 1. Again, this finding is consistent with the benefits of tax relief being progressively distributed on average.

4.5 Potential Income as a Measure of Ability to Pay

The results in section 4.4 indicate that the tax relief received by a family depends on its labor market and child care choices. In this section, we reexamine the vertical equity of tax relief using potential income (a measure of labor market opportunities) as a measure of ability to pay. We calculate potential labor income by arbitrarily multiplying each parent's hourly wage rate by 2,600 hours per year (50 hours per week for 52 weeks).[30] For parents without wage data (either because wage information is missing or a parent does not work in the market), we impute a market wage by estimating a wage equation using individual characteristics.[31] We do not include capital income in our measure of potential income for two reasons. First, to some degree differences in capital income arise from differences in households' preferences for the timing of consumption. Since we want to focus on differences in abilities rather than preferences, the concept of potential income should exclude capital income. Second, the NCCS data on capital income is sketchy, so any attempt to include capital income would be imprecise.

We focus on married families to stress the differences between single-earner and two-earner families (or families with one full-time worker and one part-time worker). Using potential income has two effects on the distributional analysis. First, the ranking of households by potential income differs from the ranking by reported income. Second, for the ESRs, it changes the denominator. Since the choice of the maximum number of hours in a year is arbitrary, the scaling of potential income is arbitrary. Therefore, we focus on quartiles of the income distribution rather than absolute income levels.[32]

Figure 4.1 compares the take-up rates for married families using actual (reported) and potential income as the ability-to-pay criterion. The take-up rates

---

30. Since we give each worker the same number of hours, the choice of 2,600 hours per year only introduces an issue of the scale of potential income.

31. In estimating wage equations for mothers, we include data on age, work experience, education, race, county of residence, and squared-values of age, work experience, and education. We correct for biases created by labor force participation by using the two-stage technique outlined by Killingsworth (1983, 148–153). We estimate similar wage equations for fathers, except we do not have data on experience. In cases where the actual wage is missing and the predicted wage is negative, we assign the parent a predicted wage of zero.

32. We approximate the quartiles of reported income for married households as $0–$25,000 (24.6 percent), $25,000–$35,000 (25.0 percent), $35,000–$50,000 (27.4 percent), and above $50,000 (23.0 percent).

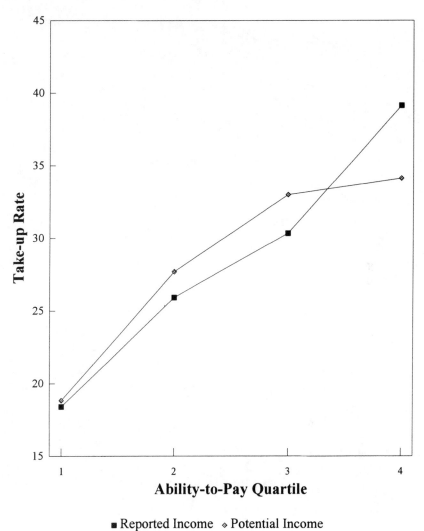

Fig. 4.1   **Take-up rates by ability-to-pay criteria**

for actual income correspond to those in column (6) of table 4.3. For both measures of ability to pay, the take-up rate increases monotonically with ability to pay. However, the difference in take-up rates between the top and bottom quartiles is smaller when ability to pay is measured by potential income rather than reported income. This difference suggests that part of the pattern of take-up rates in the reported income distribution may come from child care expenses being a cost of having two incomes, which is positively correlated with having a higher reported income.

Figure 4.2 compares the conditional ESR using the different ability-to-pay

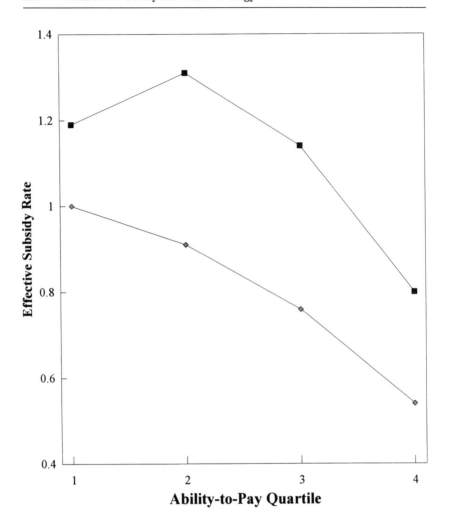

Fig. 4.2   ESRs by ability-to-pay criteria

measures. Since potential income is about two-thirds larger than reported income, the average ESR is about 30 percent lower. When households are ranked
by reported income and the subsidy rate is defined using the midpoint of the
reported income range, tax relief is regressive at low income levels (the ESR
rises with income) but is progressive above the lowest income quartile. Using
potential income to measure ability to pay leads to a different conclusion: the
ESR falls throughout the distribution of potential income. Furthermore, the
percentage difference in the ESR between the top and bottom quartiles is

higher when potential income is the measure of ability to pay. Both of these differences imply that tax relief is more progressive among married families that receive some relief when the measure of ability to pay is potential, rather than reported, income.[33] We interpret this difference as indicating that labor supply decisions are an integral part of how tax relief for child care is distributed.

4.6 Behavioral Effects of Tax Relief for Child Care

By reducing the after-tax price of child care, tax relief for child care can affect the labor market and child care decisions of households. These behavioral effects may be the unintended consequences of tax policy or they may serve certain government policy objectives. As discussed earlier, one of the government's goals in providing tax relief for child care might be to encourage work effort by low-income households. Alternatively, one of the government's goals might be to encourage the purchase of higher-priced, presumably higher-quality, care. Tax relief that is tied to labor force participation and the use of market care (as are the CCTC and the DCAP) has the potential to achieve both these goals.

Tax relief reduces the marginal cost of care and, thus, raises the net of child care wage. For example, of those households paying for care, families with an employed mother spend on average $1.56 per hour of care (Hofferth et al. 1991, 133).[34] Nearly 64 percent of employed mothers pay less than $1.50 per hour, whereas only 2 percent pay $5.00 or more per hour (Hofferth et al. 1991, 133). On the other hand, employed mothers of preschool-age children earn a median wage of $8.17 per hour, while 25 percent of employed mothers earn less than $5.50 per hour, and 75 percent earn less than $12.50 per hour.[35] Thus, for a mother earning the median wage, paying the average hourly child care cost and facing a marginal tax rate on labor income of 25 percent from the combined state and federal income and payroll taxes, a 30 percent tax credit raises the after-tax net of child care wage approximately 10 percent.[36] The question for tax policy is whether the tax relief programs are likely to induce significant changes in family labor market and child care decisions. To the extent that tax relief induces significant changes in household behavior, these

---

33. Examining the unconditional ESRs (the product of the take-up rates and the conditional mean ESRs) confirms the result that tax relief is more progressive when ability to pay is measured by potential income. For reported income, the distribution of the unconditional ESR is 0.22 (bottom quartile), 0.34, 0.35, and 0.31. For potential income, this pattern is 0.19, 0.25, 0.25, and 0.18. However, even with potential income as the measure of ability to pay, the unconditional mean of the ESRs suggests some regressivity at low ability-to-pay levels.

34. This figure represents expenditures for the primary arrangement of the youngest child under age 5.

35. These figures are based on the authors' calculations using the full sample from the NCCS.

36. This percentage increase in the wage is calculated as $(0.30)(\$1.56)/[(1 - 0.25)(\$8.17) - \$1.56]$.

behavioral responses will have implications for the distributional effects of any changes in the tax treatment of child care.

The literature on the behavioral effects of child care subsidies has been fairly limited until recently. The pioneering study in this field is by Heckman (1974). Heckman's research, which relies on an indirect measure of child care costs, provides the first evidence of a potentially large effect of child care costs on mothers' labor force participation. However, it was not until a study by Blau and Robins (1988) that direct evidence was found that child care costs have a significant effect on married women's labor supply as well as the demand for market care. Using data from the 1980 baseline household survey of the Employment Opportunity Pilot Projects (EOPP), Blau and Robins estimate a model of family labor supply incorporating both market and nonmarket care. They estimate the price elasticity of employment to be −0.38 and the price elasticity of market care to be −0.34.

Using data from the 1984 Panel of the Survey of Income and Program Participation (SIPP), more recent studies by Connelly (1992), Ribar (1992), and Michalopoulos, Robins, and Garfinkel (1992) confirm the results of Blau and Robins. The results of all of these studies are summarized in table 4.5. Connelly examines the effect of child care costs on married women's labor force participation and finds the participation rate to be sensitive to the average cost of child care. In particular, she estimates the price elasticity of employment to be −0.20. Connelly does not examine the decision to purchase market care.

Ribar analyzes the demand for market and nonmarket care as well as the decision of married women to enter the labor market. He too finds that hourly child care costs have a negative effect on the labor force participation rate of married women and on their decision to purchase market care. However, Ribar estimates elasticities considerably larger than those in previous studies. In particular, he estimates the price elasticity of employment to be −0.74 and the price elasticity of market care to be −1.86. Ribar suggests that the smaller elasticities found in the previous studies are the result of using expenditures per week or per hour of work rather than expenditures per hour of care per child. Thus, he asserts the previous studies captured combinations of cost and utilization effects.

Finally, Michalopoulos et al. estimate a structural model in which the decision to purchase market care is made simultaneously with the mother's decision to participate in the labor force.[37] Michalopoulos et al. find price effects on women's labor supply considerably smaller and price effects on child care expenditures greater than the effects estimated by other researchers. However, it should be noted that, in contrast to the other studies reported here, Michalopoulos et al. calculate elasticities for mothers who already work and purchase care rather than for the full sample of women. Michalopoulos et al. estimate

---

37. Ribar (1992) employed a partially structural approach in which a reduced-form labor supply equation and structural child care demand equations are estimated.

Table 4.5   **Behavioral Effects of Tax Relief for Child Care**

Study	Data	Estimated Elasticity of Employment	Estimated Elasticity of Market Care
Blau and Robins (1988)	1980 Baseline household survey of the EOPP	−0.38	−0.34
Connelly (1992)	1984 Panel of the SIPP	−0.20	–
Ribar (1992)	1984 Panel of the SIPP	−0.74	−1.86
Michalopoulos et al. (1992)[a]	1984 Panel of the SIPP	0.0018[b]	0.2049[c]

[a] In contrast to the other studies, the Michalopoulos et al. results are for mothers who already work and purchase child care.
[b] Estimated elasticity of hours worked with respect to child care subsidy rate.
[c] Estimated elasticity of child care expenditures with respect to child care subsidy rate.

the elasticity of hours worked with respect to the child care subsidy rate to be 0.0018 and the elasticity of child care expenditures to be 0.20.

Since Michalopoulos et al. employ a structural model to estimate the employment decision of the mother and the decision to purchase market care, they are able to estimate directly the effect of a change in child care subsidies on child care expenditures and mothers' labor supply. In particular, the structural estimates are used to simulate the effects of proposed changes to the child care tax credit. Since nonrefundability has been criticized as a particularly regressive feature of the CCTC, Michalopoulos et al. simulate the effects of making the CCTC refundable. In addition, they simulate the effects of making the declining subsidy rate (a progressive feature of the CCTC) more progressive.[38] They find the behavioral response to the refundable credit to be small, while the effects of the more progressive credit are more pronounced. In addition, most of the behavioral response is an increase in child care expenditures rather than an increase in labor supply. For example, among married mothers there is a 21.1 percent increase in hours worked and a 508 percent increase in child care expenditures.[39]

Henderson (1989) points out that if the labor market effects are large enough, tax relief for child care could pay for itself through the higher labor income taxes collected on the additional labor supply. This argument depends on the size of the labor market response, the magnitude of the subsidy, and the marginal tax rates on labor income. Using labor supply estimates from Blau and Robins (1988), Henderson calculates that by eliminating the CCTC, the government's revenue gain would be less than half the static estimate of the tax expenditure because families would reduce their labor supply and pay less in income and payroll taxes.

4.7   Conclusion

The tax treatment of child care expenditures is a complex area of tax policy. The debate over how to design these policies addresses issues of horizontal and vertical equity as well as questions of efficiency. We examine the distributional effects of the tax treatment for child care within this framework.

By evaluating the progressivity of tax relief, we address concerns regarding the vertical equity of tax relief. Using reported income as the measure of ability to pay, our results support both the critics of child care tax relief and previous research that finds the child care tax credit to be progressive: among a sample of families with children, tax relief is regressive through the lowest quintile of

---

38. In particular, Robins has proposed a refundable credit with a credit rate of 80 percent for families with incomes below $10,000. He has proposed gradually reducing the rate to 20 percent for families with incomes of $40,000 and phasing it out entirely for families with incomes exceeding $60,000.

39. The behavioral response is even more pronounced for single mothers.

the income distribution but progressive throughout the remainder of the income distribution. The regressivity at low income levels is primarily driven by nonrefundability of the credit, while the progressivity is driven by a combination of program features, including the declining credit rate and limits on qualified expenses, and the income inelasticity of child care expenses. When potential income is used as the measure of ability to pay, the benefits of tax relief appear progressive throughout the income distribution. This difference in conclusions from using the different ability-to-pay standards emphasizes the importance of defining which families are similar for interpreting equity issues.

To address some of the concerns regarding the horizontal equity of tax relief, we examine the distribution of benefits across family characteristics. We find single-parent families are more likely to receive tax relief and, conditional on income, receive larger amounts of tax relief. In addition, among families with at least one child under age 13, the probability of using the CCTC or a dependent care assistance plan decreases with the number of children. However, conditional on receiving tax relief, the value of tax relief increases with the number of children under age 13, and this increase depends on the age of the child. As one might expect, families with preschool-age children receive larger benefits than families with school-age children. Finally, larger tax relief benefits accrue to families who use child care centers or family day care homes as the primary arrangement for their youngest child than to families who use other modes of care.

Clearly, differences in family labor market and child care decisions are important in determining the distribution of benefits from the current tax policy. Econometric studies of women's labor supply and child care decisions suggest that tax policy can have substantial behavioral effects. These behavioral responses will have implications for the distributional effects of any changes in the tax treatment of child care.

References

Altshuler, Rosanne, and Amy Ellen Schwartz. 1996. On the progressivity of the child care tax credit: Snapshot versus time-exposure incidence. *National Tax Journal* 44:55–71.

Atkinson, Anthony B., and Joseph E. Stiglitz. 1980. *Lectures on public economics*. New York: McGraw-Hill.

Blau, David, and Philip Robins. 1988. Child care costs and family labor supply. *Review of Economics and Statistics* 70:374–81.

Connelly, Rachel. 1992. The effect of child care costs on married women's labor force participation. *Review of Economics and Statistics* 82:83–90.

Dunbar, Amy, and Susan Nordhauser. 1991. Is the child care credit progressive? *National Tax Journal* 44:519–28.

Garfinkel, Irwin, Daniel Meyer, and Patrick Wong. 1990. The potential of child care tax credits to reduce poverty and welfare recipiency. *Population Research and Policy Review* 9:45–63.

Hayes, Cheryl D., John L. Palmer, and Martha J. Zaslow. 1990. *Who cares for America's children? Child care policies for the 1990s.* Washington, D.C.: National Academy Press.

Heckman, James J. 1974. Effects of child care programs on women's work effort. *Journal of Political Economy* 82:136–63.

Henderson, David R. 1989. The supply side tax revenue effects of the child care tax credit. *Journal of Policy Analysis and Management* 8:673–75.

Hofferth, Sandra L., April Brayfield, Sharon Deich, and Pamela Holcomb. 1991. *National child care survey, 1990.* Washington, D.C.: Urban Institute Press.

Internal Revenue Service. 1991–92. *Statistics of Income Bulletin,* Winter.

———. 1993. *Statistics of Income Bulletin,* Spring.

Killingsworth, Mark R. 1983. *Labor supply.* Cambridge: Cambridge University Press.

Krashinsky, Michael. 1981. Subsidies to child care: Public policy and optimality. *Public Finance Quarterly* 9:243–69.

Michalopoulos, Charles, Philip K. Robins, and Irwin Garfinkel. 1992. A structural model of labor supply and child care demand. *Journal of Human Resources* 27(1): 166–203.

Ribar, David C. 1992. Child care and the labor supply of married women: Reduced form evidence. *Journal of Human Resources* 27(1): 134–65.

Robins, Philip K. 1990. Federal financing of child care: Alternative approaches and economic implications. *Population Research and Policy Review* 9:65–90.

Rowland, Mary. 1994. A tax break that few employees use. *New York Times,* November 19, p. 38.

U.S. Congress. Senate. Committee on Appropriations. 1988. *Hearing on the federal role in child care,* September 22. 100th Cong., 2d sess.

Wolfman, Brian. 1984. Child care, work, and the federal income tax. *American Journal of Tax Policy* 3:153–93.

Comment   Brigitte C. Madrian

In this paper, Gentry and Hagy examine the effective tax subsidies that result from two mechanisms designed to provide tax relief for child care expenditures: the child care tax credit and dependent care assistance plans. The paper pursues two courses of inquiry: (1) calculating the distribution of the tax subsidy and (2) examining the determinants of tax relief. Several interesting findings emerge from the analysis. First, the distribution of the tax subsidy when calculated on the basis of reported income suggests that child care tax relief is regressive in the lower tail of the income distribution. When it is calculated on the basis of potential income, however, the tax subsidy is progressive throughout the income distribution. Second, single-parent families profit more from these tax subsidies than do two-parent families: they are more likely to claim tax relief and, conditional on income, receive larger benefits. Finally, families

Brigitte C. Madrian is assistant professor of economics at the University of Chicago Graduate School of Business and a faculty research fellow of the National Bureau of Economic Research.

with more children are less likely to receive tax relief, but conditional on receiving tax relief, benefits increase with family size.

This paper presents a careful and comprehensive analysis of how tax relief for child care expenditures is currently distributed. In my remarks, I would like to extend the discussion about the progressivity or regressivity of these tax subsidies to alternative scenarios that could affect the actual distribution of benefits. First, I will consider how *potential* tax benefits are related to the progressivity of child care subsidies. Then I will discuss the progressivity implications of a child care tax subsidy designed in response to the equity and efficiency arguments that call for having tax relief for child care expenditures.

Current Tax Relief for Child Care Expenditures

Gentry and Hagy begin where any paper on tax policy should begin: by describing the tax rules pertinent to the discussion. The government currently provides such tax relief through two different means—the child care tax credit (CCTC) and dependent care assistance plan (DCAPs). As discussed in the paper, there are many common features to these two tax relief programs: qualifying expenditures must be on behalf of children under age 13, expenses must be work related, parent(s) must be working or enrolled in school, and eligible expenditures are limited by earned income.

There are other features that distinguish these two programs. Like other tax credits, the CCTC can be claimed by anyone with qualifying expenditures simply by attaching the appropriate form to the personal income tax return. In contrast, DCAPs are an employee benefit, like health insurance and pensions, and eligibility to participate is thus limited to those whose employers provide this benefit. The maximum level of expenditures eligible under a DCAP is constant for all individuals, while the level of eligible expenses under the CCTC is higher for families claiming expenditures for two or more children than for families with only one eligible child. Like other tax credits, the CCTC reduces an individual's tax liability directly. In contrast to the earned income tax credit, however, the CCTC is nonrefundable. The extent of the CCTC is thus limited by an individual's pre-CCTC tax liability. By comparison, the DCAP provides tax relief indirectly by reducing an individual's taxable income. The value of the CCTC is determined by a statutory subsidy rate that declines with income over a certain range. The value of a DCAP, in contrast, increases with an individual's marginal tax rate.

Although the main focus of Gentry and Hagy's paper is to calculate the distribution of the tax subsidy associated with the CCTC and DCAPs, it never shows exactly what the potential tax savings associated with these two programs are and how they compare. To illustrate the differences in the tax savings associated with the CCTC and a DCAP, figures 4C.1 through 4C.3 plot the tax relief available through the CCTC and a DCAP for a married couple filing jointly, assuming that all income is labor income (the value of the earned income tax credit is ignored in these figures). Figure 4C.1 assumes that the

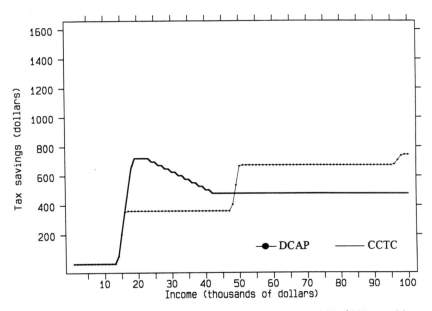

Fig. 4C.1   Tax savings comparison: CCTC vs. DCAP (one child, $200 monthly expense)

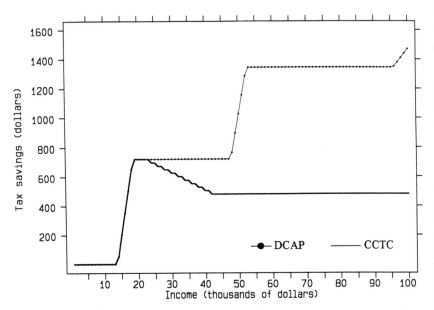

Fig. 4C.2   Tax savings comparison: CCTC vs. DCAP (one child, $400 monthly expense)

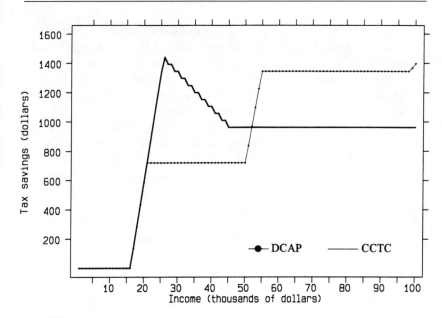

Fig. 4C.3   Tax savings comparison: CCTC vs. DCAP (two children, $400 monthly expense)

couple has $200 per month in expenses for one child, figure 4C.2 assumes $400 per month in expenses for one child, and figure 4C.3 assumes $400 per month in expenses for two children. These graphs highlight some of the differences between the two programs. Note that neither program offers *any* tax relief to low-income families who have no tax liability initially. As can be seen in all three graphs, the tax savings offered by DCAPs increases with income as marginal tax rates increase. In contrast, the tax savings associated with the CCTC is either falling or constant as income increases, except for a very narrow income range over which the value of the CCTC increases.

In figure 4C.1, for a family with one child and $200 per month in child care expenditures, the maximum tax savings offered by both a DCAP and the CCTC is abour $750 annually.[1] For middle-income families the CCTC provides greater tax relief, while at higher levels of income a DCAP provides greater tax relief. Thus, which program is "better" at reducing tax liability depends on the level of family income. If monthly expenditures rise to $400 per month (fig. 4C.2), however, the picture changes dramatically. While the tax savings derived from the CCTC remains the same, the tax savings of the DCAP increases, reaching a maximum of about $1,500 per month. Moreover, at this higher level of child care expenditures, a DCAP provides greater tax savings

---

1. Note that in all three figures, the value of a DCAP may be somewhat less than the actual tax savings graphed, to the extent that the "use it or lose it" feature of a DCAP creates uncertainty.

than the CCTC throughout the income distribution. With two children and $400 per month in child care expenditures (fig. 4C.3), the picture changes once again. In this case, the value of a DCAP is the same as it was in figure 4C.2, while the maximum tax savings provided by the CCTC increases to about $1,500. As in figure 4C.1, the CCTC is more valuable than a DCAP for middle-income families, while the reverse is true for high-income families.

These figures suggest that the resulting distribution of the tax subsidy provided by these two programs will depend on a number of factors, such as the extent to which DCAPs are provided by employers, especially for high-income families; the number of children that each family has placed in child care; how much families at various points in the income distribution spend on child care; and the actual distribution of family income. The actual distribution of the tax subsidy as calculated by Gentry and Hagy may therefore be expected to change as these factors which translate the potential tax savings into actual tax savings also change. Increased availability of DCAPs will tend to make the tax subsidy more regressive, especially if families have only one rather than two or more children in child care. Similarly, if the distribution of income shifts so that more families have sufficiently low income that they receive no tax savings from either program, the distribution of the tax subsidy will appear more regressive. In contrast, the tax subsidy will become more progressive as utilization of the CCTC increases, either because more families have sufficient income that they have positive tax liability in the absence of any child care expenses or because DCAPs are not available or offer less tax savings than the CCTC.

Designing Tax Relief for Child Care

After reviewing the nature of both the CCTC and DCAPs, Gentry and Hagy consider the various equity and efficiency rationales for providing tax relief for child care. I would like to pick up where they leave off and consider how these rationales for the provision of tax relief inform the discussion about the appropriate design of such tax relief and what they imply about the distribution of tax relief. I should first note that if all child care expenditures are considered a consumption expense, merely one more of the many costs associated with having children, then there is *no* rationale for tax relief. If, however, we believe that child care is more than just a consumption expense, there are a number of issues to be considered in designing tax relief for child care. Should tax relief be provided through a credit, such as the CCTC, or a deduction, such as a DCAP? If through a credit, should the credit be refundable? Should tax relief be unlimited, or capped (as are both the CCTC and DCAPs)? If capped, on what factors should the cap depend? Number of children? Age of children? Should expenditures on all forms of child care be eligible for tax relief?

One commonly cited rationale for tax relief is that child care expenditures represent a cost of doing business, and this cost should be deducted from taxable income just as other costs of business can be (or should be) deducted from taxable income. This justification for tax relief suggests that relief should come in the form of a deduction from taxable income rather than as a tax credit. It should be noted that many other so-called costs of doing business are not currently deductible from taxable income: travel costs for getting to and from work are not deductible, regular meals are not deductible, clothing costs (other than for uniforms) are not deductible, and other miscellaneous expenses are only deductible for those who itemize to the extent that they exceed 2 percent of adjusted gross income (unless an individual is self-employed).

One reason that many of these other work-related expenses are not deductible is that to some extent, they represent personal consumption: transportation costs are related to personal decisions regarding where to live and how to get to work; the costs of clothing and meals are likely to reflect personal tastes. Even if child care expenditures do represent a cost of doing business, they are likely to reflect some degree of consumption as well: child care providers furnish meals, diapers, and toys in addition to supervision. In addition, many forms of child care also come with large "educational" or "entertainment" components that certainly represent parental consumption decisions. The degree of consumption associated with child care is likely to be reflected in the price of child care, as the cost of better-trained providers and expensive outings is passed on to the parents who purchase these types of care. There are two ways that one could account for these consumption expenditures in the design of tax relief. One would be to make expenditures only partially deductible. A second, and perhaps more appropriate, way would be to limit the extent to which child care expenses are deductible to the expenditure level that buys basic supervision without the frills.[2] Note that both the CCTC and DCAPs have such limits.

Because there are additional costs incurred from placing additional children in child care, any limit on expenditures should be related to the number of children (the CCTC currently provides a double credit for two- relative to one-child families; DCAPs do not depend on the number of children).[3] And because older children are in school most of the day, a limit in excess of the cost of after-school supervision will result in subsidies for consumption activities. Thus expenditure limits should also vary with the age of children.

A second rationale for providing tax relief for child care expenditures is that, empirically, women with small children have higher labor supply elasticities than either men or women without children. On efficiency grounds, these women should face lower marginal tax rates. Tax subsidies for child care represent a way to effectively lower the cost of working for those individuals who are likely to have the most elastic labor supply.[4] This rationale for tax relief

2. There may be a separate rationale for wanting to subsidize educational expenditures on young children.
3. If there are economies of scale in child supervision, then the increase in the limit on allowable expenditures should decline with each additional child.
4. An alternative way to do this is through a secondary earner deduction (Feldstein and Feenberg, chap. 2 in this volume). Note that tax relief for child care expenditures may actually be more efficient than a secondary earner deduction if having a high labor supply elasticity results more from having children than from being married.

does not speak so clearly to the issue of whether relief should be provided through a credit or a deduction. That labor supply elasticities tend to increase with income, however, suggests that a deduction may be favored on efficiency grounds as well. Because participation elasticities are greater than hours elasticities, efficiency arguments also favor a limit on the level of tax relief. If labor supply elasticities decrease with the number of children, efficiency arguments call for a limit that increases with the number of children as well.

Overall, then, the equity and efficiency arguments in favor of tax relief suggest that child care expenditures should be deductible from income. There should, however, be a limit on the level of expenditures that are deductible, although this limit should vary with both the age and the number of the children in child care. While most of these features are reflected in either the CCTC or a DCAP, neither program combines them all. Under a DCAP, expenses are deductible from taxable income up to a certain limit, but there are no adjustments for the age or number of children. DCAPs also have the bizarre "use it or lose it" feature, for which I am hard pressed to find any rationale, and they are only available for a small subset of the population. The CCTC, on the other hand, is available to all but is a credit rather than a deduction. I can think of no justification for having either or both of the two different types of tax relief currently available.

What are the distributional implications of an "ideally" designed type of tax relief? In a progressive tax system, tax deductions are more regressive than tax credits. Thus, a move away from the CCTC, the form of tax relief that is used predominantly now, and toward something with the deductibility features of a DCAP will make the distribution of tax relief for child care more regressive than it currently is. A limit on the level of deductible expenditures, however, will make the distribution of tax relief progressive over the income ranges in which the expense limits are likely to bind, and a lower expenditure limit will impart greater progressivity. As shown in table 4.2 of the Gentry and Hagy paper, the expense limit binds for only about 35 percent of families with incomes greater than $100,000. This suggests that there may be considerable scope to make the distribution of tax relief more progressive by lowering the level of deductible expenditures without compromising the equity and efficiency arguments that call for relief in the first place.

5   Tax Subsidies to Employer-Provided Health Insurance

Jonathan Gruber and James M. Poterba

The value of employer-provided health insurance is excluded from an individual's federal and state taxable income and from the social security tax base. These exclusions provide an incentive for individuals and firms to structure compensation arrangements so that employees receive employer-provided insurance, rather than cash compensation that they may ultimately use to finance their health care or health insurance purchases. This incentive has important economic implications: medical care financed by insurance will generally be overconsumed because of low copayment rates under traditional insurance policies. Tax incentives for employer provision of health insurance have therefore been cited, for example by Feldstein (1973), Pauly (1986), and Phelps (1992), as encouraging overinsurance and ultimately overconsumption of medical services.

Given the central role of this tax incentive in the medical economy, it is important both to measure it and to analyze how it would be affected by various policy reforms. This task is a complicated one because the tax system subsidizes medical care purchases in two ways. The first is the exclusion from income and payroll taxes of all employer insurance premium payments, as well as some fraction of employee payments for employer-sponsored insurance. The second is the deductibility of individual expenditures on medical care and medical insurance that exceed some minimum threshold, currently 7.5 percent

Jonathan Gruber is the Castle-Krob Career Development Associate Professor at the Massachusetts Institute of Technology and a faculty research fellow of the National Bureau of Economic Research. James M. Poterba is director of the Public Economics Research Program at the National Bureau of Economic Research and professor of economics at the Massachusetts Institute of Technology.

The authors are grateful to the National Institute on Aging and the National Science Foundation for research support, to Todd Sinai for exceptional research assistance, to David Bradford, Len Burman, David Cutler, Peter Diamond, Martin Feldstein, Louis Kaplow, and Roberton Williams for helpful comments and discussions, and to Dan Feenberg for assistance with the NBER TAXSIM model.

of adjusted gross income (AGI). The net tax incentive for insurance purchase depends on the subsidy for employer-provided insurance *relative* to that for health care purchase if an individual self-insures. Most previous analyses of the tax incentive for employer-provided health insurance have focused only on the first tax incentive.

This paper presents new evidence on the net tax subsidy to employer-provided health insurance, as well as new estimates of the likely effects of various tax policy reforms. We do so by combining information from the 1987 National Medical Expenditures Survey (NMES) with data from the U.S. Treasury Individual Tax Model file to estimate how the tax system affects the after-tax price of health insurance relative to the after-tax price of out-of-pocket health care spending. We aggregate respondents in the NMES into health insurance units then use the NBER TAXSIM model to estimate the tax saving to each from employer provision of health insurance. Our procedure preserves the rich cross-sectional variation in household spending on medical care better than approaches that impute insurance and medical care outlays to households in other data sets.

This paper is organized as follows. In section 5.1, we sketch the analytical framework that we use to measure the net tax subsidy to employer-provided health insurance. We define the tax subsidies to employer-provided insurance, employer-sponsored insurance that is paid for by the employee, and out-of-pocket spending on health insurance and health care. We then measure the net tax price of employer-provided insurance as a function of these subsidies. Section 5.2 describes the data sets we analyze and outlines our algorithm for measuring the tax subsidies.

Section 5.3 reports the basic results of our analysis. We begin by providing estimates of the marginal subsidy to additional insurance purchases since this is the margin of overinsurance of most concern to health policy analysts. We then describe the recent evolution of this subsidy. We compare the period before the Tax Reform Act of 1986 (TRA86), when the top marginal tax rate under the personal income tax was 50 percent, to the late 1980s, when the 1986 tax rate reductions were fully phased in, and to 1994, after several increases in marginal tax rates had brought top marginal tax rates to nearly 40 percent. We thereby illustrate how changes in the tax structure can affect the magnitude of the tax subsidy to employer-provided health insurance.

Section 5.4 describes the effect of various tax policy reforms on the net tax subsidy to health insurance purchase and reports illustrative calculations of how such reforms might affect the demand for health insurance. We consider capping the value of insurance benefits that are exempt from federal income taxation, as well as including the full value of employer-provided health insurance in both the FICA and federal income tax bases. We describe how these changes would affect the marginal subsidies to employer-provided health insurance, and under plausible assumptions about the price elasticity of demand for this insurance, we illustrate the effect of such reforms on insurance demand. Although there is no definitive empirical evidence on the price elasticity of demand for health insurance, we present calculations using several values spanning results in the existing literature. Section 5.5 summarizes our findings and outlines several directions for future research.

5.1   Tax Subsidy to Employer-Provided Health Insurance

Employer-provided insurance is one of many ways of financing medical care services. It is therefore important to distinguish between subsidies to the purchase of health *insurance* and subsidies to the consumption of health *care* more generally. A change in the after-tax price of insurance can alter the financing of any given set of medical services, and since it changes the composite price of medical care, it may also affect the level of health care services consumed.[1] Our analysis is limited to the former effect, the impact of taxation on the financing of medical care. We assume that changes in the level of employer-provided health insurance would be offset by similar changes in household out-of-pocket spending, with little or no change in the level of health care consumed. We therefore understate the effect of tax reforms on the demand for health insurance since shifts in the aggregate demand for medical care would reinforce changes in the level of insurance demand following a tax reform.

We define the tax subsidy to insurance purchase in terms of the relative after-tax price of financing health care with insurance, and without insurance on an out-of-pocket basis. Our approach does not consider how the tax subsidy to employer-provided insurance affects the after-tax price of medical care, which prevents us from analyzing how insurance tax reforms would affect aggregate medical care spending.[2]

The current U.S. tax system subsidizes both employer-provided health insurance and out-of-pocket medical spending. Employees with employer-provided health insurance are not required to include the value of this insurance in their taxable income for federal and state income taxation, or in their wage tax base for the payroll tax.[3] The Joint Committee on Taxation estimates that in fiscal 1994, federal revenues from the personal income tax and payroll tax were nearly $90 billion lower as a result of these exclusions (U.S. Congressional Budget Office [CBO] 1994a). The tax system also subsidizes out-of-pocket

1. This distinction parallels a familiar analysis in the taxation of corporate capital income. Changing the tax treatment of debt would lead both to a shift in financing, i.e., differential use of debt and equity, as well as a shift in the ultimate level of real investment.

2. The after-tax price of medical care at the time of consumption depends on whether the patient is insured, the copayment rate and deductible level for the patient's health insurance (if insured), and whether the patient itemizes tax deductions and claims the medical expense deduction. For those who purchase insurance, there is also an ex ante price of medical care, distinct from the price at the time of consumption, that includes the price of purchasing insurance.

3. Employer-provided health insurance was encouraged by the 1942 Stabilization Act, which placed limits on wage increases but allowed employers to offer insurance plans to their employees. Scofea (1994) provides an introduction to the history of employer-provided health insurance in the United States.

spending on health insurance and medical services by allowing an itemized deduction for medical expenses. Itemizers can deduct expenditures on medical care and directly purchased health insurance in excess of 7.5 percent of AGI from their federal taxable income. The revenue cost of this provision, less than $4 billion in 1994, is much smaller than that for employer-provided insurance.

Our definition of the tax subsidy to employer-provided insurance considers both the after-tax cost of employer-provided insurance and the after-tax cost of out-of-pocket medical spending. We do not consider individually purchased health insurance, on the grounds that higher load factors and less-favorable tax treatment than for employer-provided insurance make this a dominated option for those who seek insurance.

5.1.1   After-Tax Cost of Employer-Provided Insurance

We consider an individual with a federal marginal income tax rate on earned income of τ, a net-of-federal-tax state income tax rate of τ_s, and employer and employee rates of payroll tax each equal to τ_{ss}. We assume that labor income taxes and payroll taxes are fully borne by labor, so that when an employer provides insurance that costs E dollars, the employee's wage is reduced by $E/(1 + \tau_{ss})$.[4] The employer is indifferent between purchasing $1 of insurance or paying wages of $1/(1 + \tau_{ss})$, since each dollar of wages requires a payroll tax payment as well. The change in the employee's after-tax wage income per dollar of employer-provided insurance, dw_{AT}/dE, is therefore

$$(1) \qquad \frac{dw_{AT}}{dE} = \frac{1 - \tau - \tau_s - \tau_{ss}}{1 + \tau_{ss}}.$$

Many previous studies of taxation and employer-provided health insurance, including Feldstein and Allison (1974), Taylor and Wilensky (1983), Holmer (1984), and Burman and Williams (1994), have used dw_{AT}/dE or some variant of it to define the tax subsidy to employer-provided insurance. A parallel assumption is made in the literature on taxation and the demand for fringe benefits more generally.[5]

While the reduction in after-tax wages per dollar of employer-provided insurance is a key factor determining the after-tax price of such insurance, it is not the only one. We identify two other factors that affect the after-tax cost of employer-provided health insurance, and that consequently affect the relative price of this insurance vis-à-vis self insurance. First, because insurance firms include a load factor in their policy prices, the expected value of medical care outlays from $1 of spending on medical insurance is less than the expected

---

4. Several recent studies, notably Gruber and Krueger (1991) and Gruber (1994), support this assumption with respect to various types of employer mandates.

5. Woodbury and Hamermesh's (1992) study of how the TRA86 affected the demand for fringe benefits vs. wage income at universities is a recent example in this tradition. Earlier studies that adopt similar approaches but sometimes omit either the state tax or payroll tax include Sloan and Adamache (1986) and Long and Scott (1982).

value from $1 of out-of-pocket medical spending. The load factor, λ, reflects costs of administering an insurance plan, the profits of the insurer, and any other expenses incurred in minimizing the health risk of a given group to the insurer. This load factor affects the after-tax cost of employer-provided insurance relative to self-insurance of medical care costs.

Second, contrary to the assumption of complete employer provision of insurance above, employees pay a substantial and rising fraction, currently about 15 percent, of the premiums for employer-provided insurance. Blostin, Grant, and Wiatrowski (1992) report that in 1989, nearly half of the employees who received employer-provided health care benefits contributed to the cost of individual coverage, while for two-thirds of these workers, contributions were required for family coverage. Approximately three-quarters of these employee premiums are paid after tax, and paying them is a requirement of taking advantage of the favorable tax treatment of employer-provided insurance.[6] Employees who must make after-tax contributions to their employer-provided insurance receive favorable tax treatment on a smaller fraction of their health insurance than those employees whose insurance is fully provided by the employer. Recognizing employee contributions to the cost of employer-provided insurance therefore raises the after-tax price of this insurance. In defining the after-tax price of insurance, we use G to denote employee payments for employer-provided group insurance and E to denote employer payments. We assume that a fraction δ of employee premiums can be paid for on a pretax basis through cafeteria plans and other tax-favored arrangements.

One question that arises in considering employee payments for health insurance is why employers structure health plans with such payments, despite their tax inefficiency. There are at least two possible reasons. First, within any workplace, different workers will place different values on the benefit of health insurance coverage. Unless employers can selectively lower the wages of only those employees who value insurance coverage, employers who pay the full cost of insurance will disproportionately attract workers with a high value of insurance. Employers may view this outcome as unattractive, for example because the workers who value insurance the most may be less healthy and therefore less productive workers. Cost sharing can be an effective mechanism for reducing the selection effects associated with health insurance provision.

A second reason for employers to require some employee contributions relates to employee choice of health care plan. Many employers offer a choice across plans of differing generosity and cost. Employers may not be able to

---

6. The U.S. Bureau of Labor Statistics (1993, 1994) reports that approximately 33 percent of employees of firms with more than 100 employees, and 20 percent of employees of firms with fewer than 100 employees, can deduct their own premium payments from taxes. These are employees who can pay their premiums through cafeteria plans provided by their employers. We are not able to identify which employees can make pretax premium payments in the data below, so we randomly assign individuals to the pretax employee premium group with a probability of .25. This is a weighted average of the probabilities for small and large firms.

pay lower wages to employees who choose higher cost plans, and cost sharing can be used to induce choice of cost-effective insurance.

Recognizing both the load factor on employer-provided insurance and the existence of employee contributions to such insurance yields the following expression for the after-tax price of employer-provided insurance:

$$(2) \quad P_{HI} = \left[\left(\frac{1 - \tau - \tau_s - \tau_{ss}}{1 + \tau_{ss}} \right) * \left(\frac{E + \delta * G}{E + G} \right) + \frac{(1 - \delta) * G}{E + G} \right] * (1 + \lambda).$$

We define the tax subsidy to employer-provided insurance by comparing this after-tax price with the after-tax cost of self-insurance.

5.1.2 After-Tax Cost of Out-of-Pocket Medical Spending

It is widely recognized that the income tax code provides a form of insurance against large medical costs by permitting a deduction against taxable income for medical expenditures above a certain share of AGI. This provision of the tax code discourages insurance purchase since it lowers the after-tax cost of paying high medical expenses out of pocket. Bradford (1984) and more recently Kaplow (1991, 1992) discuss the implicit insurance in the tax system, but none of the previous studies of the tax subsidy to employer-provided insurance have considered this aspect of the income tax code.

The tax subsidy to out-of-pocket medical expenses depends on whether a taxpayer itemizes. For a nonitemizer, the after-tax cost of such spending is $1. For itemizers, however, the after-tax cost of the marginal dollar of out-of-pocket medical spending is $1 - \alpha\tau$, where τ is the federal marginal tax rate and $\alpha = 1$ if the marginal dollar of spending exceeds the AGI floor and zero otherwise. We assume that medical expenses cannot be deducted in computing state taxable income.

For an individual considering the purchase of insurance, α is unknown. It is determined by the individual's taxable income and realized need for medical services during a tax year. If F denotes the AGI threshold above which medical expenses are deductible and T the individual's total medical spending, then the probability that the last dollar of health expenditures will be tax deductible ($\alpha = 1$) equals the probability that $T - F > 0$.[7] This is the probability that the marginal dollar of health costs covered by employer-provided insurance would have been deductible if it had been incurred on own account. We have no direct information on how individuals form expectations of α in contemplating insurance purchases. We therefore assume rational expectations about actual spending during the year, calculate actual values of α for all households in our data

---

7. Total medical spending is $E + G + O$, where E is the value of employer-provided insurance, G is personal spending on group insurance premiums, and O is individual out-of-pocket health care spending. We assume that out-of-pocket spending for those with employer-provided insurance would not be affected by a shift to self-insurance. The tax-deductible share of the *additional* medical spending that would result from reduced employer-provided insurance depends on the probability that $E + G + O - F > 0$, rather than the probability that $E + G - F > 0$.

sample, and use these values in place of expected values in calculating the after-tax price of insurance.[8]

Individuals with health insurance typically face lower marginal costs of health care services at the time of consumption than individuals without such insurance. This may affect their demand for medical services, and it suggests that total medical outlays, T above, may be a function of an individual's insurance regime. We address this by computing α under two different assumptions about the link between price at time of consumption and medical spending. We first assume that total medical spending is unaffected by the presence or absence of health insurance. Our second case assumes that the price elasticity of demand for medical care services is -0.33.[9] Our findings are relatively insensitive to our assumption about the link between insurance status and T because for most households α is zero.

The foregoing discussion focuses on the after-tax cost of a marginal dollar of health care spending, which we label *marginal* α. This should be distinguished from the fraction of insured spending that would be tax deductible if the individual were not insured, $(T - F)/T$, which we label *average* α. Both marginal and average α range between zero and one. Marginal α describes the after-tax cost of the medical expenses that an individual would incur if employer-provided health insurance coverage were reduced by \$1 and the resulting drop in insured medical care were replaced with out-of-pocket spending. Marginal α will only equal unity if the insured individual already has out-of-pocket spending in excess of the AGI floor. Relatively few insured individuals are in this situation. Average α corresponds to the after-tax cost of replacing all insured medical expenditures with out-of-pocket spending. Average α will be positive whenever total medical spending, including insurance, exceeds the AGI floor. When we tabulate the tax subsidy to employer provided insurance in tables 5.4 and 5.5 below, we use average α in our expressions for the after-tax price. For analyzing the effect of tax caps on insurance spending, however, we use marginal α in our calculations since individuals are adjusting insurance purchases on the margin. Using marginal α may cause us to overstate the subsidy to insurance and therefore the reduction in insurance that results from tax caps, if tax policy changes are not marginal.

5.1.3 Relative After-Tax Price of Insurance

We define the relative after-tax price of employer-provided insurance as the ratio of the after-tax price of this insurance to the after-tax cost of out-of-pocket medical spending:

8. Newhouse et al. (1989) report that the best predictor of current medical spending is past spending.

9. We measure the marginal copayment rate for those with insurance as the ratio of their out-of-pocket medical spending to total medical spending. This is likely to be closer to the average than to the marginal copayment rate, but we do not have any further information in our data set to improve this imputation.

$$(3) \quad P_{rel} = \frac{\left[\left(\dfrac{1 - \tau - \tau_s - \tau_{ss}}{1+\tau_{ss}}\right)*\left(\dfrac{E+\delta*G}{E+G}\right) + \dfrac{(1 - \delta)*G}{E+G}\right]*(1+\lambda)}{1 - \alpha*\tau}.$$

If the tax code treated insurance premia and medical expenditures symmetrically—for example, if neither were deductible from taxable income or if both could be excluded from federal and state taxable income and from the payroll tax wage base—then the cost of insurance relative to the direct outlays on medical care would be $P_{rel} = 1 + \lambda$. We therefore consider the tax-induced distortion in the relative price of insurance to be $[P_{rel}/(1 + \lambda) - 1]$, where P_{rel} is given by equation (3).

Our measures of the after-tax price of health insurance and the relative price of insurance suffer from at least four limitations. First, we fail to distinguish between marginal purchases of incremental employer-provided insurance and the discrete decision to purchase such insurance. The load factors on marginal insurance purchases may be lower than average loads if these loads in part reflect administrative costs that do not rise when a policy becomes more extensive.

Second, we assume that when expenditures on employer-provided insurance fall, employer (E) and employee (G) spending decline in equal proportion. In fact, many employers contribute a flat amount to their group health insurance plans, and employees contribute the differential cost between the plan that they choose and the lowest cost option. In such cases, if G is not tax deductible, then there is no tax subsidy to insurance on the margin. Thus, our results below will overstate the average tax subsidy to workplace insurance.

Third, our formation ignores the possibility that individuals may be able to pay for their out-of-pocket medical costs with pretax dollars, as, for example, with medical spending accounts that are provided in some cafeteria plans. This will also lead us to overstate the tax subsidy to insurance by understating the tax benefit of self-insurance. Unfortunately, we have no data on the structure of employer contributions or the availability of such pretax out-of-pocket arrangements.

Finally, we exclude any possible link between changes in the tax treatment of employer-provided insurance and the aggregate level of health care spending. We emphasize the relative cost of employer-provided insurance versus out-of-pocket spending, but our estimates of the after-tax price of employer-provided health insurance, P_{HI} in equation (2), could also be used to assess the effects of insurance tax treatment on the demand for medical care.

5.2   Data Sources on Medical Care Spending and Tax Rates

This section describes our methodology for estimating the various parameters, such as marginal tax rates, load factors, and probabilities that medical expenditures are deductible from income taxes, that enter our expression for the relative price of employer-provided health insurance. Because our analysis requires detailed information on the pattern of health care expenditures as well as the tax circumstances of individuals and households, we use the U.S. Treasury Individual Tax Model and the NBER TAXSIM program to impute tax rates to family units in the 1987 NMES. We then draw on the information on health insurance and health care spending in this database to analyze the effect of tax subsidies to employer-provided health insurance.

5.2.1 NMES Sample

We are not aware of any data set that includes detailed information on health insurance coverage, health care spending, and federal income tax status. The NMES is the best available household-level database on health care spending. This is a nationally representative household survey that followed roughly 20,000 families during 1987. It gathered information on the demographic and economic characteristics of both family units and individual family members, including information on labor force attachment and income by source. It also collected detailed data on insurance plans, and these data were cross-checked against information collected from insurance sources such as employers or insurance companies. The NMES includes information on expenditures on a variety of types of medical care. Most of this information was also cross-checked by interviews with medical providers.

To impute tax information such as marginal tax rates and itemization status to survey respondents in the NMES, we aggregate individual NMES respondents into "health insurance units" (HIUs). These units include the family head, his or her spouse, any children under age 19, and full-time students until they reach age 23. There may be multiple family heads within a household, for example, when elderly parents live with a younger nuclear family. We limit our sample to employed individuals and exclude the self-employed, families with someone who is aged 65 or over and therefore eligible for Medicare, families with anyone who is eligible for Medicaid, and families with missing information on insurance status.

Table 5.1 shows the quantitative importance of the various data restrictions that we have imposed in selecting our sample. The NMES universe contains 20,028 HIUs who represent a total of 168.5 million family heads and spouses. Since family heads and spouses are the only relevant decision makers for insurance purchases, we use only their sample weights in making our calculations. We define families as employed if either the head or spouse is employed and as self-employed if both the family head and spouse are self-employed.

We define families as insured if both the family head and that person's spouse report that they are insured in the fourth wave of the survey and if they report some spending, either by their employer or by themselves, on employer-provided group health insurance. Our analysis excludes some employed families who purchase individual insurance only since we are focusing on the tax incentives for employer-provided insurance. We define families as uninsured

Table 5.1   Sample Size and Sample Limitations from the 1987 NMES

Restriction	Families in NMES Sample	Weighted to Represent U.S. Population[a] (millions)
Total NMES sample	20,028	168.5
− Households with anyone over age 64 or oldest member under age 18	(5,688)	(32.6)
Subtotal	14,340	135.9
− Medicaid households	(617)	(3.5)
Subtotal	13,723	132.4
− Nonrespondents to insurance status questions on NMES Wave IV	(2,716)	(11.4)
Subtotal	11,007	121.0
− Families that are neither "insured" nor "uninsured" by our definitions	(3,856)	(41.9)
Subtotal	7,151	79.2
− Self-employed families	(136)	(1.6)
Subtotal	7,015	77.5
− Unemployed families	(770)	(6.5)
Subtotal	6,245	71.1
− Families with zero weight	(284)	(0.0)
Final sample	5,961	71.1

Source: Authors' tabulations using 1987 NMES.

[a]Weighted totals are weighted by sum of head and spouse weights.

if they report both the family head and spouse to be uninsured and have no employer-provided insurance. Since the NMES does not report insurance plan information for all persons, our definition excludes relatively more insured persons from the sample than uninsured persons.[10] Our final sample has 5,961 HIUs, representing a total of 71.1 million household heads and spouses.

Table 5.2 presents information on the insurance status of the individuals in the employed family units in our NMES sample. Just over 82 percent of our population-weighted sample, or 58.4 million household heads or their spouses, are part of an employed household and have employer-provided insurance. Our analysis suggests that 12.7 million employed individuals are uninsured. This translates into a higher fraction of employed individuals classified as uninsured than some other sources, but the disparity is explained by our stringent criteria for defining a household as insured.[11] Within the subsample that reports some employer-provided insurance, 42 percent have employer contributions only for insurance, and 52 percent have both employer and own contributions. Only 5

10. We also exclude NMES families with sample weights of zero. These are families that were added to the NMES during the survey year, for example, because they moved into an existing NMES household as a subfamily.

11. Our analysis yields estimates of the number of uninsured employed individuals that are similar to those in other studies.

Table 5.2　　　**Health Insurance Status of Employed Individuals in the 1987 NMES**

Status	Number (million)
Only employer premiums	24.8
($E>0$, $I+G=0$)	(1,936)
Only individual premiums	3.0
($E=0$, $G>0$)	(228)
Employer and individual premiums	30.6
($E>0$, $G>0$)	(2,360)
Uninsured ($E=G=0$) and self-reported	12.7
uninsured	(1,437)
Total	71.1
	(5,961)

Source: Estimates based on authors' tabulations from the 1987 NMES. HIUs, weighted to reflect the sampling probabilities of family heads and spouses, are the basis for tabulations. Calculations exclude individuals in households with anyone over age 65. Values in parentheses are number of NMES households in each group.

percent of the households in our sample report paying the full cost of employer-provided insurance themselves.

Table 5.3 reports the distribution of spending on tax-subsidized employer-provided insurance in our NMES sample. The subsample used to construct this table is the set of all individuals who are employed and who we classify as covered by employer-provided insurance. Column (1) shows the value of employer contributions for insurance (E), and column (2) shows the value of both employer contributions and pretax contributions by employees ($E + \delta G$). While the NMES figures are measured in 1987 dollars, all results in this paper have been inflated to 1994 dollars using the growth in personal health spending over the 1987–94 period.[12]

Table 5.3 shows that the mean value of employer-provided health insurance is $4,249. The mean value of employer and pretax employee spending is approximately 5 percent higher ($4,483). The distribution of this tax-subsidized spending is somewhat skewed, as is revealed by the lower median values. Nearly 10 percent of the sample reports employer contributions worth more than $8,000 per year, and more than one-quarter report values of less than $2,000.

5.2.2　Tax Rate Estimation

To estimate the marginal federal tax rate facing each NMES household, we must estimate each household's federal taxable income. The NMES reports

12. The CBO (1993) presents data on private health insurance expenditures in 1987 ($155 billion), along with forecasts for 1993 ($289 billion) and 1995 ($343 billion). We estimate 1994 expenditures by interpolating between the 1993 and 1995 forecasts; this yields $316 billion. We then use the ratio of 1994 to 1987 spending, $316/$155, or 2.039, to impute the distribution of 1987 spending to 1994. The estimates in table 5.3 may overstate actual employer contributions for insurance, given the rising role of insurance cost shifting to employees.

Table 5.3   **Distribution of Expenditures on Employer-Provided Health Insurance in the 1987 NMES (converted to 1994 dollars)**

Percentile	Employer Spending (1)	Employer Plus Pretax Employee Spending (2)
5th	0	602
10th	1,020	1,250
25th	1,877	2,044
50th	3,816	4,130
75th	5,872	6,021
90th	7,950	8,130
95th	9,920	10,159
Mean	4,249	4,483

Source: Authors' tabulations using 1987 NMES data. Estimates for 1994 are based on the ratio of total private health insurance spending in 1994 to that in 1987, as projected in CBO (1993).

information on a variety of family income flows, such as wage income, dividend income, and interest income, although it does not contain nearly as much detail on income sources as a tax return. In particular, it does not report capital gains income, which we set equal to zero.[13]

The NMES also asked respondents whether they itemized deductions for income tax purposes. This is a critical input to our calculation of both tax rates and the probability of deducting out-of-pocket medical expenditures. The NMES figures for itemization differ from those in the Treasury tax model, although we did not find any systematic pattern in the differences. In 1987, 58.1 percent of the joint filers in the Treasury tax model database, excluding those who claimed any household members aged 65 or over, itemized deductions; the figure is 48.5 percent in the NMES. This pattern is reversed for nonjoint filers, with the NMES itemizing share 18.3 percent and the Treasury tax model share 16.9 percent, again excluding those aged 65 and over. If the NMES understates the incidence of itemization, our results will tend to overstate the tax subsidy to employer-provided insurance.

We conduct our analysis using the reported 1987 data on medical care and insurance spending (inflated to 1994 levels, as described above), but we consider the tax subsidy to health insurance under several different income tax regimes. We ask what the tax subsidy to the level of health insurance purchased in 1987 would have been if households faced the tax rates that they faced in 1986, 1989, and 1994. To do this we "age" taxable income in the NMES database to 1986, to analyze the tax code in effect before TRA86, to 1989, when

---

13. Imputing capital gains income to individuals by income category made little difference to the estimates of after-tax insurance prices in Gruber and Poterba (1994). Besides capital gains, TAXSIM uses a number of other income items reported on a tax return, such as contributions to IRAs and Keogh accounts and self-employed business deductions, to compute taxable income and marginal tax rates. We set any tax return item for which we do not have information in the NMES equal to zero in estimating taxable income.

TRA86 was fully effective, and to 1994, the most recent tax year. Our aging procedure is a simplified version of that developed by Lindsey (1987). We assume that each family's AGI changes from year to year in the same way that average per capita AGI changes between years.

Our estimate of the marginal state tax rate facing each household is less precise than our estimate of the federal tax rate. The NMES does not report the respondent's state of residence, but rather reports four census regions. We therefore create 12 "stylized families," 6 joint filers and 6 single filers, at different income levels. We use TAXSIM to estimate state-specific marginal tax rates for each of these stylized families, and we then compute state-population-weighted averages within each census region for each of these family types. We then assign one of these averages to each NMES household by identifying them as similar to one of the stylized households.

Our calculation of each individual's marginal social security tax rate follows Feldstein and Samwick (1992a). They note that the statutory social security tax rate is not the true marginal rate since prospective benefits are linked to taxes paid. This linkage varies according to income and gender since the benefit formula is redistributive and since on average women live longer and therefore receive a higher present discounted value of benefits than men. The social security system also redistributes across households with different configurations of primary and secondary earners since secondary earners receive the higher of their benefits and one-half of the benefits of the primary earner. Feldstein and Samwick find that effective marginal tax rates vary from negative values (subsidies to labor supply) for some households to the statutory marginal tax rate for other households. As a result, our tax prices would be misspecified if we used the statutory social security tax rate.[14] We estimate the effective marginal social security tax rate facing each NMES respondent using data that Feldstein and Samwick (1992b) present on tax rates by age, sex, and family labor supply.[15]

Individuals also pay payroll taxes for disability insurance and for Medicare hospital insurance. We accounted for the former by grossing up the Feldstein-Samwick net tax rates by the ratio of the statutory tax rate for *both* OASI and disability insurance to the statutory OASI tax rate, under the assumption that disability insurance tax-benefit linkages follow the same pattern as those for OASI.[16] For individuals with labor income in excess of the taxable social secu-

---

14. Using statutory tax rate without adjustment ignores the fact that higher social security tax collections today will be offset by higher social security benefit payouts in the future.

15. We assign the Feldstein-Samwick (1992b) effective tax rate for single men to single men or to families where the wife earns more than one-half of the husband's earnings. We assign their rate for women to single women, and their rate for men with dependent spouses to those families where the wife's earnings are less than one-half the husband's earnings. One limitation of this approach is that we are using point-in-time labor supply to proxy for the relative earnings of husbands and wives over their lives, but that is all that is available in the NMES.

16. This is a crude assumption since disability insurance benefits accrue to a different population, with many more young men, than OASI benefits. In addition, there are other limitations to

rity maximum, we set τ_{ss} equal to zero. In the latter case, there is no tax-benefit linkage since all citizens receive Medicare at age 65 regardless of their work history. We therefore use the statutory Medicare tax rate in our calculation.

5.2.3   Comparison with Earlier Studies

Our methodology differs from that in the CBO's (1994b) study of tax subsidies to health insurance, the most prominent recent study of related issues, in using the NMES as the central database for analysis. The CBO study imputed information from *both* the NMES and individual tax records to a third data set, the Current Population Survey (CPS). This has the advantage of providing more detailed income information than the NMES, as well as a larger sample of respondents and the associated opportunity for more precise within-group analysis. But it has the disadvantage of compressing the substantial heterogeneity across individuals in their health care spending, and the correlation of that spending with health insurance circumstances, in the process of imputation. In addition, the CPS does not report itemization status, while the NMES does. Given our limited objective in analyzing tax subsidies to employer-provided health insurance, and our focus on national aggregates, we would not gain substantially from access to the additional information that is potentially available in the CPS.

Our analysis is closer in spirit to Taylor and Wilensky's (1983) study of tax incentives and employer-provided health insurance than to the recent CBO (1994b) study. Although Taylor and Wilensky (1983) did not consider a number of the factors we described above, such as the role of insurance loads, state taxes, and the share of employee-paid health insurance premiums, they did use an earlier data set similar to the NMES, the 1977 National Medical Care Expenditure Survey (NMCES), as the basis for their study. They imputed information on tax status to households in the NMCES and computed a variety of summary statistics on tax subsidies to health insurance.

5.3   New Estimates of the Tax Subsidy to Employer-Provided Health Insurance

We summarize our analysis of the tax subsidy to employer-provided insurance by reporting average values of the after-tax relative price of employer-provided insurance and out-of-pocket medical spending, P_{rel}, under two different assumptions about the effect of insurance status on total medical spending. Recall from the discussion above that these summary statistics use information

---

the Feldstein-Samwick net tax rate calculation, such as the fact that some social security benefits accrue to dependents of contributors, and the fact that social security may substitute for an imperfect private market for real annuities and therefore have an above-market value to recipients.

on average, rather than marginal, α. To permit comparison with earlier studies, we also report the sample average of the change in after-tax employee wage income for each dollar of employer-provided health insurance (dw_{AT}/dE).

Table 5.4 presents these summary statistics when each of the NMES families is assigned its federal marginal tax rate for 1986, 1989, and 1994. We report both the average value of the relative after-tax price of insurance and out-of-pocket care, as well as the cross-sectional standard deviation of this price. We distinguish two subgroups of the employed population, those with and without insurance, and tabulate results separately for each.

The results for insured employed families, using the 1994 federal tax code, illustrate our general findings. The average value of the reduction in after-tax wage income per dollar of employer spending on health insurance is 0.682. This implies that federal income and payroll taxes, and state income taxes, place a 31.8 percent tax wedge between the after-tax cost of all other goods ($1) and the after-tax cost of employer-provided health insurance. There is substantial disparity across households in the magnitude of this subsidy: the standard deviation of dw_{AT}/dE is .117. Comparing the results for 1986 with those for either 1989 or 1994 demonstrates that the tax rate reductions in TRA86 raised the after-tax wage cost of employer-provided benefits by an average of about four cents per dollar.[17] The changes in the structure of tax rates between 1989 and 1994, because they were concentrated on a small group of high-income households, did not substantially affect the average after-tax wage cost.

The two lower rows of table 5.4 present our estimates of P_{rel} from equation (3). This ratio is substantially higher than the after-tax wage cost of employer-provided health insurance benefits because it multiplies the after-tax wage cost by $1 + \lambda$ to reflect the insurance load factor, because it includes less favorably taxed employee contributions for health insurance in the numerator, and because the denominator $(1 - \alpha\tau)$ is less than 1.

The average value of P_{rel} for the 1994 tax code is 0.837 if we assume that medical spending is unaffected by whether or not an individual is insured; it falls to 0.811 if we assume that spending would be reduced, since the tax subsidy to self-insurance is then less valuable. There is somewhat more heterogeneity in these measures than in the simple after-tax wage cost measures in the first row; the standard deviation of P_{rel} is .151 when insurance status does not affect medical care needs and .147 when we allow this type of feedback. Moreover, the average value of P_{rel} rises less between 1986 and 1989 than the after-tax wage cost of health insurance. This is because TRA86 reduced marginal tax rates for some households but also raised the AGI threshold for deducting medical expenses from 5 to 7.5 percent. This reduced α, thereby raising the

---

17. This is consistent with Hausman and Poterba's (1987) finding that TRA86 actually raised marginal tax rates for more than one-third of taxpayers. For most of those who received rate reductions, these reductions were relatively small.

Table 5.4   **Tax Subsidies to Employer-Provided Health Insurance**

	Insured Employed			Uninsured Employed		
	1986	1989	1994	1986	1989	1994
dw_{AV}/dE	0.643	0.683	0.682	0.804	0.827	0.828
	(.123)	(.111)	(.117)	(.143)	(.157)	(.194)
P_{rel}						
η=0 to impute health spending if uninsured	0.814	0.839	0.837	0.926	0.945	0.945
	(.170)	(.149)	(.151)	(.136)	(.144)	(.173)
η=−0.33 to impute health spending if uninsured	0.779	0.813	0.811	0.932	0.949	0.950
	(.165)	(.145)	(.147)	(.137)	(.143)	(.171)

Source: Authors' tabulations based on imputation of tax rates to households in 1987 NMES. Each entry reports the average price weighted by family insurance spending. Column headings indicate which year's federal income tax and payroll tax schedule was used in constructing marginal tax rates.

Note: Numbers in parentheses are cross-sectional standard deviations.

after-tax cost of out-of-pocket medical care and partly offsetting the change in marginal rates.

We have also assessed the sensitivity of these results to variation in other tax parameters. We analyzed the effect of changing the AGI threshold for medical expenses, assuming 1994 tax rates, to illustrate how this aspect of the tax code affects incentives for insurance purchase. Lowering the AGI threshold from 7.5 to 2 percent, the pre-1983 level, raises the average value of P_{rel} for the insured employed from 0.837 to 0.902 when we assume a zero price elasticity of medical care demand, and from 0.811 to 0.868 when we assume an elasticity of -0.33. This policy change therefore has a much larger effect than the change in marginal tax rates under TRA86. It suggests that our recognition of the role of tax subsidies to out-of-pocket spending *can* be an important determinant of the after-tax price of insurance, even though at the current level of the medical expense deduction threshold, this effect is relatively small.

We also tried replacing the Feldstein-Samwick social security tax rate with the statutory tax rate. This induced a fine percentage point decline in the relative insurance price, highlighting the importance of accounting for tax-benefit linkages in the analysis of social security.

Table 5.4 makes it possible to compare the average relative prices for the insured and uninsured employed groups. The uninsured employed face higher average prices for employer-provided insurance than do their insured counterparts. This is because they are on average in lower income groups, and therefore face lower marginal tax rates, than the insured employed. Some of the observed relationship, of course, could reflect a demand curve for health insurance: those who face higher prices are less likely to buy insurance. Without more detailed analysis, however, it is impossible to disentangle the heterogeneity and demand curve effects.

For the uninsured employed, using statutory social security tax rates in place of the Feldstein-Samwick adjusted rates also causes a substantial increase in the measured tax subsidy to insurance. This is because a substantial fraction of the uninsured employed have earnings in the range over which the present discounted value of the social security benefit increment associated with an additional dollar of earnings offsets a substantial fraction of social security tax payments.

One reason for measuring the tax subsidy to employer-provided insurance is to estimate the efficiency cost associated with this tax expenditure. Table 5.5 presents the first step in any such calculation, our estimate of the price distortion induced by the tax system. Recall that if there were no tax distortions, $P_{rel} = 1 + \lambda$. We therefore use our estimate of P_{rel} with the actual tax system to compute $P_{rel}/(1 + \lambda) - 1$. The average value of this distortion declined from approximately 0.29 in 1986 to 0.26 by 1989; it has changed relatively little since then. It is notable that this estimate of the tax distortion is *smaller* than $1 - dw_{AT}/dE$, the distortion that is associated with the standard analysis of the tax incentive for fringe benefit provision (first row). In 1994, for example, the

Table 5.5   Tax Distortions in the Relative After-Tax Price of Employer-Provided
                   Health Insurance

	1986	1989	1994
dw_{AT}/dE	0.357	0.317	0.318
P_{rel}			
$\eta=0$ to impute health spending if uninsured	0.286	0.261	0.263
$\eta=-0.33$ to impute health spending if uninsured	0.321	0.287	0.289

Source: Authors' tabulations based on imputation of tax rates from various years to households in 1987 NMES. Each entry reports the difference between the price of insurance with no tax subsidy (1 for the first row and 1.101 for the second two rows) and the price with the tax subsidy. Sample is employer-insured individuals.

estimated tax subsidy is 20 percent smaller than the traditional measure of the tax price. Since the deadweight loss from this subsidy rises with the square of the size of the subsidy, our calculations imply that the deadweight loss from tax subsidization is roughly 40 percent less than would be implied using the change in after-tax wages.

Our estimate of the distortion based on P_{rel} changes less between 1986 and 1989 than the average value of dw_{AT}/dE because we recognize the role of employee contributions to employer-provided health insurance, which dampen the tax subsidy, and because we include the 1986 increase in the AGI threshold for deducting out-of-pocket medical expenses in our analysis of the relative price of insurance. Our estimates therefore imply that the reduction in deadweight loss from the package of tax changes under TRA86 is much smaller than might be supposed based only on a comparison of dw_{AT}/dE at different points in time.

5.4 Capping the Amount of Tax-Exempt Employer-Provided Health Insurance

The revenue loss associated with the tax expenditure for employer-provided health insurance, and a perception that overinsurance has contributed to the rise in U.S. health care costs during the last two decades, has led to numerous proposals to alter the current tax treatment of employer-provided health insurance. One of the most common reform proposals, and one discussed at length in CBO (1994b), is capping the value of employer-provided insurance that could be excluded from taxable income. One special case of such caps would be complete inclusion of the value of employer-provided insurance in employee taxable income. In this section, we use our augmented NMES database to explore how various tax caps would affect the after-tax price of employer-provided health insurance, the demand for such insurance, and tax revenues.

There are many ways to tax employer-provided health insurance. Burman and Williams (1994) provide a detailed discussion of several options, including changes in the corporate tax deductibility of such insurance payments, as well as including some or all of the value of these benefits in the personal income tax base. Our analysis focuses on the case in which employers report the value of employer-provided insurance benefits along with an employee's wage income and these benefits are then incorporated in the federal and state income tax base and the federal payroll tax base. In principle, there is no reason that employer-provided insurance needs to be taxed in all three forms, and one could disentangle the revenue effects associated with different types of incremental tax changes. We discuss the importance of the relative sources of revenue below.

By considering the case in which tax caps are implemented through the personal income tax, our analysis applies to tax caps that are specified for tax-filing units rather than individuals. Such family-level caps would be very difficult to implement through any system that relied on changes in the corporate rather than personal income tax. If caps were applied to individuals rather than families, two-earner couples in which both earners had an opportunity to receive employer-provided insurance could reduce the impact of the caps by choosing two individual policies rather than a single family policy. Caps on tax-unit health insurance benefits such as those we consider provide a strong incentive for households with two earners to eliminate duplicative insurance coverage since such insurance is likely to provide relatively little health benefit but could lead to a substantial increase in taxable income.

5.4.1   Analyzing Tax Caps

At the outset, we should recognize several basic points about tax caps. First, the cap should not affect the behavior of anyone who receives employer-provided health insurance benefits worth *less* than the cap.[18] Second, absent income effects, no one whose employer-provided health insurance exceeds the cap value prior to imposition of the cap should reduce his insurance outlays to less than the capped level. A system of tax caps would provide strong incentives for employers and employees to restructure benefits packages to reduce the fraction of health insurance value that exceeds the cap and to maximize the chance that the cost of coverage above this cap is paid by the employee, who may have an opportunity to deduct some insurance costs as itemized medical deductions.[19] One example of such a reaction would be scaling back the set of services covered by the employer-provided insurance plan, while introducing a cafeteria plan to allow workers to pay some of these costs with pretax dollars. We ignore any such responses to tax caps in computing the revenue and behavioral effects below, but they could be important in practice.

We estimate how tax caps of various dollar amounts would affect the average after-tax relative price of health insurance and out-of-pocket spending by

18. It is possible that caps on the excludable amount of employer-provided health insurance may reduce the demand for generous coverage from some employees who previously received benefits worth more than the cap and that this will work through the negotiation process that results in a benefits and wage package to reduce the level of health benefits.

19. We consider a tax cap that applies to federal and state income taxes, as well as payroll taxes. If the cap were only applied to federal income taxes, the incentive to reduce health insurance value above the capped amount would be smaller.

setting the relative tax price for any NMES family with employer-provided insurance above the cap to $(1 + \lambda)/(1 - \alpha\tau)$. This is just the expression for the after-tax cost of health insurance in equation (3), with $\tau = \tau_s = \tau_{ss} = 0$ in the numerator. Since the families who are most likely to be affected by any cap are those with high incomes, high marginal tax rates, and therefore high values of the tax subsidy before the cap, the change in the average after-tax relative price of insurance can be substantial even if the number of households affected by the cap is small. Throughout our tax cap analysis we use marginal α in evaluating equation (3) since this is the appropriate parameter for evaluating a marginal reduction in spending on employer-provided insurance as would be associated with a tax cap.

After describing the change in the after-tax relative price of employer-provided health insurance associated with the tax caps, we present illustrative calculations of how these caps would affect the demand for employer-provided insurance. We assume that caps would apply to all employer-provided insurance that was subsidized before the cap was enacted, regardless of whether this insurance was paid for by employers or employees making pretax contributions.[20]

For each NMES family, we compute the marginal after-tax relative price of employer-provided insurance under the status quo $(P_{rel,0})$ and under the assumption that employer-provided insurance above the cap is included in taxable income $(P_{rel,1})$. If these two prices are identical, we assume that the individual would not change his demand for employer-provided insurance (E_0). If the two prices are different, however, we estimate the individual's demand for health insurance at the new price as

(4) $$E_1 = \max (C, E_0 *[1 + \eta*(P_{rel,1}/P_{rel,0} - 1)]),$$

where C denotes the level of the cap. The parameter η is the uncompensated price elasticity of demand for health insurance. We do not consider any income effects on the demand for insurance that might be associated with the introduction of tax caps. If E_1 is greater than C, then we take E_1 as the new level of employer-provided insurance. If E_1 is less than C, however, we assume that $E_1 = C$ and that the individual will locate at the kink point on the budget set. To find the aggregate change in the demand for employer-provided insurance as a result of a cap on the value of excludable benefits, we compute the sample-weighted sum of the changes in E_1 across all NMES households.

Our calculations make the strong assumption that each household affected by the tax cap can adjust the quantity of employer-provided health insurance that it receives in response to this tax policy change. This assumption is unrealistic since most workplaces offer only a few discrete choices with respect to health insurance coverage. Moreover, since individual employees cannot deter-

---

20. Excluding pretax employee contributions from the tax cap would result in a simple tax avoidance strategy. Firms would reduce their employer-provided health insurance but permit employees to purchase equivalent insurance on a pretax basis. This would circumvent the tax caps.

mine what benefits package their employer will offer, changes in the tax circumstances of an individual worker may not be reflected in a differential level of employer-provided insurance. Recognizing the important heterogeneity in tax preferences and insurance demand within workplaces, and incorporating this into the analysis, is therefore an important direction for future work.

A critical parameter in our calculation is η, the price elasticity of demand for health insurance. There are relatively few estimates of this parameter, and available estimates differ substantially (see Gruber and Poterba [1994] for a detailed review). There are also many different margins along which employers might alter their health insurance offerings, and it is not clear that elasticities of demand would be the same on all margins. For example, employers could reduce the value of insurance coverage provided to their workers by limiting the set of services covered, by raising copayment rates or deductibles, or by requiring a higher employee contribution for a given insurance policy. Previous studies, and our analysis below, treat adjustments on all of these margins as equivalent.

Previous cross-sectional studies of the price elasticity of demand for health insurance can be grouped into three types.[21] The first set of studies compare the quantity of health insurance demanded by high- and low-income households that face different marginal tax rates; these studies have produced a wide range of elasticity estimates.[22] The second set of studies consider evidence from hypothetical offers of supplemental insurance to participants in the RAND Health Insurance Experiment, reported in Marquis and Phelps (1987). This randomized experiment assigned individuals to plans with different copayment rates, with an out-of-pocket maximum of up to $1,000. At the end of the experiment, individuals were presented with hypothetical offers for supplemental insurance to lower their out-of-pocket exposure; the price of these offers varied across participants. The resulting elasticity of demand for the quantity of supplemental insurance was −0.6.

The third source of information on the price elasticity of demand is evidence from the take-up of price subsidies that were offered to small firms under experimental pilot projects. Thorpe et al. (1992) found an elasticity of demand of insurance coverage of between −0.07 and −0.33 for these firms. Gruber and Poterba (1994) suggested a price elasticity of demand for insurance coverage of −1.0 or greater in absolute value for self-employed individuals, focusing on tax changes to identify shifts in the after-tax price of insurance for this group. In light of this variation, we set $\eta = -0.5$ in our baseline case, and we also report analyses using values of −1.0 and −0.2.

The final aspect of the tax caps that we consider is their effect on total reve-

---

21. There are also a number of time-series studies, such as Turner (1987).

22. Examples of other studies that estimate the price elasticity of demand include Taylor and Wilensky (1983), who report an elasticity of −0.2; Woodbury (1983), who reports −1.7 to −3.5; Holmer (1984), who reports −0.16; Sloan and Adamache (1986), who report −0.6; and Woodbury and Hamermesh (1992), who report −2 to −3.

nue collections. We combine FICA, federal income tax, and state income tax revenue in our tabulations. Tax caps affect tax revenues in two ways. First, they collect taxes directly on employer-provided health insurance benefits that are valued at more than the tax cap. In addition, however, if some employees decide to reduce their demand for employer-provided health insurance as a result of the tax cap and its associated increase in the marginal cost of insurance, then their *taxable wages* will rise as their employer-provided health insurance benefits decline. We assume that any reduction in employer-provided insurance will be reflected dollar for dollar in pretax wage payments to workers.

The relative importance of the taxes collected on insurance benefits worth more than the cap and on increased taxable wages depends on the price elasticity of demand for health insurance. The *total* revenue collected as a result of the tax cap is independent of this elasticity, however, and just depends on the total value of employer-provided health benefits above the tax cap in the precap setting, that is, on the sum of $E_0 - C$ across households.

Finally, one important caveat to the results below is that we are using the total insurance expenditures of the HIU to identify the effect of tax caps. For some of the HIUs in our sample, insurance expenditures reflect employer-provided insurance coverage to both spouses. A cap that was imposed on each spouse separately would therefore have smaller effects than those estimated below.[23] For our base case described below, only 16 percent of HIUs (21.5 percent of couples) have multiple insurance policies. Among those couples who face binding tax caps, however, 32 percent have more than one policy (this is 24 percent of our total sample). This calculation overstates the effect of dual policies since, in some families with dual coverage, both spouses may have policies that exceed the cap. The problem of dual policies therefore does not appear to be an important limitation in applying the calculations reported below.

5.4.2   Results on Tax Caps

Table 5.6 presents our basic findings on tax caps for the case with a price elasticity of demand for health insurance equal to -0.5. We consider four tax caps, all denominated in 1994 dollars.[24] Our base case, shown in column (2), follows the caps suggested by CBO (1994a): \$4,000 per year for joint filers, \$1,600 per year for single filers, and \$3,400 per year for heads of household. We then show the effects of (a) doubling these caps (col. [1]), (b) halving these

---

23. If the cap were imposed on insurance spending by tax-filing unit, as it would be if it were implemented through the individual income tax system, then the cap would apply to total family insurance spending. This would create a strong incentive for families to drop duplicative insurance policies and might lead to a larger response in the quantity of insurance demanded as a result of the tax cap.

24. By inflating 1987 expenditures in the NMES by the deflator for personal health care spending, we effectively index the tax caps to the medical cost deflator. If tax caps were indexed to the consumer price index rather than an index of medical care costs, the caps would become more stringent over time if health care inflation continues to outpace overall inflation.

Table 5.6   **Effect of Capping Employer-Provided Health Insurance Deduction Assumptions: 1994 Tax Code, $\eta = -0.5$**

	Level of Tax Caps (1994 $): Joint Filer/Single Filer/Household Head			
	8000/3200/6800	4000/1600/3400	2000/800/1700	0/0/0
	(1)	(2)	(3)	(4)
1. P_{rel}	0.870	0.954	1.044	1.111
	(.155)	(.146)	(.120)	(.060)
2. *Employed workers affected* (%)	0.119	0.509	0.704	0.821
3. *Employed insured affected* (%)	0.144	0.619	0.857	1.000
Changes in insurance demand[a]				
4. Average change in E	−306	−985	−1,267	−1,308
5. Average change in E if a change	−2,123	−1,590	−1,477	−1,361
Tax increase per insured employee[a]				
6. Tax on insurance benefits	30.0	190.5	532.2	1,067.0
7. Tax on higher wages	119.2	374.1	479.9	495.2
8. Total	148.2	564.6	1,012.1	1,562.2
Aggregate Revenue Raised[b]				
9. Tax on insurance benefits	1,690	11,123	31,075	62,303
10. Tax on higher wages	6,762	21,846	28,023	28,915
11. Total	8,652	32,969	59,097	91,218

Notes: Insurance market responses assume a price elasticity of demand −0.5 for employer-provided insurance. The base case value for the relative after-tax price in the first row, for the case with unlimited tax exclusion, is 0.837 (.151) as shown in table 5.4. Revenue effects on wage taxes assume that wages rise by the full amount of any reduction in employer-provided insurance. See text for further details.

[a]In dollars

[b]In million dollars.

caps (col. [3]), and (c) setting the caps to zero, so that all employer-provided health insurance benefits are included in taxable income (col. [4]).

The results show that even tax caps that affect relatively few households can have substantial effects on the average relative after-tax price of employer-provided health insurance. The 8000/3200/6800 cap, which would have been binding for 14.4 percent of employed insured workers in 1987, raises the average value of P_{rel} from 0.837 under the status quo to 0.870. The cap analyzed by the CBO has an even larger effect, with P_{rel} rising to 0.954.[25] This cap would affect over one-half of insured employees. Introducing caps first increases the variance of the relative after-tax price in the population, but as the share of

25. The relative price of insurance can in principle be greater than 1 because of the loading factor on insurance and the subsidization of self-insurance.

households affected by the cap rises and more and more households face $(1 + \lambda)/(1 - \alpha\tau)$ as their relative tax price, the variance declines. In column (4), which corresponds to eliminating the tax subsidy for employer-provided insurance, the variance of after-tax relative prices falls substantially.

Table 5.6 next reports our estimates of the change in the level of employer-provided insurance associated with each set of tax caps (rows 4 and 5). For the base case, for example, we calculate that the average reduction in insurance spending will be $565 per insured employee, or $33 billion. Because tax caps affect only a fraction of those employees with employer-provided health insurance, the decline in insurance levels for those who are affected by the caps is substantially larger than the average decline for all employees.

The entries in column (4) of rows 4 and 5 warrant particular note. Our estimates with a price elasticity of insurance demand of -0.5 suggest that eliminating the tax exemption for employer-provided health insurance would reduce the aggregate value of this insurance by 30.8 percent. This corresponds to an average per capita reduction of $1,308.[26]

Rows 6–8 present information on the revenue effects of changing the tax treatment of employer-provided insurance. We present the total revenue collected per insured employee (row 8) as well as the decomposition of this revenue between the tax on insurance premia above the cap and the tax on higher wages that result from reductions in employer-provided insurance. Rows 9–11 report the aggregate revenue consequences of each of these policies. We report the total increase in federal income tax and payroll tax revenue, as well as the small increase in state income tax revenue.

The entry in row 11 of column (4) shows that we estimate that elimination of the tax exemption for employer-provided insurance would have raised $91.2 billion (1994 dollars). More than two-thirds of this revenue is raised from taxes on the insurance that remains in force after the tax subsidy is removed. This estimate is about one-fifth higher than the estimate presented in CBO (1994b), even though the CBO includes both the revenue collected by taxing employer-provided insurance and the revenue collected from higher wage taxes. The CBO excludes some employer-provided insurance which may not be employment-related and so begins with a smaller annual flow of employer-provided insurance than we do.[27] Our estimates are quite similar to the Joint Committee on Taxation's estimates

---

26. Table 5.6 indicates that the average change in employer-provided insurance for those affected by the elimination of the tax exclusion is larger than the average change for all employed insured. There are 256 NMES respondents who report that they are insured by their employers and who have some out-of-pocket spending on insurance, but who report zero employer contributions for their insurance. The three-quarters of this group for whom out-of-pocket insurance spending is not tax preferred will be unaffected by the repeal of the tax exemption.

27. Another potential difference between our estimates and those of the CBO relates to our estimate of the prereform distribution of insurance spending. We use the actual reported distribution of employer-provided insurance premiums in the NMES, while the CBO made adjustments that lowered the estimated expenditures for high-income (and high tax rate) families. We are grateful to Roberton Williams for suggestions with regard to these disparities.

of the total revenue cost of the tax expenditure for employer-provided insurance.[28]

The revenue estimates for various tax cap proposals provide an indication of how much revenue could be raised by each alternative. Our base case 4000/1600/3400 cap raises roughly one-third as much revenue as the total elimination of the tax exclusion for employer-provided insurance. A much higher tax cap of 8000/3200/6800 only raises $8.6 billion.

It is also quite interesting to consider the implications of alternative plans for insurance expenditures and revenue raising. The base case plan, which affects only 62 percent of insured workers, reduces insurance expenditures by 75 percent as much as removing the tax exclusion altogether. This is because, due to the somewhat skewed distribution of insurance spending, the 38 percent of HIUs that are not affected by the cap do not spend much on insurance. On the other hand, fully removing the tax exclusion raises almost three times as much revenue. Thus, as the tax cap is tightened, there will be smaller marginal gains in terms of reducing "overinsurance," but larger gains in terms of revenues.

The estimates in table 5.6 assume that the price elasticity of demand for health insurance is -0.5. This is not a behavioral parameter that commands a strong empirical consensus, so we also present estimates of the change in insurance demand and the mix of increased revenues for two alternative elasticity estimates: -0.2 and -1.0. Table 5.7 presents these results. With a price elasticity of -1.0, we find that eliminating the tax exclusion for employer-provided insurance results in a decline of $2,609 in the quantity of insurance purchased, which is a 61 percent reduction. With a elasticity of -0.2, not surprisingly, the quantity adjustment is much smaller and corresponds to approximately a 10 percent decline in the value of employer-provided insurance. Whether this entire reduction in employer-provided insurance translates into a greater share of medical care being purchased on an out-of-pocket basis depends on whether individuals replace some employer-provided insurance with directly purchased insurance, an issue that we have not yet explored.

The source of increased revenue, whether taxation of insurance premia or taxation of higher wages, also is sensitive to our assumed elasticity. Using the elasticity of -1.0, more than half of the new revenue generated from eliminating the tax subsidy comes from taxing wages, while with an elasticity of -0.2, almost 90 percent of the revenue comes from the tax on insurance benefits. As we noted earlier, the total revenue collected is not sensitive to our elasticity assumptions, only the decomposition across revenue sources.

We have also explored the sources of increased revenues under our tax cap

---

28. There is one reason to suspect that our results may *underestimate* the change in taxes from tax caps. We calculate the revenue effects of taxing health insurance spending by multiplying changes in taxable income by the taxpayer's current marginal tax rate, ignoring any movements across tax brackets that might result from taxation of employer-provided insurance. Since the tax code is progressive, this should lead our calculations to underestimate the actual revenue gain.

Table 5.7   **Sensitivity of Results on Capping Employer-Provided Health Insurance Deduction to Assumptions about Price Elasticities of Insurance Demand**

	Level of Tax Caps (1994 $): Joint Filer/Single Filer/Household Head			
	8000/3200/6800	4000/1600/3400	2000/800/1700	0/0/0
Elasticity=−1.0				
Changes in insurance demand				
Average change in E	−383	−1,437	−2,318	−2,609
Average change in E if a change	−2,654	−2,320	−2,704	−2,715
Tax increase per insured employee[a]				
Tax on insurance benefits	1.9	26.7	143.3	575.1
Tax on higher wages	146.2	538.0	868.8	987.1
Elasticity=−0.2				
Changes in insurance demand				
Average change in E	−156	−437	−511	−523
Average change in E if a change	−1,083	−706	−596	−544
Tax increase per insured employee[a]				
Tax on insurance benefits	86.6	398.1	819.6	1,364.1
Tax on higher wages	61.5	166.6	193.6	198.1

Notes: Revenue effects on wage taxes assume that wages rise by the full amount of any reduction in employer-provided insurance. See text for further details.
[a]In dollars.

plans. For our base case plan (4000/1600/3400), approximately 56 percent of the revenues raised are federal income tax revenues. Another 33 percent are raised by the social security and Medicare taxes, with the remaining 11 percent being raised by state taxes. The distribution is very similar for alternative tax caps.

One final aspect of taxing employer-provided health insurance that our data can inform concerns the distribution of binding tax caps across income classes. Table 5.8 presents summary statistics on this issue. Each column corresponds to a different set of tax caps, from the previous tables, but now the entries show the fraction of NMES families in a given income category that would be constrained by each cap. For our base case 4000/1600/3400 cap in column (2), for example, the table shows that the cap would bind for 27.1 percent of the families with incomes between $10,000 and $20,000, compared with 67.8 percent of those with incomes between $75,000 and $100,000. The sample sizes for high-income groups in the NMES are relatively small, but the results at least illustrate the general pattern across income classes. All of the tax caps except the highest are binding for the majority of HIUs by approximately $35,000 in family income; removing the tax exclusion entirely binds for the majority of families with more than $10,000 of income.[29]

---

29. One potentially puzzling feature of table 5.8 is the failure to observe "100 percent" for each of the entries in col. (4) of panel B. This disparity arises because there are some NMES respon-

Table 5.8   **Distribution of Binding Tax Caps by Family Income Class**

AGI Class (thousand 1994 $)	Level of Tax Caps (1994 $): Joint Filers/Single Filers/Household Heads			
	8000/3200/6800 (1)	4000/1600/3400 (2)	2000/800/1700 (3)	0/0/0 (4)
	A. *All Persons*			
Under 10	3.4	17.9	26.5	30.3
10–20	5.9	27.1	43.7	50.9
20–30	10.4	47.6	68.9	75.8
30–40	10.3	53.4	75.9	86.1
40–50	13.0	59.9	82.8	92.9
50–75	14.2	63.0	84.9	94.2
75–100	19.9	67.8	86.1	94.1
Over 100	19.0	66.4	85.5	95.3
Total	11.8	51.1	70.6	78.8
	B. *Insured Persons Only*			
Under 10	9.9	53.2	78.6	89.9
10–20	10.9	50.0	80.5	93.9
20–30	13.0	59.0	85.4	94.0
30–40	11.5	59.8	84.9	96.4
40–50	13.6	63.1	87.1	97.6
50–75	14.6	64.6	87.1	96.7
75–100	20.6	70.3	89.2	97.5
Over 100	19.3	67.5	86.9	96.9
Total	14.4	62.2	85.9	96.0

Source: Authors' calculations using 1987 NMES data. Each entry shows the percentage of employed individuals who would be affected by tax caps of the magnitudes indicated. Results in col. (4) of panel B are not equal to 100.0 because there are 181 NMES respondents reporting employer-provided insurance but no spending ($E = G = 0$).

The rising incidence of binding caps at higher income levels reflects both the rising probability of having employer-provided insurance at higher income levels and the rising value of average premiums conditional on such insurance. In order to separate these factors, panel B of table 5.8 repeats these calculations for those with insurance. Here we can see that all except the most generous tax caps bind for the majority of insured persons at any income level, and the gradient with respect to income is much less steep.

5.5 Conclusion

Our analysis emphasizes two aspects of the current tax subsidy to employer-provided health insurance and presents new evidence on the economic effects

---

dents who have employer-provided health insurance, but who report zero employer expenditure (E). They do report positive out-of-pocket spending (G) on insurance, but given our assumption that only one-quarter of households with such expenditures make them on a pretax basis, even a zero tax cap does not bind for 75 percent of these households.

of various tax reforms. The conceptual points we emphasize suggest that the current federal tax code subsidizes employer-provided insurance less than many previous analyses would suggest. This is because a substantial and growing share of employees who receive employer-provided insurance must pay for part of this insurance with their own after-tax dollars, and because the tax code also provides a deduction for extreme medical expenses, thereby to some degree discouraging individuals from purchasing health insurance. Our empirical analysis of the effect of capping the value of employer-provided health insurance that could be excluded from taxation, or eliminating the exclusion entirely, suggests that these reforms could have substantial effects on the level of employer-provided insurance.

There are a number of important issues associated with both the determinants of the level of employer-provided insurance and the effect of tax reforms on this insurance that we have not addressed. One issue is the role of joint decision making in workplace benefits. We have not considered how to aggregate the heterogeneous changes in tax incentives for employer-provided insurance that would accompany many tax cap plans into decision rules for firms. We have also stopped short of asking whether changes in tax incentives would lead to different combinations of workers into firms or health insurance units. If tax reform led to greater heterogeneity in worker tastes for employer-provided health insurance, employers might respond by offering larger menus of insurance policies. This could be important for revenue estimation and could also have welfare implications.

A second important issue concerns general equilibrium effects in the health insurance markets. If a substantial number of currently insured workers decide not to purchase insurance under some of the tax reforms we consider, it is possible that the load factor facing those who remain in the insured pool may change. This could affect the demand for health insurance even by those who do not face tax caps.

A third issue is modeling the appropriate demand response to changes in the tax price of insurance. We have assumed a constant elasticity demand function and applied this elasticity equally to "looser" and "tighter" caps. In fact, individuals may be quite elastic with respect to insurance coverage on the margin, but less elastic when it comes to dropping their insurance entirely. Extending this analysis to consider a richer range of responses to different tax caps is an important step for future research.

Finally, this paper represents a strictly positive exercise. We have not considered any of the interesting normative issues surrounding the tax treatment of health insurance. One important argument for subsidizing workplace insurance is that workplace pooling, which is largely exogenous to underlying health, avoids the classic adverse selection problems in individual insurance markets. Rothschild and Stiglitz (1976) discuss the theoretical possibility that private insurance markets may fail, but there is little empirical evidence on the extent of such failures and their welfare consequences. Such an argument would imply welfare losses if the removal of this tax subsidy led to the breakup of workplace pools. What is not clear, however, is the extent to which the tax subsidy, as opposed to other gains from pooling, is responsible for holding workplace pools together. If they can be measured, these pooling gains must be weighed against the distortions from excess consumption of medical care in deciding on the optimal level of tax subsidies.

More generally, the question of whether private insurance purchases should be subsidized depends on a host of unresolved issues, such as the degree to which uninsured individuals consume uncompensated care, how the costs of such care are shifted to paying health care consumers, the role of health insurance in affecting labor market behavior, and the other positive and negative externalities that a more-insured population may provide. All of these issues require further investigation.

References

Blostin, Allan P., Robert B. Grant, and William J. Wiatrowski. 1992. Employee payments for health care services. *Monthly Labor Review* 117 (November): 17–32.

Bradford, David F., and the U.S. Treasury Tax Policy Staff. 1984. *Blueprints for basic tax reform,* 2d ed. Arlington, Va.: Tax Analysts.

Burman, Leonard E., and Roberton Williams. 1994. Tax caps on employment-based health insurance. *National Tax Journal* 47 (September): 529–45.

Feldstein, Martin S. 1973. The welfare loss of excess health insurance. *Journal of Political Economy* 81 (March–April): 251–80.

Feldstein, Martin S., and Elisabeth Allison. 1974. Tax subsidies of private health insurance: Distribution, revenue loss, and effects. In *The economics of federal subsidy programs,* U.S. Congress, Joint Economic Committee, 977–94. Washington, D.C.: Government Printing Office.

Feldstein, Martin S., and Andrew Samwick. 1992a. Social security rules and marginal tax rates. *National Tax Journal* 45:1–22.

———. 1992b. Social security rules and marginal tax rates. NBER Working Paper no. 3962. Cambridge, Mass.: National Bureau of Economic Research.

Gruber, Jonathan. 1994. The incidence of mandated maternity benefits. *American Economic Review* 84 (June): 622–41.

Gruber, Jonathan, and Alan B. Krueger. 1991. The incidence of mandated employer-provided insurance: Lessons from workers' compensation insurance. In *Tax policy and the economy,* vol. 6, ed. David Bradford, 111–44. Cambridge: MIT Press.

Gruber, Jonathan, and James M. Poterba. 1994. Tax incentives and the demand for health insurance: Evidence from the self-employed. *Quarterly Journal of Economics* 109 (August): 701–33.

Hausman, Jerry A., and James M. Poterba. 1987. Household behavior and the Tax Reform Act of 1986. *Journal of Economic Perspectives* 1:101–19.

Holmer, Martin. 1984. Tax policy and the demand for health insurance. *Journal of Health Economics* 3:203–21.

Kaplow, Louis. 1991. The income tax as insurance: The casualty loss and medical expense loss deductions and the exclusion of medical insurance premiums. *California Law Review* 79 (December): 1485–1510.

————. 1992. Income tax deductions for losses as insurance. *American Economic Review* 82 (September): 1013–17.

Lindsey, Lawrence. 1987. Individual taxpayer responses to tax cuts, 1982–1984: With implications for the revenue-maximizing tax rate. *Journal of Public Economics* 33:173–206.

Long, James E., and Frank A. Scott. 1982. The income tax and nonwage compensation. *Review of Economics and Statistics* 64:211–19.

Marquis, M. Susan, and Charles E. Phelps. 1987. Price elasticity and adverse selection in the demand for supplementary health insurance. *Economic Inquiry* 25:299–313.

Newhouse, Joseph P., et al. 1989. Adjusting capitation rates using objective health measures and prior utilization. *Health Care Financing Review* 10 (Spring): 41–54.

Pauly, Mark. 1986. Taxation, health insurance, and market failure in the medical economy. *Journal of Economic Literature* 24:629–75.

Phelps, Charles E. 1992. *Health economics.* New York: Harper Collins.

Rothschild, Michael, and Joseph Stiglitz. 1976. Equilibrium in competitive insurance markets: An essay on the economics of imperfect information. *Quarterly Journal of Economics* 90:629–49.

Scofea, Laura A. 1994. The development and growth of employer-provided health insurance. *Monthly Labor Review* 117 (March): 3–10.

Sloan, Frank, and Killard Adamache. 1986. Taxation and the growth of nonwage benefits. *Public Finance Quarterly* 14:115–39.

Taylor, Amy, and Gail Wilensky. 1983. The effect of tax policies on expenditures for private health insurance. In *Market reforms in health care: Current issues, new directions, strategic decisions,* ed. Jack Meyer. Washington, D.C.: American Enterprise Institute.

Thorpe, Kenneth L., et al. 1992. Reducing the number of uninsured by subsidizing employment-based health insurance: Results from a pilot study. *Journal of the American Medical Association* 267:945–48.

Turner, Robert. 1987. Are taxes responsible for the growth of fringe benefits? *National Tax Journal* 40:205–20.

U.S. Bureau of Labor Statistics. 1993. *Employee benefits in medium and large private establishments, 1991.* Bulletin no. 2422. Washington, D.C.: U.S. Department of Labor.

————. 1994. *Employee benefits in small private establishments, 1991.* Bulletin no. 2441. Washington, D.C.: U.S. Department of Labor.

U.S. Congressional Budget Office (CBO). 1993. *Projections of national health expenditures, 1993 update.* Washington, D.C.: U.S. Congress, Congressional Budget Office.

————. 1994a. *Reducing the deficit: Spending and revenue options.* Washington, D.C.: U.S. Congress, Congressional Budget Office.

————. 1994b. *The tax treatment of employment-based health insurance.* Washington, D.C.: U.S. Congress, Congressional Budget Office.

Woodbury, Stephen A. 1983. Substitution between wage and nonwage benefits. *American Economic Review* 73:166–82.

Woodbury, Stephen A., and Daniel S. Hamermesh. 1992. Taxes, fringe benefits, and faculty. *Review of Economics and Statistics* 73:287–96.

Comment   David F. Bradford

This paper presents measurements of the incentive effected by tax rules for employers to provide health insurance benefits to their employees. The problem poses conceptual and empirical challenges. The bulk of the work of the paper describes the methods by which the authors tease quantitative estimates of average subsidy rates out of, mainly, two disparate data sources (the National Medical Expenditure Survey and the U.S. Treasury Individual Tax Model file). But I propose to focus my comments on the conceptual side of the story.

I hope that my taking up conceptual issues is not taken to imply a lack of appreciation for the ingenuity and perseverance that the authors have devoted to the quantitative estimates. It is an extraordinary job, taking into account a great many fine points of the data sets and institutional setting.

The principal conceptual issues I would raise relate to the interpretation of the empirical work. The authors describe their analysis as limited to the question of the determination of how the tax system influences the division between employer-provided payments and out-of-pocket outlays by the employee in financing a *given* package of health care services. The distinction is made between this problem and that of determining the impact of the tax system on the level of health care services demanded. It is taken for granted that, from the perspective of the employee, the payments by the employer take the form of insurance, whereas the own out-of-pocket payments constitute the lack of insurance coverage that we describe as self-insurance.

The critical distinction drawn in this paper, then, is not between subsidized health care and unsubsidized health care, but between health care covered by insurance and that not covered by insurance. Although a richer set of variations is recognized in the analysis of policy experiments, the basic analysis seems to treat "covered by insurance" as a zero-one variable. Either one is covered by an employer-sponsored plan or one is self-insured.

Presumably, the reason for being interested in this distinction is the *moral hazard* associated with insurance: Put simply, a person covered by insurance has insufficient incentive to economize on health care services. Moral hazard is of particular importance in the case of health care coverage because the insured-against event has a large subjective element. One can usefully think of moral hazard as arising under health insurance at two points: First, if I am insured, my incentive is reduced to preserve my health by, for example, eating well and exercising regularly. Second, as typically structured (and it, perhaps, need not be so), health insurance alters my incentive to economize on the services deployed to deal with health problems that arise. Having concluded that I am sick, I have the option of a large range of treatments, ranging from letting

David F. Bradford is professor of economics and public affairs at the Woodrow Wilson School at Princeton University.

nature take its course to consulting a world-famous specialist. Insurance reduces, perhaps to zero, the marginal cost of choosing relatively expensive methods of dealing with any given health problem. I would guess that the second sort of moral hazard is the far more serious problem quantitatively.

If, in addition to subsidizing expenditures on health care, the tax system induces people to be covered by insurance, there is an "extra moral hazard" cost imposed on top of the usual deadweight loss. The authors discuss this overinsurance effect in connection with their simulation of the impact of various caps on employer-provided health care allowed to be excluded from the employee's taxable income.

I find myself in some doubt about the adequacy of the implicit model of insurance market equilibrium employed in the paper. (I use the term "some doubt" advisedly, given the complexity of the market and the needed analysis.)

First, as to the effect of a subsidy on the terms of insurance. Private insurance contracts may involve any of a variety of methods of internalizing the moral hazard problem. Classic approaches are to specify a deductible amount (so as to eliminate the moral hazard in the choice of service level in situations in which the loss to the insured is relatively small) and co-insurance rate (so that the extra cost to the insured of choosing expensive treatment is raised above zero). Other methods include monitoring and regulation by the insurance company, to reward my choice of a healthy life-style, to limit my freedom to identify myself as sick, and to restrict my choice of treatments according to some criterion of medical necessity.

Economic theory predicts that such devices to moderate moral hazard will be equilibrium phenomena. That is, they will be chosen by mutual agreement between insured and insurer. The insured will accept the various limits on coverage in return for the saving on the cost of the insurance. The saving will be greater than the expected cost of "necessary" treatment that will be borne by the insured, because the insured will have an incentive (or be obliged by the monitoring regime) to limit treatment to what really is necessary (as distinct from what would be chosen if there were no limit or cost to the insured).

A second classic problem of insurance is *adverse selection.* The possibility of adverse selection is due to asymmetric information, whereby I know I am at high risk of incurring health care expenses, but the insurance company cannot observe this fact. If insurance is priced to break even with average risks, I will tend to choose relatively extensive insurance coverage. The insurance company will then lose money. Adverse selection problems can also arise as a result of regulatory requirements that limit the ability of insurance companies to vary the premium charged according to the health characteristics of the insured. Adverse selection seems a likely explanation for the often-noted high loading and limited availability of individual health insurance policies.

The devices to deal with adverse selection include physical exams, limits on preexisting coverage, and similar techniques to break into the information advantage of potential insureds. These measures can be costly. An important technique that economizes on such underwriting procedures is to bundle the offering of insurance with some other choice that is likely to dominate the insurance in importance. The choice of employment is a prime example. (The point is recognized by the authors.) The fact that a particular employer offers a particular health insurance plan is not very likely to play a large role in the determination of who will become an employee. To the extent this is true, employers can offer health insurance on terms that may be better than those obtainable by employees in a private, individual insurance market. Other features of the terms of employment may also present opportunities to mitigate adverse selection. For example, good health benefits may attract high health risks, but putting a substantial part of the compensation in the form of retirement annuities will deter those who do not expect to live long.[1]

Thus, economic theory gives us grounds to expect that employer-based health insurance would be observed in unregulated equilibrium, even without any tax incentives. If I approach this analysis with the expectation that (1) most people are going to prefer some insurance coverage to self-insurance and (2) employer-based plans are very likely to be common even in the absence of a subsidy, it seems to me that I am led to a different interpretation of the results.

To isolate the point (and I cannot hope to settle it), imagine that employer-based insurance (or something economically equivalent) is exactly what we would predict in the absence of a tax subsidy. Then the subsidy rates developed by the authors are, as a first approximation, those that apply to the purchase of health care, and only secondarily to the characteristics of the insurance contract involved.

To make this point clearer, I have played devil's advocate with my tax lawyer colleagues, asking whether I could write a contract with my employer with the following terms: I will take my pay in the form of health care services to be purchased by my employer as needed, as determined by me, subject to the IRS rules about what constitutes health care. If (as I hope and expect) the employer's outlays fall short of a specific level (my current salary) the employer will make up the difference in cash. The income tax law makes explicit provision for the exclusion from the employee's taxable income of health care services supplied by the employer. *If* the plan I described to my lawyer friends were feasible from the standpoint of the tax law, it would leave me in the position of obtaining the full advantage of the exclusion of health care benefits from tax, but without any insurance beyond the implicit insurance provided by the tax rate. (Even that might be eliminated if we worked out that the cash settlement varied by *more* than the employer's outlays.) But you would not be able to observe this fact from data on employee health care outlays.

There are two problems. First, my lawyers have pretty well convinced me that my plan would not work. Second, who would want such a plan? There

---

1. Sherry Glied, who pointed this out to me, suggests that the empirical magnitudes make this a plausible balance.

may, however, be schemes as yet undiscovered that would move a good distance in the direction I described (such as a commitment to experience rating of my coverage) and that would pass legal muster. This question deserves investigation, with due cognizance of the second point: The choice is not between no insurance and full insurance. The question is how much, if any, excess moral hazard is induced by the tax law. My suspicion is, a lot, but I think the exploration of this question requires a closer modeling of the specifics of the insurance plans than has yet been addressed by the authors.

There is a second point at which I think the analysis would benefit from greater attention to the characteristics of equilibrium insurance contracts. It is assumed in the paper (and by most analysis of this issue) that one could administer a cap on employer-provided health insurance, with insurance in excess of the cap to be taxed as wages to the employee. Insurance market considerations suggest two possibilities that may merit closer analysis: First, to the extent that the employer-provided insurance is similar in anti-moral-hazard characteristics to what would be predicted in the absence of tax subsidy, we would expect the *insurance* equilibrium to be, not the locus of adjustment to the change in the rules, but rather the amount of health care services purchased. Second, since the implicit insurance policy provided to an employee depends greatly on the characteristics of the employee (coverage of an older person, e.g., is predictably much more costly than coverage of a younger person), and on the pool of employees in a plan (those in a firm with many old people, or many sick people, will face a higher average premium), it seems to me seriously doubtful that simple caps, taking no account of such differences in characteristics (let alone preferences), would constitute viable tools in practice.

6   High-Income Families and the Tax Changes of the 1980s: The Anatomy of Behavioral Response

Joel Slemrod

6.1 Introduction

It is indisputable that many high-income individuals took notice of, and responded to, certain aspects of the tax changes enacted in the 1980s. Indeed, some of the behavioral responses are now the stuff of legend, such as the 96.3 percent increase in capital gains realizations in 1986 compared to 1985, in anticipation of the tax increase on gains scheduled for 1987.

Another striking bit of evidence is the enormous increase in the real income levels of high-income families during the 1980s, both in absolute terms and relative to the real income increases of everyone else. Between 1978 and 1990 the real increase in the reported income of the top 1 percent of tax returns, ranked by income, was 91.6 percent; the real increase for everyone else was 18.9 percent. Over this period, the shares of total income received by the top 1 percent of tax returns rose from 8.8 to 13.4 percent.

In contrast to the capital gains episode, there is much controversy over the causal connection between the increased incomes of high-income families and the tax changes of the 1980s. There is a large literature ascribing the increased income inequality during the decade to technological change, particularly computerization, that increased the relative productivity of skilled labor, and a related literature associating the inequality to increased globalization of the U.S. economy. Even in the absence of any behavioral response at all, the in-

Joel Slemrod is professor of business economics and public policy and professor of economics at the University of Michigan and a research associate of the National Bureau of Economic Research.

The author is grateful for able research assistance provided by Jon Bakija, Victoria Kilgore, and Hisahiro Naito, and for helpful comments on an earlier draft from James Alm, Don Fullerton, James Poterba, and other conference participants.

creasing return to highly skilled occupations would cause increasing absolute and relative incomes of the well-to-do.

One of the objectives of this paper is to separate out the nontax and tax explanations of the increased income dispersion. I investigate this issue in section 6.3 of the paper, where I report the results of some aggregate time-series regression analysis. I conclude that, although the nontax demand factors can explain much of the increased concentration of income up to 1985, they are unlikely to be the cause of the spike in concentration of reported incomes that began in 1986.

The second objective of the paper is to characterize what behavioral response did occur by whether it was timing or likely to be permanent, and in particular whether it reflected income creation or income shifting. This characterization has important implications for the revenue, incidence, and efficiency of tax changes, and for the generalizability of the behavioral response of the tax changes of 1980s to future tax changes. This task is attempted in section 6.4.

Before I get to these tasks, I first review, in section 6.2, the existing literature on these issues.

6.2   A Critical Review of Existing Literature

The details of the two major tax bills of the 1980s have been carefully laid out elsewhere (see Steuerle 1992) and need not be repeated here. In brief, the Economic Recovery Tax Act of 1981 (ERTA) lowered the top individual income tax rate from 70 to 50 percent and lowered all other tax rates in three annual steps by a total of about 23 percent (not 23 percentage points). The reduction in the top rate overstates somewhat the decline in the effective marginal tax rate on labor income because since 1970 the maximum tax on earned income had limited the marginal tax rate nominally to 50 percent and effectively to no more than a number in the mid-50s for nearly all high-income workers.

The Tax Reform Act of 1986 (TRA86) contained scores of provisions and cannot be adequately summarized in a sentence or two. Of direct concern to this paper is the reduction of the top rate of individual income tax from 50 to 28 percent, in two steps from 1986 to 1988. The exclusion of 60 percent of long-term capital gains was eliminated, so that the top effective rate on gains increased from 20 percent (40 percent of 50 percent) to 28 percent (100 percent of 28 percent). The basic corporate tax rate was lowered from 46 to 34 percent.

There have been innumerable studies of the impact of the federal tax changes enacted since 1981. In what follows I attempt only a selective review of some of the research which focused on the response of high-income taxpayers. Lindsey (1987) was among the first to point out that the 1981 cut in the top tax rate from 70 to 50 percent coincided with a very large increase in the share of income reported by the top 1 percent of the income distribution to the Internal Revenue Service (IRS). He argued that the tax cut was a principal cause of this income increase, as it reduced the penalty for earning (to be precise, reporting) taxable income.

Lindsey's methodology did not enable him to distinguish his tax causality hypothesis from an obvious alternative—that, for nontax reasons, pretax income inequality was growing rapidly between his two years of data, 1981 and 1985. To be fair, this alternative hypothesis is more apparent in 1995 than it was at the time that Lindsey was writing. In the past decade there has arisen a voluminous literature documenting an increase in inequality in the United States, much of it summarized in Levy and Murnane (1992). As Karoly (1994) documents, data from the Census Bureau revealed that inequality among families, after reaching a postwar low in 1967–68, began to increase during the 1970s and continued to rise through the 1980s. Although the trend toward greater inequality began in the late 1960s, about two-thirds of the absolute increase in the Gini coefficient between 1968 and 1989 occurred between 1980 and 1989. Although these basic facts are now widely acknowledged, the origin of the increase in inequality remains highly controversial. The two leading explanations, which are not mutually exclusive, are (1) technological change that increased the relative return to skilled labor and (2) increased globalization of the U.S. economy, which increased the effective relative supply of unskilled labor and thereby lowered its relative return.

That inequality began to increase in 1970 does not rule out the tax causality hypothesis. As Feenberg and Poterba (1993) and Slemrod (1994b) point out, the top individual marginal tax rate has been monotonically declining since 1962. Moreover, the approximate starting time of the increase in inequality, 1970, coincides with the introduction of the maximum tax on earned income, which reduced the marginal tax rate on labor income to 50 percent (or slightly more), even though the top marginal tax rate on other income stayed at 70 percent until 1981. Thus, there is an a priori case to be made that the tax causality hypothesis applies much more generally than the period Lindsey analyzes—at least since 1970.

At this point a caveat is in order about the data commonly used to measure income inequality. The Current Population Survey (CPS) data analyzed by Karoly and others features top-coding of income amounts at a constant (although occasionally increased) nominal level. For this reason it cannot measure reliably changes in, for example, the share of income earned by the top 1 percent of the distribution. Standard summary measures of income distributions, in addition to the Gini coefficient, are the income at the 10th, 25th, 50th, 75th, 90th, and 95th percentiles, but none higher than the 95th percentile.

Thus, any conclusion about, say, the share of income earned by the top 1 percent of the population must come from some other data source other than the CPS or, because it suffers from the same sort of problem, the Panel Study of Income Dynamics. Tax researchers have made use of the public-use files of tax return data released by the Statistics of Income (SOI) Division of the IRS.

There is no top-coding problem with this data; in fact, high-income individuals are oversampled in order to produce a very precise picture of their tax returns. The tax return data, though, have their own strengths and weaknesses. They contain virtually no demographic information—marital status, state of residence, and whether the taxpayer or spouse is over age 65 being notable exceptions—and no information on labor supply or labor market status more generally. These data also exclude those households whose income is below the threshold for filing an income tax return.

Summary measures of income inequality based on the tax data show the same patterns as more commonly used data—continually increasing inequality since 1972 of all income, and also of wages and salaries by themselves. Feenberg and Poterba (1993) have recently used tax return data to calculate a time series of inequality measures that focuses on high-income households. Using interpolations of published SOI aggregated data, they calculate the share of adjusted gross income (AGI) and several components of AGI that were received by the top 0.5 percent of households arranged by income. Their plot of the high-income share of AGI is reproduced in the bold line in figure 6.1. After being approximately flat at about 6.0 percent from 1970 to 1981, it begins in 1982 to increase continuously to 7.7 percent in 1985, and then jumps sharply in 1986 to 9.2 percent. There is a slight increase in 1987 to 9.5 percent, then another sharp increase in 1988 to 12.1 percent. After 1988 there is a decline to 11.2 percent in 1989 and 10.9 percent in 1990.

Feenberg and Poterba also report that, among the top income earners, the largest increase in share is attributed to the top 0.2 percent. This fact, they assert, "casts doubt on the view that the factors responsible for the increase in reported incomes among high-income taxpayers, especially in the 1986–1988 period, are the same factors that were responsible for the widening of the wage distribution over a longer time period" (1993, 161). Rather, they argue, "it reflect[s] other factors including a tax-induced change in the incentives that high-income households face for *reporting* taxable income" (170, emphasis added). They add that with their data "it is impossible to determine how much of the increase in reported income was due to changes in tax avoidance behavior; how much was due to changes in real behavior such as labor supply; and how much was due to changing returns to the factors, labor and capital, that high-income taxpayers own" (163).

The Feenberg-Poterba calculations refer to the share of AGI received by the rich, despite the fact that the definition of AGI changed during this period.[1] A change in the definition of AGI has two distinct effects on a share measure of income concentration. These two distinct effects are nicely illustrated using the most important set of changes in AGI definition over the period in question—those pertaining to long-term capital gains. From 1970 to 1978 half of realized long-term capital gains were included in AGI. The Tax Reform Act of

---

1. This is noted in footnote 5 of Feenberg and Poterba (1993).

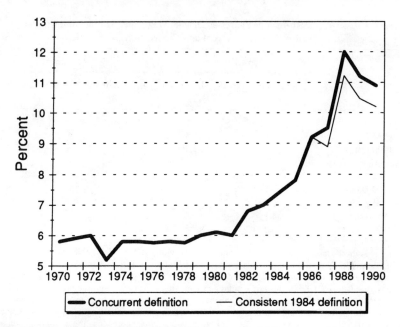

Fig. 6.1   Share of AGI received by top 0.5 percent of taxpayers, adjusted for consistency with 1984 definition of AGI
Sources: Feenberg and Poterba (1993) and author's calculations based on 1990 Individual Tax Model file from the SOI Division of the IRS.

1978 lowered the fraction included in AGI to 40 percent for gains realized after October 31, 1978. TRA86 eliminated the exclusion altogether, so that for gains realized as of January 1, 1987, all of realized long-term gains were included in AGI.

Consider the change in AGI definition made as of 1987. As long as income is measured by AGI, including 100 rather than 40 percent of capital gains in AGI increases the apparent concentration of income because capital gains are heavily concentrated among high-income households. It also changes the ranking of taxpayers, pushing toward the top of the income distribution those households whose income consists of a relatively high share of capital gains. This reranking makes the apparent share of capital gains received by high-income households increase and the share of other sources of income increase or decline depending on the cross-sectional correlation of that source with capital gains.

In order to investigate the empirical importance of these effects, I first recalculate the top income shares of AGI, wages and salaries, and capital gains in 1984 and 1990, using in each case both the 1984 and 1990 definitions of AGI. These results are shown in table 6.1, calculated separately for the top 1 percent of households ranked by AGI and (approximately) the top 0.5 percent, the Feenberg-Poterba cutoff. Consider, as an example, the AGI figures in columns

Table 6.1   **High-Income Shares of Income, Wages and Salaries, and Capital Gains Using Concurrent and Consistent AGI Definitions**

	Top 1 Percent		Top 0.5 Percent	
	1984 Definition (1)	1990 Definition (2)	1984 Definition (3)	1990 Definition (4)
AGI				
1984 Data	9.9	11.5	7.4	8.9
1990 Data	13.4	14.2	10.1	10.8
Wages and salaries				
1984 Data	6.5	6.2	4.5	4.2
1990 Data	8.7	8.6	6.1	6.0
Capital gains				
1984 Data	58.1	65.6	52.2	58.4
1990 Data	56.2	62.7	49.1	54.8

Source: Author's tabulations using 1984 and 1990 Individual Tax Model data from the SOI Division of the IRS. Not all the relevant changes in the definition of AGI were, or could be, accounted for. In converting 1984 data to the 1990 definition, the following items were accounted for: dividends exclusion, excluded long-term capital gains, moving expenses, employee business expenses, and the two-earner deduction in unemployment benefits included in AGI and gross unemployment benefits. In converting the 1990 data to the 1984 definition, the following were accounted for: capital gains, dividend exclusion under 1984 law, unemployment compensation, self-employment tax deduction, self-employed health insurance deduction, unreimbursed employee business expense deduction, and moving expense deduction.

(3) and (4). They show that the share of AGI received by the top 0.5 percent of income earners increased from 7.4 percent in 1984 to 10.8 percent in 1990, using concurrent definitions of income. But a significant fraction of that 3.4 percent increase is an artifact of changing AGI definitions. When one uses a consistent 1990 definition of income to compare concentration, the 3.4 percent increase becomes a 1.9 percent increase; when one uses a consistent 1984 definition, the 3.4 percent increase falls to 2.7 percent.

It is also insightful to compare measures of capital gains concentration using concurrent and consistent definitions of income, as is also done in table 6.1. Consider the numbers based on the top 0.5 percent of income earners. Using a concurrent definition of income, one would conclude that the concentration of capital gains increased by 2.6 percent, from 52.2 to 54.8 percent. In contrast, using a consistent definition reveals that the concentration actually declined over this period by either 3.1 or 3.6 percent, depending on which consistent definition of income is used.

Aggregate time-series data on shares should, for more accurate comparability, be evaluated with a consistent definition. As a first step toward that task, figures 6.1 and 6.2 present the Feenberg-Poterba time series on AGI and capital gains, from 1970 to 1990, and how the post-1986 figures would be adjusted to reflect the definition of income from 1978 to 1986; the adjustments in 1987, 1988, and 1989 are assumed to be proportionately the same as in 1990.

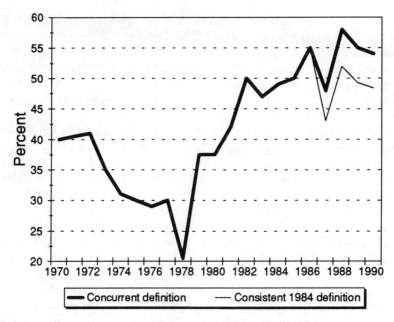

Fig. 6.2   Share of capital gains received by top 0.5 percent of taxpayers, adjusted for consistency with 1984 definition of AGI

Sources: Feenberg and Poterba (1993) and author's calculations based on 1990 Individual Tax Model file from the SOI Division of the IRS.

Adjusting the data in this way does not change the impression that the measured concentration of AGI increased sharply between 1981 and 1990; the magnitude of the increase is, though, smaller than what one would estimate using concurrent income definitions. Using consistent income definitions also clarifies the temporary upward blip of the concentration of capital gains in 1986, due to extraordinary capital gains realizations in anticipation of the tax increase scheduled for 1987. With a consistent definition, the 1986 blip becomes much more apparent, and the post-1986 era is characterized by a concentration that is no higher than the 1982–85 period.

I have argued for the importance of using consistent income definitions when doing cross-year comparisons of the distribution of income and income components. However, even when consistent income definitions are employed, there are important conceptual problems with comparing cross-sectional slices of income distributions because one is comparing different groups of households across years.

The potential problem due to rank reversals can be illustrated by an extreme example. Imagine that all of these taxpayers in the top 1 percent of the income distribution in 1990 were below the 1 percent cutoff in 1984, with marginal tax rates below 28 percent, and furthermore, as follows from the above, that all of the households in the top 1 percent in 1984, who had tax rates of 50 percent, were below the top 1 percent cutoff in 1990, with tax rates of 28 percent or lower. In this case it would certainly not be valid to conclude, from observing that the top 1 percent in 1990 received a larger share of total income than did the top 1 percent in 1984, that the reduction in the top tax rate "caused taxpayers to report more income." In this hypothetical example those households that experienced the largest increase in income had an increase in their tax rate.

There is, in fact, considerable year-to-year movement within the top income class. Slemrod (1992) reports that in the 1980s, between 28 and 40 percent of the households in the top 1 percent were new from one year to the next. Another reason to be wary of comparing cross sections of high-income households is that, in a critical dimension, this group is bimodal. In particular, as Slemrod (1994b) discusses, the distribution of the ratio of wages and salaries to total income is bimodal, with local maxima at 0–10 and 90–100 percent and a minimum at 50–60 percent. This reflects the fact that the affluent consist of both retired households, whose income is almost entirely the returns from their accumulated wealth, and well-compensated people in their working years.

There is some intriguing evidence that the set of high-income taxpayers in 1990 in fact has a very different demographic makeup than the set in 1984. According to tax return data, the fraction of tax-paying units containing at least one person aged 65 or over fell dramatically over this period, from 22.4 to 14.1 percent for the top 0.5 percent of the population, and from 20.5 to 13.4 percent for the top 1 percent; over the same period for all taxpayers the fraction rose only very slightly, from 12.0 to 12.1 percent.[2] The same demographic pattern is observed in comparing the 1983 and 1989 data from the Survey of Consumer Finances. Apparently in the highest income group the retired, coupon-clipping rentiers were to a large extent displaced by high-earning people between 1984 and 1990. Thus, the reasons to be cautious about comparing cross-sectional slices are not only hypothetical but quantitatively significant.

The potential hazards of inferring behavioral response from comparing the behavior of two distinct groups of taxpayers can be mitigated by analyzing longitudinal, or panel, data on an unchanging set of taxpayers. This has been done in the work of Feldstein (1993) and Auten and Carroll (1994).

Feldstein (1993) investigates the high-income response to TRA86 by making use of the Ernst & Young/University of Michigan tax return panel data. This panel, based on SOI tax return data, follows the same set of taxpayers from 1979 to 1988. Feldstein analyzed married couples for whom both 1985 and 1988 tax returns were available. After making several adjustments to the data, he concludes that the 1985–88 percentage increase in various measures of income, particularly taxable income excluding capital gains, was much higher, compared to the rest of the population, for those high-income groups whose marginal tax rate was reduced the most. Based on this finding, he estimates that the elasticity of taxable income with respect to the marginal tax rate is

2. The ranking of households is based on a 1984 definition of AGI.

very high and suggests that an increase in the top marginal tax rate will raise little, if any, revenue.

A few caveats must be attached to this finding. First, because the panel data is not stratified, it contains only a very small number of high-income observations. For example, the top income class on which Feldstein focuses most of his attention (nonelderly couples in the 49–50 percent tax brackets in 1985) contains only 57 observations. Because of the wide variation among this group in financial situation and in income changes over time, generalizing from such a small sample is problematic.

This difficulty is illustrated by taking a closer look at the exercise reported in Feldstein. The most striking result is a 71.6 percent increase in the taxable income of those in the top income class between 1985 and 1988, after subtracting out capital gains and indexing for per capita personal income growth. Of the total increase in this measure of income, nearly three-quarters was accounted for by an increase in two sources of income which are reported on schedule E—partnerships and S-corporations. One taxpayer, whose S-corporation income increased from about $5,000 in 1985 to over $3 million by 1988, was responsible for 47.5 percent of this growth in net partnership and S-corporation income. Just four taxpayers accounted for 87.0 percent of the increase. As the analysis of stratified cross-sectional data in section 6.4 will make clear, changes in S-corporation and partnership income were in fact probably an important part of the income gains of the affluent, although they did not dominate to the extent that this panel data, dominated by a single observation, would suggest.

The importance of S-corporation and partnership income in Feldstein's results also suggests caution regarding the interpretation that lower marginal tax rates induced the rich to engage in more real-income-producing activities. The tremendous growth in S-corporation income may simply represent a shift from C to S status among corporations, rather than the creation of new income that would not otherwise have been taxed.[3] Moreover, as Feldstein notes, some of the large reduction in partnership losses was probably due to new passive loss limitation rules rather than the reduction in rates. Other non-marginal-rate fac-

3. As discussed in detail later, TRA86 reduced the top individual tax rate below the top corporate rate, repealed the "General Utilities doctrine" (which increased the tax burden on sales of C-corporation assets), and instituted a tough alternative minimum tax for C-corporations. This made S-corporations (which face only the individual income tax) more attractive than C-corporations (which face the corporate profits tax) for many small business owners. Thus, a large increase in S-corporation income after 1986 probably represents a shifting of taxable income from the corporate to individual tax systems, rather than growth of companies that already held S status before 1986. Feldstein attempted to avoid this problem by excluding from his sample all taxpayers who reported S-corporation income in 1988 but *not* in 1985. However, the one taxpayer remaining in the sample who accounted for almost all of the growth in S-corporation income had only a nominal amount of S-corporation income in 1985 and over $3 million in 1988. Although this may represent an incredible success story for a small S-corporation of which the taxpayer was a shareholder in 1985, it is also possible that this taxpayer was also a shareholder of at least one already-large C-corporation that switched to S status between 1985 and 1988. In any event, it is difficult to make generalizations about high-income taxpayers from the behavior of any one household.

tors, such as elimination or limitation of some types of itemized deductions, also contributed to the growth in taxable income among the rich.

Auten and Carroll (1994) make use of a much larger longitudinal data set, consisting of 14,102 tax returns for the same set of taxpayers for 1985 and 1989. The sample observations are stratified, so that high-income taxpayers are oversampled. Thus, there are 4,387 taxpayers in the 49–50 percent tax rate brackets in 1985; this compares to 57 in Feldstein's panel. They regress the change in AGI between 1984 and 1989 against the change in marginal tax rate and, in some specifications, some demographic variables. They also control for occupation, as a proxy for demand-side, nontax factors that affected the change in compensation over this period. They conclude that changes in tax rates appear to be an important determinant of the income growth of the late 1980s, although the results are somewhat sensitive to the choice of sample and weighting. They caution, as I will later in the paper, that their results do not necessarily indicate that tax-induced income growth yielded a proportional rise in total tax revenues; because of the potential for shifting of income, that depends on the source of the income change.

6.3 Aggregate Time-Series Analysis of Trends in Income Inequality

Many have suggested that the changes in the pattern of income tax rates was a key causal factor behind the data shown in figures 6.1 and 6.2; they argue that the increased concentration reflects a larger behavioral response of high-income individuals due to the larger drop in their marginal tax rates. There is, though, a competing nontax explanation for the trend of increased concentration of income that began about 1970 but accelerated about 1980—a change in the structure of wage rates due to an increase in the premium on education. Between 1979 and 1988 there was a 15 percent increase in the average wage of a college graduate relative to that of a high school graduate; the high-school/ elementary-school wage differential also increased substantially. A large literature in labor economics has documented the increasing inequality in pretax earnings and has debated the underlying causes of this phenomenon; analysis of the tax changes over this period has been conspicuously absent from this debate. Instead the debate has centered around technological changes which favor skilled over unskilled labor, the increased integration into the world economy of countries with abundant unskilled labor, and changes in the U.S. supply of skilled versus unskilled workers.

Virtually all of the empirical research on trends in inequality has been based on data that does not include the high-income households that are the subject of this paper. Yet it is arguable that the same factors which have caused the increasing dispersion of income in the lower 99 percentiles are also relevant to the relative earnings of the high-income households in the top percentile. For this reason it is important in an empirical analysis of the effect of taxes to control for the exogenous nontax factors that have been affecting the distribution of income.

In what follows I describe a series of multivariate regression analyses of the time-series evidence on high-income shares of income and sources of income. The objective of this exercise is to identify the permanent and temporary impact of changes in the tax structure and anticipated changes in that structure, holding constant some nontax influences.[4] By separately performing the regressions for the years up to 1986 and for the years up to 1990, I also investigate whether there was a change in the structure of the model in 1986.

The dependent variables for the regressions are the shares of AGI and four sources of income—wages and salaries, interest, dividends, and capital gains[5]—received by the top 0.5 percent of households for 1954 through 1990. The data up to 1986 are taken directly from Feenberg and Poterba (1993). The data from 1987 through 1990 are based on Feenberg and Poterba's but are adjusted to correspond to a pre-TRA86 definition of AGI, for reasons described in section 6.2.[6]

Given the small number of observations in this analysis, a critical challenge is to identify the best small set of tax variables that captures the important aspects of a given year's tax environment. Because the focus of this inquiry is the behavior of the high-income group relative to the rest of the population, I construct a measure of the difference between a weighted-average marginal tax rate on labor income for the top 0.5 percent of taxpayers and the weighted-average marginal rate on all other tax return filers, using AGI as the weighting factor. This is denoted TL.[7]

Included as regressors are the current rate, the expected one-year-ahead change (measured by the actual change), and the change from the previous year. The maximum marginal tax rate on long-term capital gains (denoted TC) is also included, although not compared to the average rate;[8] this is also entered in concurrent, expected change, and lagged change form. The standard corporation income tax rate is not included as an explanatory variable, on the grounds that over this period it changed substantially only once, by virtue of

---

4. These regressions should be interpreted as the reduced form of a structural model in which the own inequality of each income source depends on the dispersion in how it is taxed and, via rank reversals, in which each income source's concentration as ranked by income depends on all other sources' inequality and the shares of each source in total income. Thus the right-hand side of each reduced-form equation ought to contain the set of all right-hand variables in the structural equations.

5. Unfortunately, the data do not permit an analysis over this period of the concentration of business income.

6. The adjustment is carried out as follows. The 1990 tax return data are sorted by the pre-TRA86 definition of adjusted income, and the high-income shares are recalculated. The Feenberg-Poterba shares for 1987, 1988, and 1989 are then multiplied by the ratio of recalculated 1990 share to the Feenberg-Poterba 1990 share. This procedure is carried out separately for each of the five shares.

7. The construction of TL and the other variables are described in more detail in a data appendix available from the author.

8. For 1954–78, the rate is taken from the first row in table 1.13 of U.S. Department of Treasury (1985). This measure takes into account the provisions that would commonly affect very high income taxpayers, including the alternative minimum tax and temporary surcharges in 1968, 1969, and 1970. For years after 1978, the top rate is taken from annual *Statistics of Income* publications.

TRA86; for this reason this variable would likely pick up much of the explanatory power of all of the TRA86-induced changes. I return to this issue below.

As discussed above, many economists accept that there were economic forces, unrelated to the tax system, which over this period caused increased inequality in the return to labor. The issue at hand is how to statistically control for these factors. One approach would be to include measures of the alleged causes of the earnings dispersion; for example, technological change could be proxied by the extent of computerization, globalization by the import share of GNP, and the cohort effect by the fraction of college-educated youth. I have chosen, however, to adopt a more direct approach to this problem by using as a control a measure of the dispersion of earnings in the population as a whole. Specifically, I use the difference between the logarithm of the 90th percentile and the logarithm of the 10th percentile of male weekly wages (denoted WGINEQ), based on census data, as reported in Katz and Murphy (1992), updated past 1987 using data reported by Karoly (1993), and extended before 1963 using data from Goldin and Margo (1992). Because this index is not affected by changes in the share of wages going to the very affluent, it is not endogenous. It does, however, arguably reflect the same economic forces that would affect the return to the labor of the most affluent.

As additional explanatory variables I include the real level of stock prices (RSTPR), to pick up its impact on capital gains realization behavior, and the average nominal corporate AAA bond rate (AAARATE), to account for its influence on the receipt of taxable interest. I experimented with the prime-age male unemployment rate as a business-cycle indicator, but it was not an important factor and is not included in the regressions reported here.

The results of the regression analyses are presented in table 6.2. In discussing them, I will refer to the effect of the concurrent tax rate as the permanent effect and to the effect of the expected future and lagged tax changes as timing effects. Several tentative conclusions can be drawn from table 6.2. One striking conclusion is the large impact of capital gains tax on the share of capital gains of the affluent. Using either the series ending in 1985 or in 1990, the results suggest that an 8 percentage point increase in the top capital gains tax rate (the increase due to TRA86) would permanently lower the high-income share of capital gains by about 9 or 10 percentage points; if the increase were to be expected in advance, a 6 percentage point *increase* in the high-income share would occur the year before the increase went into effect. The ultimate impact of the capital gains effect on the high-income share of AGI is, however, dampened substantially; it moves only about a tenth as much as the capital gains share itself.

I turn now to the core issue of the relative importance of tax effects and demand-side effects on the increase in inequality. Consider the determinants of the high-income share of total wages and salaries. According to the regression analyses, the relative contributions of the demand-side effect, represented by WGINEQ, and the permanent tax effect, represented by TL_t, depend entirely

Table 6.2 Time-Series Regression Analyses of the High-Income Shares of AGI, Wages and Salaries, Capital Gains, Interest, and Dividends, 1954–85 and 1954–90

Independent Variables	AGI		Wages and Salaries		Capital Gains		Interest		Dividends	
	1954–85	1954–90	1954–85	1954–90	1954–85	1954–90	1954–85	1954–90	1954–85	1954–90
TL_t	−0.00565	−0.190*	−0.0266	−0.126*	0.484	−0.277	0.312	−0.459*	0.433*	0.124
	(0.0471)	(0.0253)	(0.0179)	(0.0111)	(0.393)	(0.148)	(0.180)	(0.0832)	(0.219)	(0.0915)
$TL_{t+1} - TL_t$	0.0502	−0.0672	0.0213	−0.0571*	0.549	0.281	0.182	−0.263*	0.205	0.207
	(0.0445)	(0.0356)	(0.0170)	(0.0156)	(0.373)	(0.209)	(0.170)	(0.117)	(0.207)	(0.129)
$TL_t - TL_{t-1}$	0.0491	0.0434	0.0303*	0.0267	−0.224	−0.134	0.0193	0.148	−0.318*	−0.174
	(0.0254)	(0.0338)	(0.0112)	(0.0148)	(0.246)	(0.198)	(0.112)	(0.111)	(0.137)	(0.122)
TC_t	−0.108*	−0.0806*	−0.0154*	−0.00385	−1.20*	−1.10*	−0.265*	−0.182*	−0.193*	−0.139
	(0.0139)	(0.0196)	(0.00529)	(0.00862)	(0.116)	(0.115)	(0.0531)	(0.0645)	(0.064)	(0.0710)
$TC_{t+1} - TC_t$	0.0294*	0.0450	−0.0195	−0.0280	0.859*	0.823*	0.224	0.126	−0.0725	0.0968
	(0.0328)	(0.0423)	(0.0124)	(0.0186)	(0.274)	(0.248)	(0.125)	(0.139)	(0.153)	(0.153)
$TC_t - TC_{t-1}$	0.0813	0.0500	−0.00988	0.00582	0.516	0.239	0.258	0.245	0.00562	−0.297
	(0.0409)	(0.0459)	(0.0156)	(0.0202)	(0.342)	(0.269)	(0.156)	(0.151)	(0.190)	(0.166)
WGINEQ	0.955	−2.030	2.406*	−0.227	12.5	−6.74	−2.58	−25.1*	−19.1	−19.9
	(2.33)	(3.712)	(0.889)	(1.19)	(19.5)	(15.9)	(8.92)	(8.92)	(10.9)	(9.82)
RSTPR	−0.00705*	−0.0109*	−0.00683*	−0.00900*	0.0416*	0.0306	−0.0463*	−0.0596*	−0.00575	−0.0109
	(0.00232)	(0.00317)	(0.000884)	(0.00139)	(0.0194)	(0.0186)	(0.00888)	(0.104)	(0.0108)	(0.0115)
AAARATE	−0.0895	−0.291*	0.0227	−0.0584*	0.424	−0.217	−0.149	−0.704*	−0.774*	−1.20
	(0.0537)	(0.0585)	(0.0205)	(0.0257)	(0.449)	(0.343)	(0.205)	(0.193)	(0.250)	(2.12)
Intercept	10.2*	21.5*	2.19	9.47*	32.9	86.5*	18.0	76.1*	58.2*	−12.5
	(4.39)	(4.14)	(1.67)	(1.82)	(36.7)	(24.3)	*(16.8)	(13.6)	(20.5)	(15.0)
R^2	0.829	0.902	0.965	0.969	0.879	0.870	0.876	0.780	0.958	0.950
D-W	1.612	1.458	1.739	1.519	1.194	1.242	0.949	0.876	1.659	2.033

Note: Numbers in parentheses are standard errors.

*Significance at the 95 percent level of confidence.

on the weight placed on the experience of 1986–90. Based on the regression for the period 1954–85, the demand-side effect dominates. For example, of the 1.3 percentage point increase in the high-income share of wages between 1973 and 1985, 0.53 can be associated with the increase in WGINEQ (a 0.22 increase in WGINEQ multiplied by the estimated coefficient of 2.406), and only 0.26 can be associated with TL_t (a 9.8 decline in TL_t multiplied by an estimated coefficient of -0.0266). However, the regression using data through 1990 tells a completely different story.[9] Based on this regression, one would conclude that almost the entire increase in the high-income share of wages can be associated with the decline in TL_t, leaving no role for WGINEQ. A similar story can be told about the high-income share of AGI, although in this case the wage inequality variable is not as successful in explaining the pre-TRA86 variation.[10]

The proximate cause for the divergence in results is clear. The 1985–90 increase in the high-income share of wages exceeded the increase over the entire period of 1973–85. Yet over this period the measure of demand-side effects, the difference between the log of earnings at the 90th percentile and 10th percentile, actually fell after rising continuously for two decades, while the tax rate measure continued its downward trend, having its steepest decline of any comparable period.

These findings are open to two, not mutually exclusive, interpretations. One interpretation is that there was a fundamental break in the nature of the demand-side factor, so that up until 1985 its impact on the relative return to high-income occupations was well proxied by the changes in the overall distribution of earnings but that after 1985 the relative return to the 99.5th percentile and above continued to increase even though the relative return to the 90th percentile did not. A second possible interpretation is that the observed changes in high-income shares between 1986 and 1990 were primarily tax driven but, except for the capital gains response, were of a fundamentally different nature and/or magnitude than what had been observed until 1986.

Although I cannot rule out the first explanation, I do not explore it further in this paper. Instead, in the following section I take a closer look at the high-income behavioral response to TRA86, with the goal of learning more about its nature.

6.4   A Closer Look at the Income Gains of the Affluent: Income Creation versus Income Shifting

Table 6.3 allows a closer look at the composition of the high-income real income increases in the late 1980s by comparing the top 1.0 and 0.5 percent

---

9. A Chow predictive test (Fisher 1970) rejects the null hypotheses that the set of coefficients is the same in the pre- and post-TRA86 periods.

10. Note, though, that many of the coefficient estimates shown in table 6.2 are sensitive to the inclusion of the variable AAARATE; the qualitative conclusions discussed here are not.

of income earners in 1984 and 1990. Columns (5)–(8) reveal that the total increase in real reported income among the top 0.5 percent of taxpayers (in 1990 dollars) from 1984 to 1990 was $137.5 billion. Three sources accounted for 76.8 percent of the total increase. Wages and salaries accounted for $57.0 billion, or 41.5 percent of the total income. Small business corporation income (subchapter S corporations) accounted for $27.2 billion, or 19.8 percent of the total increase. Partnership income accounted for $21.3 billion, or 15.3 percent of the total increase.

Auten and Carroll (1994) report, using their panel data set, that of the total change in *nominal* AGI of their highest income group (those subject to the 49 or 50 percent rate in 1985), only 29.1 percent was accounted for by the increase in wages and salaries. More than that was due to the combination of S-corporation income, which by itself was 25.1 percent of the increase, and partnership income, which accounted for 12.1 percent of the increase. Strikingly, they report that the real wages and salaries of the highest income group increased by only 4.9 percent between 1985 and 1989, compared to 161.8 percent for income from S-corporations, and 351.4 percent for income from partnerships.[11] Because both the comparative cross-sectional and panel data indicate that the same three sources of income dominated the income gains of the rich over this period, I devote the rest of this section to further analysis of their trends.

6.4.1   Subchapter S Income

There are clear tax reasons for the $27.2 billion increase in the reported income of the affluent from S-corporations. The top individual income tax rate was cut by 22 percentage points, compared to a 12 point cut in the corporation income tax rate. By 1988 the top individual income tax rate was actually lower than the corporate tax rate for the first time since the introduction of the federal income tax. Because S-corporations are not subject to corporate income tax and are taxed essentially as partnerships, the tax penalty for high-income owners from operating as a corporation widened substantially upon the passage of TRA86.

There is substantial evidence of a large shift in activity from C-corporations to S-corporations. For one thing, the number of corporations filing to obtain S status increased dramatically at the time of enactment.[12] In the first six months of 1987, there were 375,000 filings, compared to a six-month change of 150,000 from 1983 to 1986.

Figure 6.3 shows that the relative number of C- and S-corporation returns

---

11. Note that, because Auten and Carroll group taxpayers by their marginal tax rate in 1985, the subsequent income growth is subject to downward bias due to the presence of transitory income and regression toward the mean.

12. These filings could be either new corporations or C-corporations changing status. Nelson (1993) reports that in 1989, 69.5 percent of the assets of new S-corporations were held by "conversions," defined as a firm electing S status more than one year after its date of incorporation.

Table 6.3   Reported Personal Income of High-Income Taxpayers, 1984 and 1990
                   (1990 dollars)

	Top 1 Percent				Top 0.5 Percent			
Income	1984 (1)	1990 (2)	Increase (3)	Percentage of Total Increase (4)	1984 (5)	1990 (6)	Increase (7)	Percentage of Total Increase (8)
AGI	265.6	445.9	180.2	100.0	198.4	335.8	137.5	100.0
Wages and salaries	145.9	226.9	80.9	44.9	101.6	158.6	57.0	41.5
Dividends	20.8	27.1	6.3	3.5	16.9	22.3	5.4	3.9
Interest	28.1	44.3	16.2	9.0	21.1	35.5	14.4	10.4
Business income	14.6	31.4	16.8	9.3	9.0	20.3	11.2	8.2
Capital gains	39.8	26.5	−13.3	−7.4	35.7	23.2	−12.6	9.1
Partnership	−0.5	26.2	26.7	14.8	−1.2	20.1	21.3	15.5
S-corporation income	10.3	40.0	29.7	16.5	9.6	36.9	27.2	19.8

Source: Author's tabulations using 1984 and 1990 Individual Tax Model data from the SOI Division of the IRS. The ranking of households and definitions of income are based on the 1984 definition of AGI. Discrepancies among cols. (1)–(3) and (5)–(7) are due to rounding error.

has changed dramatically since 1986. The number of C-returns, which had increased at an average rate of 3.5 percent in the two decades from 1965 to 1985, actually started to decrease after 1986, and fell by over 450,000 from 1986 to 1990. At the same time S-corporation returns more than doubled from 1985 to 1990. S-corporation returns, which represented 19 percent of all corporation returns in 1981 and 22 percent by 1985, had surged to 42 percent of all returns by 1990. The share of total corporate assets in S form has also nearly doubled since the early 1980s although it is still only slightly above 4 percent.[13]

As Nelson (1993) reports, much of the increase in S-corporation activity was undertaken by high-income individuals. Whereas in 1985, 56 percent of the positive income went to taxpayers with income over $200,000, in 1990 the figure was 71 percent. In 1985, of this group 23.9 percent had some S-corporation income or loss; in 1990 this percentage had risen to 31.7.

Of most direct interest is the change in where net income is reported. The net income of S-corporations has increased sharply since TRA86, from $8.3 billion in 1986 to $32.3 billion in 1990.

Non-rate-related tax changes may also have contributed to the shift from C- to S-corporations. In particular, the TRA86 repeal of the General Utilities doctrine, which allowed corporations to avoid two levels of capital gains tax on asset sales, made C-corporations a relatively less attractive organizational form. The expanded alternative minimum tax on corporations also had such an effect.

13. See Gordon and MacKie-Mason (1994) for an empirical analysis of how tax factors have affected the relative size of the corporate and noncorporate business sectors.

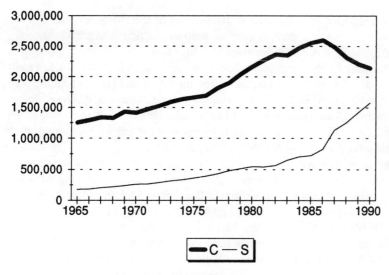

Fig. 6.3   Returns of C- and S-corporations
Source: IRS *Statistics of Income: Corporation Income Tax Returns.*

6.4.2   Partnerships

The TRA86 reversal of the relative position of the top corporate and individual marginal tax rates also increased the attractiveness of partnerships (and sole proprietorships) relative to C-corporations. As in the case of S-corporations, though, a potentially important non-rate-related change occurred—the passive loss limitations. These limitations disallowed, under certain conditions, individual taxpayers' deductions from taxable income of business losses defined as originating in "passive activities" (where the individual does not materially participate in the active conduct of the trade or business on a regular, continuous, or material basis). Before TRA86, most passive losses were allocated to the partners in limited partnerships. The limitations were phased in, beginning in 1987 and ending in 1991.[14]

As Petska and Wilson (1994) document, the total number of partnerships, which had increased by 23 percent between 1980 and 1986, started to decline markedly in 1987, and by 1990 was 9 percent lower than in 1986. Aggregate net income of partnerships averaged −$7.1 billion between 1981 and 1986 but had risen to +$16.6 billion by 1990.

6.4.3   Wages and Salaries

The comparative cross-sectional evidence, and to a much lesser extent the panel data, suggest that increased wages and salaries are an important part

---

14. See Samwick (chap. 7 in this volume) for an attempt to empirically identify how much of the change in reported partnership income is due to the change in tax rates and how much is due to the passive loss limitation rules.

of the high-income behavioral response. Part of the cross-sectional story is undoubtedly that the demographic makeup of the rich changed significantly from 1984 to 1990. This demographic change is reflected by the sharp drop in the fraction of rich households who are over age 65, from 23.4 to 14.1 percent for the top 0.5 percent of taxpayers. The mere fact that fewer of the rich are likely to be retired in 1990 will account for some amount of increased wages and salaries. There is also likely to be a rank reversal effect in which, as net partnership and S-income surges, it brings into the top income group more people who also have relatively high wages and salaries.

The preceding are cautions about inferring real behavioral changes from comparing cross-sectional slices of an income distribution. Leaving this issue aside, the key question is how much of the observed relative increase in labor income is explained by increased relative pretax rates of compensation, increased labor supply, or by some sort of income shifting.

The first explanation cannot be ruled out. However, as discussed in section 6.3, if this occurred, it occurred in the face of a decline in the dispersion of earnings between the 10th and 90th percentile of earners.

Eissa (1995) presents evidence, based on comparing cross-sectional slices of the pre- and post-TRA86 CPS, that the labor supply of those married women facing sharp marginal tax declines due to TRA86 did in fact increase their labor supply relative to other married women. The labor income of married women, though, constitutes a small fraction of the total labor income of the top 1 percent of households. Moreover, the labor supply literature speaks clearly that this is the group whose labor supply responsiveness is larger than that of any other, so that one cannot generalize from their behavior about the labor supply behavior of all members of affluent households. More definitive statements about the magnitude of labor supply response will have to await future research.

Another intriguing, and unanswered question is, To what extent is the increase in the wages and salaries of the rich itself a reflection of income shifting? For example, the TRA86 reduction in the top rate of tax on ordinary income made it relatively less attractive to receive compensation in the form of untaxed fringe benefits and relatively more attractive to receive taxed monetary compensation. The elimination of the tax rate differential between ordinary income and long-term capital gains eliminated the incentive to repackage labor income into capital gains, including the incentive to receive stock options as part of one's compensation package. These are examples of changes in the form of one's labor income payments that would show up in concurrent tax return data as an increase in labor income. More generally, the inversion of the top corporate and personal tax rates also eliminated the incentive to retain labor income within the corporation, so that one would expect that after TRA86 there would be an increase in payments from the corporations to individuals, payments that reflect neither a change in labor supply nor in the present value of labor compensation. The fact that the increase in the reported labor income of affluent individuals has been paralleled by a secular decrease in reported corporate profits is causal evidence for this income-shifting hypothesis, but there is as of yet no evidence making the causal link anything more than speculative.

6.4.4 Implications for the Regression Analyses

The preceding discussions make clear that much of the post-TRA86 increase in the income reported by high-income households on their personal tax returns was probably not due to a standard (e.g., increased labor supply) behavioral response to lower marginal tax rates. Instead there was a great deal of income shifting and changed reporting due to unique aspects of TRA86 that did not accompany previous marginal tax rate changes and are not likely to accompany future changes. According to this argument, the sharp divergence in the regression results when the post-TRA86 era is included occurs because there was indeed a new (tax) structure instituted then, one that provided very different incentives and opportunities for high-income individuals to report income (and losses) via the individual income tax system. The results do not imply that taxpayer response to marginal tax rates, holding structure constant, was different (in particular, higher) after TRA86. Instead the tax rate variables, which changed dramatically at the same time the structure changed, are picking up some of the effect of the structural change.[15]

An intriguing question is, Why, given that many of the structural changes in TRA86 concerned business income, is there a break at 1986 in the equation explaining the high-income share of wages and salaries? One possible answer is that there is a positive cross-household correlation between the share of total income that is net business income and the share that is wages and salaries. Given this correlation, any exogenous increase in the concentration of reported business income will, by pulling more households with business income into the top 0.5 percent, also increase the concentration of wages and salaries. The other answer is that there were aspects of TRA86 that affected the incentive to report labor compensation as wages and salaries, as discussed in section 6.4.3. It is unlikely that these two explanations are the whole story, implying that this paper has not completely explained the surge in the concentration of wages and salaries after TRA86.

6.5 Conclusions

The relative income gains of the affluent after the passage of TRA86 are overstated by comparing cross-sectional slices using concurrent income definitions, but they are large nevertheless. Although an index of the demand-side factors affecting inequality throughout the income distribution can explain much of the increased high-income concentration until 1985, it cannot ade-

---

15. I am grateful to the discussant of this paper, Don Fullerton, for clarifying this argument for me.

quately explain the post-TRA86 spurt. TRA86 is likely to have been a principal cause of the large increase in the reported personal income of the affluent. A close look at the sources of the post-1986 increases in the reported individual income of high-income households suggests that much of it represents shifting of income—for example, from the corporate tax base to the individual tax base—and not income creation such as additional labor supply.

This distinction is critical because knowing how much the reported individual income of a particular group of people changes in response to a tax change is not a sufficient statistic for evaluating adequately the revenue consequences. This is because the change in reported personal income may be accompanied by offsetting changes in other tax bases, in particular the corporation income tax, and by offsetting changes in reported income in other time periods. Thus, the extent to which changes in reported income are indications of the shifting of income across tax bases or time periods needs to be carefully studied.

The nature of the behavioral response is also critical for evaluating the incidence and efficiency of taxation. In Slemrod (1994a) I argue that the standard tools for measuring these concepts must be modified in the presence of what I call "avoidance," defined as responses to taxation other than altering one's consumption bundle, including income shifting.

References

Auten, Gerald, and Robert Carroll. 1994. Behavior of the affluent and the 1986 Tax Reform Act: The role of demand-side characteristics. Washington, D.C.: Department of Treasury, Office of Tax Analysis, November. Manuscript.

Eissa, Nada. 1995. Taxation and the labor supply of married women: The Tax Reform Act of 1986 as a natural experiment. NBER Working Paper no. 5023. Cambridge, Mass.: National Bureau of Economic Research.

Feenberg, Daniel, and James Poterba. 1993. Income inequality and the incomes of very high income taxpayers. In *Tax policy and the economy,* vol. 7, ed. James Poterba. Cambridge: MIT Press.

Feldstein, Martin. 1993. The effect of marginal tax rates on taxable income: A panel study of the 1986 Tax Reform Act. NBER Working Paper no. 4496. Cambridge, Mass.: National Bureau of Economic Research, October.

Fisher, Frank. 1970. Tests of equality between two sets of coefficients in two linear regressions: An expository note. *Econometrica* 28: 361–66.

Goldin, Claudia, and Robert A. Margo. 1992. The great compression: The wage structure in the United States at mid-century. *Quarterly Journal of Economics* 107 (February): 1–34.

Gordon, Roger, and Jeffrey MacKie-Mason. 1994. How much do taxes discourage incorporation? Ann Arbor: University of Michigan, Department of Economics. Manuscript.

Karoly, Lynn. 1993. The trend in income inequality among families, individuals, and workers in the United States: A twenty-five year perspective. In *Uneven tides: Rising inequality in America,* ed. S. Danziger and P. Gottschalk. New York: Russell Sage Foundation. Also data updates obtained from the author.

————. 1994. Trends in income inequality: The impact of, and implications for, tax policy. In *Tax progressivity and income inequality,* ed. J. Slemrod. Cambridge: Cambridge University Press.

Katz, Lawrence F., and Kevin M. Murphy. 1992. Changes in relative wages, 1963–1987: Supply and demand factors. *Quarterly Journal of Economics* 107 (February): 35–78.

Levy, Frank, and Richard S. Murnane. 1992. U.S. earnings levels and earnings inequality: A review of recent trends and proposed explanations. *Journal of Economic Literature* 30 (September): 1333–81.

Lindsey, Lawrence. 1987. Estimating the behavioral responses of taxpayers to changes in tax rates, 1982–1984: With implications for the revenue-maximizing tax rate. *Journal of Public Economics* 33 (July): 173–206.

Nelson, Susan C. 1993. S corporations: The record of growth after tax reform. *Journal of S Corporation Taxation* 5 (Fall): 138–61.

Petska, Thomas, and Robert Wilson. 1994. Trends in business structure and activity, 1980–1990. *Statistics of Income Bulletin* 13 (Spring): 27–72.

Slemrod, Joel. 1992. Taxation and inequality: A time-exposure perspective. In *Tax policy and the economy,* vol. 6, ed. James Poterba. Cambridge: MIT Press.

————. 1994a. A general model of the behavioral response to taxation. Ann Arbor: University of Michigan, Department of Economics, September.

————. 1994b. On the high income Laffer curve. In *Tax progressivity and income inequality,* ed. J. Slemrod. Cambridge: Cambridge University Press.

Steuerle, C. Eugene. 1992. *The tax decade: How taxes came to dominate the public agenda.* Washington, D.C.: Urban Institute Press.

U.S. Department of Treasury. Office of Tax Analysis. 1985. *Report to the Congress on the capital gains tax reductions of 1978.* Washington, D.C.: Superintendent of Documents.

Comment   Don Fullerton

Wage inequality has been increasing in recent decades, just as the top personal marginal tax rate has been falling. Some of this increasing wage inequality can be explained by tax changes, if high-income individuals in the top brackets react to rate reduction by working more hours, by working harder to get a higher wage, or even just by rearranging affairs. They might receive more of their income in the form of reportable wages and salaries instead of untaxed fringe benefits, instead of converting that income into capital gains, or even instead of retaining that income within a closely held corporation. On the other hand, some of the increasing inequality may have nontax explanations such as cohort effects, technological change, or increased globalization of the economy. To help inform future policy decisions about the effects of proposed tax

Don Fullerton is professor of economics at the University of Texas at Austin and a research associate of the National Bureau of Economic Research.

changes on economic behavior, and on the real distribution of income, we need to know how much of the increasing wage inequality can be attributed to each of these explanations.

Joel Slemrod nicely articulates the problem, summarizes what we know, and adds to that knowledge. In particular, he seeks to separate nontax and tax explanations for this increased wage dispersion and to determine whether behavioral responses are permanent changes to income or only temporary changes in the timing of income. Two aspects of the paper seem especially valuable. First, Slemrod does not try to explain everything from a single narrowly defined model with a single set of assumptions. Instead, he reaches out for any sort of information and then explains how it might apply to this problem. Second, he diverges from previous efforts that use microsimulation models with thousands of individuals in two different years. Instead, he uses overall information about wage inequality and tax rates for 37 years (1954–90) in simple aggregate time-series regressions. This approach can help shed light from a different direction.

To prepare for these regressions, Slemrod first must adjust the available measures of income inequality that show the increase in the percentage of total adjusted gross income (AGI) received by the top 0.5 percent of families ranked by AGI. The problem, pointed out by Slemrod, is that the definition of AGI changed in 1986. When he uses a consistent definition of AGI (either the 1984 definition or the 1988 definition), he shows that income dispersion did not increase quite as much as previously measured. This correction is valuable in itself. Slemrod also discusses the possibility of reranking, with different individuals appearing in the top group in a later year.

The dependent variable is the top 0.5 percent group's share of AGI (or wages and salaries, interest income, dividends, or capital gains). Independent variables include the extra tax rate paid by that group (TL) and the top capital gains rate (TC), both appearing with leads and lags. The rate in the same year indicates permanent effects, the rate in the previous year indicates timing adjustments, and the rate in the following year indicates planning ahead (to the extent that next year's rate explains this year's reported income). The other crucial variable, of course, is the measure of nontax factors. Instead of trying to measure technological change or increased globalization, Slemrod includes the difference between wages in the 90th percentile and the 10th percentile (WGINEQ). The basic idea is that *whatever* nontax factors drive wage inequality between the 90th and 10th percentiles, the same factors would similarly affect the 99.5th percentile. Those nontax factors are similar for the 90th and 99.5th percentiles, but the tax rate is different. Thus WGINEQ controls for the nontax factors, and the estimated coefficient on the tax rate of the 99.5th percentile will indicate tax factors.

And here I would make a suggestion. That use of WGINEQ is very clever, but it is not the only possibility. Technological or global forces might differently affect those in the top 10 percent (who may be plumbers, computer technicians, and college professors) and those in the top 0.5 percent (who may be doctors, business executives, and professional baseball players). Personally, I do not know. But the paper would be more convincing if it tried a number of the other possibilities for those technological and global factors it mentions, such as the extent of computerization in the workplace, the import share of GNP, and the fraction of youth who are college educated.

Also, the paper refers to "core" results for the wage and salary share regressions, noting that the nontax explanation (WGINEQ) is largest and the tax variable (TL) insignificant for the 1954–85 period but that they reverse in importance when the period is extended to 1990. This result is extremely interesting, but I am not sure exactly what it means. If tax effects or timing effects are important, then they would be important before 1986 as well as after. Indeed, if the highest tax rates induce the most tax avoidance, then the largest tax effect would appear in the earlier period when the top marginal rate fell from 90 to 70 percent (in 1964) and again from 70 to 50 percent (in 1981). In other words, how does the break at 1986 relate to the point of the paper?

I think the answer lies in the *other* changes in the Tax Reform Act of 1986 such as the passive loss rules and the smaller fall in the corporate income tax rate. In particular, 1986 marks the first time in history that the corporate rate exceeds the top personal tax rate. Doctors, business executives, and other professionals no longer have incentive to employ themselves in closely held corporations, pay themselves artificially low salaries, and retain more of their income in lesser-taxed corporate form. When the personal rate falls below the corporate rate, they just assign themselves higher salaries.

The point has a number of implications for the paper. First, I think Slemrod could better explain this reason for breaking the data at 1986. Second, instead of just pointing to the "large" changes in the tax and nontax coefficients, he could perform a statistical test for structural change in a times-series regression. Third, an implication is that the personal tax rate variables (TL and TC) may not really be the crucial tax-related determinants of reported wage inequality. Instead one might include the differential between the corporate rate and the top personal rate. Slemrod points out that this differential does not change much except in 1986, when it goes from negative to positive, so it would act like a dummy for post-1986 years. But the paper does essentially the same thing by breaking the data at 1986 anyway.

For his interpretation of these results, Slemrod uses the last section of the paper to discuss changes after 1986 in the composition of income for this top-income group, particularly the major increases in their wages and salaries, income from partnerships, and income from subchapter S corporations. He nicely describes how each of those changes can result from tax avoidance behavior. But this discussion needs to relate back to the big change in estimated coefficients after 1986. Should we infer that behavior became more responsive after 1986? No!

For my interpretation of these results, each behavior must be categorized as a response to a change in the *rate* of tax or a response to a change in the *structure* of tax. Any response in the first category should be found throughout the whole period from 1954 to 1990. Marginal rate reduction might induce shifts from untaxed fringe benefits into reportable wages and salaries, for example, or shifts from the underground economy to the market economy. But such shifts would pertain to all rate reductions in 1954–90. Thus these behaviors do not explain the break at 1986.

Most of Slemrod's other examples are responses to a change in the structure of taxation. First, changes in the passive loss rules in 1986 might induce high-income taxpayers to report more income from partnerships. Second, the inversion of the corporate rate and top personal rate in 1986 might induce them to report more income from S-corporations (instead of the more highly taxed C-corporations). Third, the same inversion might induce holders of closely held corporations to assign themselves higher salaries (instead of retaining income as corporate income). Fourth, the repeal of the General Utilities doctrine might shift activity from C-corporations to partnerships or S-corporations. Fifth, the expansion of the corporate alternative minimum tax might do the same. Sixth, the elimination of the rate differential between ordinary income and capital gains eliminates the incentive to repackage labor income to look like capital gains, such as through stock options or through renovating old houses to resell at higher prices.

All six of these structural changes occurred in 1986, and none of them relate to the tax *rate* variable in Slemrod's regressions. Without these structural changes, using only the data from 1954 to 1985, the tax rate variable is insignificant (for wages and salaries or for all of AGI). Inclusion of the 1986–90 period *appears* to make the coefficient on the tax rate much larger and highly significant, but Slemrod's regressions for 1954–90 do not allow for the important structural changes in 1986. One should not attribute those behavioral responses to the tax rate.

A logical conclusion, therefore, is that responses to changes in the rate of tax pale in comparison to responses to changes in the structure of taxation. Perhaps we have paid too much attention to theory and evidence on responses to tax rates, including efforts to measure the peak of the Laffer curve or the deadweight loss of high marginal tax rates. Perhaps instead we need to bite the bullet and tackle the more difficult issues of how the tax is designed, what is included in each tax category, and how those categories are taxed relative to each other. As Slemrod points out, we need to shift attention from optimal tax rates to optimal tax systems.

7   Tax Shelters and Passive Losses after the Tax Reform Act of 1986

Andrew A. Samwick

The Tax Reform Act of 1986 (TRA86) was the culmination of a concerted effort by the Congress and the president to improve the efficiency and perceived equity of the federal tax system. As conspicuous examples of special tax treatment for particular types of income (and particular groups of taxpayers), investments known as tax shelters received a great deal of attention in the legislative debate.[1] Tax shelters are investments designed to create losses for tax purposes that, when added to income earned from other sources in the calculation of a taxpayer's total income, "shelter" that income from taxation. Investments in real estate, oil and gas exploration, and other favored sectors, especially when debt financed, can create such tax losses even while generating positive economic income and cash flows.

Tax shelters are typically organized as limited partnerships in which the investor has no management role. An otherwise high-income taxpayer could, with very little direct effort, utilize tax shelter losses to lower his or her average tax rate below that of a low-income taxpayer without tax shelter losses, thereby undermining the vertical equity of the federal tax system. As an indication of how important tax shelters were in reducing the tax liabilities of high-income taxpayers, Petska (1992) reports that for the group of taxpayers in 1986 with

Andrew A. Samwick is assistant professor of economics at Dartmouth College and a faculty research fellow of the National Bureau of Economic Research.

The author has benefited tremendously from discussions with Martin Feldstein, Roger Gordon, George Plesko, and Ted Sims. He also thanks Dan Feenberg, Bill Gentry, Jim Poterba, and seminar participants at the NBER and Dartmouth for helpful comments; Todd Sinai for invaluable assistance with the TAXSIM programs; and Nancy Mahon of the Robert A. Stanger Company for partnership sales data and excerpts from the *Stanger Report*. Any errors are solely the author's responsibility.

1. U.S. Congress (1985) represents the legislature's perspective on tax shelters during the formulation of TRA86. McLure and Zodrow (1987) discuss the resemblance of TRA86 to the administration's proposals for tax reform.

at least $250,000 in positive income and an average tax burden of 5 percent or less on it, partnership losses offset over 40 percent of positive income.[2]

The direct assault on this type of "abuse" of tax shelters came from the new "passive loss" rules enacted by TRA86 in section 469 of the Internal Revenue Code. These rules limited the extent to which losses from activities in which the investor did not "materially participate" could offset positive income from other sources such as wages, capital gains, and dividends. For investments made after TRA86, passive losses can be offset only against income from passive activities. Any excess losses are disallowed as a current deduction until the taxpayer disposes of the activity that generates the loss or realizes sufficient passive income to apply against the losses.[3] In order to satisfy the material participation standard, a taxpayer's involvement in the activity must be regular, continuous, and substantial. Although material participation in more than one activity is possible, a taxpayer is most likely to materially participate only in his or her principal trade or business. More important, limited partnership interests are automatically presumed to be passive activities. The passive loss rules therefore effectively sever the link between the tax losses from a shelter and the tax liability due on other forms of income in a given year.

There is little doubt that investments in tax shelters have all but disappeared since the enactment of TRA86. Tabulations of form D filings with the Securities and Exchange Commission compiled by Robert A. Stanger & Co. show that public sales of limited partnerships fell from $13.1 billion in 1986 to $7.6 billion in 1989 and $2.6 billion in 1992 after 15 prior years of growth. Tabulations of partnership schedule K returns in Wheeler (1994) show a similar pattern in net income from limited partnerships. Between 1983 and 1986, aggregate net losses increased from $18.7 to $35.5 billion. By 1989 and 1992, net losses had fallen to $21.6 and $3.3 billion, respectively. It is steadfastly believed that the passive loss rules were the death blow to abusive tax shelters, where abuse can generally be said to occur when a taxpayer invests solely to lower tax liability, without any regard for economic profit.[4] According to IRS Deputy Chief Counsel Peter K. Scott, "The passive loss rules pretty much put the final nail in the coffin, in terms of the tax shelter business" (quoted in Moriarty and Rosen 1988, 920). The passive loss rules were also cited as critical to the elimination of tax shelters in economic analyses of TRA86.[5]

---

2. Positive income here refers to the total of all positive sources of income before the netting out of any losses.

3. For investments made prior to TRA86, the passive loss limitations were phased in over five years: 35 percent in 1987, 60 percent in 1988, 80 percent in 1989, and 90 percent in 1990. During the phase-in period, any passive losses not disallowed were included as a tax preference in the calculation of the alternative minimum tax. Becker (1987), Brumbaugh and Ward (1987), and Keligan (1987) provide detailed descriptions of the passive loss rules.

4. Cordes and Galper (1985) present a more systematic classification of popular and legal definitions of tax shelters.

5. See, e.g., Auerbach (1987), Musgrave (1987), and Pechman (1987) in the symposium on TRA86 in the inaugural issue of the *Journal of Economic Perspectives*.

Assigning the passive loss rules the credit for killing the tax shelters on the basis of the decline of tax shelters since its adoption may be premature because TRA86 also squeezed tax shelters in two other ways that were unrelated to the passive loss rules. The first was by reducing the magnitude of the losses that could be generated by a given tax-sheltered investment. The schedules for the depreciation of some assets typical of tax shelters, most notably real estate, were lengthened. The longer the time period over which an asset must be depreciated for tax purposes, the lower is the present value of the depreciation deductions. TRA86 also repealed the investment tax credit (ITC), which had previously allowed up to 10 percent of the cost of an investment to be deducted from the investor's tax liability in the year it was purchased. The second was by reducing the tax benefit that a taxpayer could claim from a given loss. TRA86 reduced marginal tax rates on ordinary income at the high end of the income distribution and repealed the 60 percent exclusion on long-term capital gains. These two measures reduced the after-tax value of losses while the asset was held and raised the tax rate paid on the gain generated when the asset was sold, respectively.

Accurately determining the importance of the passive loss rules in eliminating tax shelters is of economic significance because the passive loss rules do not distinguish between abusive tax shelters and legitimate economic enterprises that are organized as partnerships and happen to lose money. The passive loss limitations are so broadly applicable that they may also be disallowing the deductibility of genuine economic losses and thereby discouraging ex ante productive investment. Although the passive loss rules have been criticized by legal scholars,[6] the supposition that in the absence of these rules there would still be tax shelter abuse is held out as an offsetting benefit. The notion that the declining marginal tax rates or the repeals of the ITC and long-term capital gain exclusion could have played an important role in the demise of tax shelters is absent from the textbook legal analysis of the effect of TRA86 on tax shelters (Chirelstein 1994, 268). Given the potential for the passive loss rules to inhibit productive economic investments, that they may have been sufficient to eliminate tax shelters is not the relevant issue. The purpose of this paper is to answer the more important question of whether they were *necessary* to accomplish that goal, given the other changes enacted by TRA86.

This paper is organized as follows. Sections 7.1 and 7.2 address the issues related to legitimate tax shelters, that is, those in which transactions are assumed to take place at a fair market value. Section 7.1 illustrates with three examples the operation of tax shelters before TRA86, the impact of the changes enacted by TRA86, and the role of the passive loss rules in eliminating tax shelters. The substantive conclusion is that the passive loss limitations only affect the deferral of income. To the extent that tax shelters provide other bene-

---

6. Examples include Bankman (1989), Peroni (1988), Zelenak (1989a, 1989b), and Sims (1994). Johnson (1989) argues in support of the passive loss rules, in a response to Zelenak (1989a).

fits, such as the conversion of ordinary income to capital gains, the passive loss limitations were of secondary importance. The repeal of the ITC and long-term capital gain exclusion were more important by comparison. Section 7.2 discusses the implications of these results for the existence of a clientele for tax shelters after TRA86 by examining the change in the distribution of marginal tax rates in a panel of tax returns. Once again, the reforms other than the passive loss rules are shown to be critical, this time in removing the positive correlation between the after-tax rate of return on a tax shelter and the investor's marginal tax rate.

The emphasis is then shifted in section 7.3 to so-called abusive tax shelters, more precisely, those in which the asset's basis for depreciation can be artificially overstated to achieve arbitrarily large depreciation allowances without subsequent recapture. Such transactions are pure deferral; hence, the passive loss rules will eliminate them. As Sims (1994) argues, however, a more sensible policy could have been formulated by focusing on the loopholes that enable the basis to be overstated without sufficient penalty rather than the appearance of losses in general. Section 7.4 investigates another hypothesis for why passive loss limitations were enacted, namely, to satisfy short-term distributional goals in a comprehensive tax reform. Using cross-sectional tax return data, it is shown that approximately half of the passive losses disallowed during the phase-in period for the new rules were realized by the top 0.60 percent of the income distribution. Section 7.5 concludes.

7.1   Tax Shelters before and after TRA

The basic idea underlying a tax shelter is alarmingly simple: to take a dollar of income and lower the value of the taxes that must be paid on it. Although investments commonly known as tax shelters are not the only ways to exploit the tax preferences in the Internal Revenue Code, they are among the least straightforward.[7] This section begins by describing the salient features of a tax-sheltered investment and then illustrates these features, and the changes enacted by TRA86, using examples of tax shelters typical of the pre-TRA86 period.

7.1.1   Components of a Tax Shelter

There are two principal ways that income tax burdens can be lowered in a tax shelter. The first is by deferring the tax liability into future years. If interest rates are positive, then the present value of a tax payment can be lowered by shifting it into later years because the investor can earn interest on the tax

---

7. A much simpler way to confer a tax advantage is to simply exempt the asset's return from taxation, as in the case of municipal bonds. Fierro (1981) is an informative—and entertaining—introduction to tax shelters.

liability during the interim. The second is by converting the taxable income from ordinary income to capital gain income, which has typically been taxed at a lower rate. Without deferral or conversion, there is no tax shelter. The source of both deferral and conversion is depreciation—not the actual physical deterioration of capital—but the magnitude of the deduction from income that the owner of the asset is allowed to claim for tax purposes. If the depreciation allowances correspond to the economic depreciation of the asset, then there is no tax advantage to the investment under an income tax system.[8] In practice, the tax advantage comes from depreciation allowances that are larger than economic depreciation during the earlier years of the investment.[9] Even if the amount taken in depreciation is added (for tax purposes) to the proceeds from the eventual sale of the asset, the investor benefits by deferring the tax until the date of the sale. Depreciation allowances become even more valuable if, when the asset is sold, the proceeds are taxed at a lower rate, such as that prevailing on capital gains before TRA86. In this way, the depreciation allowances are converted from ordinary to capital income.

As will be shown in section 7.2, an investment in a depreciable asset is not likely to function as a tax shelter unless it is debt financed. By borrowing a portion of the funds required for the initial investment in the asset, the investor can claim the depreciation on the full investment, deduct the interest payments on the borrowed funds from taxable income, and pay off the debt when the shelter is disposed of. Investors with the highest marginal tax rates naturally benefit most from the deductibility of interest payments. As the leverage in the deal is increased, the tax losses grow relative to the personal funds contributed by the investor, thereby allowing more of the investor's other income to be sheltered from taxation for a given depreciable asset. The associated economic cost of leverage is that it also increases the investor's exposure to risk. Additionally, it is the use of leverage to finance tax-sheltered investments—and the notion that higher leverage might in some cases not actually imply an increase in exposure—that has historically drawn the scrutiny of the Internal Revenue Service (IRS) and motivated congressional reforms such as the passive loss rules.

Investors in tax shelters are almost always purchasing interests in limited partnerships, either publicly traded or privately placed. The pooling together of numerous investors confers the advantages of diversification and economies of scale in transactions. Beyond pooling, the limited partnership has two features that recommend it as the organizational form for tax shelters. First, the partnership itself is not a taxable entity. Instead, income and losses from the investments "pass through" to the individual partners' tax returns. There is also

---

8. This point is well demonstrated by Warren (1985) and other comparisons of income and consumption tax systems.

9. Scholes and Wolfson (1992, 393) define a tax shelter in precisely this way: "an asset in which the investment cost can be deducted from taxable income at a rate that exceeds its economic depreciation."

flexibility in the allocation of income and losses to different partners over time. If the same investment were made by a C-corporation, the investors (as stockholders) would have no flexibility in allocations and any income produced by the investment would be subject to both corporate and personal income tax. Second, the liability of a limited partner is restricted to the amount of money contributed or pledged by that partner to the partnership, just as a corporate stockholder's liability is confined to the amount of stock purchased. If the investment were made by a sole proprietor, his liability would be unlimited. The examples that follow can easily be understood as the investor's share of interests in a limited partnership.

7.1.2   Cattle Feeding

A straightforward example of a tax shelter that produces only the deferral of income tax is that of cattle feeding. The idea behind the shelter is to purchase steers that weigh up to 700 pounds, fatten them up through six months of constant feeding, and then sell them to slaughterhouses at weights of over 1,000 pounds. The investment is a shelter because the feed consumed by the cattle plus all the fees incurred for veterinary services and management of the feedlot are considered to be tax deductible in the year they are incurred. However, the income realized from the sale of the cattle will not be taxed until the date of sale. Cattle-feeding shelters are organized in July or August for potential sale in the early months of the following year. With good timing, all of the expenses can be made in the first year and all sales can be made in the subsequent year.

The risks involved with the cattle-feeding shelter are that the market for fattened cattle is highly competitive and that the actual amount of weight that can be put on a steer is subject to random events such as cold weather and disease. Although futures markets exist for both cattle and grain, they have typically locked in very slim profit margins, and the use of futures markets to hedge risk may draw the attention of the IRS. Swanson and Swanson (1985) cite a cattle-feeding tax shelter from November 1979 in which feeder cattle were selling for $0.80 per pound, the expenses for fattening were estimated at $0.47 per pound, and the futures price of fully fattened cattle for delivery in April 1980 was $0.725 per pound. Using these estimates, purchasing a 650-pound steer and adding 450 pounds to it would have cost the investor 520 + 252 = $772. Selling a cattle future for delivery in April would have yielded 1,100*0.725 = $797, for a profit of $25. For tax purposes, the investor would have shown a $252 loss in 1979 and $277 in income in 1980.

In a cattle-feeding shelter, both the loss and the income are treated as ordinary income, so there is no conversion into capital gains. Moreover, since the fattening process takes only six months, such a shelter is really useful only when the taxpayer can foresee a reduction in his marginal tax rate during the following year. A taxpayer who has temporarily high income due to a capital gain or one who is planning to retire the next year would be a good candidate for the cattle-feeding shelter. The shelter operates, in essence, by exploiting the progressivity of the tax schedule. By adding losses in the year in which the marginal tax rate is high and income in the year in which the marginal tax rate is low, the taxpayer can lower his overall tax liability.

Table 7.1 shows the extent to which taxpayer can utilize a deferral shelter in the pre-TRA86 (1986) and post-TRA86 (1988) periods. Four sets of income declines over a two-year period are presented. The first three rows of the table show the effects for a taxpayer with a first-year income of $96,000 and a second-year income of $32,000 using a deferral shelter to transfer $32,000 of this income from the first year to the second, thereby equalizing a tax liability across the two years.[10] Using the 1986 tax table for a joint return, this results in a decline in the two-year tax liability of $2,537. The three other examples in the table also show gains from the tax shelter, ranging from $850 when the taxpayer shifts only $24,000 to $3,531 when the taxpayer defers $60,000 in income. The tax savings are on the order of 5 percent of the unsheltered tax liability.[11]

To demonstrate the effect of TRA86 on pure deferral shelters, the analogous tax savings are computed for the four shelters using the 1988 tax schedule.[12] TRA86 compressed the existing tax schedule with 14 tax brackets and a top marginal tax rate of 50 percent into a 2-bracket schedule with a top marginal tax rate of 28 percent. The table shows that the tax savings are generally smaller in absolute magnitude after TRA86. The decline is particularly apparent for the last shelter, which involves the highest income and the most deferral because TRA86 lowered the marginal tax rates most dramatically at the high end of the income distribution. The exception to this pattern is the second shelter, in which the amount of deferral increases using the post-TRA86 schedule. The reason is that the 1988 schedule imposed a 5 percentage point surtax on a range of income to phase out the benefits of the lower inframarginal tax rates for taxpayers above targeted income levels. When the phase-out was completed, the taxpayer had a 28 percent average tax rate on all taxable income, but within the phase-out range, the marginal tax rate was 33 percent. Since the phase-out range for a joint return was $71,900–$149,250, smoothing income to exactly $72,000 in 1988 was particularly advantageous.[13]

To summarize, pure deferral shelters such as the cattle-feeding shelter de-

---

10. For simplicity, the discounting of the tax losses from the second year that is appropriate for these comparisons is omitted.

11. The tension between horizontal equity and a progressive tax schedule has been the subject of numerous articles on "the marriage tax." See, e.g., Rosen (1987).

12. The 1988 schedule is used because the 1987 schedule was a transitional one to allow for the phase in of the marginal tax rate changes. The top marginal tax rate in 1987 was 38.5 percent.

13. This "bubble" in the marginal tax rates also accounts for the negative gain from deferral in the fourth shelter, as this shelter shifts income in both years into the phase-out range from the 28 percent marginal rate regions on both sides of it. The bubble was replaced in 1990 by a top marginal tax rate bracket of 31 percent.

Table 7.1   Effects of Deferral Shelter before and after TRA86

	Without Cattle Shelter		With Cattle Shelter		
Item	Year 1 (1)	Year 2 (2)	Year 1 (3)	Year 2 (4)	Tax Gain from Shelter[a]
Income	96,000	32,000	64,000	64,000	
Tax (1986)[b]	29,603	5,102	16,084	16,084	2,537
Tax (1988)[b]	24,218	5,093	14,053	14,053	1,205
Income	96,000	48,000	72,000	72,000	
Tax (1986)	29,603	10,075	19,414	19,414	850
Tax (1988)	24,218	9,573	16,298	16,298	1,195
Income	120,000	60,000	90,000	90,000	
Tax (1986)	40,481	14,564	26,974	26,974	1,097
Tax (1988)	32,138	12,933	22,238	22,238	595
Income	180,000	60,000	120,000	120,000	
Tax (1986)	69,929	14,564	40,481	40,481	3,531
Tax (1988)	50,400	12,933	32,138	32,138	−943

[a]Difference between the total tax paid without the shelter (sum of cols. [1] and [2]) and the total tax paid with the shelter (sum of cols. [3] and [4]).
[b]Tax (1986) and Tax (1988) are the tax liabilities on the taxable income specified in the top row of each group according to the tax tables for the respective years, assuming the taxpayer files a joint return.

scribed here typically offered modest tax relief in the pre-TRA86 period for taxpayers confronted with a one-time change in income levels. The magnitude of the tax gain from deferral was generally reduced by TRA86, especially at high income levels, where due to an oddity in the tax schedule, deferral could have actually increased the tax liability.[14] Finally, it is important to note that the passive loss limitations put an end to short-term deferral shelters used in this manner by disallowing the loss in the first year, forcing it to be realized in the second year when the cattle were sold, unless the temporarily high income in the first year was itself due to passive income.

7.1.3   Equipment Leasing

Equipment leasing was among the most popular tax shelters other than real estate in the pre-TRA86 period, thanks in large part to the implementation of the accelerated cost recovery system (ACRS) and a more generous ITC under the Economic Recovery Tax Act of 1981. ACRS is a schedule of depreciation allowances that permits depreciation to be taken for tax purposes over 3-, 5-, or 10-year periods; in each case, the depreciation period is considerably less

14. Curiously, the enactment of TRA86 itself caused a one-time opportunity for all high-income taxpayers to profit by deferral of income from the calendar year 1986 to 1988 because TRA86 reduced top marginal tax rates from 50 to 28 percent. The *Stanger Report* discussed an investment strategy that capitalizes on this opportunity. ("Hoof It to Cattle in 1986" 1986).

than the useful life of the investment. The ITC was an even more generous tax incentive, returning up to 10 percent of the cost of an asset in the year it was purchased. Because the ITC is a credit rather than a deduction, it reduces the investor's tax liability (not the investor's taxable income) dollar for dollar. TRA86 repealed the ITC, and although it did not directly alter ACRS for equipment, the reduction in top marginal tax rates lowered the after-tax value of depreciation deductions. Because the sale of leased equipment generates ordinary income rather than a capital gain, equipment leasing did not shelter income through conversion, and TRA86's repeal of the 60 percent exclusion does not come into play.

The customers of an equipment-leasing partnership are corporations that, for any of a number of reasons, prefer not to own their machinery. The most compelling reason is that because of low income or unused tax losses, the corporation cannot benefit from depreciating the assets it owns. By leasing, it can share the benefits of the tax deductions taken by the partnership. Alternatively, the corporation may choose to lease to avoid a long-term commitment to a particular level of technology or to reduce monthly payments and conserve on cash flows. The benefits to the partnership are the rents that it charges its customers, the depreciation deductions and ITC taken on the equipment, and the residual value of the equipment at the end of the lease.

As with any tax shelter, there are several risks associated with equipment leasing. The major risk is that the equipment will become obsolete due to technological advances in the relevant industries. If the equipment becomes obsolete, then the partnership will have a difficult time setting up subsequent leases after the initial one or recouping any of the original value through the sale of the equipment. The government has also increased the risk associated with leasing by requiring that the lease be short term (no more than half the depreciable life of the asset) in order to qualify for the ITC. The other requirement for the ITC is that the lease be actively managed, which in practice requires that 15 percent of the rent on the equipment be paid out for maintenance and related expenses. The most straightforward way to avoid these risks is to lease equipment that has little chance of becoming obsolete, like a box. When was the last time technology improved on a rectangle? Commonly leased equipment includes boxcars, shipping containers, and barges. The low risk of obsolescence ensures continuity of leasing customers or potential buyers for a sale of the equipment.

The important elements of an equipment lease are presented in table 7.2.[15] The investor purchases a $10,000 interest in a partnership that uses no debt in purchasing the assets (the leveraged investment will be presented in table 7.3). The assets are assumed to have a depreciable life of five years under ACRS, and for simplicity, it is assumed that the partnership can obtain three identical

---

15. The structure of this tax shelter is based on those described in "Equipment Leasing Partnerships" (1984) and Swanson and Swanson (1985).

Table 7.2   **Unleveraged Equipment-Leasing Tax Shelter before and after TRA86**

Cash Flow	0	1	2	3	4	5	6
				Year			
A. *Assumptions*							
Initial outlay	−10,000						
Debt and interest	0	0	0	0	0	0	0
ITC		−1,000					
Rental income		1,200	1,200	1,200	1,200	1,200	1,200
Management fees		−180	−180	−180	−180	−180	−180
Depreciation (ACRS)		−1,500	−2,200	−2,100	−2,100	−2,100	0
Residual value							9,000
B. *Pre-TRA86 with ITC*							
Taxable income		−480	−1,180	−1,080	−1,080	−1,080	10,020
Taxes paid		−1,240	−590	−540	−540	−540	5,010
After-tax cash flow	−10,000	2,260	1,610	1,560	1,560	1,560	5,010
IRR	8.22						
C. *Pre-TRA86 without ITC*							
Taxable income		−480	−1,180	−1,080	−1,080	−1,080	10,020
Taxes paid		−240	−590	−540	−540	−540	5,010
After-tax cash flow	−10,000	1,260	1,610	1,560	1,560	1,560	5,010
IRR	5.64						
D. *Pre-TRA86 with PLL*							
Taxable income		0	0	0	0	0	5,120
Taxes paid		0	0	0	0	0	1,560
After-tax cash flow	−10,000	1,020	1,020	1,020	1,020	1,020	8,460
IRR	6.58						
E. *Post-TRA86 without PLL*							
Taxable income		−480	−1,180	−1,080	−1,080	−1,080	10,020
Taxes paid		−134	−330	−302	−302	−302	2,806
After-tax cash flow	−10,000	1,154	1,350	1,322	1,322	1,322	7,214
IRR	7.24						
F. *Post-TRA86 with PLL*							
Taxable income		0	0	0	0	0	5,120
Taxes paid		0	0	0	0	0	1,434
After-tax cash flow	−10,000	1,020	1,020	1,020	1,020	1,020	8,586
IRR	6.78						

Note: See text (sec. 7.1.3) for assumptions. IRR values are percentages.

two-year leases and then sell the equipment for 90 percent of the original purchase price. This generates an ITC of $1,000, available in the first year of operation. Rental income is assumed to be 12 percent of the initial outlay. In order to qualify for the ITC, management and other fees of 15 percent of gross rent are paid out each year. The depreciation schedule allowed by ACRS generates deductions of 15 and 22 percent in the first two years and 21 percent in the remaining three years.

Panel B computes the after-tax cash flows of the investment during the pre-TRA86 period with the ITC in place. Taxable income each year is the rental income less management fees and depreciation. Taxes paid in each year are simply 50 percent of the taxable income for this high-income investor. In the first year, the taxes paid are reduced by the full amount of the ITC. Note that in every year, taxable income is negative. This is the amount of income from other sources that can be sheltered, and the after-tax value of the shelter is given by the negative taxes paid. The after-tax cash flows are the rental income less management fees and taxes paid. Since the sale of the equipment in year six is treated as ordinary income, it can be added directly into the taxable income and after-tax cash flow for that year. Because the equipment was fully depreciated by the date of the sale, the full amount of the sale is taxable. This is known as "recapture" of the depreciation allowances, because every dollar taken in depreciation in an earlier year is subject to tax when the equipment is sold. Note, however, that the investor still enjoys the benefit of deferring the taxes until the sixth year.[16]

The internal rate of return (IRR) for this investment is computed to be 8.22 percent.[17] The IRR is the interest rate such that, when the after-tax cash flows are discounted at this rate, the net present value of the investment is zero. Panel C shows that if the only change made by TRA86 was to repeal the ITC, then the IRR would fall to 5.64 percent. Incorporating another change enacted by TRA86, the reduction of the top marginal tax rate to 28 percent, in the calculations in panel E increases the IRR to 7.24 percent. The seeming paradox that lowering the after-tax value of the depreciation deductions raises the IRR of the investment is resolved by noticing that, because there is no conversion of income to capital gains in an equipment-leasing shelter, the lower marginal tax rate increases the after-tax cash flow from the residual value of the equipment. The two effects tend to offset each other; if the residual value were lower, then lowering the marginal tax rate might have further reduced the IRR. Thus, a natural consequence of the base broadening (repeal the ITC) and rate reduction of TRA86 would be the shift toward the leasing of equipment with higher residual values.

Panel F demonstrates the effect of the passive loss limitations (PLL) on the IRR, assuming that the investor has no sources of passive income in any of these years. In each year, the taxable income in the post-TRA86 scenario was

16. Recapture will be a more interesting phenomenon in the real estate tax shelter discussed in the next example.

17. That is, r such that

$$\sum_{t=0}^{T} C_t (1 + r)^{-t} = 0.$$

When the cash flows have exactly one change in sign, the IRR is uniquely defined and projects with the higher IRRs have higher net present values. Some examples presented below will also have a negative cash flow in the last period, but it will never be large enough to invalidate the correspondence between a higher present value of the investment and a higher IRR. All IRRs are presented in nominal terms on after-tax cash flows.

negative. The passive loss rules prevent this negative income from being used to reduce the investor's tax liability until the equipment is disposed of in year six. As in the cattle shelter discussed in the previous example, the passive loss rules in this case simply reduce the deferral built into the tax shelter. Compared to the removal of the ITC, the passive loss rules have a relatively minor effect on the value of the shelter when viewed appropriately as an investment in a depreciable asset.[18]

Table 7.3 repeats the analysis of the equipment-leasing tax shelter assuming that the partnership borrows an amount equal to the partners' equity investments. In other words, to obtain the same equipment, the partners contribute only $5,000 and borrow $5,000 to be repaid at the end of six years. The annual interest rate on the loan is assumed to be 10 percent; the payments incurred by the loan are shown in the second row of the table. The most important feature of the leverage is that it does not necessarily reduce the value of the ITC or depreciation deductions the investors can claim; ACRS and ITC are based on the value of the equipment only. Leverage enables tax shelter investors to generate higher tax losses for a given amount of equity investment.

The second important feature of leverage is that the interest paid on the debt is tax deductible; therefore, the opportunity cost of funds is equal to $(1 - \tau)^*\rho$, where τ is the marginal tax rate and ρ is the interest rate on the debt. For the pre-TRA86 period, this amounts to 5 percent. Borrowing at 5 percent to invest in a project with an IRR of 8.22 or 5.64 or 6.58 percent is a value-enhancing undertaking; hence, the IRRs rise to 14.38, 6.81, and 7.47 percent for the three pre-TRA86 scenarios. With leverage, the loss of the ITC is even more detrimental to the IRR of the investment, and its consequences are still larger than those of the passive loss limitations. For the post-TRA86 period, the marginal tax rate is 28 percent, yielding an after-tax cost of funds of 7.2 percent. Since this rate is just slightly below the 7.24 percent IRR on the post-TRA86 shelter, the IRR is increased trivially to 7.28 percent by the borrowing. When the passive loss limitations are incorporated, leverage actually decreases the IRR on the investment to 5.81 percent. Note that if the marginal tax rate were still 50 percent, the IRR in this case would increase, but borrowing at 7.2 percent to invest at 6.78 percent is value-reducing transaction. Thus, the reduction in marginal tax rates can under some scenarios discourage the use of leverage after TRA to invest in tax shelters. By reducing the deferral and hence the IRR of a tax shelter, the passive loss limitations enhance this effect.

Before concluding the analysis of equipment leasing, a word of caution is in order about the use of debt in a tax shelter. During the tax reforms of 1976 and 1978, Congress enacted the "at-risk" rules for investments in order to curb

18. This statement is true both before and after TRA86. Panel E imposes the passive loss limitations on the pre-TRA86 shelter, yielding an IRR of 6.58 percent, under the assumption that the passive loss limitations would have also affected the ITC (if they did not, their effects would be even smaller).

Table 7.3   Leveraged Equipment-Leasing Tax Shelter before and after TRA86

Cash Flow	0	1	2	3	4	5	6
A. Assumptions							
Initial outlay	−10,000						
Debt and interest	5,000	−500	−500	−500	−500	−500	−5,500
ITC		−1,000					
Rental income		1,200	1,200	1,200	1,200	1,200	1,200
Management fees		−180	−180	−180	−180	−180	−180
Depreciation (ACRS)		−1,500	−2,200	−2,100	−2,100	−2,100	0
Residual value							9,000
B. Pre-TRA86							
Taxable income		−980	−1,680	−1,580	−1,580	−1,580	9,520
Taxes paid		−1,490	−840	−790	−790	−790	4,760
After-tax cash flow	−5,000	2,010	1,360	1,310	1,310	1,310	−240
IRR	**14.38**						
C. Pre-TRA86 without ITC							
Taxable income		−980	−1,680	−1,580	−1,580	−1,580	9,520
Taxes paid		−490	−840	−790	−790	−790	4,760
After-tax cash flow	−5,000	1,010	1,360	1,310	1,310	1,310	−240
IRR	**6.81**						
D. Pre-TRA86 with PLL							
Taxable income		0	0	0	0	0	2,120
Taxes paid		0	0	0	0	0	60
After-tax cash flow	−5,000	520	520	520	520	520	4,460
IRR	**7.47**						
E. Post-TRA without PLL							
Taxable income		−980	−1,680	−1,580	−1,580	−1,580	9,520
Taxes paid		−274	−470	−442	−442	−442	2,666
After-tax cash flow	−5,000	794	990	962	962	962	1,854
IRR	**7.28**						
F. Post-TRA86 with PLL							
Taxable income		0	0	0	0	0	2,120
Taxes paid		0	0	0	0	0	594
After-tax cash flow	−5,000	520	520	520	520	520	3,926
IRR	**5.81**						

Note: See text (sec. 7.1.3) for assumptions. IRR values are percentages.

the use of leverage to purchase depreciable assets. The at-risk rules distinguish between nonrecourse and recourse debt. A nonrecourse debt contract limits the borrowers exposure to the value of the asset. A common example is the typical home mortgage. If the homeowner defaults, he loses his house, but if the value of the house is less than the amount outstanding on the mortgage, he is not liable to make up the difference out of his other wealth. If he were, that would be recourse debt. The at-risk rules stipulate that if the investor finances the tax shelter with nonrecourse debt, then the value of the tax preferences such as the ITC and ACRS are limited to the amount of the investment for which the investor has personal recourse. In the leasing example, it has therefore been implicitly assumed that if the lessees defaulted or the equipment became obsolete and could not be sold to cover the debt payments, the investor would have been required to personally pay off the debt. The at-risk rules will be relevant in section 7.3 when the rationale for the passive loss limitations is analyzed for abusive tax shelters.

The analysis of the equipment-leasing tax shelter yielded several interesting conclusions. The most important change due to TRA86 was the repeal of the ITC, the tax refund of 10 percent of the cost of obtaining the asset. Over a short time horizon, the passive loss limitations had a relatively small impact on the rate of return in the tax shelter once the ITC was repealed and the marginal tax rates were lowered. The reduction in top marginal tax rates could actually increase the rate of return on the tax shelter by reducing the tax liability on the residual value of the equipment by more than the value of the lower depreciation deductions. This finding will be important in the discussion of tax shelter clienteles in section 7.2. This tradeoff also demonstrated that as a consequence of recapture of depreciation, there is sometimes a discrepancy across policy regimes between the size of tax losses and the rate of return on the investment. Further, the lower marginal tax rate discourages the use of leverage in obtaining depreciable assets and encourages the use of assets with higher residual values in equipment-leasing shelters.

7.1.4   Real Estate Tax Shelters

By far the most common type of tax-sheltered investment is real estate.[19] As a tax shelter before TRA86, real estate provided not only deferral of tax through depreciation allowances but conversion of income to capital gains upon the sale of the property. Additionally, the magnification of tax benefits through leverage discussed in the equipment-leasing shelter is easier to obtain on real estate shelters because real estate is less affected by the at-risk rules. Mortgages are by their nature nonrecourse loans, but the tax code permits the full value of the initial investment to be used as the basis for depreciation allowances.[20] Although the pre-TRA86 tax code was rife with special tax preferences to encourage new construction, rehabilitation of historic structures, and provision of low-income housing, a simple example of a real estate deal will suffice to show the operation of the tax advantages.[21]

---

19. Tabulations in Petska (1992) show that in every year between 1985 and 1989, over half the losses in partnerships that reported net losses were in real estate partnerships.

20. When implemented in 1976, real estate investments were exempt from the at-risk rules. TRA86 extended the at-risk rules to real estate loans under some circumstances. See Becker (1987) and Owen, Robinson, and Plache (1987) for a full discussion of the effects of TRA86 on real estate investments.

21. This tax shelter is also based on an example in Swanson and Swanson (1985).

Table 7.4   **Real Estate Tax Shelter before and after TRA86**

			Year			
Cash Flow	0	1	2	3	4	5
A. *Assumptions*						
Rental income		8,000	8,640	9,331	10,078	10,884
Mortgage payment		9,750	9,750	9,750	9,750	9,750
Interest		9,000	8,910	8,809	8,696	8,570
Principal		750	840	941	1,054	1,180
(Remaining						
balance)		75,000	74,250	73,410	72,469	71,416
Property taxes		2,000	2,160	2,333	2,519	2,721
Property value		108,000	116,640	125,971	136,049	146,933
B. *Pre-TRA86*						
Depreciation		5,556	5,556	5,556	5,556	5,556
Taxable income		−8,556	−7,986	−7,366	−6,694	−5,962
Tax (saving)		−4,278	−3,993	−3,683	−3,347	−2,981
Property basis		94,444	88,889	83,333	77,778	72,222
Capital gain						74,711
Capital gains tax						14,942
After-tax cash flows	−25,000	528	723	932	1,155	61,969
IRR at five years	**21.88**					
C. *Post-TRA86*						
Depreciation		3,175	3,175	3,175	3,175	3,175
Taxable income		−6,175	−5,605	−4,985	−4,313	−3,582
Tax (saving)		−1,729	−1,569	−1,396	−1,208	−1,003
Property basis		96,825	93,651	90,476	87,302	84,127
Capital gain						62,806
Capital gains tax						17,586
After-tax cash flows	−25,000	−2,021	−1,701	−1,356	−984	57,347
IRR at five years	**14.17**					
D. *Post-TRA86 with PLL*						
Depreciation		3,175	3,175	3,175	3,175	3,175
Taxable income		0	0	0	0	0
Tax (saving)		0	0	0	0	0
Property basis		96,825	93,651	90,476	87,302	84,127
Capital gain						38,147
Capital gains tax						10,681
IRR calculations	−25,000	−3,750	−3,270	−2,752	−2,192	63,249
IRR at five years	**13.15**					

Note: See text (sec. 7.1.4) for assumptions. IRR values are percentages.

Table 7.4 shows the cash flows associated with a real estate tax shelter that purchases a $100,000 property with a $25,000 down payment, depreciates the property for five years, and sells at the end of five years to realize a capital gain. The mortgage is assumed to be for 25 years at an interest rate of 12 percent. Such a mortgage can be paid off with a constant annual payment of approximately 13 percent. The property is assumed to appreciate in value at a nominal rate of 8 percent. Rents are assumed to be 8 percent of the property value each year, and property taxes are assumed to be 2 percent per year.[22] These assumptions are shown in panel A.

Panel B shows the after-tax cash flows and IRR for the pre-TRA86 period. The property is depreciated using straight-line depreciation over an 18-year period. This yields a depreciation allowance of $5,556 in each year. Note that the property's basis for tax purposes is reduced each year by the depreciation allowance. Taxable income is then computed as the rental income less the sum of the mortgage interest, property taxes, and depreciation. The tax liability is simply half of taxable income at a top marginal tax rate of 50 percent, and because taxable income is negative each year, the investor reduces his overall tax liability through the shelter. The after-tax cash flow is computed as rent less the sum of the full mortgage payment, property taxes, and the tax liability. In the fifth year, the property is sold for $146,933, triggering a capital gain of $74,711 once the basis is deducted. Because 60 percent of the capital gain is excluded from ordinary taxation, the capital gains tax is 0.4*0.50*74,711, or $14,942. The capital gain net of its tax liability is the largest part of the after-tax cash flow in the fifth year. The leverage and tax preferences on the real estate shelter make the IRR on this investment a handsome 21.88 percent (though maintenance and other fees which would reduce cash flows have been omitted, or inadequately included as property taxes, for simplicity).[23]

Panel C recomputes the after-tax cash flows to account for the changes in depreciation and tax rates enacted by TRA86 but does not impose the passive loss limitations. Depreciation schedules for real estate were lengthened from 15, 18, or 19 years before TRA86 to 27.5 years for residential rental property and 31.5 years for nonresidential real property.[24] Consequently, the annual depreciation allowance is reduced to $100,000/31.5 = \$3,175$. The lower depreciation allowances result in smaller taxable losses to shelter other income. Moreover, because the top marginal tax rate was reduced to 28 percent, the after-tax value of the depreciation deductions is lower. The repeal of the long-term capital gain exclusion has the effect of increasing the capital gains tax rate from 20 percent to 28 percent. This is different from the equipment-leasing shelter in which the sale of the equipment was taxed as ordinary income in both cases. In the real estate shelter, the marginal tax rates lower the after-tax cash flows on depreciation, interest payments, and capital gains. As a result of these three changes, the IRR after TRA86 falls to 14.17 percent. Another inconvenient

22. In fact, real estate investments often have much better expected appreciation and rents than in this example; the assumptions are conservative here to demonstrate how the tax advantages can generate high rates of return for even mediocre investments. The sensitivity of the main conclusions drawn from this example to the conservative assumptions will be discussed below.

23. The IRRs on real estate tax shelters were often inflated by holding the investment until death, at which time the tax basis would be "stepped up" for the heirs, or by borrowing the initial investment from the tax shelter promoter at favorable interest rates.

24. TRA86 also eliminated accelerated depreciation for real estate, requiring the use of straight-line depreciation. To keep the table as simple as possible, this change is not reflected in the calculations. Straight-line depreciation is used for the pre-TRA86 shelter as well.

feature of this shelter is that the lower tax losses have made the annual after-tax cash flows negative; this shelter actually requires inflows of cash during its years of operation.

Panel D incorporates the passive loss limitations into the post-TRA86 computations. As in the equipment-leasing shelter, the passive loss limitations disallow the negative taxable income in each year before the disposition of the asset.[25] The disallowed passive losses are deducted from the cash flow when the property is sold in the fifth year. The passive loss limitations further reduce the after-tax cash flows in the years before disposition and increase the income in the year of disposition. The IRR on the shelter is reduced by about 1 percentage point to 13.15 percent as a result of the passive loss rules. This reduction is small compared to that caused by the changes in the marginal tax rate, conversion, and the lengthening of the depreciation schedule.[26]

The examples in this section were chosen to illustrate the means through which features of the tax code generate the benefits of tax shelters and to ascertain the importance of the passive loss limitations, which are thought to have been the fatal blow to tax shelters, relative to other provisions in the tax code. For a pure deferral shelter such as cattle feeding, the reductions in marginal tax rates at high income levels from 1986 to 1988 substantially reduced the already modest tax benefits of income smoothing. Due to the 33 percent bubble, however, it was possible that deferral was in some cases a better deal after TRA86. The passive loss rules directly eliminated the benefits of pure deferral because they disallow all passive losses from offsetting one-time changes in nonpassive income.

As the equipment-leasing and real estate shelters demonstrate, deferral of a given size tax liability is only one aspect of a tax shelter. Far more important to the shelters' IRRs were the *determinants* of the size of the tax liability to be deferred—the magnitude of the ITC, the length of the depreciation period, and the after-tax cost of debt to use as leverage—and the differential between ordinary and capital gains tax rates, which determines the payoff to conversion.

---

25. If the property were held for more than five years before being sold, the taxable income from the shelter would eventually turn positive as the interest component of the mortgage payment continued to fall and the difference between the rental income and the depreciation deduction continued to widen due to nominal appreciation of the property. In that case, disallowed passive losses could be applied to income before the property's disposition. In the absence of the passive loss rules, most investors would refinance the mortgage to increase the fraction of the payment that is due to interest as soon as the investment ceased to have negative taxable income.

26. Redoing the calculations assuming disposition after 10 years does not change any of the qualitative comparisons across tax regimes. Increasing the rental rate lowers the tax losses during the years before disposition both before and after TRA86. The effects of the marginal tax rate and depreciation changes are somewhat reduced, and the effects of the passive loss rules are greatly reduced because fewer losses are disallowed. At a rental rate of 12 percent, the IRRs are 28.58, 23.65, and 23.62 percent for the pre-TRA86, post-TRA86, and post-TRA86 with passive loss limitations scenarios, respectively. Decreasing the appreciation rate on the property to 4 percent leaves the magnitudes of the IRR differences across regimes similar to those in table 7.4, as the lower appreciation creates both higher tax losses in the years before disposition but smaller gains to conversion upon disposition. The IRRs for the three regimes under this assumption are 12.26, 3.97, and 3.60 percent.

After these factors were taken into account, the effect of the passive loss rules on the IRRs of the equipment-leasing and real estate shelters was minor. The main consequence of the passive loss rules in these cases was cosmetic; the passive loss rules eliminated only the reporting of a tax loss from the investment before its disposition. But to claim that this cosmetic change is of any importance beyond the effect it had on the IRR is to require that all tax sheltering be done solely for short-term deferral reasons (as in the cattle shelter) or that tax shelter investors systematically ignore the recapture of depreciation upon disposition of their investment.

7.2   Tax Shelter Clienteles after TRA86

The illustrative tax shelters in the previous section assumed that tax shelter investors faced the marginal tax rates for the highest-income taxpayers both before and after TRA86. To the extent that some investors faced lower marginal tax rates, the IRRs on these examples will not be representative of those actually obtained. Additionally, the dispersion of marginal tax rates of investors has important implications for the pricing of tax shelters in a competitive equilibrium.[27] This section uses the University of Michigan panel of tax returns and the NBER TAXSIM program for calculating tax liabilities to determine the distribution of marginal tax rates on tax shelter investments across TRA86 and whether it is feasible for a market for tax shelters to exist after TRA86.

Tax shelters are not identified as such on an individual's tax return. After TRA86, the best indication of whether the taxpayer is engaged in tax sheltering is whether any passive income or losses are listed on schedule E, where all amounts of "supplemental income" are reported. Since the passive loss rules did not exist before TRA86, the distinction between passive and nonpassive income or losses is not made. It is therefore not possible to reliably distinguish between tax shelter investors and, say, a lawyer in an unprofitable legal partnership by examining only a cross section of pre-TRA86 tax returns. Instead, a panel of tax returns spanning years on both sides of TRA86 is required, so that the distinction between passive and nonpassive investments in the years after TRA86 can be used to classify the income and losses in the years before TRA86.

Table 7.5 presents tabulations of partnership losses from 1986 by whether the taxpayer also reported passive partnership income or losses during any of the years from 1987–90.[28] Of the 10,341 tax returns in the 1986 data set, 346,

---

27. The "price" of a tax shelter can be conceptualized as the magnitude of the fees a tax shelter promoter would require from investors. Although such fees were omitted from the initial outlays in the illustrative tax shelters, in a competitive market they are clearly endogenously determined. The size of the fees will determine how much of the tax benefits the investor will have to share with the promoter.

28. The panel of tax returns is a random subsample of the IRS *Statistics of Income* public-use files maintained by the Office of Tax Policy Research at the University of Michigan.

Table 7.5   **Change in Marginal Tax Rates (MTRs) by Partnership Status**

Has Partnership Losses 1986 (1)	Has Passive Partnership Post-TRA86 (2)	Number of Returns (3)	Percentage of Category (4)	Percentage with Passive Partnership Losses Post-TRA86 (5)	Average First-Dollar MTR	
					1986 (6)	1988 (7)
No	No	9,799	98.04	0	16	16
	Yes	196	1.96	53	26	22
	Total	9,995	100.00	1	17	16
Yes	No	100	28.90	0	22	20
	Yes	246	71.10	91	33	26
	Total	346	100.00	65	30	24
Total		10,341	100.00	3	17	16

Source: Author's calculations from the University of Michigan panel of tax returns and the NBER TAXSIM program.

or 3.3 percent, reported partnership losses in 1986. The classification excludes those returns with partnership income but no losses because the objective is to identify tax shelterers, not just partners, prior to disposition in the pre-TRA86 period. Within this group, 246, or 71.1 percent, reported income or loss from a passive partnership in the post-TRA86 period. This group will be identified as the "tax shelterers" in 1986.[29] Column (5) shows that 91 percent of this group reported actual passive *losses* after TRA86.

Having identified a group of taxpayers as tax shelterers, it is possible to determine the average marginal tax rate on partnership losses that prevailed prior to TRA86. In doing so, it is important to do a "first dollar" calculation— that is, to set partnership net income to zero—because large partnership losses lower the taxpayer's marginal tax rate. The first-dollar marginal tax rate is a better measure of the tax incentive to shelter income than is the more traditional "last dollar" calculation. Column (6) of table 7.5 shows that this rate is 33 percent on average for those who sheltered income in 1986. The NBER TAXSIM tax calculation program is used to construct this estimate.[30] One of the many useful capabilities of the TAXSIM program is that it can compute

29. Although data on S-corporations, estates, and trusts reported on schedule E are available and subject to the passive loss rules, those data are excluded from these tabulations because tax shelters are usually organized as partnerships. Unfortunately, the individual tax return data does not distinguish between limited and general partnerships.

30. TAXSIM is a detailed microsimulation model of the U.S. federal and state income tax systems, originally used to study the effects of tax deductibility on charitable giving by Feldstein and Taylor (1976) and substantially extended to study the integration of the personal and corporate income tax systems by Feldstein and Frisch (1977). Feenberg and Coutts (1993) provide an introduction to the TAXSIM model.

Table 7.6   **Distribution of Partnership Losses and Marginal Tax Rates (MTRs):**
                       Tax Shelter Investors in 1986

First-Dollar MTR 1986	Number of Returns (1)	Percentage of Returns (2)	Percentage of Partnership Losses 1986 (3)	Weighted Average MTR 1986 (4)	1988 (5)
0	21	8.54	6.72	0	5
0–5	0	0.00	0.00	–	–
5–10	1	0.41	0.02	8	15
10–15	8	3.25	2.81	14	4
15–20	22	8.94	2.65	16	16
20–25	12	4.88	2.64	21	24
25–30	21	8.54	1.37	27	28
30–35	28	11.38	2.19	32	29
35–40	38	15.45	8.24	37	32
40–45	29	11.79	8.45	42	33
45–50	32	13.01	14.39	48	31
50	34	13.82	50.52	50	28
Total	246	100.00	100.00	41	27

Source: Author's calculations from the University of Michigan panel of tax returns and the NBER TAXSIM program.

the marginal tax rates under alternative scenarios, including the tax rules prevailing in years other than that of the data. Column (7) shows that the average first-dollar marginal tax rate on partnership losses for the tax shelterers would have fallen to 26 percent under the 1988 tax rules.[31]

Table 7.6 shows the decline in marginal tax rates for the group of tax shelterers based on the level of their 1986 marginal tax rate. In this table, marginal tax rates are weighted by the taxpayer's level of partnership losses so that the marginal tax rates of taxpayers who are sheltering more income are weighted more heavily in the average.[32] As shown by columns (4) and (5) of the last row, dollar-weighting the marginal tax rates shows a decline from 41 percent in 1986 to 27 percent in 1988. Columns (2) and (3) show that although taxpayers with the top marginal tax rate constituted only 13.82 percent of the tax shelterers, they represented 50.52 percent of the partnership losses. Every taxpayer in this tax bracket would have faced a 28 percent marginal tax rate under the 1988 tax schedule with the same reported income. Thus, the tax rates assumed in the examples in the previous section do represent a majority of the tax shelter-

31. Repeating this analysis (and that in table 7.6) on the tax returns from 1984 and 1985, or requiring partnership activity in all three years, yielded only trivial differences from those reported here.

32. Dollar-weighted marginal tax rates measure the marginal tax rate on each dollar of partnership loss rather than the marginal tax rate on each taxpayer who reports partnership losses.

Table 7.7   **Tax Shelter Rates of Return under Alternative Marginal Tax Rates**

	Marginal Tax Rate			
Shelter	50	32	33	28
Equipment-leasing shelter (no leverage)				
Pre-TRA86	8.22	9.39		
Pre-TRA86 without ITC	5.64	6.97		
Pre-TRA86 with PLL	6.58	7.96		
Post-TRA86 without PLL			6.90	7.24
Post-TRA86 with PLL			6.38	6.78
Equipment-leasing shelter (50 percent leverage)				
Pre-TRA86	14.38	13.42		
Pre-TRA86 without ITC	6.81	7.21		
Pre-TRA86 with PLL	7.47	8.58		
Post-TRA86 without PLL			7.20	7.28
Post-TRA86 with PLL			5.46	5.81
Real estate shelter				
Pre-TRA86	21.88	20.04		
Post-TRA86 without PLL			13.54	14.17
Post-TRA86 with PLL			12.37	13.15

Note: IRRs correspond to the investments from tables 7.2–7.4

ing that occurred prior to TRA86, and approximately 83.79 percent of the tax shelterers faced lower marginal tax rates after TRA86 than before.

Table 7.6 also demonstrates that tax shelters are not uniformly held by investors in the top marginal tax bracket. If the demand for tax-sheltered investments by taxpayers facing the top marginal tax rate is less than the supply, then tax shelters will have to be priced to attract investors in lower marginal tax brackets. As has often been noted in discussions of tax-exempt securities, this generates a pure rent for investors in the top marginal tax brackets.[33] Table 7.6 shows that under the 1986 tax schedule, 35 percent of the partnership losses of tax shelterers were reported by individuals with marginal tax rates at least 5 percentage points below the top rate. Because TRA86 compressed the number of tax brackets, column (5) shows that, in contrast, over 85 percent of the partnership losses of tax shelterers would have been within 5 percentage points of the top rate (here, the 33 percent bubble). Thus, to the extent that the investor's marginal tax rate is an important determinant of the IRR on the tax shelter, TRA86 reduced the scope for such rents to be earned by top marginal tax rate investors (and even more so for very high income taxpayers, who did not face the top marginal tax rate).

Table 7.7 presents the IRRs from the tax shelters described in tables 7.2 through 7.4 under alternative marginal tax rate assumptions. Focusing first on the real estate tax shelter at the bottom of the table, the IRR falls from 21.88

---

33. This issue is discussed in connection with tax shelters by Cordes and Galper (1985).

to 20.04 percent when the marginal tax rate is changed from 50 to 32 percent (the average tax rate for the marginal tax rate group that saw a reduction in tax rates due to TRA86). The potential rents earned by the higher marginal tax bracket investors on this are equivalent to those obtained if the same two groups both invested in a municipal bond that offered a pretax equivalent rate of return of 10 percent to the investor with the 32 percent marginal rate.

When the same shelter is evaluated under the post-TRA86 tax rules, the investment actually has a higher IRR at a marginal tax rate of 28 percent (14.17 percent) than a 33 percent (13.54 percent). For this calculation, the passive loss rules have not been imposed; the reversal exists because TRA 86 lengthened the depreciation schedules and, most important, eliminated conversion to capital gains by repealing the long-term exclusion. Imposing the passive loss rules increases the discrepancy only slightly. The middle set of numbers shows that an analogous conclusion can be drawn from the equipment-leasing shelter that borrowed half of the initial outlay. Because the equipment lease did not involve conversion to capital gains, simply removing the ITC was enough to make the shelter less appealing at higher tax rates.[34]

Thus far in the analysis, all tax shelter investors have been individual taxpayers, but this does not have to be the case. Corporations can also purchase interests in limited partnerships, and after TRA86, may have been the more natural clientele for tax shelters than any cohort of individuals. One reason is that corporations are not subject to passive loss rules if they are widely owned.[35] Another is that the reductions in individual marginal tax rates in TRA86 were not quite matched for corporations. The top marginal tax rate for corporate income fell from 46 to 34 percent as a result of TRA86, making the corporate rate higher than the top individual rate for the first time. If depreciation allowances are available, the owner of the asset should have the highest marginal tax rate in order to maximize the value of the tax deferral.[36]

It is unlikely that this "inversion" of top marginal tax rates or the absence of the passive loss rules for corporations should have resulted in a migration of the ownership of depreciable assets to the corporate sector. The most important reason is that the higher marginal tax rate only matters if the shelter can gener-

34. The first set of IRRs shows that even in the pre-TRA86 period, the unleveraged equipment leasing investment afforded higher rates of return to the low marginal tax rate investor. If the residual value of the equipment at the end of the shelter were much less than the assumed 90 percent, the return to the high marginal tax rate investor could have been made higher than that of the low marginal tax rate investor. For example, with a residual value of 40 percent, the 50 percent marginal tax rate yields an after-tax rate of return of 2.92 percent, compared to 2.80 percent for the 32 percent marginal tax rate investor.

35. Brumbaugh and Ward (1987) provide a more detailed explanation of the rules determining whether an entity is subject to the passive loss rules.

36. I am indebted to Roger Gordon for first pointing out to me the relevance of the corporate tax rate changes to tax shelters after TRA86. As with the individual income tax schedule, the corporate schedule contained a 5 percentage point bubble to phase out the benefits of lower inframarginal tax rates for sufficiently high income corporations.

ate losses that are not recaptured at that same rate in a short period of time. The repeal of the ITC and the lengthening of real estate depreciation schedules after TRA86 affected corporations as well as individuals. Furthermore, shifting ownership of depreciable assets to high tax rate entities makes sense only if the after-tax rate of return increases with the tax rate. Another reason is that the inversion proved to be a short-lived phenomenon, and this was not wholly unanticipated. The top marginal tax rate for individuals was increased to 39.6 percent by the Omnibus Budget Reconciliation Act of 1993, a rate that is higher than the similarly increased 35 percent top rate on corporations, and a preferential 28 percent maximum rate on long-term capital gains was reestablished.

The possible migration of depreciable assets into the corporate sector notwithstanding, the implications of the comparisons in table 7.7 for the existence of a tax shelter clientele are profound. Investments that before TRA86 could be used as tax shelters are no longer most profitably held by top marginal tax rate investors. In a competitive equilibrium, these investments should be made by individuals in the lowest marginal tax brackets rather than the highest ones. High-bracket investors would likely earn higher risk-adjusted returns by holding tax-exempt bonds, especially if they were priced to attract investors from lower marginal tax brackets.[37] If the correlation between the marginal tax rate and the after-tax IRR is not positive, then it is difficult to think of the investment as a tax shelter in the traditional sense. Again, the passive loss limitations are not necessary for this change in the tax shelter clientele, given the other reforms enacted by TRA86.

The sample tax shelters discussed in this and the previous section also clearly show the potential economic dislocations caused by the passive loss rules. Because they target losses, and tax losses are magnified by leverage, the passive loss rules discourage the use of debt to purchase depreciable assets. Investors who would otherwise require debt to finance their investments are thereby hindered. Since losses and gains are treated asymmetrically, the passive loss rules also discriminate against riskier investments that yield larger and more frequent losses for a given expected rate of return. Because they discriminate between investors who happen to have passive income from other investments and those who do not, the passive loss rules create a more heterogeneous pool of potential investors, thereby impeding the full capitalization of the tax benefits (assuming any can still be found) that would occur if a given clientele of investors could absorb the entire supply of tax shelters. But, most important, the passive losses do not distinguish between genuine economic

37. This conclusion will not necessarily hold if taxpayers with higher marginal tax rates are less risk averse than those with lower marginal tax rates. In that case, the clientele for former tax shelters will be composed of the least risk-averse high-bracket investors in addition to somewhat more risk averse low-bracket investors.

losses and those that might be due solely to the tax-related incentives that have been written into the law. Noncorporate enterprises are consequently hampered relative to corporations in undertaking risky investments.[38]

7.3   Targeting Abusive Tax Shelters

An important assumption in the foregoing analysis of tax shelters has been that all assets are traded at a fair market value. In transactions without important tax consequences, a fair market value prevails because buyers have no interest in paying too much for an asset and sellers have no interest in receiving too little. Abuse of tax shelters creeps into the system when the transaction price of the asset is artificially inflated to allow the investor to claim depreciation allowances that are not only accelerated but far in excess of the fair market value of the asset. What should be apparent to the dispassionate observer is that under normal circumstances, the tax shelter promoter who sells the asset should be unwilling to agree to overstate the transaction price if he incurs an added tax liability but receives no real compensation for it. The important insight due to Sims (1994) is that the key to abusive tax shelters is therefore the mechanism that allows the seller to escape taxation on the artificially inflated price. This section shows that the mechanism identified by Sims—the combination of purchase-money debt and installment sale reporting of the gain—is in substance a pure deferral shelter.[39] Consequently, the passive loss rules were sufficient to eliminate abusive tax shelters. As in the case of legitimate tax shelters, however, they were hardly necessary.

The government has generally been aware that tax shelter abuse must be related to the amount of debt used to purchase the depreciable asset. An early attempt to curtail the use of debt in abusive tax shelters was the passage of the at-risk rules in 1976 as section 465 of the Internal Revenue Code. As discussed in the real estate shelter example, the at-risk rules restrict the amount of deductible loss from the ownership of depreciable property to the total amount of the taxpayer's economic investment, that is, the amount the investor has at risk in the transaction. The at-risk rules specify that borrowed funds are at risk only to the extent that they are secured by the investor's other personal assets or that the taxpayer is personally liable to repay them. So-called nonrecourse loans, in which the investor's obligation to the lender is limited to the asset that secures the loan, are not deemed to be at risk and cannot be counted in the investment's depreciable basis.

---

38. Limited partnerships such as venture capital funds whose objectives are to undertake risky but ex ante profitable investments exclusive of tax preferences would be less likely to be disposed of within a few years; hence, the elimination of deferral that results from the passive loss rules would have a larger effect on genuine economic losses than losses motivated by tax considerations.

39. This section draws heavily on the insights of Sims (1994), as well as helpful conversations with its author.

On the surface, the at-risk rules appear to be able to eliminate tax shelter abuse by preventing investors from using debt that they will not have to repay in full to inflate the asset's basis for depreciation. Sims (1994) shows, in contrast, that the at-risk rules were inadequate because the practical distinction between nonrecourse and recourse debt in tax shelters is small. One reason is that default on even a nonrecourse loan will harm the investor's future access to credit. Another is that even loans with personal recourse can be defaulted. But the most important reason is that any amount of nonrecourse debt that is not repaid must be included as "cancellation of indebtedness" (COD) income in the investor's gross income for tax purposes when default occurs.[40] Thus, the "giveaway" is more apparent than real; an investor cannot effectively evade taxation by defaulting on a nonrecourse loan.

The failing of the at-risk rules is that a nonrecourse loan is not substantively different from a recourse loan; there are consequences of default that make it an undesirable outcome.[41] As a result, it is unlikely to generate significant abuse of the tax advantages in a shelter. In order to facilitate abuse, the loan must be such that default is a planned event and is mutually satisfactory to the lender and the borrower. The only lender that could possibly be indifferent to default on the loan to finance a tax shelter investment is the tax shelter promoter who sells the assets. It is therefore "purchase money" financing from the seller that is the key ingredient of tax shelter abuse. But purchase money alone does not guarantee that the promoter will agree to overstate the sale price of the asset if he or she incurs an immediate tax liability on the transaction. Some mechanism must be found for the promoter to avoid this tax liability. In the most flagrant cases, that has been the installment sales treatment in section 453 of the Internal Revenue Code.[42] Installment sale reporting allows the seller to pay taxes on gain from the sale of the asset in proportion to the amount of the total contract price that is actually paid at any given time, that is, the fraction of the total price that is not purchase money.

In Sims's example, the promoter produces a teakettle for $750 and agrees to sell it for $1,000 in cash plus a $2,000 note from the buyer (payable in full at the end of the shelter) for a total contract price of $3,000. The promoter's gain for tax purposes is the $2,250 between his sale price and his production costs. However, the installment sale rules allow him to pay taxes on only the fraction of that price that he has received at the time of sale: (1,000/3,000)*2,250, or $750 dollars. As long as his tax rate is lower than 33 percent in this case, his tax liability will be less than his $250 in actual gain on the sale, that is, the

---

40. See Chirelstein (1994) for a more detailed discussion of COD income.
41. Coven (1986) critiques the at-risk rules along these lines.
42. Sims (1994) draws this conclusion based on an examination of the tax shelter case law since the passage of the at-risk rules and discusses other more-limited means by which the basis of the depreciable asset could be manipulated through purchase-money financing.

$1,000 in cash less the $750 in production costs.[43] The promoter then agrees to allow the buyer to default on the $2,000 note. In the meantime, the tax shelter investor has taken the accelerated depreciation on the inflated contract price and has only to pay tax on the $2,000 (as COD income) when he defaults on the note at the end of the shelter. As long as this can pass the at-risk rules by being recourse debt (or be done on real estate transactions, which are less encumbered by the at-risk rules), the sham transaction works. Since the promoter earns his livelihood by facilitating this type of abuse, reputational considerations will virtually guarantee that he chooses not to enforce the debt even though he is legally entitled to do so. His long-term incentive is not to expropriate his customers.

In this example, the investor was able to take $2,000 of extra accelerated depreciation and then pay tax on the $2,000 in a later year. It is a pure deferral shelter, as in the case of the cattle-feeding shelter discussed in section 7.1, with the added bonus that unlike the cattle-feeding shelter, in which the magnitude of the gain was constrained by the progressivity of the tax code, the deferral in the teakettle shelter is unlimited. As long as the promoter obtains the $1,000 in cash for the teakettle, he will always be able to cover his tax liability by using the installment sale reporting regardless of the amount of purchase money he offers the investor. The depreciable asset itself is almost irrelevant; it simply provides access to the favorable depreciation on a paper transaction. The clever point made by Sims is that it might just as well be a teakettle.

Table 7.8 revisits the equipment-leasing tax shelter without leverage from table 7.2 to demonstrate the effects of the purchase-money debt on the IRR of the shelter and the role of passive loss limitations in eliminating this type of abuse. In this case, the investor pays the same $10,000 initially, receives the same cash flows as rent and management fees from leasing the equipment, and sells the asset for the same residual value. The only change that has been made is the addition of $30,000 in seller financing, which appears only in year six when the investor defaults on the note and pays ordinary income tax on it. In the pre-TRA86 period, this inflates both the ITC and the depreciation allowances by a factor of four and increases the IRR from 8.22 to 43.08 percent. When the ITC is removed, the IRR increase is more modest, from 5.64 to 19.12 percent. If the ITC is retained but the passive loss rules are applied to the pre-TRA86 period, the IRR increases from 6.58 to 10.76 percent. It is the presence of the ITC which makes this more than just a pure deferral shelter, since the ITC is never recaptured.[44] Under the post-TRA86 period marginal tax rates, the IRR increases from 7.24 to 12.06 percent. The more modest increase is a

43. More generally, Sims shows that the promoter need only require a cash payment of at least $c/(1-t)$ to break even, where c is the cost of the asset and t is his marginal tax rate, *regardless* of the amount of purchase money in the deal.

44. Alternatively, the ITC is equivalent to an extra depreciation allowance that is recaptured at a 0 percent tax rate and therefore always "converted."

Table 7.8   **"Abusive" Equipment-Leasing Tax Shelter before and after TRA86**

Cash Flow	0	1	2	3	4	5	6
A. *Assumptions*							
Initial outlay	−40,000						
Purchase money	30,000	0	0	0	0	0	−30,000
ITC		−4,000					
Rental income		1,200	1,200	1,200	1,200	1,200	1,200
Management fees		−180	−180	−180	−180	−180	−180
Depreciation (ACRS)		−6,000	−8,800	−8,400	−8,400	−8,400	0
Residual value							9,000
B. *Pre-TRA86 with ITC*							
Taxable income		−4,980	−7,780	−7,380	−7,380	−7,380	40,020
Taxes paid		−6,490	−3,890	−3,690	−3,690	−3,690	20,010
After-tax cash flow	−10,000	7,510	4,910	4,710	4,710	4,710	−9,990
IRR	**43.08**						
C. *Pre-TRA86 without ITC*							
Taxable income		−4,980	−7,780	−7,380	−7,380	−7,380	40,020
Taxes paid		−2,490	−3,890	−3,690	−3,690	−3,690	20,010
After-tax cash flow	−10,000	3,510	4,910	4,710	4,710	4,710	−9,990
IRR	**19.12**						
D. *Pre-TRA86 with PLL*							
Taxable income		0	0	0	0	0	40,020
Taxes paid		0	0	0	0	0	−1,440
After-tax cash flow	−10,000	1,020	1,020	1,020	1,020	1,020	11,460
IRR	**10.76**						
E. *Post-TRA86 without PLL*							
Taxable income		−4,980	−7,780	−7,380	−7,380	−7,380	40,020
Taxes paid		−1,394	−2,178	−2,066	−2,066	−2,066	11,206
After-tax cash flow	−10,000	2,414	3,198	3,086	3,086	3,086	−1,186
IRR	**12.06**						
F. *Post-TRA86 with PLL*							
Taxable income		0	0	0	0	0	5,120
Taxes paid		0	0	0	0	0	1,434
After-tax cash flow	−10,000	1,020	1,020	1,020	1,020	1,020	8,586
IRR	**6.78**						

Note: See text (sec. 7.3) for assumptions. IRR values are percentages.

result of the lower value of the overstated depreciation deductions at a top marginal tax rate of 28 percent. Finally, once the ITC has been removed, the shelter becomes a pure deferral shelter and the passive loss limitations eliminate all gains from the purchase-money financing. The IRR is unchanged from table 7.2 at 6.78 percent.

In this case, the passive loss rules are effective at eliminating a tax shelter that has no function but to reduce payments to the Treasury. As long as the shelter is subject to recapture of all tax benefits at the same tax rate as they are deducted (i.e., no conversion), the passive loss rules are sufficient to remove the mechanism through which shelters become abusive. It is also clear that the passive loss rules are far more than what is necessary to accomplish this objective. The appearance of a loss is not the problem, nor is the use of debt which magnifies that loss. The two problems are the escape hatch provided by the installment sale treatment of the seller's gain and the unlimited deferral through purchase-money debt. The former was effectively repealed by the Revenue Act of 1987, which required that installment sellers pay interest on the tax liability deferred due to nonrecognition of a gain under section 453. Sims argues that in most cases (including his teakettle shelter), such interest penalties would be prohibitive and proposes an even simpler solution that focuses on the latter: disallow any basis attributable to the use of purchase money in tax shelters. Such a provision would be similar in spirit to the at-risk rules but would recognize that it is seller financing, rather than nonrecourse debt, that is the catalyst of tax shelter abuse. It would also not invalidate genuine economic losses as do the passive loss limitations. Instead, it would merely require that an outside lender provide the financing for legitimate tax shelters. As long as the outside lender has the same information about the borrower as does the seller, this requirement imposes no efficiency loss.

7.4 Distribution of Passive Losses

As suggested by table 7.6, tax shelters in the pre-TRA86 period were heavily concentrated in the high end of the income distribution. Any hypothesized effect of the passive loss rules on investments in tax shelters would therefore be borne disproportionately by high-income taxpayers. Since income redistribution is often a goal of tax policy and a requirement of major tax reforms such as TRA86, this section considers the effect of the passive loss rules on the distribution of the federal tax burden across the population of taxpayers.

Table 7.9 begins by examining the fraction of tax returns that were directly affected by the passive loss limitations during the phase-in period. Because of the concentration of passive losses at high income levels, the data are taken from the public-use files of the IRS *Statistics of Income* for the four years after TRA86. Unlike the panel data set used for table 7.6, these cross-sectional files are stratified by income level with high-income returns oversampled. The oversampling of the part of the income distribution where the losses are concentrated increases the precision of the estimates. The first line of the table shows that the fraction of returns filing schedule E declined in each year, from 13.06 percent in 1987 to 12.60 percent in 1990. As mentioned above, schedule E must be filed by taxpayers with income or losses from rental real estate, partnerships, S-corporations, trusts, or estates. Aggregate losses on schedule E declined by a much greater magnitude, from $85.3 to $69.1 billion, over the

Table 7.9   **Aggregate Passive Loss Limitations, 1987–90**

	Year			
	1987	1988	1989	1990
Returns filing schedule E (%)	13.06	12.91	12.68	12.60
Reporting passive losses	29.86	26.99	28.76	23.50
With passive loss limitation	42.84	38.97	38.69	42.00
Aggregate schedule E losses (billion 1990 $)	85.3	74.2	71.0	69.1
Aggregate passive losses	76.9	61.6	63.8	55.2
Aggregate disallowed passive losses	15.3	15.8	20.9	18.9
Passive losses disallowed (%)	19.88	25.66	32.73	42.24
Phase-in of passive loss limitations	35.00	60.00	80.00	90.00

Source: Author's calculations from the annual IRS *Statistics of Income* public-use cross sections.

same period.[45] The discrepancy is a consequence of the incentives TRA86 provided for profit-making enterprises to organize as S-corporations and partnerships rather than C-corporations by lowering the top personal tax rate below the corporate tax rate on income.[46] The fraction of returns that reported passive losses from any of these sources conditional on filing schedule E also fell dramatically over this period, from 29.86 percent in 1987 to 23.50 percent in 1990.[47] The decline in the aggregate value of passive losses was $21.7 billion, or 28.2 percent of the total in 1987.

Taxpayers who report passive losses are required to file form 8582 in order to determine whether the passive loss limitations apply to them. If the limitations bind, the disallowed amount is carried forward to the next year. In each year, the fraction of taxpayers with passive losses who reported more losses than they were allowed was approximately 40 percent, and the aggregate value of these disallowed losses was between $15.3 and $20.9 billion over this period. The fraction of passive losses that were disallowed increased steadily from 19.88 to 42.24 percent over the four-year period. In each year, this fraction was approximately half of the statutory rate of disallowance for passive losses in excess of passive gains. That roughly half of the passive losses were not disallowed suggests that investors were able to successfully match at least some passive losses to passive income.[48]

45. All dollar amounts in this section are in constant 1990 dollars.
46. See Gordon and MacKie-Mason (1990, 1994) for a theoretical discussion and an estimate of the tax distortions in the choice of organizational form before TRA86. Plesko (1994) estimates the effect of tax factors on conversions to S-corporations after TRA86. Guenther (1992) and Gentry (1994) examine the importance of tax considerations in the behavior of master limited partnerships relative to corporations.
47. These passive losses do not include passive losses carried forward from previous years.
48. After TRA86, there was a premium on passive-income generators, affectionately referred to as PIGs. As discussed by Gentry (1994), the use of PIGs was curtailed for publicly traded partnerships in 1987 by requiring that losses from a publicly traded partnership (PTP) could only be carried forward to offset income from that PTP.

Table 7.10   **Incidence of Passive Loss Limitations by Positive Income Level, 1987–90**

Positive Income Level[a,b]	Average Positive Income[b]	Share of Total Tax Returns	Share of Aggregate Passive Losses	Share of Aggregate Disallowed Losses	Share of Aggregate Taxes
1987					
Under 10	4.69	27.87	1.03	0.74	2.03
10–25	16.85	29.82	2.85	1.60	8.91
25–50	35.95	26.23	7.05	4.48	21.97
50–100	65.51	13.02	18.30	13.14	26.78
100–250	142.10	2.46	22.86	25.46	16.19
Over 250	645.75	0.60	47.91	54.59	24.12
1988					
Under 10	4.62	28.28	1.82	2.04	1.07
10–25	16.93	29.95	2.93	2.14	8.34
25–50	35.96	25.92	8.06	4.61	21.78
50–100	65.66	12.80	17.70	12.84	26.04
100–250	142.41	2.39	21.66	26.30	15.02
Over 250	733.54	0.65	47.84	52.08	24.74
1989					
Under 10	4.60	28.42	1.46	0.81	1.09
10–25	16.85	30.24	3.50	2.56	8.86
25–50	35.83	25.43	7.37	4.17	22.28
50–100	65.88	12.77	17.02	10.76	27.11
100–250	140.94	2.51	20.40	24.14	15.79
Over 250	690.05	0.63	50.24	57.55	24.87
1990					
Under 10	4.64	28.80	2.02	1.71	1.14
10–25	16.84	30.22	3.78	4.16	9.13
25–50	35.78	25.50	7.12	4.11	23.23
50–100	65.96	12.53	16.69	13.63	27.45
100–250	141.59	2.35	19.83	25.59	15.06
Over 250	682.58	0.61	50.56	50.80	23.99

Source: Author's calculations from the annual IRS *Statistics of Income* public-use cross sections.
[a]Positive income is the sum of all positive components of total income.
[b]Dollar amounts in thousands of constant 1990 dollars.

Table 7.10 presents the distribution of each aggregate by "positive income" for each year. This measure of income is simply the sum of all positive components of income, before the netting out of losses.[49] In each year, the group of taxpayers with over $250,000 in positive income—the top 0.60 percent of the distribution—reported half of the passive losses and slightly more than half of

49. Specifically, positive income is the sum of wages, taxable interest, nontaxable interest, dividends, social security benefits, unemployment insurance included in adjusted gross income, capital gains, partnership income, S-corporation income, estate income, farm rents, rental income, royalty income, and self-employment income. The last four are included only to the extent that the reported net figure is positive. This measure is similar to, but not necessarily equivalent to, that of Petska (1992).

the disallowed passive losses. This is more than double their share of the total income taxes paid, which was just under one-fourth in each year. If the group of taxpayers is expanded to those with over $100,000 of positive income (the top 3 percent), the shares of passive losses, disallowed losses, and the current tax liability rise to 70, 80, and 40 percent, respectively.

The implication of table 7.10 is that, whatever the ultimate revenue effect of the disallowance of passive losses, it will be borne almost entirely by the very highest income taxpayers.[50] Since the analysis in section 7.3 showed that the passive loss rules were not necessary to eliminate abusive tax shelters, there are only three sources of increased revenue that are appropriately attributed to them. The first is from the tax losses that are no longer reported by legitimate tax shelters that would have been reported given all changes in TRA other than the passive loss rules but will not be reported because of these rules (e.g., some cattle-feeding shelters). Since the examples in section 7.1 showed that the marginal effect of the passive loss rules on the after-tax IRR was approximately 1 percentage point, this is likely to be a very small amount of revenue. The second is from the inclusion of allowed passive losses as a tax preference for the alternative minimum tax calculation during the phase-in period. This tax preference is unfortunately not separately or easily identifiable in the public-use files of tax returns. In any event, it is explicitly a short-term revenue source. The third is the various instances in which the passive loss rules will bind in a given year and defer the investor's tax loss until a year in which the investor reports positive passive income. In those cases, government revenues will be increased by the interest on the potential tax loss during the years of deferral. Assuming an average 20 percent last-dollar marginal tax rate on passive losses (calculated from TAXSIM) and a 10 percent discount rate, this increase amounts to 2 percent of disallowed losses per year of deferral. Assuming one year of deferral and $20 billion of disallowed losses per year, this represents a $0.4 billion increase in annual revenues. This amount is trivial compared to aggregate tax revenues or the taxes paid by the top 0.60 percent of the income distribution.

7.5 Conclusion

The tax shelter examples demonstrated that the impact of the passive loss limitations on legitimate tax shelter investments was largely redundant. The passive loss rules eliminated the tax advantages of pure deferral shelters. In

---

50. It is important to note that tables 7.9 and 7.10 reflect the aging of tax shelters that were purchased under the pre-TRA86 regime. Because limited partnerships are highly illiquid in most cases, investors could not easily avoid the passive loss rules on their existing tax shelters. Although some tax shelter investors undoubtedly sold their investments in 1986 in anticipation of, or in response to, the passage of TRA86 (and are therefore not included in the tables), Damato (1995a) reports that many of these investors—and their heirs—are still burdened by these partnerships nearly 10 years later.

practice, the conversion of ordinary income to a lightly taxed (capital gain) or untaxed (ITC) form was a more important determinant of the IRR on the tax-sheltered investment, and passive loss rules do not affect conversion. TRA86's repeal of the provisions that allowed for conversion were the decisive blow to legitimate tax shelters; once these changes were incorporated, applying the passive loss rules had only a minor effect on the after-tax IRR on investment. Once conversion was eliminated, the correlation between the after-tax rate of return on investment and the investor's marginal tax rate was no longer positive; consequently, high-income taxpayers were not the natural clientele for legitimate tax-sheltered investments after TRA86.

The analysis of abusive tax shelters showed that passive losses were sufficient to eliminate the abuse because it took the form of pure deferral. As in the case of legitimate shelters, however, they were unnecessary. The changes to the installment sale treatment of gains that occurred a year later were a more direct attack with fewer unrelated consequences. The passive loss rules punish all losses, including genuine economic losses and interest deductions, rather than just those that cause the abuse. Similarly, the disallowance of basis due to purchase money for depreciation purposes would have eliminated the ability to shelter absent of economic risk without the potential for discouraging legitimate economic enterprises. Estimating the impact of the passive loss rules on risky investment in the noncorporate sector is therefore an important direction for further research.

The passive loss rules therefore represent a policy without a substantive economic purpose but with a large potential to discourage legitimate investment. Their chief effect is cosmetic; high-income taxpayers can no longer use the losses from the tax shelter to reduce the taxes paid on other income earned that year. The suggestion that this cosmetic change, in the absence of a large impact on the after-tax IRR of the investment, would help eliminate tax shelters requires that tax shelter investors systematically ignore recapture in their investment decisions. Instead, recent studies of high-income taxpayers such as Auten and Carroll (1994), Feldstein (1993), Feenberg and Poterba (1993), and Slemrod (chap. 6 in this volume) suggest a high sensitivity to tax incentives in economic activities with less of a tax component than tax-sheltered investments. Appearances aside, the important indicator of future increases in legitimate tax-sheltered investment is the introduction of opportunities for conversion, including investment tax credits and preferential tax treatment of capital gains. The recent rebound in the secondary market for real estate limited partnerships reported in Damato (1995b) suggests that the tax changes in 1993 may be having that effect.

References

Auerbach, Alan J. 1987. The Tax Reform Act of 1986 and the cost of capital. *Journal of Economic Perspectives* 1(1): 73–86.

Auten, Gerald, and Robert Carroll. 1994. Taxpayer behavior and the 1986 Tax Reform Act. Washington, D.C.: Department of the Treasury, Office of Tax Analysis. Manuscript.

Bankman, Joseph. 1989. The case against passive investments: A critical appraisal of the passive loss restrictions. *Stanford Law Review* 42:15–49.

Becker, Stuart. 1987. The effect of the Tax Reform Act of 1986 on present and future tax motivated investments. In *Proceedings of the Forty-Fifth Annual NYU Institute on Federal Taxation,* vol. 2. New York: Matthew Bender.

Brumbaugh, Mark B., and Christopher Ward. 1987. Passive activity losses: The final solution? In *Proceedings of the Forty-Fifth Annual NYU Institute on Federal Taxation,* vol. 2. New York: Matthew Bender.

Chirelstein, Marvin A. 1994. *Federal income taxation: A guide to the leading cases and concepts.* Westbury, N.Y.: Foundation.

Cordes, Joseph J., and Harvey Galper. 1985. Tax shelter activity: Lessons from twenty years of experience. *National Tax Journal* 38:305–24.

Coven, Glenn E. 1986. Limiting losses attributable to nonrecourse debt: A defense of the traditional system against the at-risk concept. *California Law Review* 74:41–82.

Damato, Karen. 1995a. Partnerships, often old dogs, are biting heirs. *Wall Street Journal,* March 3, p. C1.

———. 1995b. Real-estate partnerships begin comeback. *Wall Street Journal,* January 13, p. C1.

Equipment leasing partnerships. 1984. *Stanger Report* (Shrewsbury, N.J.) 6(6): 5–8.

Feenberg, Daniel R., and Elisabeth Coutts. 1993. An introduction to TAXSIM model. *Journal of Policy Analysis and Management* 12(1): 189–94.

Feenberg, Daniel R., and James M. Poterba. 1993. Income inequality and the incomes of very high-income taxpayers: Evidence from tax returns. In *Tax policy and the economy,* vol. 7, ed. James M. Poterba. Cambridge: MIT Press.

Feldstein, Martin S. 1993. The effect of marginal tax rates on taxable income: A panel study of the 1986 Tax Reform Act. NBER Working Paper no. 4496. Cambridge, Mass.: National Bureau of Economic Research.

Feldstein, Martin S., and Daniel Frisch. 1977. Corporate tax integration: The estimated effects on capital accumulation and tax distribution of two integration proposals. *National Tax Journal* 30(1): 37–52.

Feldstein, Martin S., and Amy Taylor. 1976. The income tax and charitable contributions. *Econometrica* 44(6): 1201–22.

Fierro, Robert D. 1981. *Tax shelters in plain English: New strategies for the 1980s.* Rockville Center, N.Y.: Farnsworth.

Gentry, William M. 1994. Taxes, financial decisions and organizational form: Evidence from publicly traded partnerships. *Journal of Public Economics* 53: 223–44.

Gordon, Roger H., and Jeffrey K. MacKie-Mason. 1990. Effects of the Tax Reform Act of 1986 on corporate financial policy and organizational form. In *Do taxes matter?* ed. Joel Slemrod. Cambridge: MIT Press.

———. 1994. Tax distortions to the choice of organizational form. *Journal of Public Economics* 55:279–306.

Guenther, David A. 1992. Taxes and organizational form: A comparison of corporations and master limited partnerships. *Accounting Review* 67:17–45.

Hoof it to cattle in 1986. 1986. *Stanger Report* (Shrewsbury, N.J.) 8(7): 7–10.

Johnson, Calvin H. 1989. Why have anti-tax shelter legislation? A response to Professor Zelenak. *Texas Law Review* 67:591–625.

Keligan, David L. 1987. A primer on the new passive loss rules. *Practical Tax Lawyer* 1(4): 9–23.

McLure, Charles E., Jr., and George R. Zodrow. 1987. Treasury I and the Tax Reform Act of 1986: The economics and politics of tax reform. *Journal of Economic Perspectives* 1(1): 37–58.

Moriarty, Michael, and R. Eliot Rosen. 1988. An interview with IRS Deputy Chief Counsel Peter K. Scott. *Tax Notes* 39 (May 23): 920–25.

Musgrave, Richard A. 1987. Short of euphoria. *Journal of Economic Perspectives* 1(1): 59–72.

Owen, Stephen L., Gerald J. Robinson, and Matthew J. Plache. 1987. Real estate tax shelters—What's left. *Practical Tax Lawyer* 1:67–80.

Pechman, Joseph A. 1987. Tax reform: Theory and practice. *Journal of Economic Perspectives* 1(1): 11–28.

Peroni, Robert J. 1988. A policy critique of the section 469 passive loss rules. *Southern California Law Review* 62:1–104.

Petska, Tom. 1992. Partnerships, partners, and tax shelters after tax reform, 1987–1989. *Statistics of Income Bulletin* 12(1): 8–24.

Plesko, George A. 1994. The role of taxes in organizational choice: S conversions after the Tax Reform Act of 1986. Boston: Northeastern University. Manuscript.

Rosen, Harvey S. 1987. The marriage tax is down but not out. *National Tax Journal* 40(4): 567–76.

Scholes, Myron S., and Mark A. Wolfson. 1992. *Taxes and business strategy: A planning approach.* Englewood Cliffs, N.J.: Prentice Hall.

Sims, Theodore S. 1994. Debt, accelerated depreciation, and the tale of a teakettle: Tax shelter abuse reconsidered. *UCLA Law Review* 42(2): 264–376.

Swanson, Robert E., and Barbara M. Swanson. 1985. *Tax shelters: A guide for investors and their advisors,* rev. ed. Homewood, Ill.: Dow Jones–Irwin.

U.S. Congress. Joint Committee on Taxation. 1985. *Tax reform proposals: Tax shelters and minimum tax* (JCS-34-85). Washington, D.C., 7 August.

Warren, Alvin C., Jr. 1985. Accelerated capital recovery, debt, and tax arbitrage. *Tax Lawyer* 38(3): 549–74.

Wheeler, Timothy D. 1994. Partnership returns, 1992. *Statistics of Income Bulletin* 13(4): 75–81.

Zelenak, Lawrence. 1989a. When good preferences go bad: A critical analysis of the anti-tax shelter provisions of the Tax Reform Act of 1986. *Texas Law Review* 67:499–589.

———. 1989b. Do anti-tax shelter rules make sense? A reply to Professor Johnson. *Texas Law Review* 68:491–507.

Comment   Roger H. Gordon

Summary of Paper

The key question addressed in this paper by Samwick is the role of passive loss restrictions, introduced as part of the Tax Reform Act of 1986 (hereafter

Roger H. Gordon is professor of economics at the University of Michigan and a research associate of the National Bureau of Economic Research.

TRA86), in ending the use of tax shelters. In the years immediately prior to this legislation, high-income taxpayers made intensive use of tax shelters that enabled them to reduce their net tax liabilities. Tax shelter activity became so important that the entire partnership sector generated net tax losses. These losses were heavily concentrated in a few sectors, particularly real estate and oil and gas.

The misinvestments that resulted in these sectors became sufficiently dramatic that TRA86 included a number of provisions that aimed and in fact succeeded at eliminating most tax shelter activity. As emphasized by Samwick, the act lowered personal tax rates substantially, making tax considerations less important. In addition, it lengthened the tax lives for new investments and eliminated the tax credit for equipment. Furthermore, it eliminated the 60 percent exclusion of capital gains income. Finally, the legislation imposed new restrictions preventing individuals from using losses generated on "passive" investments to offset positive taxable income from other sources.

Have these passive loss restrictions in fact played an important role in preventing the reemergence of tax shelters, or are the other changes sufficient in themselves? In several numerical examples that Samwick examines, the passive loss rules seem to have little effect on the net tax liabilities generated from the investments described in the examples.[1] Given that these passive loss rules likely discourage risky activities in general and have little effect on tax shelter activity, Samwick concludes that they merit reconsideration.

Nature of Tax Shelters prior to TRA86

Samwick defines tax shelters as any activity "in which the investment cost can be deducted from taxable income at a rate that exceeds its economic depreciation." Yet the sharply accelerated depreciation rates available during the early 1980s, and the fairly low inflation rates, mean that virtually all investments would be tax shelters by this definition. For purposes of discussion, I will view tax shelters more narrowly to be investments that in present value reduce the tax liabilities of the owner and that in equilibrium will be owned primarily by those in the highest tax brackets, who according to Samwick's data were in fact the principal owners of these assets.

What aspects of the tax law prior to TRA86 allowed some investments to become tax shelters? Accelerated depreciation in itself is certainly not sufficient—even with immediate expensing, the net tax payments on an investment have a present value of zero. With the tax credit, it is more plausible that some investments will on net generate tax losses in present value. All that is required is that the fraction of the initial costs paid for through reduced tax liabilities exceed the fraction of the return paid in taxes. This occurs if $k + \tau Z > \tau$, where k is the tax credit rate, τ is the personal tax rate, and Z is the present value of

---

1. In one example of a shelter with an overstated basis, passive loss rules do in fact have an important effect. But Samwick notes that other rules could eliminate these abuses more directly.

depreciation deductions. These assets would be owned primarily by those in the highest tax brackets, however, only if their attractiveness increases, relative to municipal bonds, as the investor's tax rate increases. This occurs only if $k + Z > 1$.[2] But for any plausible discount rate, this condition is not close to being satisfied during the period. In fact, in none of Samwick's examples without debt finance are either of these conditions satisfied, implying that these examples do not constitute tax shelters.

To be a tax shelter, more is needed. One important characteristic of many tax shelters is that they provide good collateral for loans, allowing the owner to finance an unusually high fraction of their cost with debt.[3] Extra debt is attractive if the net-of-tax cost of the debt is cheaper than the net-of-tax return the individual can earn on invested funds. If we characterize the available rate of return for these investors by the municipal bond rate, then extra debt is more attractive as long as $i_m > i(1 - \tau)$, where i_m is the municipal bond rate and i is the taxable interest rate.[4] In 1984, for example, the high-grade municipal bond rate was 10.15 percent while the taxable BAA corporate bond rate was 14.19 percent. At the top personal tax rate of 50 percent, the gain from borrowing an extra dollar was therefore $10.15 - 0.5(14.19) = 3.06$ cents per year; for those in a 30 percent tax bracket, the gain from borrowing a dollar is only 0.22 cents per year.[5] Therefore, financing even half of the investment with debt raises the after-tax rate of return by 1.5 percentage points for those in the top bracket,[6] while leaving the net return virtually unchanged for those in a 30 percent tax bracket.

Another important characteristic of many tax shelters was the possibility of saving taxes by periodic sales of the asset. When an asset is sold, capital gains tax liability is generated, in itself imposing a tax penalty on such sales. The resulting tax liabilities would be $g(P - B)$, where g is the capital gains tax rate, P is the sale price, and B is the remaining tax basis of the asset. In addition, however, the new owner can depreciate the asset based on the new purchase price rather than the presale tax basis, generating extra tax savings that in present value can be approximated by $\tau Z(P - B)$.[7] On net, the tax savings are $(\tau Z - g)(P - B)$ if the asset is sold. Prior to 1986, the tax savings from the

---

2. Following Hall and Jorgenson (1967), the required rate of return on an investment is $(\rho + d)(1 - k - \tau Z)/(1 - \tau)$, where ρ is the net-of-tax rate of return available elsewhere (e.g., on municipal bonds) and d is the economic depreciation rate. The derivative of this with respect to τ is negative, indicating that the asset is more attractive as τ increases, only if $k + Z > 1$.

3. As emphasized by Gordon and Slemrod (1988), partnerships had substantial debt during this period.

4. I assume here that extra borrowing allows the individual to reduce the amount of municipal bonds he needs to sell off in order to finance the investment project.

5. As seen in Poterba (1989), the value of τ where investors break even on extra debt has consistently been much below the highest personal tax rate.

6. An implicit assumption here is that the individual could not have borrowed this extra amount without undertaking the investment and thereby having an additional asset to provide as collateral.

7. When the depreciation formula is exponential, the present value of future depreciation deductions is exactly proportional to the remaining tax basis.

write-up in the basis normally more than offset the capital gains tax liabilities generated by the sale,[8] resulting in often substantial net tax savings for the buyer and seller together from the sale. In fact, assets could profitably be traded and redepreciated several times during their lives. These tax savings from "churning" were larger the greater the difference between the tax rates on ordinary versus capital gains income so were largest for those in the highest tax brackets.[9] In all of Samwick's examples, while tax liabilities on the sale of the assets are taken into account, the value of the resulting write-up in basis and redepreciation of the asset is ignored.[10] Yet during this period the value of this write-up would often outweigh the capital gains liabilities incurred as a result of the sale.

As noted by Samwick, there were a variety of more questionable strategies that could also be pursued in putting together tax shelters. One, for example, would be to hold the asset while it is generating substantial tax deductions but then to give it to one's child before the asset is sold, so that the resulting capital gains are taxable at the child's rather than the parents' tax rate. This device is also of benefit primarily to those in the highest tax brackets, for whom the difference between the parents' and the child's tax rate is greatest.

As a result of these extra devices, assets that could easily be traded on the secondary market earned as a result a much higher net-of-tax return, not only because the purchase of the asset could be financed heavily with debt but also because the asset could easily be churned and so depreciated several times. Examples of assets that can easily be traded include not only real estate and oil and gas fields, but also airplanes, computers, automobiles, and a variety of other types of capital equipment.[11] Both leverage and churning were beneficial primarily for those in the highest tax brackets, explaining the concentration of ownership of these assets in the highest tax brackets.

The resulting tax subsidy to investment in such assets does not arise from specific provisions in the tax law intentionally aimed at encouraging investment in these assets, but simply because of the existence of a dense secondary market for these types of capital. In fact, many of the academic studies of the tax reforms on 1981–83 concluded that structures faced much higher effective tax rates that equipment, contrary to the observed tax losses in the real estate industry since the reforms (see, e.g., Fullerton and Henderson 1989). Given that the academic studies did not forecast the shift of resources into tax shelters, it seems most unlikely that Congress intended such a shift when designing

---

8. See Gordon, Hines, and Summers (1987) for further discussion.

9. Since the top personal tax rates were higher than the top corporate tax rate during this period, the tax savings would be larger when the asset is owned by high tax bracket individuals rather than a corporation. See Gordon and MacKie-Mason (1994) for further discussion.

10. One further complication was the recapture rules for depreciation at rates faster than straight line. Given the short lifetimes, taking this into account would not change the calculations much.

11. The essential characteristics are that the asset not be specific to a given firm and that its condition be readily observable by potential purchasers.

these tax reforms. As a result, the pattern of subsidies to tax shelters would appear in large part to be arbitrary and capricious, resulting in a misallocation of capital across uses.

Further efficiency losses would result from the separation of ownership from control. In particular, during this period corporations faced a tax incentive to sell off nominal ownership of their buildings and equipment to noncorporate owners, even though the capital continued to be used within the corporation, since the noncorporate owners could take better advantage of the above strategies to reduce tax liabilities. This separation of ownership from control likely generated efficiency losses due to monitoring and agency costs. The sharp differences that existing during these years in the effective tax rates on different types of assets also generated substantial distortions to individual portfolio holdings and therefore to the allocation of risk across investors, generating yet another type of efficiency loss.

Normally, efficiency losses are an unavoidable cost of raising tax revenue in an equitable way. However, this tax shelter activity not only generated clear efficiency losses but also lost revenue, and reduced the perceived equity of the tax system since the gains went largely to those in the highest tax brackets.[12]

Effects of TRA86 on Tax Shelters

Given that the existing tax shelters were inefficient and inequitable and created a serious erosion of tax revenue, it is not surprising that TRA86 included many provisions that reduced the attractiveness of tax shelters. As emphasized by Samwick, personal tax rates fell, depreciation rates were decelerated, the investment tax credit was eliminated, and the 60 percent exclusion for capital gains tax rate was eliminated. Each of these changes does serve to reduce the attractiveness of tax shelters, as he shows.

The increase in the capital gains tax rate has the additional effect of making churning unattractive. After TRA86, there is a net tax loss for the buyer and seller together when they exchange an asset.

A further important provision in TRA86, not mentioned by Samwick, was the introduction of restrictions on the deductibility of interest payments. Under the legislation, mortgage payments could continue to be deducted on schedule A, but other interest payments could no longer be taken as an itemized deduction. This provision made it much more difficult to borrow to invest in lightly taxed assets, in principle putting a cap on a major form of tax arbitrage.

This cap can be effective, however, only if the individual cannot simply shift nonmortgage interest deductions from schedule A to a different part of the tax return. For example, nonmortgage debt can simply be reclassified as mortgage debt. This possibility does not completely undermine the restriction, however,

---

12. In a full incidence study of tax shelter activity, one would need to take into account as well the distributional effects of the reduced prices paid by consumers for the goods produced in these favored industries.

since many high-income investors will need to provide more collateral than their house in order to maintain the level of debt they had prior to TRA86. Another approach would be to shift the borrowing into a noncorporate business the individual participates in. As long as such a business can use any resulting tax deductions to offset other income, the restriction on interest deductions would be moot. A key function of the passive loss rules, therefore, may be to prevent such an end run around the restriction on interest deductions.

What are the efficiency consequences of this restriction on interest deductions? Restricting the degree to which individuals can take advantage of existing tax subsidies to debt finance, in itself, is likely to be an efficiency gain since it restricts the behavioral response to this portfolio distortion. Certainly some reduction in use of debt would be an efficiency gain. Jensen and Meckling (1976) explore a variety of nontax considerations that affect a firm's debt/equity choice. Whether the efficient use of debt, ignoring taxes, leads to systematic tax losses for a firm is an open question. If not, as seems very likely, then restrictions on interest deductions would shift the use of debt finance toward the efficient level.

Were it not for tax distortions, would passive loss restrictions be binding? If not, would these restrictions then tend to push individuals toward efficient allocations? To the extent that passive losses result from large interest deductions, then the same considerations as above arise, and most likely the reduction in debt finance caused by the restrictions would be an efficiency gain. But passive losses can result for reasons other than large interest deductions. Samwick argues, for example, that losses are more likely in riskier activities, so that restrictions on passive losses could inhibit risk taking by limited partnerships.[13] But individuals with tax losses from one set of partnerships need simply buy shares in other partnerships that have taxable income in order to make use of the tax losses. Any unused losses in a given year can be carried forward and used to offset positive passive income in later years.[14] As a result, the passive loss restrictions would tend to induce investors in high tax brackets to shift their portfolios into activities generating tax profits, which would push them toward the portfolios they would choose without tax distortions. Again, the response should be an efficiency gain.

The current passive loss rules are less binding than those faced by corporations, since corporate shareholders cannot use losses from one corporation to offset profits from another corporation. The passive loss restrictions therefore reduce substantially an artificial advantage to the noncorporate form.

It would be valuable to develop evidence on the extent to which passive loss restrictions have altered debt finance decisions and individual portfolios, as

13. Passive loss restrictions do not affect individual entrepreneurs since their activity would not be passive.

14. While these carryforwards are not as valuable as immediate offsets against other income, as emphasized by Altshuler and Auerbach (1990), the loss from the postponement would normally be reasonably small.

well as real investment behavior. Samwick's data suggest that individuals on average lose few deductions as a result of these restrictions. Does this suggest that the passive loss restrictions have not played an important role? It is premature to draw such a conclusion. In theory, given optimal portfolio choice in the face of these restrictions, individuals should not be observed with portfolios that generate expected passive losses. While random events may leave them with passive losses ex post, they should simply rearrange their portfolio the following year so as to generate enough positive passive income to offset the loss carryforward. Transactions costs generated from frequent readjustments in portfolios may outweigh the resulting tax savings, so some unused passive losses will remain. But evidence on the amount of these unused losses reveals information only about the size of the transactions costs faced when trying to readjust portfolios ex post and says nothing about what portfolios would look like if the passive loss restriction were eliminated. Nor does it say anything about the distributional effects of the restriction. One approach to answering these questions would be to conduct a general equilibrium simulation of portfolio holdings and real allocations with and without the passive loss restrictions. Another approach would be to look closely at the changes in behavior that followed TRA86. However, so many provisions changed in 1986 that it would be extremely difficult to isolate the effects of the passive loss restrictions in particular on all these aspects of behavior.

Conclusion

Samwick hypothesizes, and I agree, that "it is the use of leverage to finance tax-sheltered investments that . . . motivated congressional reforms such as the passive loss rules." This congressional concern with the use of leverage very much seemed justified. Allowing nominal interest to be tax deductible while taxing an approximation of the real return on other assets opens up a variety of arbitrage opportunities among investors in different tax brackets. Gordon and Slemrod (1988) found that in 1983 the resulting arbitrage was sufficient to more than offset all the tax revenue collected on the return from real investments. While other tax changes in 1986 helped to reduce the opportunity for tax shelter activity, the passive loss rules remained the key device available to limit the scope for tax arbitrage through borrowing to finance investments in more lightly taxed activities.

Clearly, passive loss restrictions are a very inelegant means of limiting the scope for tax arbitrage. They do not eliminate opportunities for such arbitrage but only limit the amount that can be done. Better would be to eliminate the opportunities entirely. Most proposals for a consumption tax or value added tax, for example, would eliminate these arbitrage opportunities. Even under the income tax, shifting to the taxation and deductibility of real rather than nominal interest would eliminate most of the problems. But as long as the tax code continues to allow the tax deductibility of nominal interest payments, it is hard to dismiss the value of the passive loss restrictions without much more concrete evidence.

References

Altshuler, Rosanne, and Alan J. Auerbach. 1990. The significance of tax law asymmetries: An empirical investigation. *Quarterly Journal of Economics* 105:61–86.

Fullerton, Don, and Yolanda Kodrzycki Henderson. 1989. A disaggregate equilibrium model of the tax distortions among assets, sectors, and industries. *International Economic Review* 30:391–413.

Gordon, Roger H., James R. Hines, Jr., and Lawrence H. Summers. 1987. Notes on the tax treatment of structures. In *The effects of taxation on capital accumulation,* Martin Feldstein, 223–54. Chicago: University of Chicago Press.

Gordon, Roger H., and Jeffrey K. MacKie-Mason. 1994. Tax distortions to the choice of organizational form. *Journal of Public Economics* 55:279–306.

Gordon, Roger H., and Joel Slemrod. 1988. Do we collect any revenue from taxing capital income? In *Tax policy and the economy,* vol. 2, ed. Lawrence Summers, 89–130. Cambridge: MIT Press.

Hall, Robert E., and Dale W. Jorgenson. 1967. Tax policy and investment behavior. *American Economic Review* 57:391–414.

Jensen, Michael C., and William H. Meckling. 1976. Theory of the firm: Managerial behavior, agency costs and ownership structure. *Journal of Financial Economics* 3:305–60.

Poterba, James M. 1989. Tax reform and the market for tax-exempt debt. NBER Working Paper no. 2900. Cambridge, Mass.: National Bureau of Economic Research.

8   The Relationship between State and Federal Tax Audits

James Alm, Brian Erard, and Jonathan S. Feinstein

8.1   Introduction

In this paper we present an analysis of state and federal individual income tax enforcement programs. We develop an econometric model of state and federal tax audit selection decisions and audit assessments and then present a detailed empirical analysis of Oregon state and federal tax audits. We investigate the degree to which the federal and state tax authorities employ similar audit selection criteria, the correlation between state and federal noncompliance, and the allocation of state audit resources between independent audits and "piggyback" audits based on federal enforcement efforts.

The majority of studies in the empirical academic literature on tax compliance have investigated compliance with central government tax obligations. We believe the study of state tax compliance and enforcement and the relationship between state and federal compliance and enforcement is important for several reasons. In the United States the magnitude of noncompliance with both state and local taxes is probably at least as large, as a percentage of total obligations, as the magnitude of noncompliance with federal tax obligations. In many cases a household's decision about how much of its state tax liability to pay may be closely related to its decision about how much of its federal tax liability to pay, especially when the state and federal tax bases are similarly defined, as they are in many states. As a result a state tax authority may find

James Alm is professor of economics at the University of Colorado at Boulder. Brian Erard is assistant professor of economics at Carleton University. Jonathan S. Feinstein is associate professor of economics at the Yale University School of Management.

The authors thank officials at the Oregon Department of Revenue and the Internal Revenue Service for the enormous amount of help they provided in assembling the data set used in this paper. They also thank the many state tax administrators who filled out the tax audit survey and returned it. Finally, they thank preconference and conference participants for helpful comments and suggestions, especially James Wetzler and Jim Poterba.

that an effective enforcement strategy is to piggyback on federal enforcement efforts, following up on federal audit cases for which a large amount of noncompliance is detected. The fact that state noncompliance is likely to be highly correlated with federal noncompliance has some important implications. First, it influences how state tax authorities allocate their limited tax enforcement budget between independent audits and piggyback audits. Second, it raises a host of policy questions about the proper balance and relationship between state and federal tax enforcement programs, questions that are especially relevant in an era in which the size of the federal government may be reduced and the role of state governments in providing basic goods and services may increase. Our analysis is intended to address all of these issues, as well as other related topics.

Since little information has been published about state tax enforcement programs, we decided to conduct a survey of the 50 states to learn more about their audit programs (a copy of this survey is available on request).[1] To date we have received responses from 32 states.[2] Table 8.1, based on these survey responses, provides some information about state enforcement programs and compares these programs to Internal Revenue Service (IRS) enforcement efforts. As indicated by the figures in the table, state enforcement levels are quite low in comparison with federal enforcement levels, especially in regard to the individual income tax. Thus, state budgets for enforcement and tax administration are smaller than average IRS state-level budgets, state audit rates are generally much lower than the federal audit rate, and the magnitude of assessments (the total of additional taxes, interest, and penalties) generated by independent state audits is much smaller than that generated by federal audits. Our focus in this paper is on the relationship between state and federal tax enforcement efforts. Our survey results indicate that the states rely extensively on information provided by the IRS through its revenue agent reports (RARs) on federal audits and its CP2000 notices on federal reporting discrepancies identified through the Information Returns Program. In particular, as shown in table 8.1, on average states conduct more piggyback audits based on federal information than independent audits, and the total magnitude of assessments generated by piggyback audits is larger than that generated by independent audits. Other results from the survey (not reported in table 8.1) indicate that, although the states obtain much information from the IRS, they provide relatively little in-

1. Note that compliance and enforcement issues surrounding state sales tax have been examined in some detail (see Due and Mikesell 1993).

2. These states are Alabama, Arizona, Arkansas, California, Connecticut, Florida, Hawaii, Illinois, Indiana, Iowa, Kansas, Louisiana, Minnesota, Missouri, Nebraska, New Hampshire, New Jersey, New Mexico, New York, North Carolina, North Dakota, Oregon, Rhode Island, South Carolina, South Dakota, Tennessee, Texas, Utah, Vermont, Washington, Wisconsin, and Wyoming. Several states (Maryland, Michigan, and Massachusetts) have declined to respond to the survey. Most of the remaining states have indicated that they will eventually provide some information. It should also be noted that the survey is not limited to the individual income tax; other major state taxes and their associated audit programs are also surveyed.

Table 8.1   **Collection and Enforcement Activities by the States and the IRS for the Individual Income Tax, 1992**

	Amount
Agency budget ($ per capita)	
State individual income tax audit budget[a]	0.40
Total state tax agency budget[a]	12.61
IRS state-level budget[a]	16.33
Audit rate (%)	
State independent audits[a]	0.33
RARs and CP2000 reports[a]	0.75
IRS audits	0.91
Additional assessments for the individual income tax ($ per capita)	
States from independent audits[a]	3.78
States for RARs and CP2000 reports[a]	5.04
IRS audits	23.66
Individual income tax collection ($ per capita)	
States in the survey[a]	539
All states[a]	486
IRS	3,738

Sources: State data on individual income tax collections, additional assessments, audit rates, and agency budgets are calculated from the survey of state tax administrators, as discussed in the text. IRS data are calculated from the *Internal Revenue Service 1992 Annual Report.*

Note: All averages are simple unweighted averages.

[a]Average across the states.

formation in return. The states also seem to follow somewhat different audit selection procedures than the IRS, relying less on computer algorithms or statistical methods for the selection of returns for audit, and instead often choosing returns based on previously productive accounts, random selection, specific tax items or filer characteristics, or a comparison of information on state returns with information from other sources. A striking result of the survey is the degree of variation in state income tax enforcement efforts. Some states undertake no independent audit efforts, even though they have significant income tax programs, while others, such as Oregon (on whom we concentrate our empirical analysis in this paper), have quite ambitious independent enforcement programs.

The survey results indicate that states rely extensively on federal enforcement efforts and that state and federal audit selection procedures may be similar but are not identical. The results also suggest that there may be much room for changing and improving state audit programs. Our analysis in this paper is designed to investigate these findings in greater detail.

Our behavioral model accounts for state and federal tax audit decisions and assessments, including state piggyback audits, in a common framework. The model consists of two periods. In the first period the federal and state tax authorities simultaneously and independently select cases for audit and make revenue assessments. In the second period the state authority has the option of performing a piggyback audit on any case for which, in the first period, the federal authority performed an audit and the state did not. We assume that each authority selects a case for audit whenever its expectation of the revenue to be earned from conducting the audit exceeds the shadow cost of audit resources. We also assume that each authority observes a private signal of the revenue associated with a case prior to making its audit decision, and we allow the signals of the two authorities to be correlated. Our empirical framework includes a careful specification of the revenue assessment distribution faced by each authority, and it contains a rich stochastic structure that allows for several different kinds of correlations between federal and state assessments.

We estimate our model using a data set that combines information on federal and state audit programs in Oregon. Oregon is a medium-sized state, containing approximately 1 percent of all U.S. households. It is a good state in which to study individual income tax compliance and enforcement, both because it collects more than two-thirds of its total tax revenues from the individual income tax (versus only about one-third on average for other states) and because it has a very active tax enforcement program. Our data include detailed federal and Oregon state tax return information for 43,500 Oregon filers for tax year 1987, as well as audit results for the 4,400 filers in the sample whose 1987 federal returns were selected for an IRS audit and the 2,800 filers whose 1987 state returns were selected for either an independent audit or a piggyback audit by the Oregon Department of Revenue (ODR).

We report estimates for three separate audit classes: a business class, a farm class, and a nonbusiness, nonfarm class. Four aspects of our results are particularly interesting. First, we find that state and federal assessments are strongly positively correlated, as expected. Second, we find that the IRS and ODR audit selection criteria overlap, but only partially. In the business and farm classes, each authority seems to rely heavily on its private signal in deciding whether or not to select a case for audit. The private signals of the two agencies are highly correlated within these classes, indicating a substantial overlap between federal and state information. However, each agency's signal appears to contain information about the other agency's revenue assessment that is unknown to the other agency, a finding which suggests that the federal and state tax authorities could improve their audit selection procedures in these classes by exchanging more information. In the nonbusiness, nonfarm class the authorities seem to rely less on their private signals and more on filers' reports of certain tax return line items in making their audit selection decisions, so information sharing seems less important. Third, using our results we are able to estimate the shadow value associated with providing additional audit resources to each tax authority. We estimate that the shadow value associated with providing the IRS with an additional dollar of audit resources is approximately $5 for the business class, $2.50 for the farm class, and $4 for the nonbusiness, nonfarm class. We estimate that the shadow value associated with providing the ODR with an additional dollar of audit resources is approximately $1, $2, and $3 for the business, farm, and nonbusiness, nonfarm classes, respectively.

For ODR piggyback audits, we estimate that the shadow value of additional resources is between $2 and $3 for the business and nonbusiness, nonfarm classes; however, we are unable to reliably estimate the value for the farm class. Our results indicate that the IRS might be able to increase its audit revenues by reallocating some of its audit resources from farm audits to business audits. In contrast, it would appear that the ODR could increase its audit revenues by shifting some of its resources out of business audits and into nonbusiness, nonfarm audits. The piggyback audit results indicate that the ODR might also benefit by performing more piggyback audits and fewer independent audits within the business and farm classes. Fourth, we report a number of interesting findings from a detailed examination of Oregon's audit programs, which suggest that the state could increase revenues by making greater use of IRS information and by increasing the number of audits of nonresident filers.

Our work in this paper is related to several other studies of compliance and enforcement. The econometric specification we develop builds on the theoretical analysis of the tax compliance game presented in Erard and Feinstein (1994b). In addition, the data employed in this study have been used in prior research by Erard and Feinstein (1994a, 1994c) on federal tax reports and audit selection decisions. Our work is also related to studies of taxpayer and auditor behavior by Alm, Bahl, and Murray (1993), Beron, Tauchen, and Witte (1991), and Dubin, Graetz, and Wilde (1990).

8.2   Modeling State and Federal Audit Interactions

In this section we present our framework for analyzing tax audit decisions and assessments. We divide our presentation into two parts. First, we present a model of auditing by a single tax authority. We then extend our model to the case in which there are two separate tax authorities, which we label "federal" and "state." These models form the basis for our empirical analysis of Oregon and IRS tax audit decisions and assessments for tax year 1987, which is presented in section 8.3.

8.2.1   Single-Agency Model

Consider a tax authority charged with collecting the taxes owed by each member of a community of individuals or households. Although many members of the community pay their full tax liability voluntarily, others do not. The authority cannot costlessly observe each member's true liability and determine whether the member is fully in compliance. Instead, the authority must use audits to detect noncompliance. In this subsection we present a simple model of the authority's audit selection decisions and assessments. We divide our discussion into four parts. First, we specify an audit assessment distribution; next, we describe the tax authority's calculation of the expected assessment to be earned from performing an audit; then, we define audit costs and derive an audit selection criterion; finally, we present the likelihood function associated with our model.

Audit Assessments

Consider first the specification of audit revenue assessments, which is the most complex part of our model. For a taxpayer who has been audited, we define R as the amount of additional taxes, interest, and penalties that the taxpayer is assessed. For a taxpayer who has not been audited, we define R as the amount that would have been assessed if an audit had taken place. The assessment R may be positive, in which case the taxpayer owes R dollars to the government; zero; or negative, in which case the individual has overpaid his taxes.

In our data, described much more fully below, approximately 70 percent of all federal audits result in a positive assessment, 23 percent result in no assessment, and 7 percent result in a negative assessment. Further, the mean positive federal assessment is more than twice as large as the mean negative assessment, and the variance of positive assessments is much larger than the variance of negative assessments, in part because there are a small number of very large positive assessments. The statistics for state audit assessments are similar, though not identical. Our specification of the distribution of R reflects these facts, in two main ways. First, in contrast to several previous studies of tax compliance, including Clotfelter (1983) and Feinstein (1991), we distinguish negative assessments from zero assessments, in order to more precisely model the assessment distribution.[3] Second, we specify a log-normal distribution for positive assessments, in order to fit the long right-hand tail of very large positive assessments recorded in our data.

We specify the distribution associated with R in terms of a two-step process consisting of three equations. The first step distinguishes positive assessments from nonpositive (zero or negative) assessments. We define the latent variable $P*$ as

(1) $$P* = \beta_1 x_1 + w$$

and assume that the assessment is positive if $P*$ is greater than zero, but otherwise the assessment is either zero or negative. In expression (1), x_1 are characteristics of the individual or household under consideration, β_1 is a parameter vector, and w is a stochastic disturbance. The second step involves one of two expressions, depending on the sign of $P*$. If $P*$ is greater than zero, the assessment R is positive and is defined by

(2) $$R = \exp(\beta_2 x_2 + \varepsilon),$$

where x_2 are characteristics of the individual or household, β_2 is a parameter vector, and ε is a stochastic disturbance. Alternatively, if $P*$ is less than or equal to zero, then the assessment R is either negative or zero, according to a Tobit specification given by

---

3. The only two previous studies of which we are aware that distinguish negative from zero assessments are Alexander and Feinstein (1987) and Erard (1995).

$$(3) \qquad R = \begin{cases} -\alpha + u & \text{if } u < \alpha, \\ 0 & \text{otherwise,} \end{cases}$$

where α is a constant and u is a stochastic disturbance. We discuss the distributions associated with the stochastic disturbances w, ε, and u below.

It is important to recognize that our specification of the assessment distribution is neither derived from nor meant to be interpreted as a structural model of reporting behavior.[4] Instead, the model reflects our view of the way in which a tax authority is likely to evaluate the assessment distribution. We believe the authority is likely first to evaluate the probability that the taxpayer has underpaid his taxes, using equation (1) and including in x_1 individual or household characteristics that affect the probability of an underreport. We believe the authority is likely next to evaluate the magnitude of an underreport, conditional on an underreport occurring, using equation (2). In equation (2), x_2 includes individual or household characteristics that influence the extent of underreporting, and the exponential parameterization captures the long right-hand tail, reflecting the small probability of a very large positive assessment. We note that x_1 and x_2 may contain some common elements but are unlikely to be identical. We believe the authority is likely to consider last the possibility that, conditional on no underreport, there is a negative assessment, evaluating both the probability and likely extent of such a negative assessment by means of equation (3). We doubt that most tax authorities develop a careful model of negative assessments, partly because such assessments are relatively infrequent and of small magnitude, and partly because it is not obvious what individual or household variables are likely to be associated with overpayments. Hence we do not include any explanatory variables in equation (3).

Note that the assessment R is not equivalent to the difference between the taxpayer's legal tax obligation and his tax payment, for four reasons. First, the tax examiner may not detect all of the taxpayer's underpayment or overpayment. Second, the examiner may tend to exaggerate the size of an underpayment, in an effort to obtain greater enforcement revenue for the tax agency. Third, the assessment may include interest and penalty charges for detected underpayments. Fourth, the examiner and the taxpayer may negotiate over the size of the assessment, in which case the final outcome will depend on the relative bargaining strengths of the two parties.[5]

4. Alexander and Feinstein (1987) and Erard (1995) both present a more elaborate model of taxpayer reporting errors and underreports. In particular, both studies present models in which errors are symmetrically distributed around zero, negative assessments are always due to error, and positive assessments are due either to error or to intentional evasion.

5. It should also be noted that the amount the taxpayer is assessed during an audit may differ from the amount that is eventually received by the tax authority, either because the assessment is later reduced following an appeal by the taxpayer, or because the taxpayer fails to pay the assessed amount. We leave it to future research to incorporate these issues into a model of compliance and enforcement.

Calculation of the Expected Assessment

As the next step in the description of our model, consider the tax authority's calculation of the expected value of the assessment associated with a particular taxpayer, a calculation that plays a central role in the authority's audit selection decision. We assume that the authority knows the form of equations (1), (2), and (3), including the forms of the distributions from which the stochastic disturbances are drawn, and knows the values of all parameters that enter into these three equations. We also assume that the authority observes the explanatory variables x_1 and x_2 prior to making its audit selection decision, but does not observe the values of the stochastic disturbances, w, ε, and u, and therefore does not observe the actual assessment R. Last, and important, we assume that prior to making its audit selection decision the authority is able to observe the value of a signal, denoted η, that provides information about the assessment R. We integrate the signal into our revenue assessment model by assuming that η is correlated with each of w and ε and therefore provides information about both the probability of a positive assessment and, conditional on a positive assessment occurring, the likely magnitude of the assessment. We do not allow for the possibility that η is correlated with u since we doubt that the authority is likely to observe information about the likelihood or magnitude of a negative assessment. Intuitively, we expect that the greater is η, the greater will be the tax authority's calculation of the expected value of the assessment to be earned from performing an audit. Although η is observable to the tax authority, we assume that it is not recorded in the data available for analysis and therefore must be treated as a stochastic disturbance in the econometric specification. The fact that η is a stochastic disturbance is important for the structure of both our econometric model and the associated likelihood function; we discuss the role of η in the model and the likelihood function below.

Having introduced the signal η, we can now specify distributions for w, ε, η, and u. We assume that w, ε, and η are jointly drawn from a trivariate normal distribution and that u is independently drawn from a separate normal distribution. We impose several restrictions on these distributions. The first restriction is that the unconditional mean of each disturbance is zero. The second restriction is that the standard error of w (σ_w) is equal to one, a normalization that is required for identification for the same reason that the standard error in a probit model is set equal to one, namely, because only the sign of P^* affects the assessment R. The third restriction, similar to the second, is that the standard error of the signal η (σ_η) is equal to one, a normalization that is required for identification because, in the likelihood function, η is associated with the tax authority's decision about whether to conduct an audit, a binary choice that is modeled in a manner analogous to a probit model. The final restriction is that (conditional on η) w and ε are independent of one another; for the trivariate normal distribution, this restriction is equivalent to the condition that $\rho_{w\varepsilon} = \rho_{\eta w}\rho_{\eta\varepsilon}$, where ρ_{ab} is the correlation between random variables a and b. We impose this final restriction primarily to ease the computational burden associated with estimating the model.

After these restrictions have been imposed, there are four remaining parameters to be estimated. Two of the parameters are standard errors: σ_ε, the standard error associated with positive assessments, and σ_u, the standard error associated with negative assessments. The other two parameters are correlations: $\rho_{\eta w}$, which measures the information contained in the signal about the probability of a positive assessment, and $\rho_{\eta\varepsilon}$, which measures the information contained in the signal about the likely magnitude of a positive assessment, conditional on a positive assessment occurring.[6] Note that, although ε is normally distributed, the distribution of positive assessments is log-normal, due to the exponential form of equation (2).

We let $E(R|\eta)$ denote the expected value of the audit assessment, conditional on the value of the signal η. Using well-known properties of the normal and log-normal distributions, $E(R|\eta)$ can be expressed as

$$(4) \quad \Phi\left(\frac{\beta_1 x_1 + \rho_{\eta w}\eta}{\sqrt{1 - \rho_{\eta w}^2}}\right)\exp\left[\beta_2 x_2 + \rho_{\eta\varepsilon}\sigma_\varepsilon\eta + \frac{\sigma_\varepsilon^2(1 - \rho_{\eta\varepsilon}^2)}{2}\right]$$
$$- \left[1 - \Phi\left(\frac{\beta_1 x_1 + \rho_{\eta w}\eta}{\sqrt{1 - \rho_{\eta w}^2}}\right)\right]\left[\alpha\Phi\left(\frac{\alpha}{\sigma_u}\right) + \sigma_u\phi\left(\frac{\alpha}{\sigma_u}\right)\right],$$

where $\phi(\cdot)$ and $\Phi(\cdot)$ are, respectively, the standard normal probability and cumulative density functions. The first term in equation (4) is the probability of a positive assessment multiplied by the expectation of the magnitude of the assessment, conditional on a positive assessment occurring. The second term is the probability of a nonpositive assessment multiplied by the expectation of the magnitude of a negative assessment, conditional on a nonpositive assessment occurring and taking into account the probability of a zero assessment.

Audit Selection Criterion

Consider now the tax authority's audit selection criterion. Our specification of this criterion is based upon the theoretical analysis of the tax compliance game presented in Erard and Feinstein (1994b). They show that a revenue-maximizing tax authority that has a fixed audit budget, is risk neutral, and cannot precommit to its audit rule will select a return for audit whenever the expected revenue to be earned from performing the audit exceeds λc, where c is the audit cost and λ is a Lagrange multiplier associated with the budget constraint. The multiplier λ is an important policy parameter because it provides a measure of the increase in tax revenues that can be achieved by increasing the tax authority's audit budget. In particular, if λ exceeds one the government can increase its total revenue by raising the tax authority's audit budget.

---

6. We note that either one of the correlations may be fully identified, but then only the absolute value of the other correlation is identified, because of the form of the likelihood function.

Therefore, a revenue-maximizing government would want to provide the tax agency with sufficient resources to make λ equal to one. This revenue-maximizing policy might not, however, be an optimal policy from a social welfare perspective. The revenue raised from additional audit resources is merely a transfer from noncompliant taxpayers to the government, whereas the audit resources employed to effect this transfer represent a genuine resource cost. The welfare-maximizing value of λ, therefore, may be well in excess of one.

Adapting the criterion of Erard and Feinstein (1994b) to our context, we conclude that the tax authority will choose to audit a taxpayer whenever the expected revenue conditional on the observed signal, $E(R|\eta)$, is equal to or greater than the shadow cost of an audit, λc. In our econometric analysis, we treat λc as a single parameter; however, we have separate information about audit costs, so we are able to deduce an estimate of λ by dividing our estimate of λc by a rough estimate of c.

We assume that the expected value of the revenue assessment is nondecreasing in η, which implies that there exists some threshold signal, η^*, such that for all $\eta > \eta^*$, $E(R|\eta) \geq \lambda c$, while for $\eta < \eta^*$, $E(R|\eta) \leq \lambda c$.[7] It then follows that the authority will choose to audit a taxpayer if and only if the signal η is equal to or larger than the threshold value η^*. The threshold value for the signal is determined implicitly by the equation

$$(5) \qquad E(R|\eta^*) = \lambda c.$$

Likelihood Function

As the final step in the presentation of our model of a single tax authority, we present the likelihood function associated with the model. Each observation refers to a particular individual or household and falls into one of four categories: no audit, audit and positive assessment, audit and zero assessment, or audit and negative assessment. The likelihood associated with no audit is simply

$$(6) \qquad L_1 = \Phi(\eta^*),$$

or the probability that the signal is below the threshold value η^*. Note that η^* is a function of the characteristics x_1 and x_2 and therefore varies across individuals and households. The likelihood associated with an audit and a positive assessment in the amount R is

$$L_2 = \frac{1}{R\sigma_\varepsilon} \phi\left(\frac{\ln R - \beta_2 x_2}{\sigma_\varepsilon}\right)$$

---

7. This assumption is always satisfied when $\rho_{\eta w}$ and $\rho_{\eta \varepsilon}$ are both positive. The condition is also satisfied if one correlation is positive and the other negative, provided that the negative correlation is not too large in absolute value relative to the positive correlation. Our econometric estimation has never produced estimates for which the condition fails to hold.

$$(7) \quad \times \text{BN} \left[-\frac{\eta^* - \rho_{\eta\varepsilon} \left(\dfrac{\ln R - \beta_2 x_2}{\sigma_\varepsilon} \right)}{\sqrt{1 - \rho_{\eta\varepsilon}^2}}, \frac{\beta_1 x_1 + \rho_{\eta\varepsilon}\rho_{\eta w} \left(\dfrac{\ln R - \beta_2 x_2}{\sigma_\varepsilon} \right)}{\sqrt{1 - \rho_{\eta w}^2 \rho_{\eta\varepsilon}^2}}, \right.$$

$$\left. \frac{\rho_{\eta w}\sqrt{1 - \rho_{\eta\varepsilon}^2}}{\sqrt{1 - \rho_{\eta w}^2 \rho_{\eta\varepsilon}^2}} \right],$$

where R is the audit assessment and $\text{BN}[\cdot,\cdot,\rho]$ represents the standard bivariate normal cumulative distribution function with correlation ρ. The likelihood associated with an audit and a zero assessment is

$$(8) \qquad L_3 = \text{BN} \left[-\eta^*, -\beta_1 x_1, -\rho_{\eta w} \right] \Phi \left(-\frac{\alpha}{\sigma_u} \right).$$

Finally, the likelihood associated with an audit and a negative assessment is

$$(9) \qquad L_4 = \text{BN} \left[-\eta^*, -\beta_1 x_1, -\rho_{\eta w} \right] \frac{1}{\sigma_u} \phi \left(\frac{R + \alpha}{\sigma_u} \right),$$

where again R is the assessment, which in this case is negative.

8.2.2   Joint-Agency Model

In the United States and many other countries most individuals and households are obligated to pay taxes to more than one political jurisdiction. When this is the case and the tax authority associated with each jurisdiction conducts tax audits, many questions arise concerning issues that are important both for the understanding of tax enforcement systems and for tax policy formulation. To what extent do the authorities employ similar selection criteria? To what extent do they coordinate their selection processes? To what extent do they share audit results and other information? When they both audit the same individual or household, do they detect the same noncompliant behavior? Finally, is the marginal value of an additional dollar of audit resources approximately the same for the different authorities?

In this subsection we present a model that addresses these and related questions. The model includes a large collection of individuals (or households), each of whom is obligated to pay taxes to two jurisdictions, federal and state. We assume that each jurisdiction has a tax authority, and each authority conducts audits. In addition, we assume that the state tax authority can use results from federal audits to perform piggyback audits. We divide our presentation into two parts. We first describe the conceptual structure of the model, which is based on the framework presented in the previous subsection. We then derive the likelihood function associated with the model.

Model Structure

Consider a particular individual or household. Our model of the state and federal tax authorities' decisions about whether to audit the individual or household consists of two periods. In the first period each authority decides whether to audit the individual or household and, if it conducts an audit, makes a revenue assessment. The authorities' period-one decisions are made simultaneously and are independent of one another. If in period one either the state authority has conducted an audit or the federal authority has not conducted an audit, then period two is not applicable and the model terminates at the end of period one. Otherwise, there is a second period, during which the state authority learns the federal period-one audit results and then decides whether to perform a piggyback audit. The piggyback audit consists of two stages: first, the federal audit results and the taxpayer's state return are used to determine the additional revenue owed to the state; second, the individual is notified of the assessment. The piggyback audit is much less expensive than a period-one audit since it involves neither direct face-to-face contact with the individual nor a careful investigation of the individual's tax records.[8]

We use the framework presented in subsection 8.2.1 to model both the federal audit assessment distribution and the federal tax authority's period-one audit selection decision. In particular, we let R_f denote the federal assessment that either is generated by a federal audit or would have been generated if the individual or household had been subjected to a federal audit. Similarly, we let x_{1f} and x_{2f} denote characteristics of the individual or household that affect the federal assessment and enter into equations (1) and (2); w_f, ε_f, and u_f denote the stochastic disturbances that are associated with the federal revenue assessment distribution and enter into equations (1), (2), and (3); and η_f denote the signal observed by the federal tax authority. Finally, we define the threshold value for the federal signal η_f^* as the value of η_f for which $E(R_f \mid \eta_f^*) = \lambda_f c_f$, where λ_f is the multiplier associated with the federal audit budget constraint and c_f is the cost of a federal audit. We assume that $E(R_f \mid \eta_f)$ is greater than or equal to $\lambda_f c_f$ if and only if $\eta_f \geq \eta_f^*$. It then follows that the federal tax authority performs an audit whenever η_f is equal to or greater than η_f^*. As should be clear from our description, the federal tax authority observes only its own signal η_f prior to making its audit decision; it does not observe the analogous state signal η_s, which is introduced below.

Our specification of the state period-one independent audit assessment distribution also is based on the framework presented in section 8.2.1; however our specifications of the state piggyback assessment distribution and the state tax authority's audit selection procedure are somewhat different. We let R_s denote the state period-one assessment; x_{1s} and x_{2s} denote characteristics of the

8. In actual practice, the state may need to contact the taxpayer if the information on the taxpayer's state return is insufficient to determine the tax consequences of the federal audit results.

individual or household that affect the period-one assessment and enter into the state versions of equations (1) and (2); w_s, ε_s, and u_s denote stochastic disturbances that enter into the state versions of equations (1), (2), and (3); and η_s denote the signal observed by the state tax authority. We define the cost of a state independent audit to be $\lambda_s c_s$, where λ_s is the multiplier associated with the state's independent audit budget constraint and c_s is the cost of an independent state audit. We expect c_s to be smaller than c_f since state audits are normally shorter and simpler than federal audits. If the federal and state governments were able to share budgets and revenues, we might expect λ_s to be approximately equal to λ_f, since, if one λ-value were larger than the other, audit resources could be transferred to the authority with the larger λ-value, increasing total government revenues. Since governments do not share budgets and revenues to this extent, however, we expect λ_s to be somewhat smaller than λ_f, because at least in most cases the state tax rate is substantially below the federal rate.

We let R_p denote the assessment that either is generated by a period-two piggyback audit or would have been generated if the state had chosen to conduct such an audit. Since the piggyback audit is based directly on the period-one federal assessment, R_p is likely to depend upon R_f. However, R_p may not be exactly proportional to R_f, due to differences in tax progressivity, differences in the tax treatment of certain issues between the federal government and the state, differences in penalty and interest charges, and possible administrative errors. We define

(10) $$\ln (R_p + K) = h(R_f, x_p; \beta_p) + \varepsilon_p.$$

In equation (10), $h(\cdot)$ is a parametric function that depends on the federal revenue assessment R_f and a vector of explanatory variables x_p, which control for differences between the federal and state tax bases, tax rate schedules, and credit structures. We assume that the state tax authority knows the functional form of h, inclusive of the values of the parameter vector β_p and the "displacement parameter" K, which accounts for the possibility that R_p is negative. The term ε_p is a stochastic disturbance. The state does not have direct knowledge of ε_p; rather it observes a signal η_p of its likely value at the beginning of period two, prior to deciding whether to perform a piggyback audit. We assume that a piggyback audit has a shadow cost of $\lambda_p c_p$. We expect c_p to be substantially below both c_s and c_f. If the state tax authority is allocating its audit resources efficiently, λ_s should be approximately equal to λ_p, since, if one λ-value were much larger than the other, the state could increase its revenues by shifting audit resources from the audit program associated with the smaller λ-value to the audit program associated with the larger λ-value.[9]

We consider mainly a *nonstrategic* model of the state tax authority's audit

---

9. The two λ-values also might differ if the shadow value associated with state budgetary resources is different in time periods one and two.

selection process. This model is based on the assumption that the state authority performs a period-one audit whenever the expected revenue assessment exceeds the audit cost, without taking into consideration the possibility that it may be able to perform a piggyback audit in period two if the federal tax authority performs a period-one audit and the state authority does not. In contrast, a *strategic* model would assume that the state does take into account the potential for a period-two piggyback audit when making its period-one audit decision. We believe the nonstrategic model is descriptive of actual state audit selection decisions but that states might be able to increase their audit revenues by adopting the audit selection rule generated by the strategic model. In the remainder of this section we describe the nonstrategic model in more detail and derive the likelihood function associated with it. In section 8.3 we present results from estimation of the nonstrategic model, and in the appendix we provide a more detailed description of the strategic model.

We define the threshold value for the state signal η_s^* as the value of η_s for which $E(R_s \mid \eta_s^*) = \lambda_s c_s$, and we assume that $E(R_s \mid \eta_s)$ is greater than or equal to $\lambda_s c_s$ if and only if $\eta_s \geq \eta_s^*$. For the nonstrategic model, it then follows that the state chooses to conduct a period-one audit if and only if the signal η_s is equal to or greater than η_s^*. Note that the state observes only the signal η_s in period one and has no knowledge of either the federal signal η_f or the federal authority's decision about whether to audit the individual. If the state authority does not perform a period-one audit but the federal tax authority does perform such an audit, then in the second period the state authority must decide whether to perform a piggyback audit. Define η_p^* to be the value of the signal η_p for which $E(R_p \mid \eta_p^*, R_f) = \lambda_p c_p$, and assume that for all values of R_f, $E(R_p \mid \eta_p, R_f)$ is equal to or greater than $\lambda_p c_p$ if and only if $\eta_p \geq \eta_p^*$. It then follows that the state authority will choose to perform a piggyback audit if and only if the signal η_p is equal to or greater than η_p^*. Note that, for a given value of the signal η_p, $E(R_p \mid \eta_p, R_f)$ is nondecreasing in R_f, so the threshold value η_p^* is a nonincreasing function of R_f and the probability of a piggyback audit is a nondecreasing function of the federal assessment R_f.

As the final step in the description of our model of state and federal tax audit decisions, consider the distribution of the stochastic disturbances in the model. We assume that $(w_f, w_s, \varepsilon_f, \varepsilon_s, \eta_f, \eta_s)$ are drawn from a multivariate normal distribution, and we impose the following conditions on this distribution: Following the specification presented in subsection 8.2.1, we normalize each of $\sigma_{\eta_f}, \sigma_{\eta_s}, \sigma_{w_s},$ and σ_{w_f} to 1. We then make the following assumptions: (conditional on η_f) ε_f and w_f are independent, (conditional on η_s) ε_s and w_s are independent, (conditional on η_s) w_s is independent of both η_f and ε_f, and (conditional on η_f) w_f is independent of both η_s and ε_s. The latter two assumptions are made primarily to ease the computational burden associated with estimating the model. The distribution then depends upon a total of eleven parameters. Six of the parameters are familiar from the model of the previous subsection: the two standard deviations, σ_{ε_f} and σ_{ε_s}, and the four correlations,

$\rho_{\eta_f w_f}$, $\rho_{\eta_s w_s}$, $\rho_{\eta_f \varepsilon_f}$, and $\rho_{\eta_s \varepsilon_s}$. The remaining five parameters are new, and they represent features of the relationship between the federal and state audit assessment processes. These five parameters are (1) $\rho_{\eta_f \eta_s}$, the correlation between the two signals; (2) $\rho_{\varepsilon_f \varepsilon_s}$, the correlation between the two ε-disturbances; (3) $\rho_{w_f w_s}$, the correlation between the two w-disturbances; (4) $\rho_{\eta_f \varepsilon_s}$, the correlation between the federal signal η_f and the disturbance ε_s in the state revenue model; and (5) $\rho_{\eta_s \varepsilon_f}$, the correlation between the state signal η_s and the disturbance ε_f in the federal revenue model. We discuss the interpretation of these parameters below.[10]

We assume that the disturbances u_f and u_s are drawn from a bivariate normal distribution with parameters σ_{u_f}, σ_{u_s}, and $\rho_{u_f u_s}$, and that each of u_f and u_s is independent of the other stochastic disturbances in the model. We also assume that η_p and ε_p are drawn from a bivariate normal distribution, and we impose as a normalization that the standard deviation of η_p is 1, leaving two free parameters in this distribution, σ_{ε_p} and $\rho_{\eta_p \varepsilon_p}$. In addition, we assume that each of η_p and ε_p is independent of the other stochastic disturbances in the model. Finally, we note from equation (10) that the assumption that ε_p is normal implies that R_p is distributed according to the displaced log-normal distribution, with displacement parameter K.

Our model provides a rich structure for analyzing the relationship between federal and state tax audit decisions and assessments. A comparison of the variables included in x_{1f} and x_{2f} with those included in x_{1s} and x_{2s}, and of the parameter vectors β_{1f} and β_{2f} with the vectors β_{1s} and β_{2s}, can provide information about the extent to which the variables that influence federal audit decisions and assessments are similar to those that influence state decisions and assessments. If the two sets of variables and parameters turn out to be significantly different, further research will be necessary to determine whether the differences are due to differences in tax law, differences in reporting behavior, or differences in audit selection and assessment procedures. If there are substantial differences resulting from different audit and assessment procedures, our models may help administrators to improve their procedures. The parameter $\rho_{\eta_f \eta_s}$ measures the correlation between the signals observed by the federal and state authorities. If this correlation is positive, it will serve as an indication that the two authorities have access to similar sources of information, and draw upon similar experiences, in evaluating assessment distributions. Conversely, if the correlation is negative, we might infer that the two authorities tend to

---

10. A consideration of the covariance matrix associated with this multivariate normal distribution may clarify the restrictions we have imposed. Order the disturbances as η_f, η_s, w_f, w_s, ε_f, and ε_s. The covariance matrix is 6×6. Consider the upper triangular portion of this matrix. The first four diagonal entries are 1. The next two diagonal entries are $\sigma^2_{\varepsilon_f}$ and $\sigma^2_{\varepsilon_s}$. In the first row the remaining elements are $\rho_{\eta_f \eta_s}$, $\rho_{\eta_f w_f}$, $\rho_{\eta_s w_s}$, $\rho_{\eta_f \eta_s}$, $\sigma_{\eta_f \varepsilon_f}$, and $\sigma_{\eta_f \varepsilon_s}$. In the second row the remaining elements are $\rho_{\eta_s \eta_f}$, $\rho_{\eta_f w_f}$, $\rho_{\eta_s w_s}$, $\sigma_{\eta_s \varepsilon_f}$, and $\sigma_{\eta_s \varepsilon_s}$. In the third row the remaining elements are $\rho_{w_f w_s}$, $\rho_{\eta_f w_f}$, $\sigma_{\eta_f \varepsilon_f}$, and $\rho_{\eta_f w_f} \sigma_{\eta_f \varepsilon_s}$. In the fourth row the remaining elements are $\rho_{\eta_s w_s}$, $\sigma_{\eta_s \varepsilon_f}$ and $\rho_{\eta_s w_s} \sigma_{\eta_s \varepsilon_s}$. In the fifth row the remaining element is $\sigma_{\varepsilon_f \varepsilon_s}$.

draw upon different sources of information and experiences in formulating their audit policies. In either case, so long as the two signals are not perfectly correlated, the potential will exist for both agencies to improve their audit policies by sharing the information contained in their signals. Comparisons of $\rho_{\eta_f w_f}$ to $\rho_{\eta_s w_s}$ and of $\rho_{\eta_f \varepsilon_f}$ to $\rho_{\eta_s \varepsilon_s}$ will indicate whether the signal observed by the federal authority is more informative than the signal observed by the state authority, a comparison which provides an interesting measure of the relative capabilities of the two authorities. The cross-correlations $\rho_{\eta_f \varepsilon_s}$ and $\rho_{\eta_s \varepsilon_f}$ measure the degree to which the signal observed by one authority provides information about the likely magnitude of a positive assessment for the other authority, conditional on a positive assessment occurring. To understand the empirical phenomena to which these cross-correlations relate, consider $\rho_{\eta_f \varepsilon_s}$. If this correlation is larger (more positive) than $\rho_{\eta_f \eta_s} \rho_{\eta_s \varepsilon_s}$, then conditional on η_s the likely magnitude of a positive state assessment is larger, the larger is η_f. Since the federal authority is more likely to audit the larger is η_f, a large positive value for $\rho_{\eta_f \varepsilon_s}$ implies that, conditional on the state's making a positive assessment, the magnitude of the assessment is expected to be larger when the federal authority has chosen to perform an audit than when the federal authority has chosen not to perform an audit. More important from the viewpoint of policy, these cross-correlations provide an indication of the value of information sharing between the two tax authorities. For example, so long as the value of $\rho_{\eta_f \varepsilon_s}$ is different from the value of $\rho_{\eta_f \eta_s} \rho_{\eta_s \varepsilon_s}$, the federal government will be able to help the state improve its audit selection procedures by sharing the information contained in the federal signal.[11] Finally, $\rho_{w_f w_s}$, $\rho_{\varepsilon_f \varepsilon_s}$, and $\rho_{u_f u_s}$ measure the extent to which federal and state assessments are correlated. We expect each of these correlations to be positive, but we are particularly interested in their magnitudes, especially that of $\rho_{\varepsilon_f \varepsilon_s}$. Of course, we do not expect federal and state assessments to be identical, or even proportional, due to differences in tax law and in the specific items of noncompliance detected during the respective audits.[12] However, a finding of large differences between state and federal assessments may serve as an indication that revenues can be increased by pooling audit results for cases subjected to independent audit by both agencies.

Likelihood Functions

The likelihood function associated with our model is rather complex. There are four qualitatively distinct outcomes possible for the federal tax authority in

11. As described previously, we have imposed restrictions on the other two cross-correlations, $\rho_{\eta_f w_s}$ and $\rho_{\eta_s w_f}$. In future analysis, we may allow these parameters to be free as well. However, when all four cross-correlations are free, the single-agency model estimates are not consistent in the joint-agency model, which significantly complicates estimation; see our discussion of estimation strategy in the main text.

12. The results of Alexander and Feinstein (1987), Feinstein (1991), and Erard (1995) all indicate that detection is quite imperfect. See the discussion of empirical results, in particular n. 20, for some information about the relationship between federal and state assessments among those individuals and households selected for audit by both authorities.

the model: (1) no audit; (2) audit, positive assessment; (3) audit, no assessment; and (4) audit, negative assessment. There are five qualitatively distinct outcomes possible for the state authority: (1) no audit; (2) independent audit, positive assessment; (3) independent audit, no assessment; (4) independent audit, negative assessment; and (5) no independent audit, piggyback audit. Since the form of the likelihood function depends on the outcomes for both authorities, there are therefore 20 potential cases to be considered. However, because the state authority can perform a piggyback audit only when the federal authority has performed an audit in period one, only 19 of these cases are relevant. We do not present the likelihoods associated with all 19 cases. Rather, we present the likelihoods for 6 representative cases and leave the remaining cases to be worked out by the reader, if interested.

Case 1. Federal audit and positive assessment, state audit and positive assessment:

$$(11) \quad L_1 = \frac{1}{R_f R_s \sigma_{\varepsilon_f} \sigma_{\varepsilon_s}} BN \left(\frac{\ln R_f - \beta_{2f} x_{2f}}{\sigma_{\varepsilon_f}}, \frac{\ln R_s - \beta_{2s} x_{2s}}{\sigma_{\varepsilon_s}}, \rho_{\varepsilon_f \varepsilon_s} \right)$$

$$\int_{\eta_f^*}^{\infty} \int_{\eta_s^*}^{\infty} \int_{-\beta_{1f} x_{1f}}^{\infty} \int_{-\beta_{1s} x_{1s}}^{\infty} f(\eta_f, \eta_s, w_f, w_s \mid R_f, R_s) \, dw_s \, dw_f \, d\eta_s \, d\eta_f,$$

where $BN(\cdot,\cdot,\rho)$ represents the standard bivariate normal distribution function with correlation coefficient ρ and $f(\cdot)$ is a multivariate conditional normal density function, derivable from the distribution functions defined above for the stochastic disturbances.

Case 2. Federal audit and positive assessment, state audit and zero assessment:

$$(12) \quad L_2 = \frac{1}{R_f \sigma_{\varepsilon_f}} \Phi \left(\frac{-\alpha_s}{\sigma_{u_s}} \right) \phi \left(\frac{\ln R_f - \beta_{2f} x_{2f}}{\sigma_{\varepsilon_f}} \right)$$

$$\int_{\eta_f^*}^{\infty} \int_{\eta_s^*}^{\infty} \int_{-\beta_{1f} x_{1f}}^{-\beta_{1s} x_{1s}} \int_{-\infty}^{\infty} f(\eta_f, \eta_s, w_f, w_s \mid R_f) \, dw_s \, dw_f \, d\eta_s \, d\eta_f,$$

where $\phi(\cdot)$ and $\Phi(\cdot)$ are, respectively, the standard normal probability and cumulative density functions.

Case 3. Federal audit and positive assessment, state audit and negative assessment:

$$(13) \quad L_3 = \frac{1}{R_f \sigma_{\varepsilon_f} \sigma_{u_s}} \phi \left(\frac{R_s + \alpha_s}{\sigma_{u_s}} \right) \phi \left(\frac{\ln R_f - \beta_{2f} x_{2f}}{\sigma_{\varepsilon_f}} \right)$$

$$\int_{\eta_f^*}^{\infty} \int_{\eta_s^*}^{\infty} \int_{-\beta_{1f} x_{1f}}^{-\beta_{1s} x_{1s}} \int_{-\infty}^{\infty} f(\eta_f, \eta_s, w_f, w_s \mid R_f) \, dw_s \, dw_f \, d\eta_s \, d\eta_f.$$

Case 4. Federal audit and positive assessment, no state independent audit, state piggyback:

$$
L_4 = \frac{1}{R_f \sigma_{\varepsilon_f}(R_p + K)\sigma_{\varepsilon_p}} \, \phi\left(\frac{\ln(R_p + K) - h(R_f, x_p; \beta_p)}{\sigma_{\varepsilon_p}}\right) \phi\left(\frac{\ln R_f - \beta_{2f}x_{2f}}{\sigma_{\varepsilon_f}}\right)
$$

$$
(14) \quad \Phi\left(\frac{-\eta_p^* + \rho_{\eta_p \varepsilon_p}\left(\dfrac{\ln(R_p + K) - h(R_f, x_p; \beta_p)}{\sigma_{\varepsilon_p}}\right)}{\sqrt{1 - \rho_{\eta_p \varepsilon_p}^2}}\right)
$$

$$
\int_{\eta_f^*}^{\infty} \int_{-\infty}^{\eta_s^*} \int_{-\beta_{1f}x_{1f}}^{\infty} f(\eta_f, \eta_s, w_f \mid R_f)\, dw_f\, d\eta_s\, d\eta_f.
$$

Case 5. Federal audit and positive assessment, no independent state audit, no state piggyback:

$$
(15) \qquad L_5 = \frac{1}{R_f \sigma_{\varepsilon_f}} \, \phi\left(\frac{\ln R_f - \beta_{2f}x_{2f}}{\sigma_{\varepsilon_f}}\right) \Phi(\eta_p^*)
$$

$$
\int_{\eta_f^*}^{\infty} \int_{-\infty}^{\eta_s^*} \int_{-\beta_{1f}x_{1f}}^{\infty} f(\eta_f, \eta_s, w_f \mid R_f)\, dw_f\, d\eta_s\, d\eta_f.
$$

Case 6. No federal audit, no state audit:

$$
(16) \qquad L_6 = BN(\eta_f^*, \eta_s^*, \rho_{\eta_f \eta_s}).
$$

The parameters of the model can be estimated jointly by maximizing the full likelihood function. However, we have chosen to estimate the model using a much simpler estimation strategy, which is based on the observation that the joint model we have outlined in this subsection nests the single tax authority model presented in subsection 8.2.1. In particular, we estimate the parameters of the model in four steps. First, we estimate the federal audit selection and assessment parameters corresponding to equations (1), (2), and (3) from the previous subsection: this estimation yields consistent estimates of β_{1f}, β_{2f}, σ_{ε_f}, $\rho_{\eta_f w_f}$, $\rho_{\eta_f \varepsilon_f}$, σ_{u_f}, and $\lambda_f c_f$. Next, we estimate the state audit selection and assessment parameters corresponding to the state version of equations (1), (2), and (3); this estimation yields consistent estimates of β_{1s}, β_{2s}, σ_{ε_s}, $\rho_{\eta_s w_s}$, $\rho_{\eta_s \varepsilon_s}$, σ_{u_s} and $\lambda_s c_s$. Note that each of these first two steps involves estimating the model presented in subsection 8.2.1. Third, we estimate the piggyback audit selection and assessment equation (10) on the subset of cases for which the federal government performed a period-one audit and the state did not; this estimation yields consistent estimates of β_p, $\rho_{\eta_p \varepsilon_p}$, and σ_{ε_p}. Finally, we estimate the full likelihood function, maximizing over the six remaining parameters,

$\rho_{\eta_f \eta_s}$, $\rho_{\eta_f \varepsilon_s}$, $\rho_{\eta_s \varepsilon_f}$, $\rho_{w_f w_s}$, $\rho_{u_f u_s}$, and $\rho_{\varepsilon_f \varepsilon_s}$. As discussed in section 8.3, we perform our estimation using a choice-based data sample. We therefore make an adjustment to the estimated standard errors associated with all parameter estimates to account for this feature of the data. The two critical assumptions that are necessary for our estimation procedure to yield consistent estimates are that $\rho_{\eta_f w_s} = \rho_{\eta_f \eta_s} \rho_{\eta_s w_s}$ and $\rho_{\eta_s w_f} = \rho_{\eta_s \eta_f} \rho_{\eta_f w_f}$. If, for example, the first of these equalities failed to hold, then $E(R_s | \eta_s, \eta_f)$ would no longer be equal to $E(R_s | \eta_s)$ and we would not be able to estimate the state audit selection and assessment process separately from the federal selection and assessment process.[13]

8.3 Empirical Results

In this section we describe the results from our empirical analysis of ODR and IRS tax audits for tax year 1987. We divide our discussion into three parts. First, we describe the data we used in our study. Second, we present and discuss results from the estimation of the model of state and federal tax audit decisions and assessments presented in the previous section. Third, we discuss a number of other interesting findings that have emerged from a detailed investigation of Oregon's individual income tax audit programs.

8.3.1   The Data

Our analysis is based on tax return and audit information that has been compiled from several different sources. Our information about federal and state 1987 tax returns comes from two sources, the ODR Personal Income Tax Return Extract File database and the IRS Individual Returns Transaction File (IRTF) database; research staff at ODR matched the taxpayer records from these two databases for us.[14] Our information about audits of federal and state 1987 tax returns also comes from two sources, the ODR Audit Casedata File database, which contains information about ODR audits, and the IRS Audit Information Management System database, which contains information about IRS audits. We obtained the IRS audit information through a match based on social security numbers that was performed by the IRS research staff. We merged the tax return data with the audit data to create the data set used in our analysis.

Our data set is a subset of the total population of Oregon filers for tax year 1987. In order to ensure that a large number of audit cases would be included

13. In fact, all that is required for the estimation procedure to yield consistent estimates is that either the two equalities in the text hold and/or the following two equalities hold: $\rho_{\eta_f \varepsilon_s} = \rho_{\eta_f \eta_s} \rho_{\eta_s \varepsilon_s}$ and $\rho_{\eta_s \eta_f} = \rho_{\eta_s \varepsilon_f} \rho_{\eta_f \varepsilon_f}$.

14. Approximately 8.5 percent of our sample of Oregon returns failed to match with any IRTF record. When weighted, these numbers indicate that approximately 9.3 percent of all Oregon returns in the population would fail to match with any IRTF record. About 70 percent of all returns that fail to match are part-year or nonresident returns, which we exclude from our analysis in any case.

in our sample, we heavily oversampled filers that were subjected to an audit. In addition, we sampled business and farm returns at a higher rate than other returns. Our sampling procedure was as follows. For returns that were subjected to any form of enforcement action by the ODR or the IRS, we selected every return that reported any business (federal schedule C) or farm (federal schedule F) income (positive or negative) and one-half of all those returns that reported neither business nor farm income. For returns that were not subjected to any enforcement action at either the state or federal level, we selected 6 percent of returns that reported business income, 25 percent of returns that reported farm income but no business income, and 1.75 percent of returns that reported neither business nor farm income.

For our econometric analysis, we have excluded returns for part-year residents and nonresidents, and returns that failed to match with the IRS IRTF database, leaving 43,587 observations.[15] This total includes approximately 4,500 returns that were selected for a federal audit, 1,700 returns that were selected for an independent state audit, and 1,200 returns that were selected for a state piggyback audit. Our data include extremely detailed tax return information. In particular, for each observation we have nearly every line item of the federal 1040, 1040A, or 1040EZ form as well as federal schedule A; selected line-item information from federal schedules C, D, E, and F; and nearly every line item from the Oregon return, which may be either a form 40F (full-year long form) or a form 40S (full-year short form). The data identify whether the return was selected for a federal audit, and if the return was selected for a federal audit, the data indicate the auditor's assessment of the additional tax, interest, and penalties owed by the taxpayer at the time the case closed. Similarly, the data identify whether the return was selected for an Oregon audit, and if the return was selected for an Oregon audit, the data identify whether the audit was an independent or a piggyback audit and indicate the final assessment made at the time the case closed.

Tables 8.2 through 8.6 provide additional information about the data sample from which we selected returns for our econometric analysis. The frequency figures in table 8.2 are unweighted and provide information about numbers of observations in our sample, while dollar amounts are weighted to reflect population statistics. The dollar figures presented in each of the tables represent the additional tax, interest, and penalties that were assessed during the relevant audits. Table 8.2 indicates that there were slightly more than one million filers in Oregon in 1987, 63,000 of whom were placed in one of the IRS business audit classes, 7,300 of whom were placed in one of the IRS farm audit classes, and 941,000 of whom were placed in one of the IRS nonbusiness,

---

15. Excluding these kinds of returns reduced our sample by 5,511 observations, the number of federal audits by 813, the number of independent Oregon audits by 94, and the number of Oregon piggyback audits by 48. We discuss part-year and nonresident filers in subsection 8.3.3.

Table 8.2   Audit Results by IRS Audit Category

Audit	Total	Business	Farm	Nonbusiness, Nonfarm
Unweighted number returns	43,587	6,492	1,945	35,150
Weighted number returns	1,012,023	63,611	7,307	941,105
Federal audit cases				
Overall frequency	4,433	1,073	148	3,212
No-change frequency	1,007	210	62	735
Negative change cases				
Frequency	259	78	9	172
Median change	283	698	319	209
Mean change	1,330	3,287	614	713
Positive change cases				
Frequency	3,167	785	77	2,305
Median change	1,021	1,444	1,240	924
Mean change	3,073	5,502	4,310	2,472
State independent audits				
Overall frequency	1,667	802	77	788
No-change frequency	563	312	37	214
Negative change cases				
Frequency	83	30	2	51
Median change	225	214	184	229
Mean change	578	428	184	651
Positive change cases				
Frequency	1,021	460	38	523
Median change	399	442	582	328
Mean change	1,051	1,060	1,317	1,032
State piggyback audits				
Frequency	1,158	280	23	855
Median change	324	374	172	319
Mean change	762	1,005	414	710

Note: Frequencies are unweighted; dollar amounts are weighted to reflect population totals.

nonfarm classes.[16] Our sample includes 6,492 returns from the business audit classes, 1,945 returns from the farm audit classes, and 35,150 returns from the nonbusiness, nonfarm classes. In total, our sample contains 4,433 IRS audit cases, of which 1,073 were audits of returns falling in a business class (business audits), 148 were audits of returns falling in a farm class (farm audits), and 3,212 were audits of returns from a nonbusiness, nonfarm class (nonbusiness, nonfarm audits). Slightly less than one-quarter of all audits resulted in no additional assessment; however, approximately 40 percent of all farm audits

16. It is important to note that many filers who possess some business or farm income nonetheless are not placed in a business or farm audit class. The IRS has specific, somewhat complex rules for assigning returns to audit classes. In general, a return is assigned to a business or farm class only if total business or farm group receipts are sufficiently large relative to the taxpayer's total positive nonbusiness income, as calculated based on the information reported on the return.

resulted in no additional assessment. Approximately 6 percent of all audits in our sample resulted in a negative additional assessment; the mean negative assessment in the population was $1,330, while the median negative assessment was $283. The percentage frequencies of negative assessments in the various categories were quite similar to the overall frequency, although the mean and median levels of these assessments for the business category ($3,287 and $698, respectively) were much larger than the overall average. In each audit category the majority of federal audits resulted in a positive assessment. In particular, 71 percent of all audits in our sample, 73 percent of all business audits, 52 percent of all farm audits, and 72 percent of all nonbusiness, nonfarm audits resulted in a positive assessment. The mean positive assessment in the population was $3,073 for all audits combined, $5,502 for business audits, $4,310 for farm audits, and $2,472 for nonbusiness, nonfarm audits. The median positive assessment was $1,021 for all audits combined, $1,444 for business audits, $1,240 for farm audits, and $924 for nonbusiness, nonfarm audits.

The ODR does not classify taxpayers into different audit classes. Therefore in table 8.2, all subsequent tables, and our econometric analysis we have placed each Oregon return in the same class as the matching federal return. Our sample includes 1,667 independent Oregon audits, of which 802 are audits of filers whose federal returns were placed in an IRS business audit class, 77 are audits of filers in an IRS farm class, and 788 are audits of filers in an IRS nonbusiness, nonfarm class.[17] Approximately one-third of all Oregon audits in our sample resulted in no additional assessment, as compared to one-quarter of all federal audits. The largest Oregon no-change rates were in the business (39 percent) and farm (48 percent) categories. Approximately 5 percent of all Oregon audits in our sample resulted in a negative additional assessment; the mean negative assessment in the population was $578, while the median negative assessment was $225. The frequency of negative state assessments and the average size of those assessments was somewhat smaller in the business and farm categories. The majority of all Oregon audits resulted in a positive additional assessment, just as for federal audits. Over 61 percent of all Oregon audits in our sample resulted in a positive assessment; the mean positive assessment in the population was $1,051, while the median assessment was $399. These figures are well below the corresponding figures for federal audits, which is not surprising because Oregon has essentially a flat tax rate of 9 percent, well below the federal rate for most income categories. Approximately 57 percent of all audits of business returns, 49 percent of all audits of farm returns, and 66 percent of all audits of nonbusiness, nonfarm returns in our sample resulted in a positive assessment; the mean positive assessments for these three groups in the population were $1,060, $1,317, and $1,032 respectively, while the median assessments were $442, $582, and $328. Our sample

17. The ODR has informed us that our sample may include a small number of coding errors in which piggyback audits were misclassified as independent audits.

also includes 1,158 Oregon piggyback audits, including 280 audits of business returns, 23 audits of farm returns, and 855 audits of nonbusiness, nonfarm returns.[18] The mean assessment for all piggyback assessments in the population was $762, which is somewhat higher than the mean assessment for all independent Oregon audits, while the median piggyback assessment was $324, again higher than the corresponding figure for independent audits. The mean piggyback assessment was $1,005 for business returns, $414 for farm returns, and $710 for nonbusiness, nonfarm returns, while the median assessments were $374, $172, and $319, respectively.

The focus of our analysis is on the relationship between ODR and IRS audits. To explore this relationship we have partitioned the returns in our sample into five groups: (1) returns selected for both a federal audit and an independent state audit; (2) returns selected for both a federal audit and a state piggyback audit; (3) returns selected for a federal audit but not selected for a state audit; (4) returns selected for an independent state audit but not selected for a federal audit; and (5) returns not selected for audit by either tax authority. For each of these groups, table 8.3 presents the population frequencies as well as the relevant mean and median audit assessments. The top two rows of the table classify returns according to whether they were or were not selected for an IRS audit, and columns (1)–(3) classify returns according to whether they were not selected for any kind of Oregon audit, were selected for an independent Oregon audit, or were selected for a piggyback audit. Note that the first row of column (3) is empty because it is logically impossible for a return to fall into the no federal audit, state piggyback audit category. For each category the table lists the population frequency and percentage frequency and, where appropriate, the mean and median assessments associated with each kind of audit performed. For convenience the table also displays the marginal totals for each row and column category.

The figures in table 8.3 indicate that there were over one million resident filers in Oregon in 1987, of whom fewer than 1 percent were selected for any kind of audit. The IRS selected approximately 6,000 returns for audit; the mean federal assessment was $2,146, while the median assessment was $596.[19] The ODR selected slightly fewer than 2,000 returns for an independent state audit; the mean assessment for these audits was $626, while the median assessment was $79. In addition, the ODR performed slightly fewer than 1,500 piggyback audits; the mean assessment for piggyback audits was $762 and the median assessment was $324.

The most interesting figures in table 8.3 are the individual cell totals. Consider first the cell including returns selected for both an IRS and an independent ODR audit. A population total of 328 returns fall into this cell. This is a

18. Our data set also contains information about Oregon audits based on the IRS Information Returns Program, but we neither list these audits in table 8.2 nor use them in our analysis.

19. Note that the mean and median figures in table 8.3 are based on information about all audits, including those that resulted in either a negative assessment or no additional assessment.

Table 8.3   **IRS-Oregon Audit Interactions: All Returns**

IRS	Oregon No Audit (1)	Independent Audit (2)	Piggyback Audit (3)	Totals (4)
No audit	1,004,408 (99.25)	1,624 (0.16)		1,006,032 (99.41)
		466 mean		
		32 median		
Audit	4,175 (0.41)	328 (0.03)	1,488 (0.15)	5,991 (0.59)
	1,572 mean	5,746 fed. mean	2,965 fed. mean	2,146 mean
	294 median	1,924 fed. median	960 fed. median	596 median
		1,419 state mean	762 state mean	
		644 state median	324 state median	
Total	1,008,503 (99.66)	1,952 (0.19)	1,488 (0.15)	1,012,023 (100)
		626 state mean	2,965 fed. mean	
		79 state median	960 fed. median	
			762 state mean	
			324 state median	

Notes: Figures weighted to reflect population totals. Figures in parentheses give number as a percentage of all returns.

far larger number than would be predicted to fall into the cell if the IRS and the ODR had selected returns for audit at random; apparently the criteria used by the different agencies to select 1987 tax returns for audit were similar. The audit assessments associated with returns in this cell were quite high, higher than the assessments associated with returns in any other cell. In particular, the federal mean assessment for returns in this cell was $5,746, well above the overall federal mean of $2,146, while the federal median assessment for returns in this cell was $1,924, well above the overall median of $596. Similarly, the ODR mean (median) assessment for returns in this cell was $1,419 ($644), well above the mean (median) for all independent ODR audits of $626 ($79).

We believe these findings make sense and are quite consistent with our model of state and federal tax audit decisions and assessments. For a return to fall into this cell, both the signal observed by IRS and the signal observed by the ODR must have exceeded their threshold values. Although the signals may be positively correlated, they are not identical, and each is likely to contain information about both the federal and the state assessment distributions, as is true in our model whenever w_s and w_f are positively correlated, ε_s and ε_f are positively correlated, or the cross correlations $\rho_{\eta_f \varepsilon_s}$ and $\rho_{\eta_s \varepsilon_f}$ are large and positive. As a result, the expected federal assessment is likely to have been larger when both signals exceeded their respective threshold values than when only the federal signal exceeded its threshold value, and the same is true for the state assessment. Although the mean assessments associated with returns in this cell were substantially larger than the overall means, the differential between the median assessments in this cell and the overall medians was even more dramatic, a finding that we interpret as follows. Whenever both authorities independently decide to conduct an audit, the probability that the assessment for that case will be negative or zero is substantially lower than if only one of the authorities prefers to audit. However, the probability of a very large "outlier" assessment is only slightly increased when both agencies decide to audit.[20]

Consider next the cell involving returns for which the ODR chose to conduct an independent audit, but the IRS chose not to conduct an audit. The mean and median assessments associated with ODR audits of returns in this cell were $466 and $32, respectively, well below the mean and median assessments associated with any other kind of ODR audits, including piggyback audits. These results are also consistent with our model.

Now consider the remaining two cells that involve returns selected for an audit, the cell including returns selected for an IRS audit but not selected for an ODR audit and the cell including returns selected for an IRS audit and an ODR piggyback audit. There are 4,175 cases where the IRS performed an audit and the ODR performed no audit of any kind, and there are 1,488 cases where the IRS performed an audit and the ODR performed a piggyback audit. Thus, the ODR chose not to conduct a piggyback audit in the majority of cases for which the IRS performed an audit. The mean federal assessment for IRS audit cases that were not followed up with an ODR piggyback audit was $1,572, while the mean federal assessment for IRS audits that were followed up with a piggyback audit was $2,965. The median figures for these two cases are $294 and $960, respectively. Although these figures indicate that the ODR did follow up on many of the most profitable federal audit cases, it nonetheless chose not to conduct a piggyback audit in many cases (several thousand) for which there was a sizeable federal assessment. We are not certain why the ODR chose not to conduct more piggybacks audits in 1987. However, we provide some additional statistics and discuss this issue further later in the paper, in subsection 8.3.3.

Tables 8.4, 8.5, and 8.6 duplicate the format of table 8.3 for each of the three

20. The returns in this cell provide interesting information about the ability of tax examiners to detect noncompliance, because each return is subjected to two independent audits, resulting in two separate assessments. We explored the relationship between the federal and state assessments for the 283 returns (unweighted frequency) in this cell. Since Oregon's tax rate is (approximately) a flat 9 percent, we multiplied the Oregon assessment by 2.5, so that the average Oregon assessment was similar to the average federal assessment. We considered first the 184 cases for which the federal assessment exceeded $1,000. For these cases, 14 Oregon assessments were nonpositive, 25 (of the adjusted assessments, multiplied by 2.5) were less than 0.25 as large as the federal assessment, 17 were between 0.25 and 0.50 as large, 107 were between 0.75 and 1.5 times as large, and 21 were more than 1.5 times as large. Next we considered the 35 cases for which the federal assessment was nonpositive. For these cases, 17 Oregon assessments were also nonpositive, 7 were between $0 and $400, and 6 were greater than $1,000. Since the federal tax rate varies with income, we examined how our results varied with variations in the reported federal tax balance and adjusted gross income but found that the results were not sensitive to the levels of these variables.

Table 8.4   **IRS-Oregon Audit Interactions: IRS Business Class Returns**

	Oregon			
IRS	No Audit (1)	Independent Audit (2)	Piggyback Audit (3)	Totals (4)
No audit	61,829 (97.2)	629 (1.07) 430 mean 1 median		62,508 (98.27)
Audit	693 (1.09) 3,131 mean 337 median	126 (0.20) 5,830 fed. mean 2,431 fed. median 1,478 state mean 857 state median	284 (0.45) 4,551 fed mean 1,527 fed. median 1,005 state mean 374 state median	1,103 (1.73) 3,805 mean 777 median
Total	62,522 (98.29)	805 (1.27) 594 state mean 52 state median	284 (0.45) 4,551 fed. mean 1,527 fed. median 1,005 state mean 374 state median	63,611 (100)

Notes: Figures weighted to reflect population totals. Figures in parentheses give number as a percentage of all returns.

Table 8.5   **IRS-Oregon Audit Interactions: IRS Farm Class Returns**

	Oregon			
IRS	No Audit (1)	Independent Audit (2)	Piggyback Audit (3)	Totals (4)
No audit	7,094 (97.09)	63 (0.86) 252 mean 0 median		7,157 (97.95)
Audit	113 (1.55) 874 mean 0 median	14 (0.19) 13,987 fed. mean 2,007 fed. median 4,797 state mean 777 state median	23 (0.31) 1,757 fed. mean 728 fed. median 414 state mean 172 state median	150 (2.05) 2,233 mean 1 median
Total	7,207 (98.63)	77 (1.05) 624 state mean 0 state median	23 (0.31) 1,757 fed. mean 728 fed. median 414 state mean 172 state median	7,307 (100)

Notes: Figures weighted to reflect population totals. Figures in parentheses give number as a percentage of all returns.

Table 8.6   **IRS-Oregon Audit Interactions: IRS Nonbusiness, Nonfarm**
                       Class Returns

	Oregon			
IRS	No Audit (1)	Independent Audit (2)	Piggyback Audit (3)	Totals (4)
No audit	935,485 (99.40)	882 (0.09) 508 mean 76 median		936,367 (99.50)
Audit	3,369 (0.36) 1,274 mean 310 median	188 (0.02) 5,077 fed. mean 1,698 fed. median 1,305 state mean 448 state median	1,181 (0.13) 2,607 fed. mean 849 fed. median 710 state mean 319 state median	4,738 (0.50) 1,757 mean 570 median
Total	938,854 (99.76)	1,070 (0.11) 648 state mean 99 state median	1,181 (0.13) 2,607 fed. mean 849 fed. median 710 state mean 319 state median	941,105 (100)

Notes: Figures weighted to reflect population totals. Figures in parentheses give number as a percentage of all returns.

main categories of returns in our sample: business returns, farm returns, and nonbusiness, nonfarm returns. Most of the qualitative features of these tables are similar to the features of table 8.3, so we do not discuss them in detail. However, we note that while the ODR performed many more independent audits than piggyback audits in both the business and the farm classes, it actually conducted more piggyback audits than independent audits in the nonbusiness, nonfarm classes. Apparently the ODR allocates most of its audit resources to the business and farm classes. We also note that the mean assessments on independent state audits were fairly similar across audit categories. In contrast, the mean assessment on federal audits was much larger for the business audit category than for either the farm or the nonbusiness, nonfarm category.

8.3.2   Model Estimation Results

In this subsection we present and discuss results from the estimation of our model of state and federal audit selection decisions and assessments. We present results for three different audit categories. The first category includes all returns in our sample that fall into the middle IRS business audit class; this IRS class includes all business returns with reported schedule C total gross receipts between $25,000 and $100,000.[21] The second category contains all

21. There are two other IRS business audit classes. One consists of all business returns for which the reported total gross receipts are below $25,000, and the other consists of all business returns for which the reported total gross receipts are above $100,000.

returns that fall into either of two IRS farm audit classes; we have pooled together the returns for these two classes in order to obtain an adequate number of degrees of freedom for estimation. The final category includes all observations for which the IRS placed the federal return in the middle IRS nonbusiness, nonfarm class; this IRS class includes all nonbusiness, nonfarm returns from which the calculated total positive income is between $25,000 and $50,000.[22] For each category we first present and discuss results from the estimation of the single-agency model, estimated separately for the IRS and for the ODR, then briefly discuss the estimation of the piggyback equation (10), and then present and discuss results from the estimation of the remaining parameters of the joint-agency model. All of our econometric results are based on a weighted analysis that accounts for the choice-based sampling scheme we employed in collecting our data.

Table 8.7 presents results from estimation of the single-agency model for each audit class, while table 8.8 presents the results for parameters included in the joint-agency model but not in the single-agency models, with one exception. The exception is that no results are presented in table 8.8 for $\rho_{u_f u_s}$, the parameter that measures the degree of linear association between audit assessments when both agencies make a nonpositive audit assessment. Because our data include very few observations where both agencies make such an assessment, we were unable to reliably estimate this parameter. We have therefore restricted the value of this parameter to zero for all audit classes. Notice that table 8.7 does not list the explanatory variables included in x_{1f}, x_{2f}, x_{1s}, and x_{2s} for any of the classes and also does not present the estimates of the associated parameters β_{1f}, β_{2f}, β_{1s}, and β_{2s}. Our contract with the ODR requires us not to disclose any information that might be used by others to infer the audit selection criteria of either the IRS or the ODR. As a result, we cannot reveal either the explanatory variables or the parameter estimates associated with the explanatory variables included in the federal and state revenue assessment models. We will discuss certain qualitative features of these variables below. Note also that both IRS and ODR audit assessments are measured in thousands of dollars in our analysis. The standard error estimates in tables 8.7 and 8.8 have been adjusted to account for choice-based sampling. However, we have not adjusted the standard error estimates in table 8.8 to account for the use of a multistage estimation procedure. Consequently, the estimated standard errors in this table may tend to overstate the precision of our parameter estimates to some extent.

We first discuss the results for the business class. There are 2,640 observations in our data set in this class, of which 441 include federal returns that were selected for an IRS audit, 221 include state returns that were selected for an ODR independent audit, and 127 include state returns that were selected for

---

22. There are four other nonbusiness, nonfarm IRS classes. The majority of returns in our sample from this class reported some schedule C income.

Table 8.7   Estimation Results for the Single-Agency Model

	Business Class	Farm Class	Nonbusiness, Nonfarm Class
	IRS Results		
Correlation $\rho_{\eta_f w_f}$	.1992	.1571	.1824
	(0.181)	(0.216)	(0.107)
Correlation $\rho_{\eta_f \varepsilon_f}$	.2695	.3910*	0.00[a]
	(0.158)	(0.097)	
Standard deviation σ_{u_f}	.9841*	1.334*	1.465*
	(0.252)	(0.403)	(0.445)
Standard deviation σ_{ε_f}	2.205*	2.210*	1.776*
	(0.166)	(0.298)	(0.089)
Shadow cost $\lambda_f c_f$	5.227*	2.518*	2.347*
	(1.560)	(1.270)	(0.341)
Number of observations	2,640	1,945	9,239
Number of audit cases	441	148	856
Log-likelihood value	−318.4	−268.6	−375.3
	Oregon Results		
Correlation $\rho_{\eta_s w_s}$	.6654*	.8191*	.3296
	(0.229)	(0.087)	(0.262)
Correlation $\rho_{\eta_s \varepsilon_s}$	.2144	0.00[a]	0.00[a]
	(0.125)		
Correlation $\rho_{\eta_p \varepsilon_p}$	.9772*	.9690*	.9876*
	(0.007)	(0.012)	(0.006)
Standard deviation σ_{u_s}	.4951*	.3868*	.7307*
	(0.184)	(0.068)	(0.219)
Standard deviation σ_{ε_s}	1.810*	2.015*	1.938*
	(0.179)	(0.333)	(0.178)
Standard deviation σ_{ε_p}	.4409*	.1391	.3785*
	(0.065)	(0.078)	(0.057)
Shadow cost $\lambda_s c_s$	.6842*	.9382*	.9612*
	(0.176)	(0.458)	(0.260)
Shadow cost $\lambda_p c_p$	.2705*	−.4124	.2801*
	(0.039)	(0.687)	(0.052)
Number of observations	2,640	1,945	9,239
Number of independent audits	221	77	200
Number of piggyback audits	127	23	279
Log-likelihood value	−174.5	−136.8	−121.1

Note: Numbers in parentheses are adjusted standard errors.

[a]Parameter is constrained to zero.

*Significant at the 5 percent level.

an ODR piggyback audit. To determine what variables to include in x_{1f} and x_{2f} we used a specification search to determine which tax return characteristics were significantly related to IRS audit decisions and assessments. We used a similar procedure to determine which variables to include in x_{1s} and x_{2s}. Ultimately, only a few x-variables were included in the model, indicating that within this relatively narrowly defined audit class only a few return characteristics were relevant for explaining audit selection decisions and assessments.

Further, the set of variables that were included in x_{1f} and x_{2f} only partially overlapped with the set of variables included in x_{1s} and x_{2s}, indicating that the IRS and the ODR relied on somewhat different variables in making their audit selection decisions for 1987 returns.

Now consider in more detail the results presented in table 8.7 for the business class. Three features of the results are especially noteworthy. First, the four correlations $\rho_{\eta_f w_f}$, $\rho_{\eta_f \varepsilon_f}$, $\rho_{\eta_s w_s}$, and $\rho_{\eta_s \varepsilon_s}$ are all positive, indicating that, for each of the IRS and the ODR, the value of the signal observed by the tax authority was positively correlated with both the likelihood of a positive assessment and, conditional on a positive assessment occurring, the magnitude of the assessment. The fact that the correlations are all relatively large suggests that both tax authorities possess extensive information about noncompliance behavior that we are unable to observe in our data. The largest of these correlations is $\rho_{\eta_s w_s}$, the correlation between the state signal and the likelihood of a positive state assessment, which equals .665; the other three correlations are all approximately equal to .2, though they are somewhat imprecisely estimated. Second, the correlation between the piggyback signal η_p and the stochastic disturbance ε_p in the piggyback equation is extremely large (.977). The fact that this correlation is so close to 1 indicates that the state knew almost exactly how much revenue it would earn from a piggyback audit of a 1987 return, a fact which is not particularly surprising because the piggyback audit is based on the federal audit results and does not typically involve the examination of tax records. Third, the estimates of the audit cost variables $\lambda_f c_f$, $\lambda_s c_s$, and $\lambda_p c_p$ are all precisely estimated and sensible. The estimate of $\lambda_f c_f$ is 5.23 (recall that the revenue assessment variable is measured in thousands of dollars). From independent IRS data sources we have learned that the cost of a federal business audit of a 1987 return was approximately $1,000. Hence we estimate that the shadow value associated with increasing the IRS audit budget in this audit class by $1 is approximately $5, suggesting that if the IRS were allocated additional funds for business audits, net federal government revenue would increase. Our estimate of 5 for the shadow value of additional audit resources is far below previous estimates made by Dubin et al. (1990), which were based on the analysis of aggregate state-level data on federal audit assessments.[23] Our estimate is also somewhat below an estimate of 8 made by Erard and Feinstein (1994a) based on estimation of a slightly different audit selection model and using data from the same business audit class. The estimate of $\lambda_s c_s$ is 0.684. Although we do not at the present time posses reliable information about the cost of independent state audits, we believe that these audits are less expensive than federal audits and that c_s was probably in the neighborhood of $500 for audits of 1987 returns. Therefore we estimate that the shadow value

---

23. It should be noted that the estimate by Dubin et al. (1990) is intended to account for both the direct gain in audit revenue and any revenue resulting from increased deterrence. In contrast, our measure accounts solely for the direct gain in audit revenue.

associated with increasing the ODR budget for independent business audits by $1 is approximately equal to $1, suggesting that state revenue could not be increased through greater enforcement within this class. Finally, the estimate of $\lambda_p c_p$ is 0.271. As for independent state audits, we do not possess reliable information about the cost of state piggyback audits; however, we doubt that this cost exceeded $100 for 1987 returns. Hence we estimate that the shadow value associated with increasing the ODR budget for piggyback business audits is between $2 and $3, which indicates that the ODR could have increased audit revenues within the business class by reallocating resources from independent audits to piggyback audits. This conclusion corroborates our earlier remark, made with respect to table 8.4, that the ODR appears to conduct many independent audits but relatively few piggyback audits of business filers.

Now consider the results presented in table 8.8 for the business class. The estimates for all five of the correlations listed in table 8.8 are positive. The correlation $\rho_{\eta_f \eta_s}$ appears to be quite precisely estimated at .449. The estimates of the two cross-correlations $\rho_{\eta_f \varepsilon_s}$ and $\rho_{\eta_s \varepsilon_f}$ are .189 and .316, respectively, which are similar in magnitude to the estimates of the single-agency correlations $\rho_{\eta_f \varepsilon_f}$ and $\rho_{\eta_s \varepsilon_s}$ reported in table 8.7. The large positive estimate of $\rho_{\eta_f \eta_s}$ indicates that much of the information that the IRS possesses about 1987 business filers that we are unable to observe is also possessed by the ODR. The positive estimate of $\rho_{\eta_f \varepsilon_s}$ indicates that the information the IRS possesses is positively correlated with the size of the state assessment. An interesting question is whether this information adds anything to the knowledge already possessed by the ODR about the state assessment. To find out, we have used our results to compute an estimate of the partial correlation between the federal signal η_f and the state error term ε_s, conditional on the value of the state signal η_s.[24] The estimated value of this partial correlation is .11, which indicates that the federal signal contains some information about the state assessment that is not contained in the state signal. Thus, it would appear that the ODR could improve its business audit selection procedures if it were made privy to more federal information. Similarly, the large positive estimate of $\rho_{\eta_s \varepsilon_f}$ indicates that the state may possess information that would be helpful to the IRS in predicting federal assessments. Indeed, our computations indicate that the implied partial correlation between the state signal η_s and the federal error term ε_f conditional on the value of the federal signal η_f is equal to .23, which confirms that the state signal contains information about federal assessments not contained in the federal signal. These findings are consistent with the figures presented in

24. The partial correlation coefficient is defined as

$$\frac{\rho_{\eta_f \varepsilon_s} - \rho_{\eta_f \eta_s} \rho_{\varepsilon_s \eta_s}}{\sqrt{1 - \rho_{\eta_f \eta_s}^2} \sqrt{1 - \rho_{\varepsilon_s \eta_s}^2}}.$$

Table 8.8   **Joint-Agency Model Results**

	Business Class	Farm Class	Nonbusiness, Nonfarm Class
$\rho_{\eta_f \eta_s}$	.4486*	.5485*	.4611*
	(0.043)	(0.074)	(0.033)
$\rho_{\eta_f \varepsilon_s}$	.1890	.4509	−.0485
	(0.155)	(0.270)	(0.095)
$\rho_{\eta_s \varepsilon_f}$	.3156*	.6763*	−.0486
	(0.087)	(0.154)	(0.087)
$\rho_{w_f w_s}$	.7876*	.6371	.7087*
	(0.051)	(1.111)	(0.078)
$\rho_{\varepsilon_f \varepsilon_s}$	.5921	.2722	.8795*
	(0.315)	(0.322)	(0.056)
Log-likelihood value	−461.0	−348.3	−470.0

Note: Numbers in parentheses are partially adjusted standard errors.
*Significant at the 5 percent level.

table 8.5, which indicate that in the business classes revenue assessments are much higher, for both the IRS and the ODR, when both authorities conduct an audit than when only one of the two conducts an audit.

Two conclusions follow from these observations. First, the results in table 8.8 for the joint-agency model are consistent with the results presented in table 8.7 for the single-agency models. In particular, both sets of results indicate that both the IRS and the ODR possess extensive information about compliance characteristics of 1987 business filers beyond what we are able to infer from individual tax reforms. Second, although much of this information is possessed in common by the two authorities, each authority also possesses some unique information that is correlated with the other agency's revenue assessments. This second conclusion leads us to believe that for business classes additional information sharing between the two tax authorities might significantly improve audit selection procedures. The estimates of the two remaining correlations for the business class listed in table 8.8, $\rho_{w_f w_s}$ and $\rho_{\varepsilon_f \varepsilon_s}$, are both very large and positive (.788 and .592, respectively). These results are sensible and are consistent both with the hypothesis that taxpayers who cheat on their federal return also cheat on their state return and with the complementary hypothesis that taxpayers who make a mistake on their federal return carry the mistake over to their state return.

Having discussed the results for the business class in some detail, we now discuss the results for the farm and nonbusiness, nonfarm classes. Our data set includes 1,945 observations pertaining to the farm audit class and 9,239 observations pertaining to the nonbusiness, nonfarm class. These data include information on 148 federal farm audits, 856 federal nonbusiness, nonfarm audits, 77 independent state farm audits, and 200 independent state nonbusiness, nonfarm audits. The data also include information on 23 farm and 279 nonbusiness, nonfarm state piggyback audit cases. As for the business class, we used specification searches to determine the variables to include in x_{1f}, x_{2f}, x_{1s}, and x_{2s} for our farm and nonbusiness, nonfarm classes. For the farm class our search resulted in the inclusion of a relatively small number of tax return characteristics as explanatory variables in both the federal and state assessment equations, just as for the business class. However, for the nonbusiness, nonfarm class, our search resulted in the inclusion of a fairly large number of explanatory variables in the federal assessment equations and a quite small number of explanatory variables for the state assessment equations. We do not think it is surprising that more tax return characteristics were needed to explain federal audit selection decisions and assessments in this class than in the business and farm classes, because this class includes a much wider variety of tax returns and patterns of noncompliance. We also do not find it surprising that few variables were important in explaining state audit selection decisions in this class, because the ODR appears to devote most of its independent audit resources to business and farm returns.

Consider now the results for the farm and nonbusiness, nonfarm classes reported in table 8.7. For the farm class the results indicate that the private signal of the IRS has a positive and significant correlation with the size of a positive audit assessment. In contrast, the private signal of the ODR for this class is positively and significantly related to the probability of a positive assessment. The estimated correlation between the state signal η_s and the error term w_s (.819) is very large and quite precise, indicating that the state possesses very good information about the likelihood of a positive farm audit assessment. We do not find it surprising that the state possesses better information than the federal government about the likelihood of farm noncompliance, because farmers are spread across the state, and while the ODR maintains more than a dozen separate tax offices, the IRS operates out of a single district office located in Portland. This is one filer group for which local information seems especially important. Interestingly, while the ODR seems to possess superior information about the likelihood of a positive audit assessment, the IRS seems to possess better information about the probable magnitude of such an assessment. Indeed, the estimated correlation between the ODR signal η_s and the error term ε_s converged to zero in estimation, indicating that the ODR has no private information beyond what can be obtained from tax return data about the likely magnitude of a positive assessment. For the nonbusiness, nonfarm class the results indicate a positive correlation between each agency's private signal and the likelihood of a positive assessment. However, the values for $\rho_{\eta_f \varepsilon_f}$ and $\rho_{\eta_s \varepsilon_s}$ converged to zero in estimation for this audit class, indicating that neither agency possesses private information about the likely magnitude of a positive audit assessment for a nonbusiness, nonfarm return. The estimated value of $\rho_{\eta_p \varepsilon_p}$ is very close to 1 for each of these classes, again indicating that the state has extremely accurate information about the potential revenue associated with a piggyback audit. The estimated values of the audit cost parameters $\lambda_f c_f$ and $\lambda_s c_s$ are approximately 2.5 and 0.95, respectively, both for the farm class and the nonbusiness, nonfarm class. Farm audits tend to be about as costly as business audits for the IRS, suggesting that the shadow value associated with increasing IRS farm audit resources by $1 is approximately $2.50, only about one-half as much as the corresponding figure for the IRS business class. Federal nonbusiness, nonfarm audits tend to be the least costly type of federal audit. Based on an estimate of $600 as the average cost of such an audit, the implied shadow value of increasing IRS nonbusiness, nonfarm audit resources by $1 is approximately $4, somewhat below the estimated shadow value for business audits but well above the estimated shadow value for farm audits. Apparently the IRS could have obtained greater revenue by performing more audits of business returns for tax year 1987 and fewer audits of farm returns. We assume that state farm audits cost about the same as state business audits (roughly $500) and that state nonbusiness, nonfarm audits are somewhat less expensive (perhaps $300). Based on these assumptions, we estimate that the shadow value of an additional $1 of state audit resources is about $2 for a farm audit and $3 for a nonbusiness, nonfarm audit. Our estimates imply that the state could have obtained greater revenue by allocating more resources to nonbusiness, nonfarm audits and less to business audits. Our estimate of $\lambda_p c_p$ is negative but very imprecise for the farm class. For the nonbusiness, nonfarm class the estimate is 0.28, quite similar to the value obtained for the business class. Based on an assumed piggyback audit cost of about $100, we estimate that the shadow value of an additional dollar of piggyback audit resources for the nonbusiness, nonfarm class is between $2 and $3.

Now consider the results for the farm and nonbusiness, nonfarm classes presented in table 8.8. For both classes, the estimated correlation between the state and federal signals is high, indicating a substantial degree of overlap between the information sets of the two agencies. For the farm class, the estimated cross-correlations $\rho_{\eta_f \varepsilon_s}$ and $\rho_{\eta_s \varepsilon_f}$ are quite large, indicating that each agency has information that pertains to the other agency's audit assessment distribution. To determine whether the information the IRS possesses would be useful to the ODR in formulating its audit strategy, we have again computed the implied partial correlation between the federal signal η_f and the state error term ε_s conditional on the value of the state signal η_s. The value of this partial correlation for the farm class is .54, indicating that the federal signal contains a great deal of information about state audit assessments not contained in the state signal. We have also computed the implied partial correlation between the state signal η_s and the federal error term ε_f conditional on the value of the federal signal η_f for the farm class. The value of this correlation is .60, which indicates that the state signal contains a great deal of information about federal assessments not contained in the federal signal. Thus, it appears that greater information sharing between the two agencies might result in substantial improvements to state and federal farm audit selection procedures. On the other hand, the estimated cross-correlations for the nonbusiness, nonfarm class are small in absolute value and statistically insignificant. Apparently, there is less scope for improved audit selection through information-sharing arrangements for this class. Just as for the business class, the estimates of the two remaining correlations listed in table 8.8, $\rho_{w_f w_s}$ and $\rho_{\varepsilon_f \varepsilon_s}$, are positive and generally quite large for the farm and nonbusiness, nonfarm audit classes, indicating a strong link between compliance behavior on federal and state tax returns.

8.3.3 Additional Findings

We have recently conducted a detailed analysis of the ODR individual income tax audit programs. Our analysis has generated two findings that we believe may be of some general interest and applicable to other states. First, as was previously indicated during our discussion of table 8.3, our data indicate that the ODR did not follow up on a significant number of cases for which the IRS conducted an audit and made a significant positive assessment. Table 8.9 provides some additional information about this finding. According to the statistics presented in the table, of the 198 federal audit cases in our data for which the IRS assessed more than $10,000, Oregon did not follow up on 106, or more than half. Of the 249 federal audit cases in our data for which the IRS assessed between $5,000 and $10,000, Oregon did not follow up on 142, again more than half. Of the 1,428 federal audit cases for which the IRS assessed between $1,000 and $5,000, Oregon did not follow up on 845. Surprisingly, Oregon did follow up on many cases for which the IRS made far lower assessments, as is also indicated in the table. Of course it is possible that our data are wrong, and that Oregon did follow up on many of the audits in question. We are still discussing this possibility with Oregon officials but, at the present time, have discovered no evidence in support of this hypothesis. We believe that the more likely explanation for the above finding is that the ODR either did not receive information about many of these audits or did not retain the information for later use. We wonder whether the results presented in table 8.9 are similar for other states.

Our second findings is that for tax year 1987 ODR audits of part-year and nonresident filers generated larger mean and median assessments than were generated by audits of any other filer groups. Table 8.10 presents additional information related to this point. The figures in the table indicate that the ODR conducted very few audits of part-year and nonresident filers for tax year 1987 but made large revenue assessments. If this second finding is correct and carries over to more recent years, it suggests that the ODR might be able to increase its revenue assessments by shifting some of its audit resources to these two groups. Again, we wonder whether the statistics for other states are similar.

Table 8.9   Taxpayers in Sample with a Positive Federal Audit Assessment by
               Whether They Were Subjected to a State Audit of Any Kind

Federal Audit Assessment (in dollars)	Number of Cases	
	No State Audit	State Audit
1–100	183	61
101–500	405	320
501–1,000	596	275
1,001–5,000	845	583
5,001–10,000	142	107
Over 10,000	106	92
All cases	2,277	1,438

Note: Figures weighted to reflect population totals.

Table 8.10   State Audit Results by Type of Form

	Form 40F	Form 40S	Form 40P	Form 40N
Number of audits	1,913	100	36	75
Mean audit assessment	733	340	1,175	1,871
Median audit assessment	88	77	215	744

Note: Figures weighted to reflect population totals.

8.4   Conclusion

Little is known about state audit programs and about the relationship between these state programs and federal tax enforcement activities. In this paper we use data provided by the Oregon Department of Revenue and the Internal Revenue Service to examine various aspects of these programs. In particular, we find that there is substantial—though not complete—overlap between the information employed by the ODR and the IRS for audit selection and that the information used by one agency is not always made known to the other. This result suggests that the enforcement activities of each agency could be improved through greater information sharing. We also find that the ODR may have foregone substantial amounts of audit revenue by not following up on more returns for which IRS had made large audit assessments. Finally, we find that each agency could increase its collections by reallocating its enforcement budget among the various audit classes, although the efficient reallocation is not the same for the ODR and the IRS.

It should be remembered that these results are based on an analysis of the interactions between federal and state enforcement efforts in a single state (Oregon). The results might differ if other states were examined. Indeed, our survey of state audit programs clearly indicates that the individual income tax enforcement programs in Oregon are far more extensive and effective than in most other states. The shadow value of additional audit resources, the scope for resource reallocation, and the benefits from additional federal-state information sharing may actually be much higher for some of these other states than we have found for Oregon.

Appendix

In this appendix we analyze in somewhat greater detail the *strategic* version of our federal and state model, which was mentioned previously in subsection 8.2.2. Recall that in this version of the model the state tax authority makes a decision whether to perform an audit in the first period, taking into account the possibility that it may have the opportunity to piggyback on a federal audit in the second period if it should choose not to audit in the first period. Figure 8A.1 illustrates the decision tree associated with the auditing choice faced by the state tax authority in the first period of the model.

The top branch of the tree corresponds to the decision to conduct a period-one audit; the expected value associated with this branch is $E(R_s|\eta_s) - \lambda_s c_s$, which is identical to the expected value associated with a period-one audit in the nonstrategic model. The bottom branch of the tree corresponds to the decision to wait. In the nonstrategic model, the value associated with this branch is zero, and the state chooses to conduct a period-one audit whenever $E(R_s|\eta_s) \geq \lambda_s c_s$. However, in the strategic model this branch has a more complex structure, and the value associated with waiting is typically positive.

To demonstrate that the value associated with this branch is generally positive, we describe the logical structure of this branch in detail. The wait branch leads first to a random event involving the federal authority's period-one audit decision. If the federal authority chooses not to audit, the value associated with the wait branch of the tree is zero. However, if the federal authority chooses to audit, the federal assessment R_f is revealed, and the state authority faces a further decision in period two, whether to conduct a piggyback audit. The federal authority's audit selection decision is the same as in the nonstrategic model, and therefore there is a threshold value η_f^* such that the federal authority chooses to conduct a period-one audit if and only if $\eta_f \geq \eta_f^*$. Since the signal

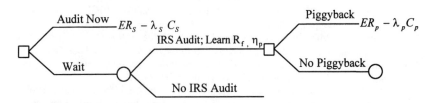

Fig. 8A.1   State's decision tree under strategic audit selection

η_s is observed by the state authority and is correlated with the signal η_f, the state authority assesses the probability of a federal audit as $\text{Prob}(\eta_f \geq \eta_f^*|\eta_s)$, which can be written as a function $L(\eta_s)$. Suppose now that the federal authority has conducted a period-one audit and has made a revenue assessment R_f. At the beginning of period two the state observes the signal η_p and computes the net expected value of performing a piggyback audit to be $E(R_p|R_f, \eta_p) - \lambda_p c_p$. Since the net value associated with no piggyback audit is zero, the state will choose to perform a piggyback audit whenever $E(R_p|R_f, \eta_p) > \lambda_p c_p$, or whenever η_p exceeds the threshold value η_p^*. The threshold value η_p^* is itself a function of R_f, denoted $\eta_p^*(R_f)$. What expected value should the state authority then assign to the option of performing a piggyback audit in period two, as of period one? Since the option is relevant only when the federal authority conducts a period-one audit, the state authority must evaluate the distribution of R_f, conditional on the signal η_s and on the event $\eta_f > \eta_f^*$, and then use this conditional distribution to compute the expected value of the piggyback option. Applying the logic of this argument, the expected value of the piggyback option may be denoted $Q(\eta_s)$ and be expressed as

$$(\text{A1}) \quad Q(\eta_s) = \int_{R_f=-\infty}^{+\infty} \int_{\eta_p=\eta_p^*(R_f)}^{+\infty} E(R_p|R_p, \eta_p) g(\eta_p) f(R_f|\eta_s, \eta_f > \eta_f^*) \, d\eta_p \, dR_f.$$

The expected value associated with the wait branch of the decision tree is then $L(\eta_s)Q(\eta_s)$, which in general is positive.

References

Alexander, Craig, and Jonathan S. Feinstein. 1987. A microeconometric analysis of income tax evasion. Cambridge: Massachusetts Institute of Technology. Mimeograph.

Alm, James, Roy Bahl, and Matthew N. Murray. 1993. Audit selection and income tax underreporting in the tax compliance game. *Journal of Development Economics* 42(1): 1–33.

Beron, Kurt, Helen Tauchen, and Anne D. Witte. 1991. The effects of audits and socioeconomic variables on compliance. In *Why people pay taxes*, ed. Joel Slemrod, 67–89. Ann Arbor: University of Michigan Press.

Clotfelter, Charles. 1983. Tax evasion and tax rates: An analysis of individual returns. *Review of Economics and Statistics* 65(3): 363–73.

Dubin, Jeffrey A., Michael A. Graetz, and Louis L. Wilde. 1990. The effect of audit rates on the federal individual income tax. *National Tax Journal* 43(4): 395–409.

Due, John F., and John L. Mikesell. 1993. *Sales taxation: State and local structure and administration*. Baltimore: Johns Hopkins University Press.

Erard, Brian. 1995. Self selection with measurement errors: A microeconometric analysis of the decision to seek tax assistance and its implications for tax compliance. Ottawa: Carleton University. Mimeograph.

Erard, Brian, and Jonathan S. Feinstein. 1994a. Econometric models of compliance and enforcement: Reporting behavior and audit selection decisions. Mimeograph.
————. 1994b. Honesty and evasion in the tax compliance game. *RAND Journal of Economics* 25(1): 1–19.
————. 1994c. The role of moral sentiments and audit perceptions in tax compliance. *Public Finance* 49 (Supplement): 70–89.
Feinstein, Jonathan S. 1991. An econometric analysis of income tax evasion and its detection. *RAND Journal of Economics* 22(1): 14–35.

Comment   James W. Wetzler

One of the mildly exasperating rituals of my tenure as New York State Commissioner of Taxation and Finance involved the State Division of the Budget's annual request for suggestions on how the Tax Department could increase tax collections in the upcoming fiscal year by expanding its audit program. The department's Audit Division would respond with proposals to start new audit programs and would attach revenue estimates implying that these audits would be far more productive than the audits that would have been conducted under a proportional expansion of the existing audit effort. Indeed, sometimes the numbers would indicate that the new audits would be more productive than the *average* productivity of the existing effort.

I would ask why, if these new audits were expected to be so productive, the Audit Division had not seen its way through to undertake them by rearranging priorities within its existing budget. A generally unsatisfactory discussion would ensue, in which the division would point out various reasons why these highly productive new audits could only be done with additional resources. Finally, overcoming my skepticism, I would agree to forward the proposals to the Budget Division; after all, there are worse bureaucratic outcomes than an increase in one's budget. The Budget Division would then tell the governor (correctly) that they had really put pressure on the stodgy bureaucrats over at the Tax Department and, by doing so, had produced more money for him to spend.

Similar Kabuki dances occur at other tax administration agencies. Sometimes, the difference between the concepts of average and marginal productivity, and their link to audit selection processes, are simply not well understood; sometimes, they are just ignored or fuzzed up for bureaucratic reasons. Hence, you can imagine my enthusiasm at being asked to discuss a paper that attempts a rigorous characterization of the audit selection process.

There is some conventional wisdom that deserves to be subjected to analysis: the overwhelming consensus among present and former tax administrators

James W. Wetzler is Director of Economic Consulting and Multistate Tax Policy Initiatives in the New York City office of Deloitte & Touche LLP and is adjunct professor of law at the New York University Law School.

is that dramatic increases in audit coverage would be beneficial. As tax commissioner, I was frequently asked why I could not address New York State's chronic budget problem by "doing something" about tax evasion. Conversely, in some quarters, support is growing for "getting the IRS off our backs," a sentiment that is likely to be translated into budget reductions and, ultimately, a further reduction in audit coverage.

It is not clear to what extent either support for, or opposition to, expanded audit coverage is based on a proper differentiation between average and marginal productivity. Just how productive is the marginal audit? Answering this question requires modeling the audit selection process, the task attempted in this paper by Alm, Erard, and Feinstein (hereafter AEF). Moreover, by focusing on the interaction between federal and state audit decisions, the paper addresses an aspect of the problem that is likely to become increasingly important as federal-state cooperation in tax administration expands.

Let me start by describing the individual income tax enforcement program in New York State, which forms the basis of my experience. In recent years, New York's strategy has been to assume that the federal government does its job properly and achieves accurate measurements of federal taxable income. The state's job, therefore, is to fill in the gaps and monitor features of the state income tax that the federal government ignores—residency, failure to file state returns, and the adjustments that lead to differences between state and federal taxable income such as the exclusion of interest on Treasury securities and the inclusion of interest on out-of-state municipal bonds. New York State uses information from the IRS to reconcile mismatches between items reported to the IRS and to the state, along with a variety of data sources to identify nonfilers. The principal field audit effort consists of audits of taxpayers who file as nonresidents but are suspected of being residents, a very productive but controversial audit program. New York does not generally attempt independent estimates of federal taxable income.

When a New York taxpayer is audited by the IRS, he or she is required to file information about the federal changes with the New York State Tax Department. Periodically, the department receives tapes from the IRS on federal audit adjustments and conducts desk audits of those taxpayers who had not voluntarily reported the federal changes. With modern computer technology, these audits are extremely inexpensive and very productive.

This appears to be approximately the program that AEF recommend for Oregon on the basis of their analysis. That is reassuring.

This paper models the audit selection process for the IRS Oregon district and the Oregon state government. Each tax administrator is assumed first to attempt to identify taxpayers who have underreported their tax liability on the basis of information on the tax returns along with "signals" based on other information, intuition, astrology, or whatever. Then, for the taxpayers expected to have some positive underreporting, each tax administrator estimates the expected tax assessment from an audit of that taxpayer, based on information and signals that may overlap but are not necessarily identical to those used in step one. Presumably, at the federal level the information on the tax returns used for audit selection corresponds to the scoring of each return under the DIF (or discriminant function) program, while the signals reflect the fact that the IRS district offices do not mechanically select for audit only those returns with the highest DIF scores. Finally, the state tax administrator is assumed to decide whether to conduct a piggyback audit to make state adjustments corresponding to federal audit changes for those taxpayers who were subjects of a federal audit and owed additional federal tax.

This appears to be an accurate characterization of the process and, by separating the positive from the zero or negative audit changes, makes the analysis more mathematically tractable.

What is, or should be, the objective of the tax administrator in making audit selection decisions? AEF are a little fuzzy on this point because they lack data on how much audits cost and, therefore, are forced implicitly to assume that the tax administrator faces a constant cost per audit.

One possible objective would be to maximize tax assessed per audit, an approach that would focus audit activity on those taxpayers believed to have the worst compliance. A second possibility would be to maximize aggregate tax assessed for the audit effort as a whole, which would require selecting for audit those taxpayers for whom assessments per dollar of audit cost were expected to be highest. (The authors note, but leave to future research, the problems of reductions in assessments after the audit is completed on account of appeals or litigation and the possibility of failure to collect the amount of tax owed, problems that are quite important in practice.) If all audits involved the same cost, the two objectives would lead to the same audit selection rule, which is what is modeled in AEF's paper; but if costs vary, it is necessary to distinguish between the two objectives. (Properly measured, the costs should include costs of appeals and litigation of audit assessments and costs of collecting the tax debts arising from the audits.)

An objective of maximizing aggregate audit assessments would require foregoing some expensive audits of taxpayers with larger amounts of underreporting in favor of cheaper audits of taxpayers with smaller but easier-to-detect underreporting. Were taxpayer behavior independent of the audit process, this would maximize the productivity of the audit program; however, it would run the risk of encouraging taxpayers to engage in hard-to-detect forms of noncompliance. (Presumably, the most egregious cases of tax evasion could still be addressed outside the audit process through criminal prosecutions for tax fraud.) It would also be perceived as unfair: taxpayers expect enforcement to concentrate on the worst offenders, not just the ones whose offenses are easiest to detect.

My understanding is that the IRS generally tries to select for audit those returns with the highest expected noncompliance. The New York State Tax Department tries to maximize revenue per dollar of audit cost. This difference probably reflects the state's greater focus on short-run budgetary objectives arising from its need to achieve annual cash flow budget balance. The state also does a better job than does the IRS of distinguishing between assessments on the one hand and actual collections arising from audits on the other. It might be helpful to secure the State of Oregon's characterization of what it thinks it is trying to maximize in its audit selection process.

This issue of exactly what should be optimized in an audit program can be analyzed at ever greater levels of sophistication. A sensitive issue involves situations where enforcement activity can be expected to indicate that taxpayers have overpaid. Correcting these mistakes is presumably of some social value, but how does one account for this benefit? In the AEF model, tax administrators never audit a taxpayer expected to have a negative assessment, but they are aware of the fact that, statistically, some of their audits will produce negative assessments. (In the data, negative assessments for any given year often represent the flip-side of an audit that produced a positive assessment for another year by changing the timing of income or deductions, and these negative assessments really should be netted against that other year's positive assessment.) Accounting for penalties is also tricky; presumably, tax administrator should not audit merely to obtain revenues from penalties, whose purpose is not to raise revenue but rather to encourage voluntary compliance.

It may also be the case that some types of noncompliance should be considered less worthy of correction than others. Random errors, that can be expected to even out over a taxpayer's life, might be less serious than systematic errors. Underpayments by lower income taxpayers may be less serious than underpayments by the rich, although the concern over noncompliance with the earned income credit suggests that public concern with low-income noncompliance grows when the tax system is used to deliver income maintenance benefits.

The paper does not make completely clear what it is that state auditors do. Do Oregon's auditors attempt to verify federal taxable income, the adjustments to federal taxable income needed to compute Oregon taxable income and other items idiosyncratic to the state tax return, or both? To the extent that Oregon's audits address items that are needed only to compute state tax, then the AEF strategic model of state auditing neglects a potentially important choice. Under the strategic model, state auditors wait to see if a return is subject to federal audit, observe the result, and then decide whether to conduct a piggyback audit based on federal audit changes. However, an additional choice exists as long as the statute of limitations has not expired—conduct a state audit to verify the state tax items. Indeed, a large federal audit adjustment may well be a strong signal that state tax adjustments are inaccurately reported as well.

The AEF model produces an estimate of the expected productivity of the marginal audit. When divided by audit cost (assumed to be constant), this equals the shadow price of audit resources (λ). Given the administrators' approach to audit selection, λ measures how much revenue can be raised by a \$1 expansion of the audit effort. AEF's estimated λs are surprisingly low, which is an important result. It may well be that the conventional wisdom is wrong and that a quantum expansion of audit coverage is not called for. However, the low λs may just reflect the particular middle income and small business audit classes that AEF chose to analyze.

The low estimates of λ may also be an artifact of the assumption that all audits have the same cost. If the marginal audit costs less than inframarginal audits, a likely scenario, the assessment per dollar of cost of the marginal audit will be higher than estimated by AEF.

AEF's policy recommendations are based on the judgment that λ should be equalized across audit programs. This would be true if the tax administrator's objective were to maximize assessment per dollar of audit cost, but not if the objective were to maximize assessment per audit, except in the special case where all audits cost the same.

A very interesting feature of the AEF model is that it permits the estimation of the state revenue gain from additional piggyback audits that would result from an expansion of federal audit coverage. Arguably, the IRS should take this gain into account in its resource allocation decisions. In any case, a measure of the state benefit would give the IRS an argument to use when going to the Office of Management and Budget and Congress to defend its budget.

It is worth noting that the IRS has recently changed its approach to tax enforcement. Reconciling itself to the fact that low audit coverage is likely to be the case for the foreseeable future, the IRS is restructuring its enforcement program to emphasize targeting enforcement efforts so as to maximize voluntary compliance. This involves identifying market segments of taxpayers, measuring their level of noncompliance, identifying the causes of that noncompliance, and taking systematic actions to address those causes. The new approach, termed Compliance 2000, will require a significant investment in research and analysis and much greater use of information provided by states, which possess much of the data needed to analyze individual market segments. I am enthusiastic that the new approach can achieve significant improvements in the level of nationwide tax compliance.

The Internal Revenue Service and the State of Oregon are to be commended for funding AEF's research. The rigorous analysis of audit selection, such as is provided here, will enable tax administrators and their critics to be much more rational in their management of the audit function.

Contributors

James Alm
Department of Economics
University of Colorado at Boulder
Campus Box 256
Boulder, CO 80309

David F. Bradford
Woodrow Wilson School
Princeton University
Princeton, NJ 08544

Gary Burtless
Brookings Institution
1775 Massachusetts Avenue NW
Washington, DC 20036

Nada Eissa
Department of Economics
521 Evans Hall
University of California
Berkeley, CA 94720

Brian Erard
Department of Economics
Carleton University
1125 Colonel By Drive
Ottawa, ON K1S 5B6
Canada

Daniel R. Feenberg
NBER
1050 Massachusetts Avenue
Cambridge, MA 02138

Jonathan S. Feinstein
Yale School of Management
Box 20-8200
New Haven, CT 06520

Martin Feldstein
President and Chief Executive Officer
NBER
1050 Massachusetts Avenue
Cambridge, MA 02138

Don Fullerton
Department of Economics
University of Texas
Austin, TX 78712

William M. Gentry
Graduate School of Business
Columbia University
Uris Hall 602
New York, NY 10027

Roger H. Gordon
Department of Economics
University of Michigan
Ann Arbor, MI 48109

Jonathan Gruber
Department of Economics
Room E52-274c
MIT
Cambridge, MA 02139

Alison P. Hagy
Department of Economics
Pomona College
Claremont, CA 91711

James J. Heckman
Department of Economics
University of Chicago
1126 East 59th Street
Chicago, IL 60637

Brigitte C. Madrian
Graduate School of Business
University of Chicago
1101 East 58th Street
Chicago, IL 60615

Gilbert E. Metcalf
Department of Economics
Tufts University
Medford, MA 02155

James M. Poterba
Department of Economics
Room E52-350
MIT
Cambridge, MA 02139

Harvey S. Rosen
Department of Economics
Princeton University
Princeton, NJ 08544

Andrew A. Samwick
Department of Economics
Dartmouth College
Hanover, NH 03755

Joel Slemrod
Office of Tax Policy Research
School of Business Administration
University of Michigan
Ann Arbor, MI 48109

James W. Wetzler
Deloitte & Touche
2 World Financial Center
New York, NY 10281

Author Index

Subject Index

Ability to pay: criterion to measure progressivity, 106; effective subsidy rates by, 120–23; potential income as measure of, 120–23

Accelerated cost recovery system (ACRS), pre-TRA86, 200

Adjusted gross income (AGI): as basis for child care credit rate, 109–14; definition changes, 172–74, 190; effect of secondary earner deduction on, 60n30, 64–66; Feenberg-Poterba time series on capital gains and, 174; marriage bonus and penalty by, 59–60, 64–66; as minimum threshold for medical deductibility, 135–36; shares received by top income earners (1984–90), 173–74

Adverse selection: devices to deal with, 166–67; as health insurance problem, 166

At-risk rules, U.S. tax code, 216–20

Audit likelihood: joint-agency audit model, 250–53; single tax authority, 244–45

Audit model: estimation results, 261–69; joint-agency model, 245–53, 271–72; by single tax authority, 239–45; state and federal tax audit decisions, 237–39

Audit programs: federal-level, 236; survey of state-level, 236–37

Audit selection: single tax authority, 243–44; strategic decision tree, 271–72

Bracket creep, 11

Capital gains: based on consistent definitions of income, 174; effect of repeal of General Utilities doctrine, 17n3, 184; eliminated exclusion in AGI definition, 173; Feenberg-Poterba time series on AGI and, 174; percent exclusion in AGI definition, 173; rationale for tax reform, 1

Cattle feeding, 198–200

C-corporations: shift in activity from, 183–85; under TRA86, 177n3

CCTC. See Child care tax credit (CCTC)

CES. See Constant elasticity of substitution (CES)

CEX. See Consumer Expenditure Survey (CEX)

Child care expense, current treatment, 101

Child care tax credit (CCTC): benefits and determinants of benefits, 100, 111–20; compared to dependent care assistance plans, 101–2; by income level (1989), 112–14; nonrefundability, 114–15; progressive features of, 105; for tax relief (1989), 107–11; tax savings comparisons with dependent care assistance plans, 129–32; U.S. households taking, 99

Compensation, cash alternative, 135

Constant elasticity of substitution (CES), 82–86, 94–95

Consumer Expenditure Survey (CEX), 83–86, 95

Consumption: intertemporal elasticity of substitution, 82–86; maximization in two-